Shakespeare's Eden

BLANDFORD HISTORY SERIES
(General Editor R. W. Harris)

PROBLEMS OF HISTORY

THE REIGN OF HENRY VII	R. L. Storey
THE DISSOLUTION OF THE MONASTERIES	G. W. O. Woodward
PAPISTS AND PURITANS UNDER ELIZABETH I	Patrick McGrath
COLONIES INTO COMMONWEALTH	W. D. McIntyre
THE EXPANSION OF EUROPE IN THE EIGHTEENTH CENTURY	Glyndwr Williams
FRANCE AND THE DREYFUS AFFAIR	Douglas Johnson
THE CHURCH AND MAN'S STRUGGLE FOR UNITY	Herbert Waddams
ROYAL MYSTERIES AND PRETENDERS	S. B.-R. Poole

HISTORY OF ENGLAND

REFORMATION AND RESURGENCE 1485–1603 England in the Sixteenth Century	G. W. O. Woodward
THE STRUGGLE FOR THE CONSTITUTION 1603–1689 England in the Seventeenth Century	G. E. Aylmer
ENGLAND IN THE EIGHTEENTH CENTURY 1689–1793 A Balanced Constitution and New Horizons	R. W. Harris
REACTION AND REFORM 1793–1868 England in the Early Nineteenth Century	John W. Derry
DEMOCRACY AND WORLD CONFLICT 1868–1970 A History of Modern Britain	T. L. Jarman

HISTORY OF EUROPE

RENAISSANCE, REFORMATION AND THE OUTER WORLD 1450–1660	M. L. Bush
ABSOLUTISM AND ENLIGHTENMENT 1660–1789	R. W. Harris
THE AGE OF TRANSFORMATION 1789–1871	R. F. Leslie
THE END OF EUROPEAN PRIMACY 1871–1939	J. R. Western
RUIN AND RESURGENCE 1939–1965	R. C. Mowat

HISTORY AND LITERATURE

THE TRIUMPH OF ENGLISH 1350–1400	Basil Cottle
THE CHORUS OF HISTORY 1485–1558	A. M. Kinghorn
SHAKESPEARE'S EDEN 1558–1629	B. L. Joseph
REASON AND NATURE IN EIGHTEENTH-CENTURY THOUGHT 1714–1780	R. W. Harris
ROMANTICISM AND THE SOCIAL ORDER 1780–1830	R. W. Harris
DOCUMENTARY AND IMAGINATIVE LITERATURE 1880–1920	J. A. V. Chapple

1558-1629

Shakespeare's Eden

The Commonwealth of England 1558-1629

B. L. JOSEPH

Chairman of the Department of Drama and Theatre,
Queen's College, Flushing

BLANDFORD PRESS
LONDON

First published 1971
First paperback edition 1971
© 1971 Blandford Press Ltd
167 High Holborn
London WC1V 6PH

ISBN 07137 3607 0 *Hardback*
07137 3627 5 *Paperback*

Printed and bound in Great Britain by
C. Tinling & Co. Ltd, London and Prescot

Contents

ACKNOWLEDGMENTS 6

LIST OF ILLUSTRATIONS 7

PREFACE 9

1 INTRODUCTION 11

2 THE COMMONWEALTH OF ENGLAND 34

3 THE ROYAL GOVERNMENT 115

4 DEGREE, HIGH AND BASE 153

5 EVENTS AND EXPLANATIONS 192

6 MAN, THE COSMOS AND PROVIDENCE DIVINE 244

7 LITERATURE IN THE AGE OF SHAKESPEARE 273

8 DRAMA IN THE AGE OF SHAKESPEARE 304

9 SHAKESPEARE IN HIS AGE 326

BIBLIOGRAPHY 361

INDEX 365

Acknowledgments

Acknowledgment is due to the following for their kind permission to reproduce photographs:

The National Portrait Gallery, No. 3
Radio Times Hulton Picture Library, No. 6
The Trustees of the British Museum, Nos. 1, 2, 4, 5, 7, 8, 9, 11, 12

List of Illustrations

(*Between pages* 200-201)

1 The presentation of the Speaker, 1584

2 Westminster Hall in the early seventeenth century

3 The Spanish Treaty Commissioners

4 A bachelor dinner party

5 English costumes *c.* 1580

6 A royal hunting party: the kill

7 Elizabeth at a hunt picnic

8 James I and Charles entertaining the Spanish ambassadors

9 Charles I dining in public

10 Diagram of the Copernican Universe by Thomas Digges

11 Peter Apian's diagram of the Universe

12 James I signing the Spanish Marriage Treaty

Preface

THIS book is an account of those aspects of life, art and thought in England in the age of Shakespeare which seem to me of most importance to a student of literature or history.

To try to cover every topic with as much detail as possible would be to produce a vast, unwieldy work and would involve some treatment of matters in which I am assured I am not always sufficiently competent. Selection is necessary.

I have therefore chosen to treat those subjects of whose importance I have become increasingly aware during a quarter of a century of research, teaching, reading, directing, each in its own way a form of intense enjoyment. These selected matters are also those of which I have found it most necessary to inform pupils wishing to become at home in the culture of Elizabethan and early Stuart England.

My practice is to offer sufficient factual details to explain my conclusions. I have tried not to give information as an end in itself, or in the vain attempt to cover everything. The treatment of literature, dramatic and non-dramatic, is therefore centred on the comparatively few topics which I believe to be of the utmost importance. These in my experience are too often not understood. This restriction is also founded in a belief that the person who aspires to an understanding enjoyment of any art needs the minimum of second-hand experience from teachers, but should be goaded and encouraged to apply himself to responding to as many works of art as possible. He will thus gain his own first-hand experience.

I have therefore tried to provide the few generalized statements on Elizabethan drama and literature which I believe to be valid, and which do not conflict with my assurance that little that I can write can be as important to a reader as his or her own response to enough individual works of art.

I have great pleasure in acknowledging my debt to the published works of a number of scholars: to C. T. Onions, to E. M. W. Tillyard and to J. B. Bamborough. These are English scholars; my debt is as great to historians, to J. W. Allen, J. B. Black, E. P. Cheyney, G. Davies, G. R. Elton, G. Griffiths, C. Hill, Sir John Neale, A. L. Rowse, L. Stone, R. H. Tawney, H. R. Trevor-Roper. It has been a privilege to have their combined scholarship at my disposal. I cannot help remarking, however, that they bear no responsibility for my mistakes, such as these may turn out to be.

B. L. Joseph
Flushing 1971

1 : Introduction

T HIS work treats many aspects of the social, political, economic and cultural life of England from about 1558 (the date of Elizabeth's accession) until about 1629 (the year in which Charles I dismissed his third Parliament). In this action Charles followed the custom of his two immediate predecessors, his kinswoman and his father, governing the realm as he had every right to do without consulting or informing his faithful Commons. The situation in which he made this decision, like the decision itself, developed quite consistently out of much in the way of precedent and cause with which this study concerns itself. It is not difficult to perceive, for instance, how much Elizabeth's exaltation of the monarchy as well as James' published views on the Divine Right of Kings conditioned Charles' thoughts and actions, not only in 1629, but right on up to the very moment in 1649 when, before laying his head on the block, he delivered the attestation: 'I die a Christian according to the profession of the Church of England, as I found it left me by my father.'[1]

We can find between 1558 and 1629 many reasons why both Charles and his enemies behaved as they did, why his death became unavoidable. They thought that, powerless and imprisoned, he would accept their demands, demands which seemed to them entirely just. But he, thanks to his own character responding to doctrine and behaviour to be found in our period, the age of Shakespeare, was confident that God had given paramount power to the monarch—to him—and that to relinquish any part of that divinely ordained power was to commit a grave sin. He was brought to trial without being deposed, with no attempt at forcing an abdication, as King, with his title duly acknowledged. The self-confidence of his judges in proceeding thus derived from seeds of thinking and conduct which had germinated before he came to the throne. Even his executioner acknowledged his royalty in reply to the King's last words. 'Stay for the sign', Charles directed; and the reply came: 'I will, an' it please Your Majesty.'[2] The assurance of the King that 'a subject and a sovereign are clear different things', that a 'share in government' pertains in no way to the people, is equalled by the self-confidence with which his judges described him as King of England, not only in the charge, but in the warrant for his execution. His assurance and their self-confidence are not surprising when we consider events and statements to be found in the history of England between the accession of Elizabeth and the end of Charles' third Parliament.

Our terminal dates may suggest that the main interest of this book is in economic, constitutional, political and social history. But this is not the case; a fruitful understanding of the age demands a more than superficial attention to literature, drama, religion, philosophy and scientific thought and practice. And it would be imprudent to restrict ourselves to Shakespeare's lifetime, when, in fact, the period indicated has a true unity of its own.

A historian of deserved repute has recently declared that we should look to the years from 1603 to 1714 if we wish to understand the changes which set England on the road to becoming the power known to the world after the accession of Queen Victoria. In these years from James I to the death of Anne can be found explanations for the development in England of 'Parliamentary government, economic advance and imperialist foreign policy, of religious toleration and scientific progress.' (C. Hill, *The Century of Revolution 1603–1714* [1966], pp. 1–5.) If this is so, then it emphasizes the importance of the age of Shakespeare as treated in this book. We see the groundwork for much that developed in Stuart England as a whole; we see what existed before James came to the throne, what changed and what persisted. The historian of politics, of the constitution, and of society cannot give his attention for long to our period without the thought that here is something that leads to the Civil War, or that is changed by it. The historian of Edwardian England writes beneath the shadow of Sarajevo; he knows it is to come. The historian of Georgian England between the wars knows he is treating the prelude to 3 September 1939.

Even so does the historian of Elizabethan and Jacobean England know that the Civil War lies not far ahead. And in that history we can learn why the conflict came and why the victory went to that part of the population represented in the Commons. In the age of Shakespeare England starts to move towards parliamentary government and religious toleration. The last victim to be burnt for heresy suffered as late as 1613, it is true. But the very fact that this was the last shows the change that was taking place. If we are to understand the age we must take notice of much that vanished as well as what endured in addition to the innovations. The England that vanished, or was to vanish, was ruled by monarchs exercising despotic rights. Exercise of the right of imprisoning a subject without trial was not peculiar to Charles I; and when Queen Elizabeth imprisoned Raleigh and his wife, her maid of honour, for begetting a child out of wedlock and then marrying in secret, neither of the subjects disputed the royal prerogative. A gross affront to the royal dignity was punished without anyone demanding that the prisoners be allowed to exercise a subject's right to habeas corpus and correct judicial process.

The England that was vanishing, the England in which church courts were still powerful, was as yet no more than a second-class state. To its own inhabitants and foreign visitors it appeared much over-populated, small as the population was in fact. Certain changes were taking place in the ownership and use of land; there was some movement of people to urban areas, some small development of industry; but the economy was largely rural, and what is regarded today as backward. Production was limited almost to immediate needs. Certainly the more modern attitude to work as an admirable and moral way of life had hardly awakened.[3]

So much, for the moment, for the England that was to be changed. It was already involved from 1588 to 1604 in the first of the new kind of war, a war of commercial and colonial rivalry. This war between England and Spain has been described as a 'naval war between rival naval powers for the control of wealth of distant lands'. It is not surprising that the new kind of war was accompanied by a rapid expansion of overseas trade with the exploring and opening up of new routes to unfamiliar parts of the world.

At home the period of most important change was from 1580 to 1620. These years have recently been described (by L. Stone in *The Crisis of Aristocracy* [1965] pp. 15ff.) as the real watershed between mediaeval and modern England. It was a period in which the state established itself against local magnates as well as lesser subjects, and by the end of which not even the most aristocratic of law-breakers could any longer rely on his prestige among neighbours to save him from reprimand and punishment emanating from the central government through its judicial administration. The new unfortified houses of the *élite* classes were a true sign of the more peaceful state of the land; so was the disappearance of large retinues of armed retainers, whose function was to maintain the status and enforce the will of great aristocrats who were now content with a coach, footmen and page. By 1620 no nobleman was strong enough for personal rebellion against his sovereign. Old landlord-tenant relationships had been undermined not only by inflation and population growth, but also capitalist ethics and new methods of estate management. Over half a century of education in accordance with a new ideal had produced an intelligentsia among the propertied classes. The Grand Tour was becoming established as part of a young man's training; and the dilettante virtuoso English nobleman so prominent later in English cultural life had already made his appearance.

The story is the same with politics and the constitution. As Great Britain, England, Scotland, Ireland and Wales were now united under one sovereign, if not so solidly as by the Act of 1707 which was to come. London and the Court were becoming the social centre of the newly united realm. In politics whatever particular liberties and ancient customs might be asserted, the assertions tended more and more to be made in terms of liberty in the abstract and the interest of the public as a whole. In this period the House of Commons began to dominate the Upper House, and stretch out for political initiative from the executive, in which the Lord Treasurer was becoming the monarch's leading servant. At the same time the Exchequer was emerging as the most important administrative section of what was still regarded in many ways as the monarch's private business rather than a separate public matter of governing the realm. In these years of Elizabeth and James I, trade became the concern of the statesman and the gentleman, and merchants amassed as much wealth as a nobleman. Usury was legislated for, and interest rates fell. Of no less importance was the development of that moral concern for one's duty in relation to others as well as to God that has become known as the workings of the non-conformist conscience. Non-conformity showed itself, too, in a new assurance that the guidance of the individual conscience was to be followed rather than obedience in family, church and state as traditionally understood. To add that between 1580 and 1620 English literature and drama became something different from, however strongly linked to, that of the past, is merely to add more detail to a picture in which we will also find place for philosophic, scientific and technological innovation.

Let us next consider the new ways of describing and thinking about man and the universe, the new facets of knowledge, the new conjectures. But we must not forget how strongly the greater part of the population still took for granted those older ideas often spoken of as mediaeval. To understand the age we must not ignore, but must at times use our imagination seriously to consider, notions which have long been exploded. The very fact that so much of the old existed side by side with the new makes it essential not to concentrate on innovation any more than on the older world picture. It is equally essential not to try to imagine any representative Elizabethan or renaissance mind with the implication that on certain matters all people between 1558 and 1629 thought alike, or that the majority of them did. Nevertheless certain basic assumptions were taken for granted then which we do not take for granted now. Even if all adults did not share the beliefs in order and hierarchy treated by Dr E. M. W. Tillyard in *The Elizabethan World Picture* (1943), they knew that these beliefs were common to the greater part of their fellow-countrymen. There is a difference between the unbelief which comes from ignorance, and that which is the result of a conscious choice. The Elizabethan who did not believe in the so-called Aristotelian-Ptolemaic description of the universe knew what that was. Similarly the Elizabethan understood completely why Protestant Europe delighted in emphasizing the fact that Providence had intervened in the defeat of the Armada, completing with gales what had been started by human determination. This is not to say that the belief in the working of Providence which we find in Elizabethan and Jacobean Anglicanism was peculiar to that age. But despite the survival of the doctrine in later centuries, many a student of *Hamlet* in those centuries has had to have his attention directed to its importance in understanding that play.[4] It is safe to say that the average Elizabethan lived at a time when many of his contemporaries shared beliefs and assumptions which have not existed side by side in any later period; and even if he did not share every belief with his countrymen he knew what they accepted nevertheless. Simply by enumerating and expounding what the Elizabethan took for granted we cannot re-create the Elizabethan mind or acquire an Elizabethan consciousness. Yet to understand the age we need to know what the Elizabethan was conscious of, particularly if we wish to respond as fully as is possible to us in this century to the literature and drama of Shakespeare's age. That the age abounded in inconsistencies need not surprise us; it is human nature to be inconsistent. The changes which have taken place since the Second World War allow us no surprise that Spenser, that most sensitive of men, could be quite savage about the Irish; we are not shocked to learn of the 'wild man' of the Druries, the family of John Donne's benefactor. It appears that one of the forms in which they sought to honour Elizabeth when she visited Hawstead Place in 1578 was by setting up a stone figure of Hercules in the inner court facing the entrance: 'in one hand a club across his shoulders, the other resting on one hip, discharging a perennial stream of water, by the urinary passage, into a carved stone basin.' (R. C. Bald, *Donne and the Druries* [1959], p. 159.) There is no record that the Virgin Queen took exception to this piece of sculpture.

This earthy quality of Elizabethan society has to be set in the balance with the poetic adulation of the Queen in verse as Gloriana, Diana and other ideal abstractions. Similarly we must not ignore the savagery with which Sidney threatened his father's secretary with cold steel if he so much as touched any letter which the father received from his son; but we must set it beside Sidney's thought for the greater need of a common soldier, in an age when common soldiery counted for very little.[5]

We must remind ourselves that human beings tend to be illogical and inconsistent when we consider that scientific and philosophical activity which has come to be described as the New Philosophy, almost certainly as the result of a misreading and misunderstanding of John Donne's famous lines in the first *Anniversarie*. The hypothesis put forward by Copernicus, even when it was accepted as fact before 1630, did not lead at once to fundamental and widespread change. Nor did a conflict between religion and science immediately develop. Despite what hindsight makes very obvious to us today, few men (if any) among Copernicus' contemporaries perceived immediately that a clash between science and religion was inevitable. The new cosmography did not make man insignificant and thus lead to a loss of confidence which had repercussions in literature. So far as men were deeply disturbed this was not because the earth was no longer to be regarded as the centre of the universe and man as unique in his home, but rather because the doctrine of divine accommodation had accustomed men to perceiving God in the accepted account of His universe. If God accommodates Himself to human understanding in our apprehension of His works, then the new astronomy rejected an important channel of knowledge of Him. Now God had become more incomprehensible again. In this situation it was no wonder that Newton was to be hailed with relief by the religious as well as with delight by the scientist, for presenting human beings once more with an intelligible account of the universe; God's presence in His works was once more to be perceived in an understanding of His works; the Divine was once more accommodated to the human intellect.[6]

When considering the new science of this period we find ourselves confronted with evidence of the renaissance habit of seeking to present novelty as the rehabilitation of what existed and became outmoded in the past. A typical example is to hand in the insistence of the supporters of the Anglican Church that their breach with

B

Rome was nothing more than a return to the pristine theology and practice established in England before the Norman Conquest. The claim was backed by documents in Old English relating to church matters, and led not surprisingly to the establishment by Parker of Old English studies in Cambridge.

An inescapable breach with the past may present itself to our eyes when we examine any particular philosophic or scientific activity in the sixteenth and early seventeenth centuries; but the actual innovator did not regard himself as such, or did not intend to substitute something fundamentally new for something old. Copernicus turned to the past when he was moved to do something about the inadequacy of the Aristotelian-Ptolemaic picture and theory of the heavens. He returned to earlier philosophers and cosmographers whom Aristotle and Ptolemy had displaced. Philolaus the Pythagorean, Heraklides of Pontus and Elephantus the Pythagorean are cited as having declared far back in antiquity that not the earth but the sun was the centre of our planetary system, and that the earth moves round the sun.[7]

Moreover, the fact that Copernicus rejected Aristotle on one count did not mean that he did so on all others. The Copernican theory is based on an acceptance of Aristotle's pronouncement that planetary orbits are circular and uniform. And Copernicus actually defended the accuracy of Ptolemy's astronomical observations. The difference was over one detail of the old picture, not with the picture as a whole.

To the age of Shakespeare Copernicus seemed to be reviving Pythagorean and Platonic thinking rather than putting forward something new. Thomas Digges, possibly the most devoted of Copernicus' English adherents, actually printed a diagram of the infinite Copernican universe in 1576 under the caption, 'A perfit description of the Coelestiall Orbes (*i.e. orbits*), according to the most ancient doctrine of the Pythagoreans, &c.' Similarly, the development of the corpuscular atomic theory in the seventeenth century was confused with a revival of such ancient atomism as that of Epicurus, as well as with Aristotle's account of *minima* which had been much discussed in the later Middle Ages.[8]

It was probably because the 'new' scientists went to times before

Aristotle for part of their inspiration that they were able so easily to retain elements of his system. Although Tycho Brahe was a meticulous observer of phenomena he put forward a cosmography in which, while the planets circled the sun, the sun itself was in orbit round the earth. And Kepler did not seem to realize how radically his system conflicted with the Greek conception of the universe. His thinking was actually seriously obstructed so long as he retained the notion that planetary movement was invariably circular, and this despite his dedication to Pythagorean and Platonic philosophy as a species of religious truth. The idea which derived from Aristotle, that motion is circular, was hard to uproot. Even Galileo consistently ignored his friend Kepler's account of the planetary orbits as elliptical. Despite his own work on magnetism, Gilbert accepted so much from Aristotle that he tried to discover whether the electrical property of rubbed amber, still known as the 'soul', really was peculiar to amber, and found by experiment that it was not. Gilbert's own work was undertaken with the intention of showing that the observed phenomenon of magnetism was an extension of rather than a contradiction of the Aristotelian system. As late as 1635, John Swan's *Speculum Mundi* (other editions 1643, 1665 and 1670) denounced Aristotle's doctrine of the changeless heavens, of the distinction between sublunary matter and the pure fifth element of the heavens. Swan repeats and accepts the accounts given by Brahe, Kepler and other astronomers of the newly observed stars and comets, and yet, on religious grounds, he maintains that the earth is motionless, employing traditional Aristotelian arguments to prove this. And despite this opinion he was still able to accept Tycho Brahe's system of the universe and insisted that the old theory of solid planetary orbs was false.[9]

Where we might least expect it we find the enduring power of a notion from the past, despite the fact that it was soon to be utterly exploded. No less a person than William Harvey was guided towards his discovery of the circulation of the blood to some extent by his acceptance of the Aristotelian doctrine that motion is circular. And, for all his development of modern scientific method, Harvey did not doubt that the heart is more than a pump, that it changes the blood while pumping it. Harvey was largely instrumental in displacing Aristotle and Galen, but he continued to believe in the presence of 'spirits' (substance at once body and soul) in the blood, which he thought was recharged with them and with heat by the heart, in accordance with the old physiology if not with the old anatomy.[10]

We must abandon the modern assumption that for a man of the age of Shakespeare to question one element of the old philosophy was tantamount to questioning it as a whole. Very often men whom posterity has recognized as responsible for exploding some essential part of the old system of things neither intended, nor were even aware of the possibility of, change so fundamental and so widespread. This is true of Bacon in respect of the modern materialism which grew out of his desire to guide mankind into realizing the full potential of Adam, who, even after the Fall, was seen as immeasurably superior in knowledge and ability to his sixteenth- and seventeenth-century descendants. Bacon, who rejected the Copernican hypothesis, genuinely saw no conflict between religion and science; he was confident that man could profit from the lesson of the fall of the angels, in which knowledge was sought without charity (or love of God). But thanks to Jesus, man could preserve charity in his search for knowledge, and in that there was no danger. Knowledge without pride was beneficial.[11] Like Milton in *Of Education*, Bacon believed that the end of learning is 'to repair the ruins of our first parents', to undo, so far as is humanly possible, under God, the degeneration in human intellectual activity since their Fall. We need not be dismayed, nor patronisingly edified, by the failure of past men of genius to realize what they have been instrumental in making obvious to the conforming mediocrity of the twentieth century. As it is in the nature of the human mind to work illogically unless stern discipline be unremittingly applied, so is it our habit to hold self-contradictory ideas quite happily in neighbouring watertight mental compartments. The juxtaposition of the contents gives rise to no disconcerting upheaval. We must also beware of allowing our hindsight to endow fallible human beings of four centuries ago with powers of foresight which in fact they did not possess. And why should they have had such powers?

It is extremely hard, if at all possible, to rethink from top to bottom a whole new cosmography, chemistry, geography, physics, medicine, physiology, almost every branch of existing knowledge, even if we limit that to what existed in the age of Shakespeare. Not only did older notions endure through our period; some lasted into the eighteenth century, when it was still possible to practise medicine in accordance with a belief in the humours. How the old lingered is admirably exemplified by an entry in Bailey's *Dictionary* (1721), which preserves opinions on physiology and psychology current in Shakespeare's lifetime. *Common Sensory* (among Naturalists) is defined as:

> that Place in the Brain where all Sensation is suppos'd to be performed, where the Soul takes Cognizance of all Objects which present themselves to the Senses.

Elsewhere Bailey defines *Naturalist* as 'One skilled in natural Philosophy', and *Natural Philosophy* as:

> that Science which contemplates the Powers of Nature, the properties of natural bodies, and their mutual action one upon another.

Here is a remnant of the old Aristotelian belief in 'common sensibles', that is, such qualities as size, shape, duration, movement, which were thought to be perceived by the Common Sense. This, one of the Five Wits in Shakespeare's time, was the faculty which combined and selected what was reported by the senses, which transmitted without recognizing what they perceived. Sir John Davies (in *Nosce Teipsum* [1599], p. 46) sings that:

> One *Common* power doth in the forehead sit
> Which all their proper forms together brings.

He is talking of the forms transmitted by the senses.

The immediate reaction to Copernicus, particularly in England, was not fear or delight at the prospect of the old system crumbling. Before the telescope made possible the observations of new evidence, even after the nova of 1572, people who knew of him for the most part regarded his work as merely providing a mathematical explanation of observed phenomena. Even after the telescope was used in astronomy, many scientists regarded the compromise of Tycho Brahe as a sensible solution of the problem. Widespread acceptance of Copernicus' findings did not come in Europe until after 1630. And until Newton's pronouncements of 1687 it was justifiable to consider at least three alternative systems.

At first Protestants in Europe showed no sustained hostility to Copernicus, nothing more than some intermittent suspicion. Real opposition came only with the growth of a Protestant scholasticism after 1560, when the Bible was defended as literally inerrant (this was not the practice of Luther and Calvin). Now the theological and assumptions of scientists seemed to imply inherent conflict with Christianity.[12]

The settlement of 1559 protected the new astronomers in England from both the threat and the reality of Papal hostility, and in fact English theologians raised little opposition to the Copernican system for a long time.

Robert Recorde the mathematician was not a thorough-going Copernican, but he defended the hypothesis as early as 1556 in his *Castle of Knowledge*. In the same year John Feild's *Ephemeris anni 1557* was published with a preface by John Dee in Latin, in which Copernicus' mathematics were accepted; but there is no certainty that Dee ever accepted the heliocentric account as a physical reality. From 1558 onwards his home at Mortlake became the centre of a circle favourably disposed to the new astronomy.

Much of the writing of the English scientists of this period was in English, which meant a larger audience for their ideas. A translation from the Latin of Palingenius' *Zodiacus Vitae*, which was not strictly scientific, was of great influence in preparing Englishmen for the eventual exploding of Aristotelianism. This translation, by Barnaby Googe, appeared in 1560 and went through several editions by the end of the century; it denies the infallibility of Aristotle and refers to earlier Greek philosophers, who as we have seen, are relevant to the work of Copernicus. This modest piece of verse had much the same effect on the popular reader as the more sustained and learned attack on Aristotelianism carried on in learned circles by Peter Ramus. Another English work was Dee's

Preface to Henry Billingsly's translation of Euclid (1570), which gives an account of those aspects of Platonic philosophy associated with the new astronomy.

The new star in Cassiopeia in 1572 stimulated Englishmen such as Dee and Thomas Digges; and the latter dedicated himself to observing the heavens in the hope of finding indisputable evidence of the correctness of Copernicus' system. Digges dedicated his *Alae seu Scalae Mathematicae* to Lord Burghley; in it he declares his hope that observation of the new star would in fact confirm the new system. A year later Digges published as a supplement of his father's *Prognostication Everlasting* that *Perfect Description of the Celestial Orbs* already referred to, in which he asserts that Copernicus both revived the 'most ancient doctrines of the Pythagoreans' and proved it 'by Geometrical Demonstrations'. He sets forth the doctrine of the infinity of the universe in this work which was reprinted six times, right up to 1605. Digges thus seems to have anticipated the views of Bruno in England, for this Italian did not visit the country until 1583, and even then his work was in his native language, not in English.

Without going into great detail it is possible to assert at this point that by 1600 Copernicanism was firmly established in England. That year saw the publication of Gilbert's work on magnetism. The year 1609 is usually associated with the next great step forward in astronomy, thanks to Galileo's account of his observations through the telescope. It appears, however, that this instrument had already been worked on and used by various Englishmen, among them Thomas Harriott who used it for terrestrial observation in Virginia in 1575. Exact details and dates are unknown but there is evidence that he and his friends possessed and used telescopes for astronomy no later than 1609. It is certain, too, that Francis Godwin's story, *The Man in the Moon*, was written before 1610 (published 1638), at least those parts which accept much Copernicanism and those which follow Gilbert in a refusal to accept that part of the theory which has the earth revolving round the sun.[13]

After 1610 the new data provided by the telescope, whether in the hands of Galileo or of his fellow experimenters in England, was incorporated into the new pictures of the cosmos. Notably Marke Ridley in his *Short Treatise of Magnetical Bodies and Motions* (1613) applied the new information to Gilbert's conclusions on magnetism. How firmly the new scientific ideas had taken hold is shown by Barclay's complaint in *Icon Animorum* (1614) that the English in particular had adopted the erroneous ideas of Copernicus, Tycho Brahe and Gilbert. There was a certain amount of religious opposition to the new astronomy, but religion and science were not inevitably in conflict. For instance, Digges and Brahe had each regarded the *nova* of 1572 as a miracle, despite the fact that it made them question the old cosmography. Samuel Purchas was typical of much English religious thinking when he asserted in the second edition of *Purchas his Pilgrimage* (1614) that there was no essential conflict between Brahe, Gilbert, Copernicus, Galileo and the biblical account of creation (pp. 9ff.).

It would be idle to attempt to prove that there was no religious opposition to the new ideas; but it is equally inaccurate to assert that their advance led to consternation in intellectual England. To some extent a false picture of the impact of the new ideas has been given in modern times by a misreading of Donne's first *Anniversarie* (1611), in particular of the lines:

> And new Philosophy calls all in doubt.
> The Element of fire is quite put out;

In this poem, Donne did not express consternation at the disappearance of old certainties crumbling into chaos; his consternation was at human pride, his own in particular; satirically as well as mournfully, he surveys a world which has decayed further and further since the Fall. So far from being 'put out', the 'Element of fire' continued to be accepted by many scientists until Boyle's *Sceptical Chymist* (1661). Paracelsus had believed in four elements in theory, but in practice had assumed the presence in bodies of three principles, salt, mercury, sulphur (the latter an equivalent to fire). Eventually the Flemish scientist van Helmont declared that there were only two elements, air and water, but he did not start his researches till 1609, and there is little likelihood that Donne was thinking of him. More probably he was referring to the denials of the existence of the element fire made by Cardan, Brahe and John Pena, whom he mentions in a sermon. But so far as Donne experienced apprehension this came not from fear of new ideas but of his own damnation. His state of mind is excellently communicated to us in the sonnet which starts with a reference to 'the round earth's imagined corners'. So far from decrying the new astronomy, his *Ignatius his Conclave* (1611) denies that Copernicus was responsible for men coming to believe that there is no hell, or to deny the punishment of sin. 'Do not men believe? Do they not live just as they did before?'

As we begin to realize just how much scientific and technological activity preceded or accompanied the composition of *The Advancement of Learning* (first published in English 1605; expanded, written in Latin and published as *De Augmentis Scientiarum* in 1623), it grows obvious that the place and achievement of Bacon must be reconsidered. Craftsmen and scholars had started collaborating before he wrote his demands for a new technology; but his plans were more thorough and far-reaching than what was being done. He seems to have been able to grasp essentials more clearly and more completely than his contemporaries, seeing a more complete and more integrated whole. His inspiration was not to his contemporaries but to later generations. The new developments of the age of Shakespeare were virtually untouched by, and owed nothing to, Bacon; but his thinking affected those who took advantage of the work of his contemporaries. Particularly was this so after the translation of his Latin back into English by Wats in 1640. And one result of that translation was the decision of John Bulwer to write two books, *Chirologia* (1644) and *Chironomia* (1644), on the hand and arm in what he calls 'manual rhetoric', but which we should understand as 'non-verbal communication'. Bulwer actually quotes Bacon's call for an account of this art as it had been in the past and was in the early seventeenth century (*Chirologia*, p. 8). The two works which resulted do not so much teach how the art should be practised as give an account of what existed at the time of writing, as well as what had been done in the past. They have proved a valuable aid to an understanding of the acting of the pre-Restoration theatre in our own day. Bacon's thinking was not materialistic; it certainly blended with and inspired much later materialistic thought, but that was not his aim. Looking back we can see that, intended or not, this result is logically to be expected. But, lacking our hindsight, Bacon and his contemporaries did not realise this.

The age of Shakespeare was too complex for us to hope to explain it with a single key, or with any small number of keys. We must be wary, in particular, not to fall victim to the temptation of adopting some fashionable (but evanescent) theory of history to explain the period or some large aspect of it. For instance, it is not really helpful to find in alleged changes of 'Philosophy' or in the 'New Science' an explanation for developments in literature. As we shall see in Chapter 7, the heroic couplet was written in English long before Dryden; and it is rash to ascribe certain qualities of Augustan writing to a theory of imagination associated with Hobbes, when in fact these qualities are to be found in the Elizabethan period, and when Hobbes' theory of imagination agrees with, not differs from, earlier theories in a common assumption that reason should be in control. For centuries before Hobbes, imagination was regarded as sensual, as distinct from rational, activity. Milton apparently coined the term 'sensuous' in order to avoid the pejorative connotations of 'sensual', not denying that the senses are involved in the creating of and the responding to a poem.

A specialist in one discipline is in danger of making serious mistakes when he accepts in good faith the findings of specialists in others, and when, without consulting their first-hand sources, he applies these findings to his own subject. In the recent past, literary historians and critics have tended to interpret literature in terms of theories of sociology exploded by professional sociologists. The literature and drama of the age of Shakespeare have been interpreted in accordance with theories and readings of Stuart economic, social and political history no longer accepted by historians. An orthodoxy has developed in which literature is related to a postulated rise of the middle classes and to a new mercantile morality, despite the fact that historians of the sixties are of the well-advised opinion that we still do not have enough conclusive evidence covering enough relevant fields to justify an attempted explanation of what was happening in England between the accession of Elizabeth and the start of the Civil War. Whatever changes took place in the position of the English middle class in Shakespeare's time it is certain that they did not dominate politics, economics, society or morality. They were, indeed, increasingly charitable and compensated for deficiencies shown by their more selfish or spendthrift social superiors.[14]

It is equally inaccurate to speak of the aristocracy as bad businessmen, losing ground irretrievably to the merchants or to one section or other of the gentry. In fact the titular nobility lost power, status and wealth temporarily relative to some of the gentry and merchants, but their economic position had been restored by the early 1620s. Not all noblemen were bad businessmen; they included among their number some of the most successful of all entrepreneurs. While some merchants were indeed wealthier than many aristocrats by 1630, the aim of the *parvenu* was to be accepted by, not to displace, his superiors. Aristocratic ways of thinking and behaving were taken over, not rejected, by the new men of wealth so far as they succeeded in establishing themselves among the *élite*. All this is commonplace for historians at the moment of writing; but little of it has percolated into standard works seeking to relate Elizabethan and Stuart literature and drama to the society in which they were produced.

We must aim at avoiding generalizations which are based on too few particulars. Generalization is justified when it derives from sufficient individual details of fact, but is to be abandoned when they are contradicted by too many of such details. So far as generalizations have been formulated in this book they should be accepted by the reader only so long as they are not contradicted by factual details unknown to the present writer, or by details of whose relevance he has not been aware. One generalization seems to be valid, however; England in the age of Shakespeare was a society dominated in almost every detail of its existence by a small *élite* numbering at the most five per cent of the population, but probably no larger than two per cent, according to reputable modern authorities. This is the consensus of opinion among historians at the moment of writing. Wherever we turn, the England of Shakespeare's age affords evidence of the domination of this *élite*, composed of the gentry, the titular nobility and the monarch. Nevertheless, there is no intention here of putting forward the fact of this domination as a key to an understanding of the age. It is stated as a fact which itself demands explanation (though that can easily be provided) rather than as in itself an explanation of every other fact which can be shown true of Elizabethan and Stuart England.

This book covers roughly three main fields of study, three different academic disciplines, history, thought and literature (dramatic and non-dramatic). Any coherence which it may have will be justifiable only if it derives from the fact that each of these fields of activity is centred on the same age. Certainly no attempt has been made consciously to subordinate any one field either to the interests of another, or to the need to present a coherent picture.

The studies of history, of thought and of literature are three distinct activities; obviously they cannot be usefully undertaken in watertight separation from one another, but the fact that they are related ought not to lead us to confuse them with one another. History concentrates on factual evidence of what existed, possibly as an end in itself, but more fruitfully for most of us when it involves some explanation of what happened. To study thought means to follow other minds through the convolutions of abstract discourse, to learn to understand what they were thinking and why. But the study of literature, dramatic or not, involves response to an artist's communication of his own reaction to the world in which he lives; this response is not part of the study of history and thought, unless we are studying the history of an art.

The way in which the three activities are related and yet separate can be illustrated by considering Goneril's words which begin Act I, Scene iii of *King Lear:* 'Did my father strike my gentleman for chiding of his fool?' The social historian relates this to his knowledge that in Shakespeare's England anyone below the rank of gentleman might expect to be exposed to a beating, to be struck in one way or another, by a superior or a superior's servants before he had lived his whole life. But a member of the *élite*, from gentleman upwards, could expect normally to be exempt from this indignity; even those of gentle birth might be beaten until they were accepted as adult; but those who were adult and gentle were not to be struck or beaten. The student of political thought fused to theology will see in Lear's reported action a breach of order; he will relate the statement to what he understands of Elizabethan thinking about hierarchy and order in the universe. The student of drama needs to share the knowledge possessed by the student of history and of thought; but he uses it to respond imaginatively to one moment, one incident, in a complex artistic statement.

To take advantage of such historical knowledge in responding to *King Lear* should not be confused with any sort of attempt to turn ourselves into Elizabethans, or to think with an Elizabethan mind. Instead we remain firmly in our own century, imagining a play which was written in another; we imagine a situation in which the King's behaviour apparently justifies complaint; he seems to have gone too far; he should not have struck Goneril's gentleman; it is an affront to her rank, to her, personally, just as the stocking of Kent later is an affront to the King. Similarly, factual historical knowledge is integrated into our imagining of the play when Lear is answered by Oswald that he is not a knave, slave, whoreson dog or cur, 'I am none of these my lord; I beseech your pardon.' Lear bursts out: 'Do you bandy looks with me, you rascal?' and strikes him (I, iv). To 'bandy looks' is to look the superior straight in the eyes, to give back look for look. To know this is to be able to imagine the appalling situation which is developing, when Goneril's steward behaves so outrageously to the King. Another example of the need to have factual knowledge in order to imagine the play occurs when Gloucester refers to Cornwall as 'my worthy arch and patron' (II, i. 58-9). To the historian this is a reference to a client-patron relationship, such as existed among gentry and noblemen in Shakespeare's lifetime. The person of lesser rank attached himself as 'client' to the fortunes of the 'patron.' Great magnates were attended in their own neighbourhood, on journeys and at Court or on ceremonial occasions in the provinces, by noble persons of lesser rank, wearing their colours; the lesser men attested by their presence to the status, the 'worth' of the patrons.[15] Where the historian might care to use this statement in *King Lear* as evidence of the existence of this sort of relationship, the student of drama finds that the factual historical information lets him imagine the complexity of the relationship between Gloucester and Cornwall and Cornwall's wife; Gloucester's submission to Cornwall and entertainment of him, his wife and entourage is not merely the behaviour of subject to ruler, it involves the relationship of client to patron; and Gloucester's decision to help Lear is more than treachery to Cornwall, the ruler of half the country; here is a repudiation of a deep-rooted mutual acknowledgment of ties and obligations. The intensity of Cornwall's resentment is partly against the client who denies his patron. (III, ii.)

There can be no disputing the fact that to obtain the fullest picture of Shakespeare's age we must consider its literature and drama as well as its history and the state of thought. But it seems necessary to exercise caution not to confuse these with one another, or to misunderstand their relationship. Possibly the most important of the differences to be kept in mind is that between drama and non-dramatic literature on the one hand and history and thought on the other. The Homily on Obedience is quite a different statement from the words which state the subject's duty of obedience in *Richard II* (III, ii, 54-62; III, iii, 74-90; IV, i, 114-133). The sermon is a non-poetic abstract discourse on this topic; the play is a complex imagining in which the artist communicates by means of his medium much that cannot be communicated verbally as well as much that can. And that part which can be communicated verbally is more than an abstract statement on the need for obedience. We can isolate that part of the whole statement and refer to it as an element of the total meaning which Shakespeare emphasizes and to which he directs our attention as something of importance in relation to everything else in the play. When we respond to Richard's assertion of the Divine Right of Kings, or to Carlisle's insistence on the subject's duty of obedience as we imagine the play, we relate these individual elements to the whole to which they belong. But when we attempt to explain in our own words their significance we cannot simultaneously state the meaning and communicate an imagining of the play. Too many things have to be said simultaneously if our account of their meaning is to be complete; and the only way of using words to communicate all these elements of meaning simultaneously has already been adopted by Shakespeare. Even if it were possible to make a separate abstract statement of the meaning of every individual element of a whole play, the reader or listener responding to each element separately in sequence would receive a communication quite different from that which comes from imagining these elements as they are integrated into the complex but single statement of the work of art, that is, a single, complex, coherent statement of many things at once.

It remains to ask why we should give attention to any or all the aspects of the age of Shakespeare treated, why we should study its history, its thought or its literature and drama. First let me answer that any of these activities is justifiable as an end in itself; it is enough to want to know about and to understand the history for its own sake, or the thought, or the literature or drama, simply because we want to. But some people may wish to find in them a guide which helps to an understanding of the modern world. Others may want to study any one or more as an aid to an understanding of one of the others. As we have seen, historical information helps our imagining of a play, and a passage in a play contributes to the historical account. There is a danger, however, in studying one subject in order to apply it to our interest in another. We are apt to notice only those aspects of it which relate to our major interest. It seems preferable to pursue the study of each aspect of this age as a separate endeavour undertaken for its own sake; then when a real knowledge has been achieved, the time has come to subordinate it to the major interest. It is tempting to find in Gloucester's reference to the lunar and solar eclipses in *King Lear* an expression of Shakespeare's reaction to the development of new scientific thinking about the stars, and to associate that thinking with such figures as Bacon and Raleigh.[16] But study of English thought on this matter in the time of these men, and study of Raleigh and Bacon themselves, in order to have an accurate knowledge of this field, will soon show us that these two believed in the influence of the stars; further study shows us that what Gloucester says about eclipses must not be confused with what people said about the stars. He is talking about something else; the way in which divine warnings against sin are given by portents such as earthquakes and eclipses; as we know more of the Elizabethans we find that Elizabeth and responsible statesmen (Bacon and Raleigh among them) shared Gloucester's view of portents (whether eclipses or earthquakes).[17] Whatever Shakespeare may or may not be doing with Gloucester will not alter the fact that Bacon believed in the influence of the stars, in the significance of portents. Conversely, the fact that Bacon believed in portents does not mean that Shakespeare shared that belief, or that he is denying it in his imagining of Gloucester. The lesson here is that if we are to use one kind of knowledge in the service of another, we must not let our intention mislead us into accepting incomplete knowledge as sufficient for our purposes.

Every writer writes with a bias, whether consciously or not. My own bias is obvious by now, I hope. I am reluctant to agree that there is any one key to all that is of importance in the age of Shakespeare. As I have said it seems to me that in this study three separate disciplines are involved, history, thought and literature. The differences between these three need to be observed even while we relate one to another. If we are not yet able to relate every aspect of the age consistently to all the others it may be for two reasons; we do not yet have all the necessary evidence (a view which historians of the 1960s are tending to adopt) and the age was one of such inconsistencies in fact that they cannot be reconciled but must merely be acknowledged.

REFERENCES

[1] C. V. Wedgwood, *The Trial of Charles I* (1964), p. 192.
[2] *Ibid.*, p. 193.
[3] See P. Ramsey, *Tudor Economic Problems* (1963).
[4] B. L. Joseph, 'The Theme' in *Twentieth-Century Interpretations of Hamlet*, ed. D. Bevington (1968), pp.
[5] *Miscellaneous Works*, ed. Gray (1829), pp. 277f.
[6] See J. Dillenberger, *Protestant Thought and Natural Science* (1960), pp. 118ff.
[7] *Ibid.*, pp. 24ff., 31ff; F. R. Johnson, *Astronomical Thought in Renaissance England* (1937), pp. 93ff.
[8] See A. G. Van Melsen, *From Atmos to Atom* (1960), pp. 58ff., 73ff.
[9] F. R. Johnson, *op. cit.*, pp. 275ff.

[10] A. R. Hall, *The Scientific Revolution 1500-1800* (1966), pp. 144ff; R. Willis, *The Works of William Harvey* (1877), pp. 47, 68.

[11] Bacon, *The Advancement of Learning*, tr. Wats (1640), pp. 18ff.

[12] Dillenberger, *op. cit.*, pp. 31ff.

[13] Johnson, *op. cit.*, pp. 227f.

[14] See, for instance, W. H. Coates, 'An Analysis of Major Conflicts in Seventeenth-Century England', in *Conflict in Stuart England*, ed. Aiken and Henning (1960), pp. 15ff.

[15] See Sir John Neale, 'The Elizabethan Political Scene', in *Essays in Elizabethan History* (1958), pp. 59ff; L. Stone, *The Crisis of Aristocracy* (1965), pp. 210ff., 257-263, 385ff.

[16] See, for instance, J. Danby, *Shakespeare's Doctrine of Nature in King Lear*, (1949).

[17] See pp. 262f., 343f.

c

2 : The Commonwealth of England

Social Divisions

THE Elizabethans had a tendency to speak of their society as if it were virtually an ideal conception of a commonwealth realized in fact, as if they and their countrymen organized in rigid hierarchy beneath their monarch had achieved a superb state of perfect order. We shall be concerned more particularly with theory of government, of order and hierarchy, in Chapter 4, but it is fitting at this point to turn our attention to a typical account of the ideal of a commonwealth as it occurs in a homily of 1547:

> Every degree of people in their vocation, calling, and office hath appointed to them their duty and order. Some are in high degree, some in low; some kings and princes, some inferiors and subjects; priests and laymen, masters and servants, fathers and children, husbands and wives, rich and poor; and every one hath need of other so that in all things is to be lauded and praised the goodly order of God without the which no house, no city, no commonwealth, can continue and endure. (*Certain Sermons or Homilies*.)[1]

Here is the pattern which the contemporaries of Shakespeare were apt to find repeated in the body politic of their land; and to some extent they were not mistaken. Elizabethan, Jacobean, early Caroline society distinguished sharply between superior and inferior, subordinating the latter, whether as wife to husband, servant to master, gentleman to nobleman, or nobleman to king. The great distinction was between those who were 'gentle' and those who were 'simple' or 'base'. Theory and traditional attitudes set an almost unbridgeable gap between these two sections of the population; but in fact there was considerable movement up and down, not only between these two large categories themselves, but within them on the many rungs of the ladder separating and connecting the lowest of bedlam beggars and the king. To move from one of the strata to another was not to call the whole structure into question; the newcomer was absorbed into the group which he joined; and if he had moved up rather than down he had every incentive to maintain the barrier he had surmounted as a mark of his own achievement as well as an obstacle to those below. It is true that Elizabethans tended to regard examples of such mobility as unfortunate aberrations rather than as evidence of a flexibility preferable to the rigid stratification which nothing but upheaval could break. In our period (*c.*1558 – *c.*1629), there was little demand for such an upheaval, partly because it was possible to move up the ladder, but even more because those who were regarded as 'gentle' (a small minority) were in a position to dominate the majority of the population in almost every element of national life.

In the age of Shakespeare England was dominated by a small *élite*, the 'gentle'. In this chapter we shall concern ourselves with the organization of English society, the hierarchies within it, the mobility within the hierarchies and from one to another, noting not only the alliance of monarch and 'gentles' in their domination of their countrymen, but the mental attitudes, the distribution of economic, political, legal and military power which evolved from it, made it possible and maintained it. We shall find ourselves noticing the weaknesses of this alliance, the issues which generated tensions, which were eventually to lead to its disruption. But the evolution and development of conflict between the monarch and various important sections of the gentle *élite* as well as parts of the population designated 'base' or 'simple' will be treated in a later chapter.

In *Positions* (1581), the celebrated schoolmaster of Plymouth, Richard Mulcaster, tells us with assurance (p. 198): 'All the people which be in our country be either gentlemen or of the commonalty. The common is divided into merchants and manuaries generally.' By 'manuaries' he means those who work with their hands. A contemporary has been quoted in his confidence that the division goes right back to the beginning of the human race (Inner Temple

MS 53844, f. 13): 'All sorts of people created from the beginning are divided into two: Noble and Ignoble.' Cain was the first of those lacking gentility: 'As Adam had sons of honour, so had he Cain destinated to dishonour.'[2]

De Republica Anglorum (1583), by Sir Thomas Smith, gives a standard Elizabethan account of the stratification of contemporary society. Smith does not refer explicitly to the division into noble and ignoble, but the arrangement of the book distinguishes one from the other:

> We in England divide our men commonly into four sorts, gentlemen, citizens, yeomen, artificers, and labourers. Of gentlemen the first and chief are the king, prince, dukes, marquises, earls, viscounts, barons, and these are called the nobility, and all these are called lords and noblemen: next to these be knights, esquires and simple gentlemen. (Bk. 1, chapter 16; ed. Alston, 1906, p. 31.)

The next five chapters deal with the different kinds of gentlemen in detail, explaining the qualifications required for gentility in Elizabethan England, before anything like a full account is given of those who were not gentle, 'citizens and burgesses', yeomen and 'the fourth sort of men', day-labourers and poor husbandmen.

Nobilitas maior is Smith's term for the higher strata of the 'gentlemen of England', those, that is, whose titles were hereditary.

> Dukes, marquises, earls, viscounts, and barons either be created by the prince or come to that honour by being the eldest sons, as highest and next in succession to their parents. For the eldest of duke's sons during his father's life is called an earl, an earl's son is called by the name of a viscount, a viscount's son is called a baron, or else according as the creation is. The creation I call that first donation and condition of honour (given by the prince, for good services done by him and advancement that the prince will bestow upon him) which with the title of that honour is commonly (but not always) given to him and his heirs, males only: the rest of the sons of the nobility by the rigour of the law be but esquires, yet in common speech, all dukes and marquises'

sons, and the eldest son of an earl be called lords. The which name commonly doth agree to none of lower degree than barons, excepting such only as be thereunto by some special office called.

During this period as a whole there was a large increase in the number of those holding hereditary titles, particularly after James I's creation of the new rank of baronet in 1611. Elizabeth created few peers, and it has been said that her policy to some extent intensified the pressure for titles which her successor was tempted into satisfying. There were fifty-seven males peers on her accession in 1558, but no more than fifty-five when she died in 1603. From 1573 onwards she created only three new peers. In the whole of her reign Elizabeth created, revived, recognized or admitted only eighteen hereditary titles: six of these were restorations, two peers inherited in the female line, three were younger sons of peers; two titles went to heirs or co-heirs of existing noble houses and three to cousins of the Queen. Only two titles went to persons possessing none of these qualifications; but they, Lord Burghley and Lord Compton, each came from knightly families. During Elizabeth's reign fourteen noble families became extinct, six lapsing by attainder.[3]

For the first twelve years of his reign James I was not niggardly, but did not create too many new peerages; but from 1616 onwards the situation changed. From 1616 to 1630 James and Charles between them made seventy-five new peers, the numbers rising from eighty-one to one hundred and fifty-six, not counting the large increase in Irish peers, who did not sit in the English House of Lords. By 1629 England had about twenty-five peers to every million of its population. A year earlier the Venetian Ambassador noted that the number of 'councillors and titled persons' had been 'so constantly multiplied that they are no longer distinguishable from the common people' (CSPVen., 1626-28, p. 607; quoted Stone, p. 121). Where there had been twenty-seven earls at the end of 1615, there were now sixty-five. Another idea of the changes can be given by comparing the numbers of new creations: in 1558 forty-six per cent of the peers were in the first or second generations;

by 1603 the percentage had dropped to eighteen but it had risen by 1628 to fifty-seven; and now forty-four per cent of the total peerage consisted of new creations in the first generation.

Smith has a chapter in *De Republica Anglorum* 'Of the second sort of gentlemen which may be called *nobilitas minor*, and first of knights'. *Nobilitas minor*, the 'second sort of gentleman', also included Esquires and plain Gentlemen. Smith emphasizes the point that knighthood is not hereditary: 'No man is a knight by succession, not the king or prince.' Knights, he observes, 'therefore be not born but made, either before the battle to encourage them the more to adventure their lives, or after the conflict, as advancement for their hardiness and manhood already showed: or out of the war for some great service done, or some good hope through the virtues which do appear in them. And they are made either by the king himself, or by his commission or royal authority given for the same purpose, or by his lieutenant in the wars, who hath his royal and absolute power committed to him for that time.'

Smith compares the knights of England to the order of ancient Rome, *equites Romanos*, who were chosen 'according to their substance and riches'. Similarly English knights were chosen according to their financial ability to maintain the dignity of the rank. But the mere financial position itself did not qualify for knighthood. 'No more are all made knights in England that may spend a knight's land or fee, but they only whom the king will so honour. The number of *equites* was uncertain, and so it is of knights at the pleasure of the prince.' Any Englishman with the requisite wealth could be compelled to accept a knighthood or pay a fine:

> *Census equester* was among the Romans at divers times of divers value: but in England whosoever may dispend of his free lands £40 sterling of yearly revenue by an old law of England either at the coronation of the king, or marriage of his daughter, or at the dubbing of the prince, knight, or some such great occasion, may be by the king compelled to take that order or honour or to pay a fine, which many not desirous of honour as of riches, had rather disburse. Some who for causes are not thought worthy of that honour and yet have

ability, neither be made knights although they would, and yet pay the fine. (Bk. I, chapter 19, pp. 38f.)

One order of knighthood was nearer in dignity and honour to an hereditary title; this was the order of Knights of the Bath. Elizabeth created eleven of these knights in 1559; but as she made no more for the rest of her reign, the order was almost extinct by 1603. The monarch alone could make a Knight of the Bath and only at coronations, royal marriages, christenings, and the knighting of the Prince of Wales. The unmarried Elizabeth had no opportunity to increase the numbers of the order once her coronation was past. Sixty-two were made at James' coronation; by 1640 there were one hundred and ninety, not an excessive number.

In 1558 there were about six hundred other knights in England. By 1573 one hundred and fifty-three knights had been made, forty of them by bearers of the Queen's commission in Ireland. By 1583 there were one hundred and seventy-eight more, of whom twenty-nine were 'Irish'. But the total number of knights in the country fell to about three hundred. Between 1574 and 1603 only three hundred and thirty-two knights were created in England by or with the approval of the Queen; but another three hundred and ninety-three had been made, largely to the Queen's disgust, by her generals campaigning abroad, particularly by Essex in Ireland in 1599 and with Lord Howard of Effingham earlier. By the end of the reign, despite these controversial creations the number of knights had fallen from about six hundred to about five hundred and fifty.

James I actually dubbed nine hundred and six knights in the first four months of his reign, and by December there were eleven hundred and sixty-one new creations. During the whole of Elizabeth's reign eight hundred and seventy-eight knights were made by the Queen, her generals and lords-lieutenant; her two successors created no less than three thousand two hundred and eighty-one between 1603 and 1641.[4]

The next lower rank among the gentle classes was that of Esquires, described by John Selden in *Titles of Honour* (1614) as 'The first step in eminency before common gentry' (p. 343). Smith has a chapter, 'Of Esquires':

Escuier or esquier (which we call commonly squire) is a French word, and betokeneth *scutigerum* or *armigerum*, and be all those which bear arms (as we call them) or *armories* (as they term them in French) which to bear is a testimony of the nobility or race from whence they do come. These be taken for no distinct order of the commonwealth, but do go with the residue of the gentlemen: save that (as I take it) they be those who bear arms, testimonies (as I have said) of their race, and therefore have neither creation nor dubbing: or else they were at the first costerels or the bearers of the arms of lords or knights, and by that being taught in arms had that name for a dignity and honour given to distinguish them from a common soldier called in Latin *gregarius miles.* (Bk. I, chapter 19, pp. 38ff.)

Smith could be clearer, for arms were also borne by a gentleman who was not an esquire. In theory the rank of esquire included legitimately only the younger sons of peers and their heirs male, the heirs male of knights, esquires of the body (Court functionaries) and such officials as judges, sheriffs and officers of the royal household.

The lowest rank of the *élite* is treated by Smith in his chapter, 'Of Gentlemen': they are 'those whom their blood and race doth make noble'. In Latin they are *nobiles*, in French, *nobles*. The Greek and Latin terms for nobility can be defined as 'honour or title given, for that the ancestor hath been notable in riches or virtues, or (in fewer words) old riches or prowess remaining in one stock'. The quality of nobility, once developed in the progenitor is virtually perpetuated in the genes; the renaissance doctrine of nobility assumed the possibility of acquired characteristics. According to Smith, the word 'gentle' derived from the Latin *gens* (a race or surname), owing to the custom of the Romans of adding the surname of a noble ancestor, to maintain the link and assert their nobility. Those who did this 'were also *gentiles:* and remaining the glory of their progenitors' fame, were gentlemen of that or that race.' Nevertheless, in Rome as elsewhere, virtue must be honoured where it is seen among 'new men', and so it is possible to raise deserving men to gentility by desert as it is possible to raise them high to what were called 'titles of honour.'

But as other commonwealths were fain to do, so must all princes necessarily follow: that is, where virtue is to honour it: and although virtue of ancient race be easier to be obtained, as well by the example of the progenitors, which encourageth, as also through ability of education and bringing up, which enableth, and the lastly enraced love of tenants and neighbours to such noblemen and gentlemen, of whom they hold and by whom they do dwell which pricketh forward to ensure in their fathers' steps. So if all this do fail (as it were great pity it should) yet such is the nature of all human things, and so the world is subject to mutability, that it doth many times fail; but when it doth, the prince and commonwealth have the same power that their predecessors had, and as the husbandman hath to plant a new tree where the old faileth, so hath the prince to honour virtue where he doth find it, to make gentlemen, esquires, knights, barons, earls, marquises and dukes, where he seeth virtue able to bear that honour or merit, and deserves it, and so it hath always been used among us. But ordinarily the king doth only make knights and create barons or higher degrees: for as gentlemen, they be made good cheap in England. (Bk. I, chapter 20, pp. 38ff.)

Like all other titles of honour, that of simple 'gentleman' can be bestowed by king or commonwealth formally in recognition of 'virtue'. In fact, however, the practice of conceding gentility in England (or of acquiring it) was less formal, demanding less rigorous procedure.

For whoever studieth the laws of the realm, who studieth in the universities, who professeth liberal sciences, and to be short, who can live idly and without manual labour, and will bear the port, charge, and countenance of a gentleman, he shall be called master, for that is the title which men give to esquires and other gentlemen: . . . (and if need be) a king of heralds shall also give him, for money, arms, newly made and invented, the title whereof shall pretend to be found by the said herald in perusing and viewing of old registers, where his ancestors in times past had been recorded to bear the same: or if he will do it more truly and of better faith, he will write that for the merits of that man, and certain qualities which he doth see in him, and for sundry noble acts which he hath performed, he by the authority which he hath as king of heralds and arms giveth to him and his heirs these and these arms, which being done I think he may be called esquire, for he beareth ever after those arms. Such men are sometimes called in scorn gentlemen of the first head. (Bk. I, chapter 21, pp. 40f.)

It did not matter what they were called in scorn, so long as they were accepted by 'tenants and neighbours . . ., of whom they hold and by whom they do dwell'. For the moment we need merely note that it was easier to move up into the ranks of gentleman and esquire than from those into knighthood or the steps of hereditary peerage above. This remained true even when the Stuarts allowed knights, baronets (the new rank), and the various ranks of the peerage to purchase their titles for money.

During the whole of this period the so-called noble or gentle classes never totalled more than a small proportion of the whole population of England and Wales. Modern authorities have calculated the *élite* as numbering as little as two and a half per cent of the population; another suggested figure is five per cent.[5] It is even possible, with the increase in the habit of more and more merchants, shopkeepers and professional men of calling themselves 'Master', that the proportion of 'gentle' to 'base' rose, but not very significantly.

De Republica Anglorum places 'Citizens and Burgesses' at the top of the large majority of the population who were not gentle:

Next to gentlemen be appointed citizens and burgesses, such as not only be free and received as officers within the cities, but also be of some substance to bear the charges. But these citizens and burgesses be to serve the commonwealth in their cities and boroughs or in corporate towns where they dwell. Generally, in the shires they be of none account, save only in the common assembly of the realm to make laws, which is called the parliament. The ancient cities appoint four and each borough two to have voices in it and to give their consent or dissent in the name of the city or borough for which they be appointed.

In some respects the yeomen were the rural equivalent of the citizens and burgesses, inasmuch as they were immediately below the lesser gentry in rank, and movement was not difficult up or down. Smith has this to say 'Of Yeomen':

> Those whom we call yeomen, next unto the nobility, knights, and squires, have the greatest charge and doings in the commonwealth, or rather are more travailed to serve in it than all the rest: as shall appear hereafter. I call him a yeoman whom our laws do call *legalem hominem*, a word familiar in writs and inquests, which is a freeman born English, and may dispend of his own free land in yearly revenue to the sum of forty shillings sterling: this maketh (if the just value were taken now to the proportion of moneys), six pounds of our current money at this present. This sort of people confess themselves to be no gentlemen, and yet they have a certain pre-eminence and more estimation than labourers and artificers, and commonly live wealthily, keep good houses, and do their business and travail to acquire riches: . . . These be not called masters, for that (as I said) pertaineth to gentlemen only: but to their surnames men add goodman: as if the surname be *Luter, Finch, White, Brown*, they are called goodman *Luter*, goodman *Finch*, goodman *Brown*, amongst their neighbours, I mean, not in matters of importance or in law. But in matters of law and for distinction, if one were a knight they would write him (for example) Sir *John Finch* knight, so if he be an esquire, *John Finch* esquire, if he be not esquire, *John Finch* gentleman, if he be no gentleman, *John Finch* yeoman. For amongst the gentlemen they which claim no higher degree, and yet be exempted out of the number of the lowest sort thereof, be written esquires. So amongst the husbandmen, labourers, lowest and rascal sort of the people

such as be exempted out of the number of the rascability of the popular sort be called and written yeomen, as in the degree next unto gentlemen. (Bk. I, chapter 23, pp. 42f.)

In *King Lear*, Kent, in disguise, pretends not to know Edmund, deliberately addressing him as 'goodman boy' and then, sarcastically, as 'young master'.

> With you, goodman boy, an you please; come,
> I'll flesh ye; Come on, young master. (II, ii. 45-6)

In what Smith calls 'matters of importance or in law' his definition was upheld by the opinion of lawyers of the learning, prestige and authority of Sir Edward Coke; the forty-shilling freeholder was theoretically entitled to style himself 'yeoman'. It seems, however, that in practice farmers who farmed more than one hundred acres which they owned in freehold were styled yeomen, those who farmed less did not have the status. The yeomen's wealth in land showed itself in the term 'yeoman bread', used of the bread they ate which contained a high proportion of wheat, when rye was cheaper.

Contemporary writers celebrated the yeoman class as something particularly English, honest, solid and dependable in peace and war, the descendants of those whose skill with bow and arrow and general toughness had won victories in France in the past. Smith does not stint his praise:

These are they which in the old world gat that honour to England, not that either for wit, conduction, or for power they are or were ever to be compared to the gentlemen, but because they be so many in number, so obedient at the lord's call, so strong of body, so hard to endure pain, so courageous to adventure with their lord or captain going with, or before them, for else they be not hasty nor never were, as making no profession of knowledge of war. These were the good archers in times past, and the stable troop of footmen that afraide all France, that would rather die all than abandon the knight or gentlemen their captain, who at those days commonly was their lord, and whose tenants they were, ready (besides perpetual shame) to be in danger of undoing of themselves and all theirs if they should show any sign of cowardice or abandon the lord, knight, or gentleman of whom they held their living. And this they have amongst them from their fore-fathers told one to another. The gentlemen of France and the yeomen of England are renowned, because in battle of horse-men France was many times too good for us, as we again alway for them on foot. And howsoever it was, yet the gentlemen had always the conduction of the yeomen, and as their captains were either afoot or upon a little nag with them, and the kings of England in foughten battles remaining always among the footmen, as the French kings amongst their horse-men. Each prince thereby, as a man may guess, did show where he thought his strength did consist. (*ibid.*, pp. 44f.)

'These were they that in times past made all France afraid',[6] wrote Harrison of this class which Thomas Fuller described as 'An estate of people almost peculiar to England living in the temperate zone betwixt greatness and want'.[7] Bacon declared that France's larger population had not availed her in struggles with England, because 'the middle people of England make good soldiers, which the peasants of France do not'.[8] The value of the yeomen lay in the fact that while rich and owning considerable land, they were content to be 'middling', a valuable link between peasant and gentleman. Lambarde comments with admiration on the yeoman's satisfaction with his status: 'A man may find sundry yeomen although other-wise for wealth comparable with the gentle sort that will not yet for all that change their condition, not to be apparelled with the titles of gentry.'[9] A. L. Rowse has called attention to the two most pros-perous yeomen of Peatling Magna and Peatling Parva, who were 'the squires of their respective villages by 1567, owning practically all the land, yet they continued to call themselves yeomen as they had done all their lives'.[10]

On the other hand, it was not difficult for the yeoman of such eminence to ascend to the status of gentleman. Dr Rowse mentions the Bales of Carlton Curlieu who were newcomers to the village in the time of Henry VIII: 'the head of the family was a yeoman in that generation, a gentleman in the next, knighted in the next with a baronetcy in 1643—all achieved within a hundred years.' Between 1543 and 1551 a yeoman of Cosby, Thomas Bent, bought land until he had possession of the manor, the village, more than a thousand acres of land and successfully took the style of 'Thomas Bent, gent'. Dr Rowse remarks that Bent's son built himself a 'mansion house' still standing in the main street of Littlethorpe.

Sir Thomas Smith deals with what he calls 'the fourth sort of men' in chapter 24:

> The fourth sort or class amongst us is of those which the old Romans called *capite censii proletarii* or *operae*, day-labourers, poor husbandmen, yea merchants or retailers which have no free land, copyholders, and all artificers, as tailors, shoemakers, carpenters, brickmakers, bricklayers, masons, etc.

The rest of this short chapter, despite its title, 'Of the fourth sort of men which do not rule', gives a succinct account of the distribution of authority throughout the other three classes. We shall consider Smith's words on this subject later when we come to examine the organization of rule and government in Shakespeare's England. At the moment it is important to note that all authorities and actual fact support his declaration that those with no free land belonged in this class; yet he is too sweeping, in that it also contained some who owned land, such as those who farmed less than the hundred acres required to elevate them into the yeoman class; presumably some merchants and professional men who owned less than the hundred acres were regarded as less than a yeoman or burgess and citizen. Nevertheless he conforms to contemporary custom in making no distinction between wage-earners and small independent producers, despite the fact that the latter were twice as numerous as those who were employed. Smith has also left out the large number of those who had no work, the deserving and the undeserving poor in need of charity, whether they stayed in one place or joined the host of vagrants moving about the country. In fact, the lowest group, which may well be called 'the masses', made up much more than half the total population of the country.

All modern accounts of Elizabethan society accept the Elizabethan distinction between those who were gentle and those who were not. One school of historians next sees five distinct strata of hierarchy in addition to which there are four groups of semi-independent professional hierarchies integrated in or related unsystematically to the upper groups of the other five. Smith's account of greater and lesser nobility is accepted, though a county *élite* and lesser gentry are now spoken of respectively. This treatment of Elizabethan society puts husbandmen (greater and lesser farmers of less than one hundred acres) and yeomen together. There is also a group of urban and rural artisans. The fifth group consists of those dependent on charity, apprentices and agricultural, industrial and domestic servants who lived in the 'family' of their employer. 'Family' then applied to all who had some function in a superior's household in the widest sense. It has been estimated that somewhere between 15 per cent and 25 per cent of the total male adult population was to be found in this group. Smith treats them to some extent in chapter 8 of his third book, *Of Bondage and Bondmen*. After declaring that no man in England is any longer a slave or a villein, he adds:

Another kind of servitude or bondage is used in England for the necessity thereof, which is called apprenticehood. But this is only by covenant, and for a time, and during the time it is *vera servitus*. For whatsoever the apprentice getteth of his own labour, or of his master's occupation or stock, he giveth to him whose apprentice he is; he must not lie forth of his master's doors, he must not occupy any stock of his own, nor marry without his master's licence, and he must do all servile offices about the house, and be obedient to all his master's commandments, and shall suffer such correctment as his master shall think meet, and is at his master's clothing and nourishing, his master being bound only to which I have said, and to teach him his occupation, and for that he serveth some for seven or eight years, some nine or ten years, as the master and the friends of the young man shall think meet or can agree. . . . And the pactions agreed upon be put in writing, signed and sealed by the parties, and registered for more assurance: without being such an apprentice in London and serving out such a servitude in the same city for the number of years agreed upon, by order of the city amongst them, no man, being never so much born in London, and of parents Londoners, is admitted to be a citizen or free man of London: the like is used in other great cities of England. Besides apprentices, others be hired for wages, and be called servants or serving men and women throughout the whole realm, which be not such bondage as apprentices but serve for the time for daily ministry, as *servi* and *ancillae* did in the time of gentility and be for other matters in liberty as full free men and women.

But all servants, labourers and others not married must serve by the year: and if he be in covenant, he may not depart out of his service without his master's licence, and he must give his master warning that he will depart one quarter of a year before the term of the year expireth, or else he shall be compelled another year. And if any young man unmarried be without service, he shall be compelled to get him a master whom he must serve for that year, or else he shall be punished with stocks and whipping as an idle vagabond. And if any man married or unmarried, not having rent or living sufficient to maintain himself, do live so idly, he is inquired of and sometimes sent to the jail, sometime otherwise punished as a sturdy vagabond: so much our policy doth abhor idleness. . . .

That which is spoken of men-servants, the same is also spoken of women-servants. So that all youth that hath not sufficient revenues to maintain itself, must needs with us serve, and that after an order as I have written. (Bk. III, chapter 8, pp. 130ff.)

One's position in the structure of ranks was decided by title, by legal and fiscal privilege, by ownership of land. Artists and stage-players were not allowed for as such. The latter were either treated as vagabonds or given a status inasmuch as they conformed to customary qualification. Under the patronage of the great they were treated as legally entitled to the rights of a great person's 'servant'; and their own system of apprenticeship preserved the younger members of the stage from the penalties enjoined for those below the rank of gentlemen who were so unfortunate as to live 'idly'. Individual players tended to be given the status to which their birth, wealth and other activities outside the theatre entitled them, as is obvious in the case of two of the most famous, Edward Alleyn and William Shakespeare.

Those modern historians who divide the population of Shakespeare's England into the five groups treated above remind us of the existence of what were virtually four semi-independent hierarchies of persons engaged in the same respective occupations, and who do not fit consistently into the main categories. These were the merchants, lawyers, clergy and office-holders, who would be called administrators today.

There was a sharp line between the moneyed merchants and the poorer ones whose status was that of artisans. The richer merchants controlled local politics and formed a group from which it was possible to enter the ranks of the gentry, and, like Lionel Cranfield, even rise to an earldom. Nevertheless, they were still regarded as inferior to gentlemen, however obscure these might be. It has been suggested recently that such figures as are available do not support the view that rich merchants easily penetrated the *élite* of society. Moreover, it has been pointed out by A. Everett in 'Social Mobility in Early Modern England' (*Past and Present* No. 33 [April 1966], p. 22) that despite the myth of the traditional Elizabethan merchant's rise from rags to riches, the story of Dick Whittington himself did not get into print until 1605. It must be observed, however, that eight per cent of the aldermen of Jacobean London had as apprentices married their masters' daughters. On the other hand several of the richest merchants of Exeter had founded their fortunes by marrying a wealthy widow. Gradually, but only gradually, the richer merchants received some social recognition and acquired some say in political decisions. They had very little formal power, but economically their interests were those of the landed classes who were regarded as their superiors; the price of land depended to some extent on the price of wool, which itself was linked to the export trade in cloth which was fostered by the central

D

government, both as a source of revenue and of employment, some sort of insurance against discontent and rioting. Gradually as the seventeenth century wore on, leading London merchants advanced money to the government, acquiring influence behind the scenes, even giving advice on economic and military matters and on foreign affairs. As a result this merchant *élite* won a measure of recognition from the landed gentry and rose in status. This rise may have been due also to the fact that in the time of James and Charles younger sons of gentlemen increasingly took to trade without reconciling themselves to a loss of gentility, especially when they prospered materially.

The upper ranks of those engaged in the law also rose in status in a typically English and inconsistent manner. This was in part due to the fact, noted by Smith, that 'whosoever studieth the laws of the realm . . . shall be taken for a gentleman' (pp. 39f.), and in part due to the profits which enabled lawyers to buy land. Like everything else, the profession of law was a hierarchy, from the country attorneys and solicitors up to the highest of luminaries, the Master of the Rolls and the Lord Chancellor. Little is known of the social origins of the country lawyers, who were not accepted as gentle merely in virtue of their study of the 'laws of the realm'. But those who had read law at the universities and had become members of the Inns of Court used the style 'gent.' and the title 'Master'.

The number of these lawyers who had been called to the bar increased by forty per cent during our period;[11] they formed three-quarters of the whole profession. The increase was obviously connected with the substitution of litigation for violence as way of disputes between members of the gentle classes. Lawrence Stone points out that 'by any standards the growth of litigation between 1550 and 1625 was something rather exceptional.' He has evidence to suggest a sixfold increase in cases in the Court of Common Pleas, a doubling in the King's Bench, a tenfold increase in the Court of Request and that of Star Chamber, 'while by 1621 Chancery was issuing about twenty thousand subpoenas a year.' No wonder that Westminster Hall was 'our cockpit of revenge' for John Smyth of Nibley, with the comment, 'the civil wars of my days there raging, wasting more treasure and time than the disunion of the houses of York and Lancaster ever did the uniting'. (Stone, pp. 240-1) Thomas Heywood's *A Woman Killed with Kindness* (1607) shows us members of the gentry involved in both violence and litigation which are typical. Another well-known play, *A New Way to Pay Old Debts* (1633), by Philip Massinger, has Overreach planning the destruction of Frugal by a deliberate trespass on his land which will lead to a multiplicity of law-suits which only a man of the aggressor's wealth can hope to survive: 'These trespasses draw on suits, and suits expenses which I can spare but will soon beggar him.' Stone (p. 241) gives an example of the number of suits in different courts which could arise out of a single quarrel. 'Lord Berkeley's dispute with Thomas Throckmorton over the tithes of Oldminster led to thirteen bills in Star Chamber, twelve in King's Bench and Common pleas, others in Chancery, and suits 'almost numberless' at the County Assizes and Quarter Sessions.' Even William, Earl of Salisbury, whom Stone (p. 242) describes as 'not an unduly litigious person, had twenty-nine in train in 1621, twenty in 1634, thirteen in 1637. Stone quotes the Earl of Huntingdon to his son, 'suits in law are grown so common that he that hath not some is out of fashion'.

Much work for lawyers was also provided by the transfers of land taking place, which have been described as 'massive'. The lack of a central registry and the fact that land law was not completely clear resulted in a situation at the beginning of the seventeenth century which provoked from John Norden in *The Surveyor's Dialogue* (1618) the comment: 'in these days there go more words to a bargain of ten pound land a year than in former times were used in the grant of an Earldom.'[12]

There was much contemporary comment on the increase in the number of lawyers and on their wealth, their acquiring land. And there can be no doubt that in addition to occupying a high position in the hierarchy of their profession, which was in part social, many lawyers were accepted at different levels of the gentry and nobility. And as law became regarded as an occupation for a gentleman, both elder and younger sons of the gentry chose legal careers for themselves from the early seventeenth century onwards.

A third semi-independent hierarchy of what were becoming

virtually professional men was that of the administrators. There were about seven hundred of these in the country as a whole, including greater and lesser office-holders in the royal household and in what we now regard as major departments of state. About one hundred of the national total were full- and part-time officials in the provinces. By the early seventeenth century they came largely from the squirearchy with some non-gentry such as yeomen and merchants. These men should not be confused with those members of the gentry and nobility who were fortunate enough to acquire a place at Court. For such, office meant merely a source of revenue with which to maintain their existing way of life according to the standards of gentle birth. But those whom we are considering as administrators saw their source of income as a profession; moreover it was one which they and society were more and more inclined to regard as fit for men of gentle birth. This meant that those who came from lower down could win acceptance more easily in virtue of their professional activity. The status attached to administrators really derived from the number of men of gentle birth in their number. More government servants were obtaining their office by the early seventeenth century as a result of patronage, by what was virtually inheritance from a father, and to a much smaller extent by purchase. Two-thirds of the administrators were of gentle birth; about one half were sons of men no lower in rank than esquires. Half of those officials who were sons of peers or of knights had themselves been preceded by their fathers in government service if not in exactly the same office.[13]

The clergy were in a less favourable position, but they did not fit neatly into the hierarchy of the main five groups either. At one end of the ecclesiastical scale, the rural priests were not of gentle blood, were not regarded as gentry as a matter of course, and when they were, must still defer to the lord of the manor. According to Notestein the behaviour of a gentleman of Tolleshunt, in Essex, was not regarded as a flagrant denial of hierarchy when he walked up to a curate who was conducting the service, and struck him with his hand, saying, 'Thou art a dunce, and a bold dunce. I will make thee neither parson nor vicar. But I will not call thee knave'.[14] Indeed, parish priests were higher than a knave (a base person) even if they were not accepted as gentry, and despite the fact that they might earn no more than a labourer, as little as eight pounds per annum in some cases, and many not more then ten pounds. In 1585 Whitgift actually put on record the fact that more than half of nine thousand benefices had incomes of not more than ten pounds, of which most had no more than eight pounds. A Church which was habitually plundered to reward services to the Crown or the demands of royal favourites not unnaturally lost status. Even the highest ranks of the clergy were regarded as inferior to those of the lawyers. In our period only one clergyman became Lord Chancellor, Bishop Williams in the reign of James I, though the office was once habitually held by a cleric.

The physicians formed another profession with its own hierarchy which did not fit easily into the kind of structure envisioned by Smith. No exact figures of their numbers are known, but one admittedly rough calculation suggests a possible one to every eight thousand of the total population.[15] The bishops licensed two-thirds of the physicians; the rest received their licences from the universities, and with them a claim to gentility if they did not already have this. The College of Physicians and Surgeons (set up in 1518) functioned in London, examining and licensing graduates.

As the training was long, only the well-to-do could afford it, many coming from the lesser gentry in all probability. Physicians did not necessarily find any difficulty in being accepted as gentle-folk, but apothecaries were regarded as 'base'; so were surgeons for the most part. After 1605 surgeons became independent of the so-called barber-surgeons (who were restricted to pulling teeth), but still had a much lower status than that of physicians.

The various classes of the population of England and Wales during our period can be separated out into a different stratification, with landowning as the qualification for the highest group. Beneath them we can place lawyers, with those who engaged in big business next. This last group contained those who practised agriculture on a large and profitable scale and about one hundred great merchants. The fourth group has been designated 'middle-class', consisting of those in trade and professions in the towns and cities who had won for themselves the style of 'Master'. Their rural equivalent consisted of gentlemen, yeomen and the more prosperous husbandmen. Fifth and largest group, 'the masses' comprised well over half of the population, with a rapidly increasing proletariat.

Much has been written, and not without reason, of the Elizabethan poor, for between one third and one half of all the households in the kingdom did not earn enough to be liable for direct taxation at a time when members of the same family were in the habit of engaging in mixed occupation according to season and demand.[16] We can divide the poor into two main divisions; those able-bodied who had some semi-skilled or unskilled occupation, but whose employment was intermittent or so badly paid as to provide no reserve for hard times, let alone the real needs of times of lesser hardship. The other division contains those dependent upon charity, whether by choice or misfortune.

Most servants, most of the poorer peasantry, most semi-skilled and unskilled workers, all who were wage-earners in casual work in textiles, including some peasants with land which was inadequate to support them, lived between poverty and penury. Many independent tradesmen or rural and urban craftsmen were in no better state. Unskilled labourers earned ten pounds per annum,[17] while price rises depressed the purchasing power of their wages by about two-thirds during the progress of the sixteenth century.

Dr Rowse points out (in *The England of Elizabeth* [1962], pp. 228ff.) that independent producers outnumbered wage labourers by two to one. He tells us that in Gloucestershire the leading occupations numerically were in the following order: 'agriculture, textiles, masons and stonelayers, millers, farmers, vintners and innkeepers, glovers, mercers, bakers, and so on down to tinkers and bellows-menders. The clothiers, as we might expect, differed little from manual workers.' Towns differed from large villages, with fewer farmers and farm labourers, miners or fishers; they had less manufacturing than the countryside, where textiles were much manufactured in individual homes. The towns were chiefly centres for finishing and distributing, and of retail trade.

Notestein points out (*The English People on the Eve of Colonization* [1962], pp. 84ff.) that a farm labourer employed the whole year round would be paid between thirty shillings and two pounds. But by the early seventeenth century farmers were employing more casual labour at a daily rate of three pence with food or eightpence without. Daily casual labour was available from March to November. The three darkest months of the year were also the hardest.

Two-thirds of the employees in the country were either in agriculture or served the gentry or nobility. Manors existed in which a quarter, a third, five-sixths, even the total male adult population served one family.[18]

Although so many households were too poor to pay direct taxes, they were hard hit by indirect taxation on the necessaries of life, even if that taxation was not paid directly to the government but in the form of fees levied at some point in distribution by courtiers and government servants as monopolies or patents as rewards, or by others who farmed various taxes. Expectation of life for the poor was less than the average for the population of thirty-five years; 'the percentage of the population under fifteen was nearly double what it is today', writes Christopher Hill (*The Century of Revolution* [1966], p. 25). He adds that labouring life was so short that the Devon justices of the peace did not even trouble to fix wages for women over thirty, as if no such woman was expected to be able to work in the fields.

So many people lived so near the starvation line for a number of reasons; the end of villeinage meant that many descendants of former villeins now held land as copy-holders, that is the terms of their leases were recorded in a copy of the role of the manorial court. These leases were usually for a stated number of lives, often for no more than one. As leases fell in and prices rose, the new terms were often too high for the tenants. They had the right to appeal to the Court of Star Chamber or to the Lord Chancellor in Chancery, but more often than not they were ignorant of this, or lacked funds or confidence, or the legal process took too long to help them. Even if landlords had not wanted to engross, that is combine two farms into one unit, or to enclose or charge extortionate 'gressons' for renewing leases, the normal course of events would have removed many copy-holders from the property they farmed. Enclosure took place mostly in the Midlands and in Leicestershire, affecting more than one third of the villages of these areas. It should be realized, however, that the mid-century collapse of the wool market overseas removed the incentive to turn arable land over to pasture; and by 1600 to grow grain was more profitable than sheep-keeping. Nevertheless the decline in the export of wool increased rather than alleviated unemployment; and the recovery of the grain market was a consequence of the famine and near-famine of the 1590s and not a symptom of economic improvement which might alleviate the lot of the poor. By the end of Elizabeth's reign and in the early years of that of James I their number had been increased by crippled and disbanded able-bodied soldiers as the wars ended, who, like those who deserted in time of war, took to vagrancy. The increase in the number of the unemployed poor, dependent on or demanding charity, was reaching alarming proportions.

The 'aged and impotent' (those who were too young, too old, or not physically fit to work) did not constitute the same threat to civil order as the able-bodied unemployed. How many there were of both (apart from the vagrants) is indicated by the fact that in the small town of Aylsham, according to *The Official Papers of Sir Nathaniel Bacon*, 'there be of poor people that have need of the charity of others to the number of 300 persons' (ed. H. W. Saunders [1915], p. 60).

By the end of the sixteenth century, England had evolved a method of dealing with the poor, which was designed as much to avoid disorder as to alleviate their hardships. The method evolved gradually as a result of deliberate attempts at exhaustive planning for the country as a whole by parliamentary statute, and partly piecemeal by individual cities to meet their respective needs. In addition, however, the monarch and the Privy Council kept a watchful eye open to remedy special cases where the normal system did not operate satisfactorily for one reason or another. Although we can distinguish three separate areas of activity, in the cities, in Parliament and in the Privy Council, we have to remember that in fact they operated simultaneously, and were not insulated from one another. The point about the measures taken in the cities is that they did not wait upon legislation in Parliament which applied to the country as a whole. In London, for instance, existing hospitals were reorganized as the four 'Royal Hospitals' established by Henry VIII on his deathbed, to which Edward VI added a fifth when he lay dying himself not long after. The city acquired enough Church property to endow St. Bartholomew's for the sick, St. Thomas for those permanently infirm, Christ's Hospital to maintain and educate children, Bridewell for vagrants and unemployed and Bedlam for the insane. What the government gave was matched by city funds.[19]

In Ipswich and Norwich affairs were also systematically organized for the relief of the poor, and for dealing with vagrants and workless; but these two towns levied a compulsory rate to provide finance. Ipswich had a combined hospital and house of correction, an asylum for the aged, a training school for the young—all as early as 1569. In addition a count was made of the numbers of beggars, who were given a badge of identification, and relief of the poor was organised. When Norwich found itself with over two thousand beggars in 1570, the poor in the city were numbered by a careful census; the able-bodied were set to work, the women spinning, the men to weaving, carpentry and similar occupations. Natives of the city unable to work were supported; beggars from elsewhere were ordered away.

Gradually similar measures were applied to the country as a whole as the result of a series of Acts of Parliament, stretching from 1531 to 1601. A survey of the whole period during which this legislation was enacted reveals a conflict between two fundamental attitudes to poverty, one that it is virtually immoral, a matter of choice by the individual who must therefore be punished into changing his ways; the other view, more humane and possibly of longer standing in human history, sees poverty as a misfortune to be relieved rather than cured by charity. The first view sees poverty as curable if only by punishment. The Elizabethans managed to combine the two by making a distinction between the deserving and the undeserving poor; as a result they were able to satisfy normal human impulses to pity and charity inside the framework of conviction that every member of the commonwealth has a place from which he should not venture, and in which he should function according to his station. Once the distinction was established, Tudor legislation concerned itself with providing a system which would enable the commonwealth to treat both deserving and undeserving poor in ways which would preserve order. And as it became obvious after the collapse of the wool trade in the middle of the century that there was not enough work to go round, measures were taken to supply the able-bodied with materials and employment in their proper place of residence; as the deserving poor were less and less cared for by charity and 'hospitality' it became apparent that money must be collected and disbursed by some sort of official organization. Despite the fact that Shakespeare's contemporaries were accustomed to thinking of their country as over-populated, it was not difficult for them simultaneously to regard punishment as a cure for unemployment. The ability of human beings to cherish contentedly notions which are in fundamental conflict has shown itself with regard to unemployment right into the twentieth century. The present writer can remember hearing an otherwise humane person declaring of South Wales during the disastrous 1920s and 1930s that no man who really wanted work need be without it.

The punitive cure for poverty is to be found in a Statute of 1495 which provides for the punishment of vagrants and their removal to their place of birth or established residence. The first distinction between the two kinds of poor was made officially in an Act of 1531. The able-bodied who were deemed capable of work were to be stripped, tied to the end of a cart and whipped. By 1536 it was beginning to be realized that mere punishment was not enough; work would have to be provided for the able-bodied poor. Eleven years later, the most vindictive of all Tudor measures was passed, largely as the result of a reaction against the attempts of Somerset and Hales to prevent enclosures and to protect tenants' rights. Vagabonds were now to be branded and enslaved for two years. Escape was to be punished either with death or with enslavement for life. This Act was repealed in 1550. The first real attempt to deal with poverty and unemployment by regulating the employment of labour and the provision of work throughout the country as a whole was made in the Statute of Artificers of 1563. Apprenticeship and wage-fixing were enjoined in order to prevent unemployment. Where men fell out of work, however, the Statute aimed at preventing their becoming vagrants with the insistence that they should remain in the locality in which they were born. Those who transgressed this order must expect the normal punishments.

Nine years later, in 1572, ten classes of persons were designated as liable for corrective or deterrent punishment as vagrants. First, all those wandering beggars who called themselves scholars; next came seafarers claiming to have been shipwrecked. Third are named all fortune tellers; fourth, persons claiming to be collectors for prisons and hospitals. Fifth are mentioned such vagabonds as bearwards, minstrels, and common players not in the service of some noble person. The next category is that of wandering craftsmen such as tinkers. In the seventh we find all workmen of any kind who refused to work for legal wages when work was available. The eighth consisted of men on parole from gaols who were begging for their fees to pay their gaolers and obtain their release. Next came wanderers who claimed loss and impoverishment by some accident such as fire. The last group contained all vagrants calling themselves gypsies. Four years later (1576) an Act enjoined that all municipal authorities must provide materials and work for those of the able-bodied unemployed who were born or had become established in the respective town or city.

The most comprehensive of all the attempts to deal with poverty and unemployment were made law in a series of Acts of the Parliament of 1597-98. Among other things the ten categories enumerated in 1572 were repeated. Punitive measures involved the arrest of the vagrants by the justice of the peace or appropriate parish officer; then with the approval of the minister and one other person of the parish the offender was to be 'stripped naked from the middle upwards and shall be openly whipped until his or her body be bloody.' Presumably Shakespeare had seen enough of these punishments and had observed with insight the satisfaction with which the local officers laid on the whip, for he imagines Lear in his own vagrant suffering coming to realize what good government permitted in the name of order:

> Thou rascal beadle, hold thy bloody hand!
> Why dost thou lash that whore? Strip thine own back!
> Thou hotly lusts to use her in that kind
> For which thou whipp'st her.   (IV, vi. 162-5.)

Once the vagrant had been whipped, a testimonial was to be signed and sealed by the justice of the peace, constable or minister, or any two of the three; this should give the date of punishment and require the vagrant to go by the most direct route to the parish in which he or she was born, where he had lived the last year, or through which he had last passed unpunished; he was given a prescribed time in which to do so. Disobedience of the requirements in any respect meant that the vagabond was liable to a repetition of the whipping in every parish until he returned to his legal place of residence and found employment. When no legal place could be discovered the vagrant was subject to the authorities of the last parish in which he had not been whipped; they were to send him to the local house of correction, or to the county gaol for one year or until he should be placed in some kind of employment.

The justices of the peace in quarter sessions were given the authority to deal with any rogue or vagabond regarded as a leader of such people, and therefore a danger to order. They were empowered to banish such delinquents overseas, not to return upon pain of death. They might also be sent to the galleys. The destination of those criminals who were banished was to be decided by at least six members of the Privy Council, with either the Lord Chancellor or Lord Treasurer as one of the number. From now on no begging for money at all was legal, whether by deserving or undeserving poor. The various provisions of the individual Acts of 1597-8 were codified and repeated in 1601.

Between 1531 and 1597 those poor who were regarded as 'deserving' were permitted to beg with a licence. These were those who were 'lame, impotent, old, blind,' who were 'not able to work.' But as the century wore on it became obvious that they and the children required something more than mere permission to beg. In 1536 it had been left to curates to exhort their parishes to show charity. In 1550 the task was handed over to the bishops. But they were no more successful, and in 1563 for the first time compulsion was used; justices of the peace were given authority to make what they considered reasonable assessments for the uncharitable to pay; refusal could be punished by imprisonment. In 1572 a compulsory poor rate was substituted for the less systematic action of the magistrates; according to the Act of 14 Elizabeth (cap. 5) the money was to be applied to the relief of those too old or too ill to work; pauper children were to be apprenticed. The measures of 1597-8 developed further the raising of money by a poor rate and the method of using it for relief of the poor. Legal provision was made for a small sum of money to be collected from each parish every month, to be paid to the High Constable, who handed it to certain justices of the peace who had been elected county treasurers. The money was to be divided between hospitals and almshouses of the county and the poor prisoners in King's Bench and Marshalsea in London. Another law passed by the same Parliament enabled private individuals to incorporate and endow hospitals, almshouses and working houses for the poor.

Between 1501 and 1601 the developing awareness of the problems of unemployment and poverty resulted not only in measures planned for the two kinds of poor, but also in the gradual emergence of a system of administering and applying the solutions decided upon. In 1501 justices of the peace were empowered to punish beggars. The Act of 1531 made them responsible for the punishment of vagabonds, and for the relief of the impotent poor. But adequate statistics were lacking and no provision was made in the Act for work for the 'sturdy' unemployed. Legislation of 1535-6 established the parish as the administrative unit; each parish to relieve its own helpless by voluntary charity; work was to be found for the able-bodied. The Act of 1552 went further, arranging for every parish to have two collectors of alms, 'gently to ask and demand and ask of every man and woman what their charity will be contented to give weekly towards the relief of the poor'. In 1563 a much more complicated organization was called for, not only to relieve the deserving, and to punish the workless, but to ensure that work at a fair wage existed for everybody. The Statute of Artificers tried to cure poverty by a complete reorganizing of the whole labour force of the country. It provided for a seven-year apprenticeship for all craftsmen under the control of a master of the relevant craft. All able-bodied subjects not employed in a craft must work in agriculture. To prevent unemployment in the crafts, apprenticeship was open only in those short of labour, or in guilds and companies which were prepared to admit apprentices. Apprenticeship was not required for unskilled jobs; and the judges ruled later that it was not necessary for entry into new crafts which developed after 1563. The justices of the peace were empowered to regulate wages annually. Pauper children were to be forced to work in agriculture. Men were to stay in the locality and occupation into which they were born.

These measures were designed to make it virtually impossible for the able-bodied to suffer involuntary unemployment. Those sturdy beggars who chose vagabondage were to be dealt with as before. But the new legislation addressed itself much more realistically to the plight of the deserving poor. Now a compulsory levy was to be made to support 'impotent, aged and needy persons'. Anybody of 'froward and wilful mind' who did not pay willingly could now be coerced by the justices of the peace, who were given power to levy contributions by distraint of property and to send offenders to prison.

Well-intentioned though these measures were, their application suffered from lack of reliable information and of a civil service, in addition to the fact that they could not affect the root causes of inflation and failure of textile exports. It was soon found that more precise instructions were needed to ensure that local authorities were successfully compelling men of sufficient means to pay the poor rate. The next piece of legislation in 1572 instructed all justices, mayors, sheriffs, bailiffs and other competent officials to levy a reasonable rate on all the inhabitants of their respective districts; the impotent poor were to be lodged in permanent places of residence. Vagabonds were to be treated with greater severity (with death as the ultimate penalty for continued refusal to mend their ways). Four years later (1576) a statute enacted that every city or incorporated town must provide a store of hemp, wool, flax, iron or other material, to enable the honest poor to work for a fair wage. Rogues were to be sent to 'houses of correction' (two to be built in each county) to be disciplined to work.

The results of nearly a century of statutory arrangements for the poor became law finally in the series of bills passed by Parliament in 1597-8. Most important was the fixing of a contribution of a poor rate of twopence per parish, with provision for wealthy parishes to subsidize their poorer neighbours. In addition to the rate for the impotent, taxation was to be imposed to raise money to provide work for the able-bodied. In each county justices of the peace were to appoint 'overseers of the poor' who actually collected the taxes, bought stocks of materials to provide work in the workhouses and managed their supply and consumption. Charitable private persons were to be encouraged to endow hospitals, houses of correction, *maisons de Dieu*, or places in which the poor could live, but the endowment must be at least of the value of ten pounds per annum. In addition the quarter sessions were empowered to arrange for the erection of workhouses.

All this was the result of hard work by a large committee comprising almost all the members of the Commons, which met in Middle Temple for the purpose, carefully examining and throwing out more than a dozen draft bills before the final piece of legislation was passed.

To put the principles to work was the task of the Privy Council, by overseeing, reminding, exerting pressure on employers to keep their people in work even in depression, on justices of the peace not to let regulations go by default. The overseers of the poor in each parish (from two to four in number) shared with the church-wardens the duty of raising taxes to bind poor children out as apprentices, to buy the raw materials for the work-houses, to support the impotent and to build cottages for them on common land. Overseers and churchwardens met once a month on a Sunday afternoon, keeping accounts of the money levied, collected and spent; they gave licences to the poor to beg in their own parishes, but only for food. Three years after the passage of this legislation it was re-enacted with small changes (1601).

But the England of Shakespeare's day knew other subjects of the monarch who were either able-bodied vagrants or impotent poor, apart from those who have been considered. The various campaigns against Spain and in Ireland produced a number of incapacitated soldiers and sailors, as well as deserters claiming to be incapacitated; moreover, the fact that there were many genuine servicemen no longer able to work provided vagabonds with the opportunity of passing themselves off as having become sick or been wounded in the wars. Society's reaction to these true and false ex-servicemen was exactly the same in principle as to the deserving and the undeserving poor. Again there is the demand for those who were able to work. Sturdy vagabonds who were unsuccessful in their attempts to be accepted as servicemen were penalized in the usual ways; sufferers from physical disabilities who were not totally disabled were found such occupations as they were capable of. There were pensions for the former servicemen whose disabilities put them among the impotent poor.

The problem of ex-servicemen became more and more acute after the country's full involvement in the Netherlands in the second half of 1585. By November 1586 so many beggars claimed to have suffered in the Netherlands that the Privy Council ordered the Lord Mayor of London to call before him those who begged in the busiest streets and investigate their claims. If these were true, audiences of sermons at Paul's Cross and other public places were to be asked for contributions to send the disabled back to their counties. In July 1589 the Lord Mayor reported to the Council how ineffective his measures had been in dispersing increased numbers of soldiers and sailors in the city. He was instructed to apply to the nearest justices to enforce the existing statutes and ordinances. But it seems as if the situation was getting worse. Soldiers from the recent Portugal expedition marched towards Nonesuch where the Court resided, demanding their pay. Proclamations that month and the next forbade these marches and ordered sailors to go to the admiralty for pay or relief; soldiers were to apply to the lords lieutenants of their respective counties. Guards were placed barring the roads to Nonesuch.[20]

By November London and the Home Counties were plagued by troops of 'vagrant and masterless men' who claimed to have been soldiers. As what remained of Willoughby's forces were about to reach London from France, Elizabeth issued a proclamation to deal with the situation. All 'vagrants and ill disposed persons calling themselves soldiers' were to obtain passports within two days from the nearest justices, and were then to proceed to the counties in which they were born, moving at least twelve miles a day. Men who had been pressed into the services and were now workless must be employed again by the masters whom they had left (with Star Chamber action for employers who did not comply); servicemen too disabled to work must apply to their official parishes for relief, as deserving but impotent poor. They were all placed under martial law. Immediately following the proclamation, commissions were issued under the great seal to the Lord Mayor of London and the lords lieutenant of the seven counties affected in south-eastern England, they were authorized to appoint provost marshals, each of whom was given a force of ten mounted men who knew the county well, paid for by funds raised by the local justices. The sheriffs and justices were to set watches on the highways from sunrise to sunset, and to search once a week in towns, villages and hamlets where the offenders were likely to be found. The provost marshalls were empowered to arrest and execute by martial law, not only offending soldiers and sailors, and those without passports, but 'other vagrant and masterless persons and sturdy vagabonds.' Although these measures were intended initially for only three months they were continued as long as seemed necessary despite the expense.[21]

In 1591 and 1592 the disorderly servicemen, or vagrants claiming to have been in the services, became so troublesome that two more proclamations were deemed necessary. Local authorities in places where soldiers landed were instructed to advance money to let them reach their homes; the justices were to hold special sessions of enquiry into the facts about men claiming to have served; again the absence of a passport meant indictment. New commissions were issued for the appointment of provost marshals to hang disorderly London apprentices and servants who were impervious to other forms of justice; death was to be meted out not only to civilians attempting to rescue prisoners but to any members of the lower classes creating disorder, whether military or civilian.

E

These measures show the threat which the government felt from deserters and disaffected disbanded servicemen. But the sick and maimed were regarded as deserving; when forces returned from abroad, their commanders, the mayors, justices and appropriate officials where they landed were ordered strictly to make sure that they were given funds to let them return home. Cheyney mentions (pp. 248ff.) that in October 1592 the sum of five shillings apiece was given to one hundred and fifty-two poor and disabled soldiers returning from Normandy. In September 1593 the behaviour of two justices in Sussex suggests that much humanity was involved as well as care for civil order. They cared for eighty-six sick and wounded men from Dieppe for two days at government expense, nine of whom were too weak to leave until they had cost the considerable sum of five pounds. The other seventy-seven left for their homes on the third day, having had distributed between them thirty-four pounds eighteen shillings for their expenses on the way.

These measures, however, were not sufficient. When the attention of the Queen and Council was brought to individual cases, pressure was exerted to find almsmen's positions in ecclesiastical establishments; these were urged to support the servicemen until positions became vacant. Although the Council might order the ex-serviceman a pension, the absence of any organized finance for the purpose meant that he was often given the substitute of a permit to beg. Sometimes he might have, at least on paper, a government pension for life (which would almost certainly be short). The establishment of hospitals by private charity was encouraged to provide disabled soldiers with pensions.

By the time that Parliament met in 1593 the conscience of the governing classes had been affected. It was proposed that a general subscription should be taken up in both Houses for the relief of the unfortunates. In the Lords it was agreed that every earl should pay forty shillings, every bishop thirty shillings and every baron twenty shillings. Peers who had not attended, having missed the expense of living in London, should pay double; those who had attended less than half of the session were to pay one third again. The Commons decided that all who were privy councillors should pay thirty shillings; members who were knights or serjeants-at-law paid twenty shillings; burgesses each paid five shillings. Any who had left without license were to pay double. So strong was feeling, that one burgess who pleaded inability to pay more than two and six-pence was almost placed in custody for disobeying the orders of the House.

The lower clergy of Convocation also collected money; London butchers were given license to kill and sell meat during Lent in order to collect funds to the sum of one hundred and twenty pounds. The Privy Council urged the mayor, aldermen and heads of city companies to contribute generously to a fund opened in the Guildhall.

When all this money had been collected, the Council appointed a mixed commission of fourteen well-known military leaders, lawyers and citizens of repute to meet on a certain day in the New-gate Sessions House. Names and claims of applicants were then recorded; a week later, between sixty and seventy disabled soldiers were given papers authorizing their receiving two shillings each Saturday for twenty weeks; they were also given a penny or two-pence per mile (in accordance with their health) to journey to their home counties. Funds were sent to fifteen lords lieutenant with requests to appoint a deputy lieutenant to see to local distribution. After twenty weeks further arrangements would be made where necessary.

A proclamation through the Lord Mayor ordered civilian beggars to comply with existing legislation by going to their native parishes for relief; but disabled soldiers were to present themselves to be supported for twenty weeks. Anyone found to be claiming falsely to be a soldier would be whipped and treated as a vagrant. Twenty-nine sailors were added to the list, to receive money from Sir John Hawkins. Soldiers living in London, Southwark and Westminster received their money from three city men.

At this point the Privy Council was anxious to deal with ex-servicemen as part of the whole problem of poor relief. But a com-mittee of the House of Commons, over forty in number with some of the most distinguished members among them, gave its attention only to the plight of the soldiers and sailors, leaving the larger problem for the next parliament. A first bill was rejected as not adequate; a new committee proposed more satisfactory measures which were introduced in the House by Bacon. After more changes a military pension Act was passed. Poor, sick and maimed ex-servicemen were to be cared for from funds raised by a weekly tax in every parish, the annual amount for each to be fixed by the justices in quarter sessions. While this was to be not less than one penny nor more than sixpence weekly per parish, the actual amounts to be paid by individuals could be decided by the inhabitants or their officials. If they neglected to do so the nearest justices of the peace made the decisions. Churchwardens were to collect the money, pay it to the high constables of the hundreds, and from them to one or two of the justices who had been elected county treasurers. To be paid relief an ex-serviceman must show a certificate from his former officer; pressed men were to apply to the treasurer of the county from which they had been recruited; volunteers to the treasurer of the county of birth or in which they had lived for the past three years. A man's injuries and service record (in the certificate) were taken into account for the justices in quarter sessions or the treasurer to establish for him a rate of payment payable quarterly for the time that the law remained in force. Normally the limit for common soldiers was not to exceed ten pounds a year; officers below lieutenants were limited to fifteen pounds, lieutenants to twenty pounds. Nothing was provided for higher ranks, who were presumably unlikely to have been drawn from a class which could not look after itself (either from private fortune or the fruits of office, honest or dishonest).

The Act also arranged for discharged soldiers to journey from their place of discharge from county to county to the one in which their homes lay. Administrators who failed in their duty were to be fined. Soldiers granted a pension were to lose it if they begged, and were to be treated like other vagrants.

This law came into force two months after the parliamentary session ended, and was stated to be valid only until the end of the next (in fact four years). The next Parliament re-enacted it, increasing the maximum assessment possible in each parish, owing to the increase in applicants as a result of the wars. For the same reason another increase was made in 1601.

However comprehensive this legislation might have been in principle, in practice it did not succeed because it depended upon the efforts of an unpaid body of officials, including the justices of the peace. The Privy Council urged sheriffs and justices of the peace of every county and the presidents of the Councils of the North and the Marches, to put the law into effect. All officials were reminded by royal proclamation of their responsibilities; the Lord Mayor ordered all ex-servicemen affected to leave London. But in the counties the justices, whether from muddle or ill-will virtually sabotaged the law, sending some former soldiers from the place in which they had been pressed to their place of birth and *vice versa*, refusing to sign certificates and ignoring the order to maintain registers. One justice complained of promulgation through the sheriffs instead of the justices as the reason for general ignorance of its very existence. The Privy Council would send reminders of their obligations to the counties, to receive the reply that the limits of payment required by law had already been reached. Towns and counties tended to go for years without collecting their assessed contributions.

There was a similar tendency not to put into practice the legislation designed to alleviate the problem of poverty as a whole. Here, however, we must remember that the actual number of able-bodied unemployed who chose not to work but to be vagrants has almost certainly been exaggerated. It may well be true that, as Tawney says, the sixteenth century 'lived in terror of the tramp'; but a few tramps may easily have preyed on the fears of their more fortunate contemporaries. There is much evidence that many Englishmen and women of the nineteen-twenties lived in terror of the communists; but we know for a fact that the communists themselves were few and hardly effective in England during those years. The Privy Council was particularly sensitive when it came to a possibility of public disorder, knowing that a minor riot could snowball into a major breakdown of order in a time in which communications were not swift, in which there was no standing army or reserve of police, and in which those who were politically disaffected might take advantage of any opportunity to undermine the regime. Conditions for unrest existed throughout the period, with the threat of turbulence increasing when enclosures and decline of the export trade in textiles made the lot of the masses harder. It was no coincidence that the Statute of Artificers came in the sixties, the years when the textile industry fell on evil times; similarly the disastrous weather of the 1590s as well as the wars increased the miseries of the poor, as a result of which the poor laws which we have discussed were passed by Parliament.

Although we today cannot be certain whether there really was any danger of widespread disorder or of anything like the overthrow of the regime, there is no doubt that enough rioting and turbulence occurred to worry the Privy Council in the middle years of the last decade of the sixteenth century. The Lord Lieutenant of Devonshire asked for country gentlemen to be forced to stay on their estates, among other reasons to oppose 'the fury of the inferior multitude, if they should happen to break out into a sudden outcry for want of relief, as, without good circumspection, many suspect they may and will do.' In any part of the country where times were very hard and the masses on the verge of rioting, rumours tended to be rife to the effect that 'the poor were up' in some other distant part, only waiting for a signal to march on London. Cheyney (*op. cit.*, II, p. 25) gives an account of the report of a justice of the peace of Somerset of the name of Hext, how at their trial a group of thieves admitted that they had stayed for three weeks at a particular alehouse stealing and eating a sheep every night. Hext also reports that a group of between forty and sixty vagrants made a remote barn their headquarters from which they emerged to steal food, returning to cook and eat it. When, in answer to complaints from the surrounding population, the justices of the peace ordered the arrest of these outlaws, the local township officers were afraid to attack them. Hext estimated that there were between three and four hundred of such vagrants in Somerset, apart from tinkers, gypsies, pedlars and soldiers. As the decade wore on there were also protests on constitutional grounds from gentlemen, disturbed that the wars led to encroachment on their privileges.

Turbulence among the poor continued through the first third of the seventeenth century, though the end of foreign wars for many years removed the problem of dealing with disbanded and disabled soldiers. Nevertheless, there were the disorders of the 'Levellers' in Northamptonshire, and of the 'Diggers' in Warwickshire in 1607, and similar troubles among the workless in Gloucestershire in 1622. There were also what have been described as minor revolts in the south-west of England in 1628-31.[22] There is an account on record of an incident which happened to William Hill, a Tewkes-bury attorney, managing the Forthampton estate of Lionel Cranfield, first Earl of Middlesex. One November day in the early sixteen-thirties, Hill took shelter from heavy rain in a wretched cottage inhabited by a shepherd serving a neighbour, Sir Richard Tracy of Stanway: 'the rain came so fast down the chimney that it forced us from the fire, and we had much ado to be dry in any other part of the house.' As the barns were weather-proof Hill went to one where he found about thirty people, men, women and children, living there, who wandered in 'a close band' and who would not allow strangers to join them.[23]

It is obvious that the governments of Elizabeth and of the first two Stuarts were concerned to avoid upheaval, but charitable impulses were not excluded from their minds and behaviour. In the fifteen-nineties to encourage the import of cheap grain the Queen renounced the usual import duties, a considerable sacrifice of finance at a time when there were enormous demands on the Treasury by the various military undertakings in Ireland and against Spain. Throughout these years the Government attempted to alleviate distress by forbidding enclosure, forestalling, regrating and engrossing, in the belief that sales in the open market would make grain cheaper.

Elizabeth held it to be part of the duty of a gentleman to relieve the distress of the poor in such unusually hard times by the exercise of hospitality. The Privy Council tried to ensure that the country gentlemen lived up to her ideal of a man staying in his own manor house (not an absentee) whose duty did not end with repelling enemies from abroad and suppressing disorder at home, but who kept a generous, though not wasteful household, entertaining his friends and giving to the poor. At the end of the Trinity law term, on 1 July 1596, the Lord Keeper of the Great Seal addressed in the Star Chamber those justices about to leave London on circuit. He instructed them that it was the Queen's will that gentlemen should return from the cities to their country dwellings. In addition a royal proclamation was issued to this effect. The Privy Council did its best to ensure that the reluctant country gentlemen complied, but there is much evidence to show that the policy was none too successful. For instance, on Christmas Day of the same year the Privy Council ordered the Lord Mayor and the aldermen of the City of London to furnish a list of those gentlemen living there who ought to have returned to their country estates. This measure seems to have failed, for the order was renewed shortly after.[24]

Looking back on the way in which the poor were treated and on attempts to solve the problems of poverty and unemployment in the age of Shakespeare, what is our verdict? By absolute standards the poor and infirm were treated with barbarous harshness. It is obvious that the capitalist tendencies of the age prevented the ruling classes from perceiving that they were offering sops and sub-terfuges; that charity and harshness could not solve what required fundamental change. Charity, however sincere, cannot cure with one hand the harm being perpetrated with such vigour by the other. There is no doubt that the governments of Elizabeth, James I and Charles I were determined to keep order; and for the most part their measures were successful. It is also true that much which they did was the result of their inability to distinguish between poverty and immorality or sin. But how fiercely shall we blame them, when over three centuries later, Beatrice Webb (one of the founders of the Welfare State) was convinced that poverty is a matter of morale, that the poor suffer from a shiftless inability to use their energy fruitfully. The true causes of poverty were not recognized in Shakespeare's England, and the existence of the poor seemed to be a natural element in a divinely created world which had suffered a fall, an element which makes demands on the ability of all human beings to feel and to demonstrate that love of God and man expresses itself in charity. Before we judge the Elizabethans as distinct from pronouncing on actual social conditions, we have to remind ourselves once again of the fallibility of human beings, which we share, and of the inexhaustible human ability to be illogical. When we denounce the Elizabethan system of hierarchy which made it easy for a gentleman to be immune to the poverty and punishment of a vagrant, we must pause and recall how easily all human beings become inured to the misfortunes of others, especially when they have become commonplace. The test of humanity is to see if a man will go short himself to relieve the distress of others; it is not a matter of curtailing profits, of giving 'from one's abundance' or denying oneself luxuries, but of actually suffering privation in order to relieve the wants of others. Judged by such standards the Elizabethans themselves are our equals. But there is no doubt that their social policies involved and inflicted much misery and distress. Professor Stone (pp. 46ff., 49) has observed that although the amount given in charity was 'pitifully small' relative to the wealth of the landed classes, 'there is no reason to suppose that it was any less than that of similar classes at other times or in other places.'

The Elite

Nevertheless, there was an enormous difference between the life of the masses and that of the small minority of the nation who were accepted as gentle. As Sir Walter Raleigh asserted on one occasion, the *élite* by no means bore a fair share of the burden of taxation.[25] Indeed, the estates of noblemen and gentlemen had not been taxed at their true value since the fifteen-twenties.

It is not surprising that the total number of the ruling class, the 'gentlefolk', increased during this period. It has been estimated that, between 1500 and 1620, the population of England and Wales rose from about 2,500,000-3,000,000 to about 5,000,000, after which the increase was slower. During that time and for about another decade the upper classes produced more surviving children than the poor. The proportion of the increase in numbers of the *élite* to that of the rest of the population was three to two. Of course some of this came from the upward thrust into the ranks of the gentry, but living conditions meant that the rich increased more than the poor. In the late sixteenth century, twenty-one was the average age at which the eldest sons of peers married; this probably holds good for those of squires; between 1550 and 1625 the average age at which gentlewomen married was twenty to twenty-one. Women of lower classes married at twenty-four to twenty-five, and as we have seen, if they belonged to the labouring classes, were not likely to be capable of child-bearing much after thirty. Below the gentry the marriage of men was delayed by conditions of work. Artisans had to serve a seven-year apprenticeship; in rural areas young people working in agriculture or as domestic servants were obliged to live in as members of the employers' households (of 'families'). The eldest sons of free-holders and tenant farmers needed to wait for the death of the father before entering into the inheritance which would permit marriage and the setting up of a household. Both marriage and remarriage were easier for gentlefolk. When we take into account the fact that between 1580 and 1630 the children of peers were producing fifty per cent more children per generation, in addition to the details already mentioned, there need be no surprise at the increase in the proportion of the *élite* to the masses. Notwithstanding this increase, the *élite* remained a very small ruling minority.[26]

There were enormous differences between the life of the average peer with an income of five thousand pounds per annum and that of the average day-labourer who earned no more than ten pounds annually. Lawrence Stone (pp. 548ff.) has pointed out that in fact a great nobleman was expected to fulfil so many obligations that it would cost him not far from every penny of his five thousand pounds. Professor Stone's examination (*op. cit.*, p. 547f.) of a large number of account books of noble families in the later sixteenth and early seventeenth centuries suggests the following expenditure: '£500 for clothes and other personal needs; £1,000 allowance to wife and family; £1,500 to £2,000 for the kitchen; £500 for the stables; £500 for miscellaneous tradesmen's bills; £500 for wages and liveries; £400 for repairs to houses; and £100 for gifts and alms.' Parliamentary taxation might come to £200 a year. There were also a number of other varying but recurrent expenses. A great nobleman was expected by society to have at least one great house in the country and a house in London, requiring between sixty and one hundred servants to run them. He had to live in appropriate dignity, giving generous hospitality in the country and dispensing artistic and political patronage in town.

The material standard of living for gentlefolk rose enormously in our period. This is to be seen in building alone, an activity shared to some extent by yeomen and merchants. There is evidence to suggest that there was more building of country houses by gentry and nobility between 1570 and 1620 than in any later half-century.[27] Enormous amounts of food, much of it rich and exotically cooked and served, was eaten in the great noble establishments. Throughout the period foreigners commented on the amount of meat eaten in the houses of the well-to-do in England. Apparently it was not unusual for a household of eighty to consume five sheep and one ox per week. From twenty-five to thirty animals would be required to provide pork for a year; thirty to forty animals a year were needed to provide the veal and lamb. From the second half of the sixteenth century there is evidence of enormous quantities of poultry and rabbits being consumed. In 1573 Burghley's establishments got through two thousand five hundred birds. Three years later he supplied about one thousand six hundred; much the same number were consumed by those feeding at the expense of Lord Lumley in 1608. In 1611 the Earl of Rutland's households used two thousand four hundred, and in 1626 about one thousand six hundred went to those who partook of the generosity of Lord Spencer. Very large quantities of dairy products were also consumed and much beer and wine, in addition to fine quality bread, quite out of reach of the poor households. Professor Stone (pp. 557ff.) points out that 'an aristocratic dietary of the period lists sixty-three varieties of bird and seventy-two of fish.' He adds that thirteen different kinds of wildfowl were offered to the guests at the marriage feast for Burghley's daughter in 1581. The weekly formal dinner provided for the judges of Star Chamber on Friday (a fish day) 7 June 1594 consisted of 'ling, green-fish, salmon, pike, gurnard, dory, carp, tench, knobberd, grey-fish, plaice, perch, sole, conger, flounder, turbot, whiting, lobster, crab, and prawns—to say nothing of eggs, capons, chickens, rabbits, artichokes, peas, strawberries, apples, gooseberries, oranges, lemons, quinces and barberries.' Stone gives many other similar details of this sort of luxury, including the employment of a hundred cooks for eight days concocting a hundred and sixteen dishes. This was in 1621 for Lord Hay's entertainment of the French Ambassador at Essex House: twelve pheasants made up one dish; another contained twenty-four partridges; another had a hundred and forty-four larks, yet another contained two swans. 'There were half a dozen enormous salmon from Russia, six feet long.'

It is well known that the Courts of Elizabeth, James and Charles were the scene of lavish masques; and during the reigns of the two latter, over one hundred performances are known to have taken place. There were probably as many as ninety others on special occasions out of Court. This was merely a continuation of the kind of luxury which cost the Earl of Leicester over six thousand pounds entertaining the Queen and her Court at Kenilworth in 1571.

When it comes to clothes the story is much the same. Rowse notes (p. 255) that seven doublets and two cloaks for Leicester were valued at £543. Such doublets, like ladies' stomachers, were sewn with pearls. It was asserted by a contemporary that Lord Hume, Keeper of the Wardrobe to James I, sold off the dresses of Queen Elizabeth for sixty thousand pounds. The enormous sums paid for fashion can be seen in Professor Stone's pages (562 ff.)

Shakespeare was writing in terms of such luxury when he imagined Edgar in *King Lear* descending into the penury of a Bedlam-beggar, scarcely more than beast. Kent gives up more than dignity when he takes on the guise of a serving-man to 'serve his enemy-king'; he gives up luxury for a hard life. And Lear himself is astounded to find himself wanting the comfort of a bed of straw with the same longing as he had previously experienced for a soft luxurious bed when tired. All three proceed out of a life of luxury into one of hardship and indignity such as few of their class were ever likely to know in Shakespeare's England.

The vast difference between the life of the gentleman and that of the poor could be justified in Shakespeare's lifetime, only by the theory that gentle blood involved real virtue, carrying obligations as well as appropriate privileges. To some extent ostentation and prodigality could be confused with the obligation to 'generosity' and 'hospitality' which was part of the ideal of gentility. Looking back from the twentieth century there is a temptation to insist that, for all its talk of virtue and nobility of blood, the age of Shakespeare was really concerned with nothing more than respect for wealth combined with land, rank and power, that, in essence, hierarchy was nothing more than the apotheosis of snobbery. There is some truth, but not the whole truth, in this judgment. It was possible for an idealistic and honest worship of honour as wholly divorced from material gain to go hand in hand with respect for wealth and power. Throughout this age an ideal conception of 'virtue' as the quality of nobility persists and even determines behaviour despite the corruption of rank, wealth and power.

As we have noted earlier, Sir Thomas Smith speaks of the virtue of nobility as a quality first discerned in the progenitor of a noble line; his virtue is transmitted to his descendants, and the longer they preserve it the more it dominates them. Although Smith speaks of gentlemen as 'those whom their blood and race doth make noble and known,' it will be recalled that virtue should be recognised and honoured where it exists in men not born of families themselves held to be noble. This is also the view of Harrison.[28] Much of his fifth chapter was the basis of Smith's chapter 20, to which we have just referred. Harrison says (p. 113) somewhat more succinctly: 'Gentlemen be those whom their race and blood, or at least their virtues, do make noble and known.' There is the same logic in the account of nobility given by Gervase Holles as not only a quality descending from one whose virtue was recognized in the past, but as something to be recognized where it truly exists in a person who proves it in his own actions whoever his progenitors may have been: 'race and lineage are the matter of nobility, though the form (which gives life and perfect being) is virtue and qualities profitable to the commonwealth' (*Memorials of the Holles family* [1937] p. 4.) This is fundamentally a view shared by H. Peacham in *The Compleat Gentleman* (1622): for him, nobility, 'taken in the general sense, is nothing else than a certain eminency, or notice taken of someone above the rest, for some notable act performed' (p. 2). It can be preserved only by a perpetual record of service, maintaining the standard set by the first and successive ancestors of the line; noble blood alone will not preserve nobility in a family.

Virtue can show itself only in action: 'For since all virtue consisteth in action and no man is born for himself, we add—beneficial to his country; for hardly they are to be admitted to be noble who (though of never so excellent parts) consume their light, as in a dark lantern, in contemplation and a stoical retiredness' (p. 14). To be descended of a noble line is in itself not enough, unless the descendant shows in fact that he is a true heir of his family's virtue in his own conduct. This is the thinking behind Richard Pace's declaration: 'A true nobility is that made by virtue rather than by a famous and long pedigree.'[29] But the contrast is meaningless by Elizabethan standards; long lineage in a family which has constantly reproduced the quality of its founder must necessarily involve the virtue which makes true nobility.

In theory the existence of virtue in any person is enough to make him noble. It is recognized by both noble and base in his manner of life, his behaviour. Honour is paid to his quality of spirit; it is a reflection back on him of the impact which he makes upon others. Once honour has been won by noble action, it can be preserved only by maintaining the standard of behaviour which first gained it. While the base can show respect to their superiors, the fine essence of honour can be conferred only by those who themselves possess it to an equal or greater degree. They alone can distinguish between a willingness to act on all occasions indiscriminately and that fine 'heroic' discrimination which perceives that action is demanded solely by honour. As Hamlet puts it:

> Rightly to be great
> Is not to stir without great argument,
> But greatly to find quarrel in a straw,
> When honour's at the stake.
>
> (IV, iv. 53-6.)

He comments that the army of Fortinbras is making the mistake of risking itself in a cause that will not bring honour, 'for a fantasy and trick of fame' (for a delusion, and an illusion of fame). They are stirring 'without great argument' (in two senses, without much debate, and without a great theme or cause). The honourable person, the man of nobility, can recognize when his honour is involved, and then though the superficial cause may seem trivial and carry no financial gain, his virtue will endow it with grandeur. But, however else nobility might show itself, there was general agreement in Shakespeare's England that it was most obviously to be discerned in service to the commonwealth, to what we would call the state.

Of course snobbery was involved in the assertion, often made, that true nobility came from descent through at least three generations. While, as we have seen, the ideal basis for worship of ancestry was provided by the assumption that the virtue of the founder of a noble line is increased and intensified by his descendants, yet human fallibility meant that noble lineage in itself was regarded as a guarantee of virtue whether that was shown in action or not. The mixture of idealism and worldliness is perfectly exemplified by the title which John Ferne chose for his popular book on heraldry, *Glory of Generosity* (1586). Generosity is the ideal quality associated with nobility, an utter lack of envy, parsimony or meanness of spirit, a readiness to put oneself and one's possessions at the disposal of others. Generosity is the very opposite of servility in every sense. It carries its own glory with it. Yet this work on heraldry caters for those who found the glory of nobility inseparable from, even to consist in, being well descended. Stone tells us (p. 23) that Sir Simonds d'Ewes, 'ever accounted it a great outward blessing to be well descended, it being the gift only of God and nature to bestow it'. And Sir John Wynn, of the prominent family of North Wales, also congratulated himself on his descent: 'a great temporal blessing it is, and a great heart's ease to a man to find that he is well descended.' (*The History of the Gwyddir Family* [1878], p. 57.)

There was a mixture of snobbery and idealism in the whole cult of heraldry and genealogy. Not unnaturally as a result, throughout the reigns of Elizabeth, James I and his son, Charles, a family tree stretching far back, either imaginatively or truthfully, into time was prized. Older families consoled themselves with their genealogy in their resentment against newcomers from beneath who suddenly equalled or passed them in titular rank. And for their part the newcomers were prone to discover or pay others to discover that they, too, possessed a lengthy pedigree denoting a family old enough to justify new status. A belief in noble virtues, sincere enough to be called idealistic, is fused to the snobbery and self-delusion which led the hard-headed Burghley to allow himself to be convinced that his noble ancestry started with a certain Owen White, who allegedly, 'came with Harold that was Earl Godwin's son out of Cornwall.' Burghley shared with thousands of noble contemporaries a delight in contemplating the genealogies and coats of arms of the great families of his own and other countries. Stone (p. 24) tells us that James I was so irritated by the perpetual boasts of Lord Lumley and his relatives that he once remarked, 'I did na ken Adam's name was Lumley'.

In the relation of wealth to nobility we find the same mixture of idealism and snobbery. Wealth alone did not bring honour; and honour in itself depended on virtue expressed in action; nevertheless in practice it was not possible to live a life of 'generosity' without wealth. Snobbery made wealth reputable when it was derived largely from ownership of land. This was partly because political and social life were geared to land-owning; and it took centuries for the notion to die in England that suffrage and political power should be allowed only to those subjects of the Crown whose ownership of land gave them 'a stake in the country'. But wealth and land were inseparable from nobility in practice because without them it was impossible to demonstrate virtue in action. The noble person had obligations to play a part in the life of his area of the country, providing work, charity and example for inferiors, entertaining equals and superiors. Stone (p. 42) has pointed out that 'the prime test of rank was liberality, the pagan virtue of open-handedness.' It is another aspect of the life of luxury lived by the élite, their well furnished new houses, their hosts of servants, vast quantities of food. Memorials often extol the generosity of the dead in our restricted modern sense of open-handedness as evidence of their generosity in that larger renaissance sense of virtue unflawed by any trace of servility. Lionel Tollemache II was made to attest to his own virtue at Helmingham in Suffolk: 'Frank house, frank heart, free of my purse and port'. 'Free', like 'liberal' and 'generous' is the epithet to use of the noble. Like Chaucer's knight they held it an honour to be known for their 'freedom'. Stone lists a number of gentlefolk of this period who are commemorated for their way of life. In the house of Roger Manners, 'plenty ever was maintained'. Sir George Selby was 'everywhere most celebrated for his splendid and ever-abounding style of living'. Sir Henry Poole was 'much given to hospitality'. Eleanor Parker was praised because throughout her life with her husband, 'she agreed with his dispositions to spend with great plenty and bounty on hospitality'.[30]

But after admitting the existence of an element of sincere respect for an ideal in the gentleman's way of life, we must not blind ourselves to the amount of snobbery and self-indulgence which were equally inseparable from it; the snobbery showed itself when men who did not scorn to scheme and manoeuvre to snap up grants and monopolies, who saw no dishonour in peculation and battening on public funds, prided themselves on never having stained themselves by engaging in trade. When the ideal degenerated into self-indulgence it led to the attitude expressed by Viscount Conway: 'We eat and drink and rise up to play and this is to live like a gentleman; for what is a gentleman but his pleasure?'[31]

The truth lies somewhere between the ideal of 'generosity' and the actual pursuit of 'pleasure'. Rank must be shown in a way of life. Burghley was neither cynical nor snobbish in his statement: 'For gentility is nothing else but ancient riches.' The founder of the line needed wealth to maintain his noble way of life; without 'ancient riches' there would have been no way for his descendants to preserve their gentility, their virtue in action. Burghley refused an earldom because he declared himself too poor to live up to the obligations of so high a rank. Not that he was mean. On each of the twelve occasions on which the Queen honoured him with a state visit, he spent between two thousand and three thousand pounds (the sum should be multiplied by more than thirty to reach the modern equivalent). The higher nobility might have to maintain as many as a hundred gentlemen if sent on a foreign embassy. On his embassy to France in 1584 the Earl of Derby provided his train of a hundred and thirty gentlemen with one livery of purple and gold lace and a second of black satin and taffeta as well as a gold chain each. The Earl of Northumberland gave his deafness as an excuse to evade being sent as ambassador abroad. Huntingdon's

F

twenty years of service as President of the North left him about twenty thousand pounds in debt to the Crown. Leicester's exact debt on his death is not known, but it is said to have amounted to as much as seventy thousand pounds, an enormous sum by sixteenth-century values. No wonder Sir Philip Sidney's mother pleaded with Burghley to stop her husband, Henry, being raised to the peerage, because his extravagant nature and his small fortune would lead to disaster.[32]

Wealth was inseparable, not only from the peerage, but from the rank of knight. Some might refuse a knighthood on the grounds of poverty. Conversely, a large enough yearly revenue from land to allow a man to maintain his estate might attract to a gentleman the honour of knighthood as an obligation not to be evaded. Sir Thomas Smith remarks on this (pp. 33f.):

> in England whosoever may dispend of his free lands 40. 1. sterling of yearly revenue by an old law of England either at the coronation of the king, or marriage of his daughter, or at the dubbing of the prince, knight, or some such great occasion, may be by the king compelled to take that order and honour, or to pay a fine, which many not so desirous of honour as of riches, had rather disburse. Some who for causes are not thought worthy of that honour and yet have ability, neither be made knights though they would, and yet pay the fine.

Smith notes that in his day £120 represented the value of £40 at the time when it had been fixed as the requirement for knighthood (about £4,000 in modern money).

A man of gentle birth too poor to maintain what his contemporaries regarded as a noble way of life was inevitably in danger of forfeiting his rank by the strictest standards. The law of primogeniture meant that any son but the first might find himself in the unenviable position of Orlando in *As You Like It*, though not necessarily as the result of his elder brother's malice. Orlando complains to Adam that his father left him, 'but poor a thousand crowns', charging the eldest brother, 'to breed me well'. Yet not only is Orlando kept 'rustically at home', but everything is done to depress him out of the class into which he was born:

Besides this nothing that he so plentifully gives me, the something that nature gave me, his countenance seems to take
from me. He lets me feed with his hinds, bars me the place of
a brother, and as much as in him lies, mines my gentility with
my education.   (I, i. 1–22.)

When he confronts Oliver, Orlando admits that he should show
respect to his father's heir as above him in rank, but insists that he,
too, possesses gentle virtue which the elder brother should respect:

I know you are my eldest brother; and in the gentle condition
of blood you should so know me. The courtesy of nations
allows you my better in that you are the first-born; but the
same tradition takes not away my blood, were there twenty
brothers betwixt us. I have as much of my father in me as you,
albeit I confess your coming before me is nearer to his reverence.   (I, i. 47–57.)

Orlando will not let himself be called a 'villain', one devoid of
nobility, for that is a slur on his father. 'You have train'd me like
a peasant, obscuring and hiding from me all my gentleman-like
qualities.'

Whatever distinction of rank might set one member of the gentle
classes above another, they were literally differences of degree and
not of kind, such as that between noble and base. Orlando is
refusing to let himself slip out of gentility altogether. In avoiding
that descent he maintains himself as one, who though no higher
than a gentleman, is still accepted as worthy of the hand of the
daughter of the Duke, his rightful ruler. Similarly, in *Twelfth
Night*, Viola, as the young man Cesario, is deemed worthy in blood
of the elevated Countess Olivia. When Olivia asks: 'What is your
parentage?' the answer comes confidently, even with pride:

Above my fortunes, yet my state is well:
I am a gentleman.   (I, v. 298–9.)

Left alone, Olivia remembers this answer, addressing the Duke's
messenger in her fantasy:

I'll be sworn thou art;
Thy tongue, thy face, thy limbs, action and spirit,
Do give thee five-fold blazon.   (I. v. 261-3; 275-7.)

She plays on the word *blazon*, which can mean 'announce' as well as having the sense of a coat of arms. Each of Cesario's noble qualities is like a coat of arms; all five attest to gentility. The principle holds good for Viola's twin, Sebastian, who is accepted immediately as gentle enough to marry a countess.

There is modern misunderstanding of this play whenever it is not realized that Maria is a gentlewoman, not a waiting servant, and that Malvolio, too, is gentle. His blood is not inferior. It is not possible to imagine or play the dialogue between the Doctor and the Gentlewoman in *Macbeth* accurately, unless we give due weight to her superiority in rank.

In a society in which so much depended upon being accepted as gentle there was obviously pressure for recognition from those whose parents had been considered 'base'. The barrier could be crossed by those who had land. And by the early seventeenth century it was becoming easier for a merchant, lawyer or physician to make the crossing, to some extent because younger sons of gentlemen were no longer being left enough to maintain their way of life. Economic change had affected the earlier habit of settling small landed estates on younger sons, either as a gift or for life or a stated number of lives. Instead, like Orlando, they were given a modest life annuity. Like Orlando (who had but a thousand crowns) these younger sons were determined not to forfeit their claims to gentility; but, unlike him, not fortunate enough to marry their ruler's daughter, they were constrained to engage in trade or a profession. The fact that they continued to sign themselves 'Gent.', referred to themselves, and were referred to by others, as 'Master' strengthened the pretensions of members of the same occupations who were not of gentle parentage. When Hugh, the sixth son of a Cornish gentleman, Edward Herle of Prideaux, was apprenticed in London, and another younger son of a gentle family became, 'Thomas Bonython of London, goldsmith in Cheapside' (and these were but two of many), it was not so difficult for the 'base born' to assert that trade was not necessarily ignoble.[33]

Earlier, in Elizabeth's reign, a man could be recognized as a gentleman if he satisfied three requirements; he must have the wealth or occupation to be able not to engage in manual labour, to support the gentle way of life, and to pay the fees required by the College of Heralds with whom his new status was formally registered. Smith points out that knights and higher ranks of nobility could be created only by the Crown, but one who was not born a gentleman could become one if he met the requirements:

> But ordinarily the king doth only make knights and create barons or higher degrees: for as for gentlemen, they be made good cheap in England. For whosoever studieth the laws of the realm, who studieth in the universities, who professeth liberal sciences, and to be short, who can live idly and without manual labour, and will bear the port, change and countenance of a gentleman, he shall be called master, for that is the title which men give to esquires and other gentlemen, and shall be taken for a gentleman . . . (and if need be) a king of Heralds shall also give him for money, arms newly made and invented, the title whereof shall pretend to have been found by the said Herald in perusing and viewing of old registers, where his ancestors in times past had bin recorded to bear the same: Or, if he will do it more truly and of better faith, he will write that for the merits of that man, and certain qualities which he doth see in him, and for sundry noble acts which he hath performed, he by the authority which he hath as king of Heralds and arms, giveth to him and his heirs these and these arms, which being done, I think he may be called a squire, for he beareth ever after those arms. (pp. 39ff.)

Sincerity to an ideal allowed the virtue of a man seen in action to be taken as justifying a grant of arms and the status of gentleman, but snobbery demanded the pretence of a discovery of noble ancestors. And where the newcomer was honest enough to let his gentility rest on his own virtue he suffered at the hands of the snobs. 'Such men are called sometime in scorn gentlemen of the first head.'

Smith found no fault with this manner of making gentlemen, who adopted the way of life of their new status. The new gentleman, like those born to the rank, had to conform to maintain honour and reputation:

In any show or muster or other particular charge of the town where he is, he must open his purse wider and augment his portion above others, or else he doth diminish his reputation. As for their outward show, a gentleman, if he will be so accounted, must go like a gentleman . . . and if he be called to the wars, he must and will (whatsoever it cost him) array himself and arm him according to the vocation which he pretendeth: he must show also a more manly courage and tokens of a better education, higher stomach and bountifuller liberality than others, and keep about him idle servants, who shall do nothing but wait upon him. (p. 41.)

The association of the well-known coat of arms with William Shakespeare is the result of a transaction between his father and the Heralds' Office. John Shakespeare, the dramatist's father, had been bailiff (an office under the Crown) and justice of peace in Stratford; he also held lands and tenements to the value of £500. In addition he married a daughter and heir of Robert Arden of Wilmcott, 'a gent. of worship'. The law of primogeniture applied only to sons. Until 1926 English law enjoined that daughters (in the absence of an heir) should inherit equally. (This is one of Lear's problems; he has three daughters and no heir.) Arden's formal possession of gentility could therefore be transmitted to his posterity through his daughter, the poet's mother. The documents concerning this certificate of gentility to John Shakespeare involve at different times Clarenceux Cooke, Dethick, Garter King-of-Arms, and Cooke's successor, the renowned historian, William Camden. The documents suggest in a not wholly satisfactory way that John Shakespeare's family deserved the grant of gentility in its own right for past services to the Crown. But what matters is that he owned more than enough land and that he had held a royal office, that of bailiff of Stratford. More important, service as justice of the peace suggests that he was regarded as a gentleman by his neighbours. In other parts of England a man of his wealth not married to a gentle-man's heir might not have been accepted by neighbours as anything more than a successful and respected yeoman, the other side of the dividing line.[34]

The case of John Shakespeare affords a fine example of the way in which conservatism could insist on the preservation of forms, apparently rigidly, while at the same time there was considerable compromise. The point is that if sufficient grounds existed a new-comer's pretensions could be regularized, and the College of Heralds was the instrument chosen to prevent too many new-comers rising in status unchecked. It was simple enough for Eliza-beth to restrict the number of knights and peers in her realm; nobody was likely to assume any of these titles arbitrarily and hope to be accepted. But it was much easier to exercise wealth and owner-ship of land in order to live like a gentleman and assume a style which required no formal ceremony or grant from the monarch. The Queen forbade the use of the style 'esquire' to those not legally entitled to it. She used the College of Heralds to inquire into the claims of all those who styled themselves 'Gent.'

The College of Heralds was founded in 1417 when it was already becoming necessary to regulate the claims of parvenus to gentility. By providing coats of arms and a pedigree the Heralds issued virtual certificates of gentility. This side of their activity was continued throughout our period. Between 1560 and 1589 over two thousand grants of arms and gentility were made. At least one thousand seven hundred and sixty followed in the next forty-nine years. In the hundred and ninety years between 1433 and 1623 the number of families claiming gentry status in Shropshire rose from forty-eight to four hundred and seventy. There were comparable increases elsewhere.[35]

Human nature being what it is there should be no surprise at the fact that the Heralds were capable of providing what the parvenus wanted in return for money. From time to time the Earl Marshal tried to impose some standards to prevent the more obvious care-lessness. In 1597 one such attempt caused great alarm when doubt was cast on the authority of the Garter King-of-Arms to sell coats of arms. Stone gives details of the scandal of 1616, when it was revealed that Sir William Segar, Garter King-of-Arms, had been misled by the York Herald into providing arms (at a cost of twenty-two shillings) to the common hangman of London; he was granted those of the Kingdom of Aragon with a Canton of Brabant. Despite his initial fury at this affront, James I did nothing more than imprison those involved for a few days in the Marshalsea. Naturally the public respect for the Heralds decreased. Corruption and carelessness combined to exploit the possibilities exposed by the fact that in England it was possible to make gentlemen 'good cheap', in Smith's words. The result was that by 1617 it could be commonly lamented: 'if a man be rich, though unknown from where he came, the officers-at-arms can easily be persuaded for a gratuity, to afford him the title and arms of a gentleman' (*Memoirs of Bulstrode Whitelocke*, ed. R. H. Whitelocke, [1860], p. 36) Even worse was the fact that would-be gentlemen exposed themselves to fraud from bogus heralds. Stone (pp. 247f.) mentions one who managed to swindle nearly ninety applicants for coats of arms in Cheshire in 1579. Rowse recounts that a certain William Dawkins compiled pedigrees without authority for a hundred families in the eastern counties. He suffered imprisonment and the loss of an ear.

The College of Heralds existed not only to regulate the provision of coat armour to newcomers to the gentry, but to maintain some kind of continuous inquiry into the legality of those which were in use. From 1530 onwards they conducted visitations which took place in every county of England about once in a generation. In 1566 a new drive resulted from an Act of Parliament restating the privileges and duties of the College of Heralds. Three years later newcomers whose credentials were not satisfactory were given a year in which to justify their assumption of arms. It is probable that what took place at Stafford in 1583 was normal procedure. The names of forty-seven families whose claims were rejected were made public in a very humiliating manner:

These names being written on a sheet of paper with four great letters, was carried by the Bailiff of the Hundred and one of the Heralds' men to the chief town of that hundred; where in the chief place thereof the Heralds' men read the names (after cry made by the Bailiffs and the people gathered) and then pronounced by the said bailiff every man's name severally contained in the same bill; that done, the Bailiff set the said bill of names on a post fast with wax where it may stand dry. (BM. Harl. MSS. 1173, f. 85.)

This was done in 'the chief place of the said town'.

The visitation of Cornwall in 1620 resulted in the verdict *ignobilis* against fifty-six would-be gentlemen, while two hundred and fifty claims were allowed. Rowse (p. 248) points out that 'hardly a single name among the disclaimed subsequently appears among the county families'. The public humiliation apparently remained in local memory long enough to deter most families from a second attempt, or established once and for all their ignobility beyond discussion. Three years later a visitation branded ninety-five families as ignoble in Shropshire out of the four hundred and seventy whose claims were investigated.

The Heralds were used with some effect in their visitations to prevent the unopposed rise of base persons to the status of gentry. But the College was less successful in attempts to restrict appropriate types of dress to the various ranks in society. In 1463 there had been a fairly comprehensive codification of sumptuary laws to regulate in detail not only the dress but the food to which English men and women were legally entitled. More legislation took place in 1533. The aim was not only to preserve class distinctions, but to protect home industries, restrict extravagance and reduce import of luxuries.It was typical, of course, that wealth combined with rank was regarded as immune to what was corrupting and immoral if permitted to the 'base' mass of the nation. By the middle of the sixteenth century the regulations were being flouted more than in the past, with the government taking action as a result. In 1552 Norroy, King-of-Arms, was given the duty of preventing anyone below the rank of esquire from wearing hood and tippet. In 1562 orders were given to local authorities in Surrey to search strictly for women's clothes which broke the restrictions. Smith naturally assumes that clothing should be appropriate to rank: 'As for their outward show, a gentleman (if he will be so accompted) must go like a gentleman, a yeoman like a yeoman, and a rascal like a rascal' (p. 41).

Elizabeth issued ten Proclamations insisting on the enforcement of the Sumptuary Act of 1533, chiefly to perpetuate social distinctions rather than as economic policy. In this she was for once in agreement with her puritan subject, Philip Stubbes, who also deplored the confusing of distinctions; he complained that there was:

> such a confuse mingle mangle of apparell . . . that it is very hard to know who is worshipful, who is a gentleman, who is not; for you shall have those . . . go daily in silks, velvets, satins, damasks, taffetas and suchlike, notwithstanding that they be both base by birth, mean by estate and servile by calling. This is a great confusion and general disorder, God be merciful to us. (*The Anatomy of Abuses* [1583], sig. CIIv.)

Weapons as well as clothes and food should be restricted to appropriate ranks. A Proclamation of 1600 regulating the carrying of fire arms comments that 'the indecent and disorderly confusion among all sorts and degrees of men (every mean and base person taking to himself that which belongeth to men of the best sort and condition) as is very unseemly and unmeet in a well-governed state'. Three years later the Statute of 1533 was repealed. But in the universities distinctions of rank continued to be shown in dress. And as late as 1636 Charles I forbade the sale and wearing of imitation jewellery which enabled the lower sort to seem as sumptuously garnished as their betters. Sport was also regulated by rank. Legislation allotted archery to the base; only gentlemen with an income of over one hundred pounds per annum might legally play tennis and bowls.[36]

To own land was not only essential to status; without land it was impossible to take part legitimately in any kind of political activity. For both reasons attempts were made to restrict sales of land to persons of gentle birth. In 1529 the first draft of the Statute of Uses contained clauses making the existing lands of the nobility inalienable in perpetuity; these clauses did not become law, because the landowners themselves were apprehensive of too great an encroachment on their own freedom. Nevertheless for some forty years there were plans to legislate against merchants buying land. The need for laws to this effect is mentioned in memoranda of the fifteen-thirties, in the writings of Edward VI and in a memorandum presented to Elizabeth's first Parliament in 1559. As late as 1576 a clause in an Act of Parliament actually prohibited West of England clothiers from buying more than twenty acres.

But all such measures (including visitations by the Heralds) could do little more than delay developments. In our period the merchant class as a whole might not rise in status, but many individual merchants who acquired land by the early seventeenth century had a good chance of establishing their families as gentle. This does not mean that we should accept contemporary and modern accounts of a vast surge upwards. Existing figures are admittedly incomplete, but they suggest that the barriers of status held. Out of fourteen of the richest squires in Yorkshire in 1642, no more than two enjoyed family wealth which derived originally from trade; and this is the source of the wealth of only one of the twenty-five leading squires in Somerset in the sixteen-thirties. A mere 7 per cent of the early Stuart baronetage, and no more than 4 per cent of the early Stuart peerage owed their family wealth originally to commerce.[37]

The title, 'Merchant', often occurs in legal usage as an official description, but it was not given indiscriminately to all who were strictly 'base' and who engaged in a money-making occupation. Many of the more important London magnates in the reigns of James I and Charles I were knighted, 'and many others of the business *élite* called themselves Esquires or Gent.'[38] Although Charles I ordered another thorough visitation by the Heralds in 1633, two years later nearly one thousand two hundred residents of London were calling themselves 'Gent.' and 'Master', many without authorization.[39]

The most effective of the attempts to maintain degrees of status was the most formal and most restricted; this was the Act of Precedence of 1539, establishing the exact status of officers of the Court. Everyone was put in his exact place, so that there could be no contesting precedence. But in the country as a whole there were innumerable opportunities for dispute and violence, despite the custom of making some attempt to give precedence in public gatherings to the man with the highest title. Enemies might seek pretexts for scoring over one another and for fighting; arrogance might attempt to rise above equals and so make enemies, even over so trivial a matter as giving precedence when going through a doorway in the presence of others in what was not strictly a public gathering. A member of the Drury family lost his life as a result of his insistence on preceding an enemy through a door.[40]

To give precedence was to defer; one equal might defer as courtesy to another. Conversely, to bid another of equal or higher rank not to defer was an insult. For normally deference was recognition of inferiority. The inferior deferred consistently to all above him, in many other ways than in giving precedence at a doorway. All those who were base deferred to all who were gentle. Above the line the gentle also deferred to their superiors, with the greatest noble, even the heir apparent, admitting in behaviour his inferiority to the monarch.

The great distinction between the gentle and the base showed itself in punishments and legal penalties. No person of base rank could expect to be immune from a beating from an irate superior or his servants, and to mutilation or whipping by officers of the law. But any gentle person accepted as adult in this society was not expected to tolerate or be exposed to such treatment. That is why in *King Lear* Goneril is so outraged to hear that her father has beaten her gentleman for chiding of his fool. A gentleman should not have been beaten. The tabu against beating or whipping the gentle gives Hamlet's remark to Polonius its sting; 'Use every man after his desert, and who shall scape whipping?' (II, ii. 523). Primero in Middleton's play is appalled at the possibility of gentlemen being whipped: 'Whipping? you find not that in the statute to whip satin' (*Your Five Gallants* [pub. 1607], V. ii).

It has been pointed out that Sir Henry Wotton 'was shocked' at the treatment of the ringleaders of a mutiny in the English fleet in the pay of Venice in 1618; no distinction was made between officers (by definition gentlemen) and men; they were all hanged in public.[41] The axe was considered a more honourable form of execution than the rope; and if it came to hanging, peers were allowed a silken rope, which was not only swifter, but held to be appropriate to their status. Among the privileges of peers was immunity to arrest, except for treason, felony and breach of the peace. They were not tried before a jury of inferiors for criminal offences. They were not exposed to torture; and if found guilty of a capital offence, their bodies were not dismembered after death.

In Shakespeare's day men of base rank were treated in some respects almost as if they were sub-human. Stone (p. 30) reminds us of an appalling instance of this in the *Autobiography of Lord Herbert of Cherbury*. When Herbert was shipwrecked off Dover in 1609 he got first into the only rescue boat, and with drawn sword permitted Sir Thomas Lucy alone to follow him. The two men of rank then left the crew with the sinking ship and saved themselves. It seems that Herbert was not ashamed of this action, and did not expect it to outrage contemporaries. The same attitude can be seen in Tybalt's contempt for Benvolio who is contaminating his honour in drawing his sword against serving-men: 'What, art thou drawn among these heartless hinds?' (*Romeo and Juliet*, I, i. 64). The scorn of the nobleman for his inferiors and his heartless indifference to their fate was not confined to pre-Restoration England. We find it, together with an enormous personal courage, in the behaviour of the Earl of Cardigan who led the charge at Balaclava. After riding, with parade-ground meticulousness of dressing, right into the Russian guns, he did not see fit to sully his sword with ignoble blood. His duty was to lead his men to their objective; theirs was to fight their base equals. He returned to his ship and took a hot bath, utterly uninterested in the number or condition of the survivors.

In Elizabethan and early Stuart England all who were base showed their respect to all who were gentle by kneeling, removing their hats, bowing low, where appropriate, serving with lowered eyes, not looking a superior in the face nor meeting his gaze. Oswald in *King Lear* is almost certainly accepted as gentle (he wears a sword and is Goneril's steward); he therefore objects to the names which Lear heaps on him. Oswald's determination to assert himself, looking the King straight in the eyes, enrages Lear who is not accustomed to such behaviour by inferiors: 'Do you bandy looks

with me, you rascal?' (I. iv). As on other occasions in this play,
Lear is incited by a gentleman's misbehaviour into breaking the
letter of the law himself. He ought not to treat Oswald like a menial;
but Oswald has provoked him by ignoring his royalty, calling him,
'my lady's father' and neglecting to serve him efficiently.

The depth of Kent's love for and loyalty to Lear should not be
measured merely by his readiness to risk death in the service of his
'enemy king'. Far more important by the standard of Shakespeare's
day is Kent's willingness to serve this master as a menial. In Edgar's
words, Kent, in disguise:

> Follow'd his enemy king, and did him service
> Improper for a slave. (V, iii. 220–1.)

Kent has exposed himself to all the indignities which the gentle
imposed on the base as a matter of course. He accepts duties far
beneath his real rank, duties which would be regarded by Shakespeare's contemporaries as so dishonourable as to justify any man
of gentle birth from refusing to perform them. But Kent is ready to
submit in love and loyalty, just as in *The Tempest* Ferdinand can
descend without rancour to the base task of carrying logs in the
service of his lady, Miranda.

For the Elizabethan, and for the subjects of the early Stuarts, the
hat was part of the costume, particularly for 'gentles', and was
normally worn indoors and out, just as in England well into the
present century a hat was regarded by women as part of an en-
semble, required to give unity to the whole appearance, and worn
formally indoors. To remove the headgear, to 'uncover', was a sign
of deference to a superior; the hat might also be removed as a
salutation between equals. Every subject, however high his rank,
went uncovered in the presence of the monarch. Gheeraerts' picture
of one of Elizabeth's processions in 1600 shows this clearly; all the
nobility surrounding her have their heads bare. The only exceptions
were ambassadors from rulers not regarded as inferior to the throne
of England. A well-known print shows the Spanish ambassadors
wearing their hats when dining with James I and his son, Charles,
then Prince of Wales. James wears his crown, the prince his
coronet, but the rest of the Court are bareheaded. Charles, as

King, was confronted by a difficult piece of punctilio, when about to receive an Ambassador Extraordinary from the Duke of Mantua. The Master of Ceremonies, Sir John Finett, was consulted as to the exact prestige of the Duchy. He informed the King that the King of France had directed the Mantuan Ambassador to remain covered, and not to stand, but sit, on being received at the royal bedside. On the other hand, the King of Spain had not permitted an Ambassador from Mantua to be covered in an audience. Charles followed the French example, bidding his visitor remain covered.[42] Obsequiousness to Queen Elizabeth could go so far as the behaviour of Dr Dawson of Trinity College, Cambridge. When he preached at Paul's Cross on 14 November 1602, he did not remove his head-covering throughout his prayer, 'until he came to name the Queen, and then off went that, too; when he had spoken before both of and to God with it on his head'. (H. Manningham's *Diary*, quoted by Cheyney, I. 62).

When we read and perform Elizabethan drama it is important to remember that others uncovered in the immediate vicinity of the monarch. That is why Richard II bitterly tells his companions to cover their heads when he returns from Ireland to hear of disaster. At that moment he despairs, abandons all pretensions to power, without which he cannot survive as King.

In *Hamlet* Ophelia finds the fact that Hamlet is bareheaded ('No hat upon his head') only less disturbing than his shuffling along, wide-legged and knock-kneed, his trunk hose having slipped down to his ankles, acting as gyves, fetters connecting the two legs ('downgyved to his ankles'). Once Claudius has formally declared to Hamlet in public: 'Be as ourself in Denmark', the Prince is the only man who may wear his hat in the presence of the monarch. It was often good manners (condescension in the best sense of the word) for a superior to ask inferiors not to uncover in his presence. And so Hamlet bids Osric to replace his hat upon his head. But Osric's uneasy affectation leads the Prince to make a fool of him (V, ii. 92–104). The sensitivity of the 'gentle' was such, however, that in real life, the recipient of a genial permission to remain covered might take it as insulting patronage, if he did not admit the giver's superiority and had no intention of removing his hat in any case. Of such minutiae and trivialities were duels and quarrels born. Gentlemen, esquires and knights had no objection to uncovering to their superiors, but deference could be irksome for one who found himself allied by marriage to a great noble. Thus Sir William Holles would not give his daughter's hand in marriage to an earl. Stone quotes him as follows (p. 746): 'Sake of God, I do not like to stand with my cap in my hand to my son in law. I will see her married to an honest gentleman with whom I may have friendship and conversation.' When the letters of great noblemen were read out to the public, the listeners removed their hats in respect.

Deference to superiors also required suppleness of knee and back in bowing, particularly in the deep and humble bows known as 'cringes'. The Elizabethan word 'tender' bore the sense of 'pliable, supple', with the result that we find in Shakespeare the term, 'tender courtesies' (supple bowing with bended knee as a sign of respect).

At Court the subject showed his deference to the monarch by kneeling. On such formal occasions as when the Commons attended Elizabeth in the Lords at the end of a session, they knelt through the whole of the long address.[43] Similarly, when the Queen visited Cambridge in 1564 she was met at the entrance to Queen's by two scholars who knelt before her, kissing papers which they handed to her. The beadles of the University knelt to her and gave their staffs to Mr Secretary, who handed them to her.[44]

Elizabeth had every reason to expect from her subjects what she had paid as humbly to the monarchs from her own family whom she had served. The Venetian Ambassador who witnessed an interview between the Princess and her royal father was very surprised when she knelt three times on this one occasion. 'As it was the manner of those times for all men to kneel down before the great Queen Elizabeth,' so Edward, Lord Herbert of Cherbury, recalled, 'I was likewise upon my knees as she passed by to the Chapel at Whitehall. As soon as she saw me, she stopped, and swearing her usual oath, demanded, "Who is this?" ' (*Autobiography*, ed. Lee, pp. 81f.)[45] When the Queen wished to talk to any member of her Court during what might be regarded as her less formal semi-domestic hours, she might sign to him to approach, whereupon he would fall on one knee while engaged in conversation with her. This custom impressed Thomas Platter:

> As soon as the Queen had seated herself her lady in waiting, very splendidly arrayed, stood on her right; those with the white staffs and several other knights on her left; and one of the knights handed her some books, kneeling when he approached her, as did likewise the Admiral and my lord Cobham, who were also present. I am told that they even play cards in this posture. (Clare Williams, *Thomas Platter's Travels in England, 1599* [1937], p. 193.)

When William Lambarde had an audience of the Queen not long after the Essex conspiracy to present her with a copy of his *Pandecta*, she treated him with unusual esteem, 'having forbidden me from the first to the last to fall upon my knee before her, concluding: "Farewell, good and honest Lambarde" '.[46] No less humility was shown by twelve august judges in the presence of Elizabeth's successor, James, when he summoned them to Whitehall to express his anger at their refusal to consult him in the Case of Commendams in April 1616. They certainly fell on their knees, and report had it that they were actually on all fours.[47] Certainly Sir Thomas Smith was not exaggerating when he declared:

> And to no prince is done more honour and reverence than to the King and Queen of England, no man speaketh to the prince nor serveth at the table but in adoration and kneeling, all persons in the realm be bareheaded before him: insomuch that in the chamber of presence where the cloth of estate is set, no man dare walk, yea though the prince be not there, no man dare tarry there but bareheaded. (pp. 62f.)

Elizabeth treated Lambarde with the most generous condescension. Indeed, she was in the habit of raising a kneeling courtier with her hand to let him speak to her standing, as was noted by the German traveller, Paul Hentzner, who was in England in 1599. His account of what he saw at Greenwich Palace gives us an understanding of an element of 'ceremony' which is all too often over-

G

looked. We see that the person of grandeur was preceded by those of lesser status, as well as followed by a train:

> We were admitted by an order, which Mr Rogers (Daniel Rogerius) had procured from the Lord Chamberlain, into the Presence-Chamber hung with rich tapestry, and the floor, after the English fashion, strewed with hay, through which the Queen commonly passes in her way to chapel. At the door stood a gentleman dressed in velvet, with a gold chain, whose office was to introduce to the Queen any person of distinction that came to wait on her. It was Sunday [Sept. 6, N.S.], when there is usually the greatest attendance of nobility. In the same hall were the Archbishop of Canterbury, the Bishop of London, a great number of Counsellors of State, Officers of the Crown, and Gentlemen, who waited the Queen's coming out, which she did from her own apartment when it was time to go to prayers, attended in the following manner:—
>
> First went Gentlemen, Barons, Earls, Knights of the Garter, all richly dressed and bareheaded; next came the Lord High Chancellor of England, bearing the seals in a red silk purse, between two, one of whom carried the royal sceptre, the other the sword of state in a red scabbard, studded with golden fleur-de-lis, the point upwards; next came the Queen, in the 65th year of her age (as we were told), very majestic. . . . As she went along in all this state and magnificence, she spoke very graciously, first to one, then to another (whether foreign ministers, or those who attend for different reasons), in English, French, and Italian; for besides being well skilled in Greek, Latin, and the languages I have mentioned, she is mistress of Spanish, Scotch, and Dutch (*Belgicum*). Whoever speaks to her, it is kneeling; now and then she raises some with her hand. While we were there, William Slawata, a Bohemian baron, had letters to present to her; and she, after pulling off her glove, gave him her right hand to kiss, sparkling with rings and jewels—a mark of particular favour. Wherever she turned her face as she was going along, everybody fell down on their knees. The ladies of the court followed next to her, very handsome and well-

shaped, and for the most part dressed in white, She was guarded on each side by the gentlemen pensioners, fifty in number, with gilt halberds. In the ante-chapel, next the hall where we were, petitions were presented to her, and she received them most graciously, which occasioned the acclamation of *God save the Quene Elizabeth*! She answered it with *I thancke you myn good peupel*. In the chapel was excellent music; as soon as it and the service were over, which scarcely exceeded half-an-hour, the Queen returned in the same state and order, and prepared to go to dinner. ('Extracts from Paul Hentzner's Travels in England, 1598', tr. W. B. Rye in *England as seen by Foreigners in the Days of Elizabeth and James I* [1865], pp. 103ff.)

Here is much which should not be ignored by those who intend to stage a play such as *Macbeth* or *King Lear*. Lear's entry in the first scene ought to be in a procession of this kind, preceded not only by the symbols of kingship, but also by great officers of his household, flanked by the bodyguard, and followed by more subjects, whose presence attests to the grandeur of the monarch. Status in the time of Shakespeare was shown by harbingers who went ahead to announce the approach of greatness on journeys across country, and by a troop of lesser persons immediately ahead of the great one, with a train following, on any occasion of formality or semi-formality. Where the monarch was preceded by subjects, the man of gentle birth let officers of his household and his clients, wearing his colours, go before to attest to his worth. Clients were men of lesser rank who accepted the protection of a great magnate. The great man would advance the interests of the lesser by means of patronage; in turn the lesser would serve those of his patron where they did not conflict with loyalty to the throne. Rank was shown in public by the number and splendour of attending clients wearing a great man's livery. In *King Lear*, Gloucester is in an awkward position when both Lear and Cornwall visit his home. Lear is no longer King, but habits of loyalty and service make it impossible for the Earl to turn against him. On the other hand, Cornwall is Gloucester's 'worthy arch and patron'; he also rules now that the

King has abdicated; Gloucester is therefore tied to him as both client and subject. Part of Cornwall's displeasure when Gloucester sides with the King comes from what could be regarded as the ingratitude of a client as well as the treachery of a subject. In this play we have to imagine (and show on stage) Gloucester himself attended like a great noble, with not only followers, but led by those inferior to him, as in his own splendour he moves about the Court, the countryside or his own palace. For only then do we understand what Edgar means when he first sees his father, blinded and turned out of doors: 'My father poorly led'. Before, when Edgar last saw him, and in the years of splendour, his father was preceded by evidence of his importance, by harbingers, by his own clients and servants (themselves gentle); now he is miserably led by one unimpressive aged tenant. All the glory has gone.

What Henry V means by the 'idol Ceremony' cannot be understood by anyone today who has no idea of the way in which meals were laid, not even served, in the houses of the great. As may be expected the monarch's state was greater than that of any subject. Hentzner describes how the Queen's table was 'set out with the following solemnity,' while she was still at prayers:

A gentleman entered the room bearing a rod, and along with him another who had a table-cloth, which after they had both knelt three times, with the utmost veneration, he spread upon the table, and after kneeling again, they both retired. Then came two others, one with the rod again, the other with a salt-cellar, a plate and bread; when they had knelt as the others had done, and placed what was brought upon the table, they too retired with the same ceremonies performed by the first. At last came an unmarried lady of extraordinary beauty (we were told she was a countess) and along with her a married one, bearing a tasting knife; the former was dressed in white silk, who, when she had prostrated herself three times, in the most graceful manner approached the table and rubbed the plates with bread and salt with as much awe as if the Queen had been present. When they had waited there a little while, the yeomen of the guard entered, bareheaded, clothed in scarlet, with a golden rose upon their backs, bringing in at each turn a course of twenty-four dishes, served in silver most of it gilt; these dishes were received by a gentleman in the same order as they were brought and placed upon the table, while the lady-taster gave to each of the guards a mouthful to eat of the particular dish he had brought, for fear of any poison. During the time that this guard, which consists of the tallest and stoutest men that can be found in all England, 100 in number, being carefully selected for this service, were bringing dinner, twelve trumpets and two kettle-drums made the hall ring for half-an-hour together. At the end of all this ceremonial, a number of unmarried ladies appeared, who with particular solemnity lifted the meat off the table and conveyed it into the Queen's inner and more private chamber, where after she had chosen for herself, the rest goes to the ladies of the court. The Queen dines and sups alone with very few attendants; and it is very seldom that any body, foreigner or native, is admitted at that time, and then only at the intercession of some distinguished personage. (*ibid.*, p. 103.)

The solemnity accompanied by trumpets and kettle-drums might also be expected at a feast such as that which Macbeth gives in honour of Banquo; this is actually called a 'solemn supper', though we today mistakenly refer to it as a banquet. A banquet was a refreshment with desert after the main meal. Although Macbeth has announced in the afternoon that the meal will be one of great ceremony, for his own purposes he decides to dispense with all formality for himself, but not for his queen ('Our hostess keeps her state').

Ceremony equal to that at Elizabeth's dinner was shown when her successor entertained the Constable of Castile at Whitehall Palace to a banquet (fruit and wine) in 1604 to celebrate peace with Spain:

The audience chamber was elegantly furnished, having a buffet of several stages, filled with various pieces of ancient and modern gilt plate of exquisite workmanship. A railing was placed on each side of the room in order to prevent the crowd from approaching too near the table. At the right hand upon entering was another buffet, containing rich vessels of gold, agate and other precious stones. The table might be about five yards in length and more than one yard broad. The dishes were brought in by gentlemen and servants of the King, who were accompanied by the Lord Chamberlain, and before placing them on the table they made four or five obeisances. ('Banquet and Entertainment given by James I to the Constable of Castile at Whitehall Palace, Sunday, August 19, 1600,' tr. Rye, *op. cit.*, pp. 118ff.)

The King and Queen (she on his right) sat at the head of the table some distance apart but both under the canopy of state. At the Queen's side, also a little apart from her, the Constable sat on a 'tabouret of brocade with a high cushion of the same'; the Prince sat likewise beside the King. Other Spanish dignitaries were seated, as were the great noblemen of the kingdom. Fruit was shared, toasts were drunk ceremonially. At the appropriate moment the people 'shouted out: *Peace, peace, peace! God save the King! God save the King!* and a king-of-arms presented himself before the table'; this dignitary requested with formality to be given permission to publish the peace. It was given. The toasts continued for some time; when about three hours had passed, the cloth was removed and the meal was over.

Ceremony accompanied the monarch's meal even when the occasion was much less splendid, as we see from an account of James I at dinner one Sunday after having touched for the King's evil:

Soon afterwards, a person having a small white narrow towel on each shoulder, entered the room and spread the table. Every time that he placed anything upon the table, he made a low obeisance; then several of the King's bodyguard came to the door of the room with the dishes. The foremost of these called out, 'The King's dinner is coming', whereupon some lords went and took the dishes from them at the door (for they were not permitted to enter this room), and placed them on the table. When this was announced to his Majesty, he came without his cloak and seated himself behind the table close to the wall. Then a person took his Majesty's hat from him, and the before-named bishop standing before the table said grace and then placed himself close to the King's right hand, His Highness standing on his left. It is the custom to set before his Majesty at first three dishes only, one of which is usually a piece of beef. After he has partaken of that, from eight to ten delicate dishes are then put before him. The carver cuts very small pieces, to which at the same time, the King helps himself out of the dish with his own hand, and he is seldom seen to eat any bread. His first drink is beer, which he takes from a cup turned out of a peculiar kind of wood, and after that he. drinks a thick sweet French wine called Frontignac, which is presented to him by a chamberlain, who kneels all the while his Majesty is drinking; the small table upon which the drinks are placed stands in the presence-chamber from which they are fetched. As a bishop is required to wait during every meal, his Majesty generally converses with him at table, and occasionally with others.' ('The Visit to England made by Otto, Prince of Hesse, 1611', tr. Rye, *op. cit.*, 152ff.)

The monarch continued to dine with this formality long after Shakespeare's death. Although he was a prisoner in Hurst Castle not long before his death, Charles I still 'dined alone and in state, in the best room available, seated beneath a canopy, served on bended knee'. By this time his attendants numbered no more than sixteen; among them were two gentlemen of the bed-chamber, a carver, a cupbearer, a sewer, two pages, three cooks. On Christmas Day, which he passed in Windsor Castle he still dined 'under his canopy in formal state'. But now his attendants were reduced to six. For the whole of his captivity visitors had been allowed to watch the setting of the royal chair, the holding of gloves, uncovering of dishes, the formal tasting, carving, pouring, presenting on bended knee. At Hurst Castle, Farnham and Winchester the public ceremony had continued as it had taken place earlier in Charles' own reign, and in those of his father and of Elizabeth. Now the monarch's subjects were not permitted to watch him eat with ceremony.[48]

Throughout our period the households of great noblemen were organized on almost as magnificent a scale as those of the monarchs, with prescribed ceremony at meals, a host of gentle servants acting as stewards, ushers, chamberlains and so on. Anthony, Viscount Montague, had a *Book of Orders and Rules* for the regulation of his household. Between seven and eight in the morning a groom and page were to be ready to serve in the great hall. The Viscount's chamberlain directed the grooms of the chamber and wardrobe to look after clothes. *A Breviate touching the Order and Government of a Nobleman's House* which appeared in 1605 was comparatively modest, calling for no more than a steward, a gentleman usher, eleven yeomen of the cellar, pantry, wardrobe, two yeomen ushers, various cooks, a caterer and slaughtermen.[49] Olivia's establishment in *Twelfth Night* seems to have been of this size, but possibly somewhat larger.

The ceremony of setting the table for Elizabeth's dinner reminds us that Englishmen of Elizabethan and Stuart England behaved as if it was necessary to honour the possessions and servants of the great as well as their persons. To slight a royal servant was tantamount to insulting royalty itself. That is why Gloucester is outraged to find Cornwall determined to set Kent in the stocks. Kent, disguised as Caius, has already declared:

> Call not your stocks for me. I serve the king,
> On whose employment I was sent to you.
> You shall do small respect, show too bold malice
> Against the grace and person of my master,
> Stocking his messenger.   (II, ii. 136–140.)

Finding Regan and Cornwall determined to insult the King through him, Kent adds, 'Why, madam, were I your father's dog, You should not use me so.' But they are determined to subject Lear to their will. Gloucester objects in vain:

> Your purpos'd low correction
> Is such as basest and contemned'st wretches
> For pilf'rings and most common trespasses
> Are punish'd with. The king must take it ill

That he, so slightly valu'd in his messenger,
Should have him so restrain'd.

Regan replies implacably:

My sister may receive it much more worse
To have her gentleman abus'd, assaulted
For following her affairs.   (II, ii. 149–157.)

Not unnaturally, when Lear finds Kent in the stocks, he bursts out:

They durst not do it!
They could not, would not do't. 'Tis worse than murder
To do upon respect such violent outrage.
(II, iv. 22–24.)

In an age when it was customary for citizens to remove their hats while listening to letters read out from a noble patron, it is not too surprising that the Earl of Arundel felt almost as enraged as King Lear when, in 1635, the Mayor of Chester did not appear obsequiously to greet him as he went through the town. When the Mayor eventually appeared the Earl in his rage snatched the staff of office from his worship and shouted: 'I'll teach you to know yourself and attend peers of the realm.'[50]

It is well to remember that distinction between superior and inferior was demanded and shown from top to bottom of society. At the top it might result in each Lord of the Garter making three obeisances to the empty seat of the Queen in the chapel at Whitehall on St George's Day, 1597;[51] lower down we find the same principle at work when Drake dined at sea. A Spanish prisoner related that he carried with him 'nine or ten cavaliers' who sat with him: 'None of these gentlemen took a seat or covered his head before him, until he repeatedly urged him to do so'. (K. R. Andrews, *Drake's Voyages* [1967], p. 61.)

Just as Goneril was affronted when her father beat her gentleman, and Lear objected to his 'knave' (not even a gentleman) being put in the stocks, so Queen Elizabeth felt herself personally impugned when the actions of her servants were questioned. When

Leicester threatened to have the Gentleman of the Black Rod dismissed for not admitting one of his followers into the Privy Chamber, the Queen assured him she would allow nobody to dictate to her whom she would choose as servants: 'God's death, my Lord, I have wished you well. I will have here but one mistress and no master.' A similar principle was involved when in 1589 the Commons passed two bills dealing with abuses in the offices of the Exchequer and Purveyances. The Queen ordered them not to touch 'the officers and ministers of her own household' or 'the officers and ministers of her own court of her own revenue'.[52]

No officer of the Crown had been imprisoned by Parliament since 1388; and not since 1449 had there been a parliamentary complaint against a servant of the Crown. The responsibilities of officers and ministers were solely to the monarch, not to Parliament; and the monarch not Parliament had the sole right to remove them. In the period of Shakespeare the ministers were still regarded as literally the royal servants; to attack them could be construed as to attack Elizabeth, James or Charles, thanks to the contemporary assumption that the treatment of a great man's servant was not to be separated from the status of the great man himself. To remain in office a servant of Queen Elizabeth needed only to have her confidence, not that of Parliament; this assumption was generally accepted in her reign, but occasions arose when it was disputed in the reigns of her successors.

In the first half of Elizabeth's reign Parliament was regarded as a court, but not as one in which members might take the initiative in proceedings against the Queen's ministers or officials. Smith's chapter, 'Of the Parliament and the authority thereof', says only that it 'restoreth in blood and name as the highest court, condemneth or absolveth them whom the Prince will put to that trial' (Bk. II, p. 49). Smith obviously does not consider the possibility of private members putting anybody in the service of the Prince 'to that trial'. In a later chapter, 'Trial or judgment by Parliament', he considers disputes between 'private and private man, or between the Prince and any private man, be it in matters criminal or civil, for land or for heritage', whatever is decided must still be 'at the last day confirmed and allowed by the Prince' (*ibid.*, p. 64). Again there does not seem to be any envisaging of the kind of action contemplated against royal 'servants' later in Elizabeth's reign and those of James and Charles.

Education

It is obvious that the *élite* dominated in Parliament as elsewhere. It was a Parliament representing the *élite*, consisting of the monarch, the Lords and, in the Commons, the elected representatives of those owning land. By the end of the sixteenth century the members for the towns as well as those for the counties were drawn overwhelmingly from the ranks of the gentle. And just as the *élite* dominated every other aspect of the national life, so it dominated education.

We find two fundamental justifications of education in this period and they are not mutually exclusive. The first is idealistic; we meet it in Milton's assertion that the end of learning is to 'repair the ruins of our first parents' so far as, with divine grace, that is possible in a fallen world.[53] The other justification is not really more practical, though it may seem so at first sight; it is to develop the potential of the servants of the monarch to serve the crown, either directly in some office or other, or indirectly in contributing soberly to the well-being of the commonwealth. We read the first view of learning in John Brinsley's *A Consolation for our Grammar Schools* (1622):

> For what maketh a nation to be a glorious nation, but that the people are a wise and understanding people? What is it whereby we come so near unto the Highest, or to that blessed estate from which by our first parents we are so fallen, and to which we must be renewed and restored, if ever we shall inherit again the tree of life, as by true understanding and knowledge, especially if the same be sanctified unto us? Yea, what is it else whereby we excel the beasts, but by this divine reason, with which the more we are enlightened by the spirit of the Lord, through the means of learning, the more we differ, the more we do excel?

In *The Education of Children* (1588), the Plymouth school-master, Kemp, gives us a more practical view:

> Knowest thou not what profit and commodity learning bring-eth to the children of Adam? Look upon the barbarous nations, which are without it; compare their estate with ours; and thou shalt see what it is to be learned, and what to be unlearned. They for want of learning can have no laws, no civil policy, no honest means to live by, no knowledge of God's mercy and favour, and consequently no salvation nor hope of comfort. We by the means of learning have and may have all these things. Therefore in that thou dost enjoy thy lands and livings, in that thou mayst procure such things as thou wantest, it is the benefit of learning. In that thou sleepest quietly in thy bed, in that thou travelest safely on the way, in that thieves and enemies do not spoil thine house and household, kill thy children, take away thy life, it is the benefit of learning. Nay, go further. In that thou thyself runnest not to the like excess of iniquity—art no thief, no murderer, no adulterer, it is the benefit of learning. Dost thou not here see what a plentiful harvest of all good fruits learning bringeth forth? (Sig. D4r°.)

There was general agreement on the need for education, on the fact that an educated person had repaired some of the consequences of the Fall, and on the basic kinds of learning to be encouraged. That learning was all to the good of the commonwealth was also generally agreed; but there was not complete agreement as to those who should and those who should not be educated. The earlier humanists in England, Colet and More, under the influence of Erasmus and other Continental educationalists, have the same certainty as to the importance of learning as such later men as Elyot, Cheke, Ascham, Kemp, Mulcaster; but where the latter seem to be concerned chiefly with an *élite* to serve the monarch, the earlier men do not insist on the need to educate those whose fathers own no property. There were certainly some Protestant humanists who were anxious not to restrict education to those who were 'gentle', or who were managing to get themselves accepted as such. Partly out of pure idealism and partly out of a practical concern with providing competent clergy and with enabling as many of the laity as possible to read the Gospels, there were reformers who agreed with Bishop Latimer:

> For if ye bring it to pass that the yeomanry be not able to put their sons to school . . . I say, ye pluck salvation from the people, and utterly destroy the realm. For by yeomen's sons the faith of Christ is and hath been maintained chiefly. Is this realm taught by rich men's sons? No, no; read the chronicles; ye shall find sometime noblemen's sons which have been unpreaching bishops and prelates, but ye shall find none of them learned men. ('First Sermon Preached before King Edward, March 8th, 1549' in *Sermons*, ed. G. E. Corrie [1884], p. 179.)

Even Latimer is not suggesting educating the propertyless; his concern is with the yeomanry. But the corporation of London went further, trying to make useful members of the commonwealth out of the poor. Christ's Hospital was founded in 1552 to give an education to 'all the fatherless children and other poor men's children that were not able to keep them'.[54] They were given a petty and a grammar school education.

Children normally went to the petty school at the ages of four and five to learn reading, writing and the rudiments of spelling in accordance with the practice of the individual teacher. Girls as well as boys could attend. The A B C with catechism was taught by means of a horn book; the other text was the Primer, a collection of prayers and metrical versions of the psalms. Specially forward boys could also be taught the parts of speech and the accidence of Latin. Girls did not go to grammar school. Boys started there at the ages of seven or eight; they learned chiefly Latin grammar and literature. The educationalists also wanted to form the mental and moral attitudes of their charges, and therefore chose only those classical texts which taught an approved morality in addition to a pure style. What was known as 'vulgars', the translating from a classical language into the vernacular, had an influence on the writing of the latter. In some schools Greek or Hebrew could be substituted for Latin; in very few, both Latin and Greek could be learned in the upper forms. In some few places arithmetic and penmanship were also taught. The foundation on which grammar school education was built can be read in the assertion of Erasmus: 'All knowledge falls into one of two divisions: the knowledge of 'truths' and the knowledge of 'words': and if the former is first in importance the latter is acquired first in order of time.' (*De Ratione Studii* [1511], tr. Woodward, *Desiderius Erasmus concerning the Aim and Method of Education* [1904], p. 162.) The emphasis on a verbal education may seem misguided to us today; but renaissance England was saved from verbal intellectualism by the fact that the verbal was not separated in theory or practice from its very intimate connexion with all those other ways, which are non-verbal, by means of which human beings communicate with one another. Hence the emphasis on what was called Action or Pronunciation, communication by appearance, movement, posture, expression of eyes and face in addition to tone of voice, volume, intensity and pace.[55]

Although England lost schools with the breach with Rome, the losses were being made good throughout our period by founding and refounding. Modern authorities confirm the assertion of William Harrison in 1586: 'there are not many corporate towns now under the Queen's dominion that have not one grammar school at the least, with a sufficient living for a master and usher appointed to the same.'[56] By 1600 there were three hundred and sixty grammar schools in the country, one for every thirteen thousand of the population. But the numbers and ratio varied from county to county. Between 1529 and 1604 a series of ecclesiastical canons, royal injunctions and parliamentary statutes gave real uniformity to the curriculum in these schools as a whole. According to T. W. Baldwin:

> Grammars, vulgars and Latins, and parsing and construction are its uniform tools for attaining Latinity, and these are used according to a definite and systematic scheme. Whether there was to be one master or many, a few pupils or a large school, three forms or six or eight, the curriculum and its methods remained fundamentally the same. (*William Shakespeare's Small Latine and Lesse Greeke* [1944], I, 435.)

As has been indicated, for the most part the sons of the poor and the propertyless did not go to the grammar school. There was, however, a broad representation of sons of leaseholders and yeomen as well as gentlemen in the country; in urban areas the grammar school was open to sons of artisans (Ben Jonson was a bricklayer's son), small shopkeepers and larger merchants as well as those of lawyers and doctors. And, of course, there was nothing but pride to stop the gentle classes from using it. Many of the founding statutes show that the intention was to make an education available to boys who would later become apprentices and not necessarily go to university. It is not certain that we can take Shrewsbury school as typical, but there the children came from the gentry of North Wales and the north-west of England, in addition to those from the burgesses and other inhabitants of the town. This school also numbered sons of the nobility among its pupils. For instance Philip Sidney, Fulke Greville (later Lord Brooke) and James Harrington all entered Shrewsbury School on 17 October 1564.

While there was a general demand for the education of the children of the governing *élite*, not everybody supported equal education for those of the lower classes. By the fifteen-eighties a famous headmaster, Richard Mulcaster of Merchant Taylors', saw a threat to order in the possible disaffection of over-educated young men unable to earn a living from their training. 'To have so many gaping for preferment, as no gulf hath store enough to suffice, and to let them roam helpless, whom nothing else can help, how can it be but that such shifters must needs shake the very strongest pillar in that state where they live, and loiter without living?' (*Positions* [1581], p. 134.) This was also the view of Sir Francis Bacon, when thirty years later he was asked for an opinion as to the advisability of carrying out the will of the founder of Charterhouse. Bacon declared that there were already too many grammar schools, as a result of which there was a shortage of workers and a 'superfluity' of unemployed educated men, which was a danger to the state:

For by means thereof they find want in the country and towns both of servants for husbandry, and apprentices for trade: and on the other side, there being more scholars bred than the state can prefer and employ; and the active part of that life not bearing a proportion to the preparative, it must needs fall out, that many persons will be bred unfit for vocations and unprofitable for that in which they were brought up; which fills the realm full of indigent, idle, and wanton people, which are but *materia rerum novarum*. (*Works*, ed. Spedding [1841], I, pp. 495f.)

Throughout the sixteenth century, as the need for educating the gentle classes became more and more apparent, there was a growing demand to exclude those not of gentle birth. When the Canterbury Cathedral School was refounded (*c.* 1549), some of the commissioners tried to exclude sons of artisans, but were successfully opposed by Cranmer.[57] There were various proposals for special academies to educate men of gentle birth to serve the state, notably those of Sir Humphrey Gilbert and Burghley. Gilbert proposed to the Queen about 1570 an 'Achademy' [*sic*] for young gentlemen to bring them up in obedience to their monarch, learned in Latin, Greek and Hebrew, logic and rhetoric, the four chief contemporary European languages, natural philosophy; to these he wanted to add a knowledge of contemporary military and political institutions in Europe, civil and common law, arithmetic and geometry for ballistics, astronomy and cosmography, navigation, surgery and medicine. These gentlemen were also to master the gentle accomplishments of horse-riding, fencing, shooting, music, dancing, vaulting, not to forget heraldry.[58]

Although the grammar schools were never closed to persons not of gentle birth, their betters tended to overwhelm selected schools and the universities, and also the Inns of Court. At the universities the 'gentles' tended to patronize certain fashionable colleges; their social inferiors were usually scholars and often sizars; these latter acted as servants to their betters, with whom they did not mix.

This short survey of education is sufficient to establish that here as elsewhere the small *élite* dominated. Those men not of gentle birth who received a grammar school or university education were subjected to indoctrination of the morality and ideals regarded as suitable for those who were born gentle. They all learned to 'fear God and honour the King' (or Queen), to admire, in theory, the virtues of patience, loyalty, chastity, honesty and suchlike; they were also conditioned to an admiration of the heroic virtues exemplified in classical epic, the 'heroic poem'. And it was possible for contemporaries to speak of the learning they admired as 'heroic education'.

REFERENCES

[1] Quoted by C. Read, *The Government of England under Elizabeth* (1960), p. 2.

[2] Quoted by Stone, *op. cit.*, p. 49.

[3] See Stone, *op. cit.*, 'The Inflation of Honours', pp. 97ff.

[4] See Stone, *op. cit.*, pp. 64ff.

[5] See A. Everett, 'Social Mobility in Early Modern England', *Past and Present*, No. 33 (April, 1966); Stone, *op. cit.*

[6] W. Harrison, *The Description of England* (1587), ed. Edelson (1968), p. 118.

[7] T. Fuller, quoted by A. L. Rowse, *The England of Elizabeth: The Structure of Society* (1962), pp. 226f.

[8] F. Bacon, *Essays* ed. Reynolds (1890), 'Of the True Greatness of Kingdoms and Estates'.

[9] W. Lambarde, *The Perambulation of Kent* (1596 ed.), p. 14; quoted by Rowse, *op. cit.*, p. 23.

[10] See Rowse, *op. cit.*, pp. 226f.

[11] See A. Everett, *op. cit.*, p. 22.

[12] Quoted by Stone, *op. cit.*, p. 241.

[13] See G. E. Aylmer, *The King's Servants* (1966).

[14] W. Notestein, *The English People on the Eve of Colonisation* (1962), p. 66.

[15] Everett, *op. cit.*, p. 22.

[16] *Ibid.*, p. 22.

[17] Stone, *op. cit.*, p. 7.

[18] Rowse, *op. cit.*, p. 229.

[19] Here and in the following paragraphs see Rowse, *op. cit.*, pp. 196ff., 325f.

[20] E. P. Cheyney, *A History of England from the Defeat of the Armada to the Death of Elizabeth* (1926), II, pp. 245f.

[21] For the following pages see Cheyney, *op. cit.*, pp. 247-255.

[22] C. Hill, *The Century of Revolution* (1966), pp. 25ff.

[23] M. Prestwich, *Cranfield: Politics and Profits under the Early Stuarts* (1966), pp. 528ff.

[24] Cheyney, *op. cit.*, II, pp. 13ff.

[25] Rowse, *op. cit.*, p. 335.

[26] See Everett, *op. cit.*, p. 40.

[27] Rowse, *op. cit.*, pp. 253ff; Stone, *op. cit.* pp. 549ff.

[28] Harrison *op. cit.*, ed. cit., p. 113.

[29] Quoted by B. W. Beckingsale, *Burghley* (1967), p. 272.

[30] Stone, *op. cit.*, pp. 42-3.

[31] See M. Ashley, *England in the Seventeenth Century* (1952), p. 18.

H

[32] See Rowse, *op. cit.*, pp. 253ff; Beckingsale, *op. cit.*, p. 274.
[33] Rowse, *op. cit.*, p. 249.
[34] See Sir Edmund Chambers, *William Shakespeare* (1951), II, pp. 18ff.
[35] Stone, *op. cit.*, pp. 66ff.
[36] For this and the following paragraph, see Stone, *op. cit.*, pp. 28ff., 27.
[37] Everett, *op. cit.*, p. 40.
[38] Aylmer, *op. cit.*, p. 262.
[39] Everett, *op. cit.*, p. 52.
[40] I. Dunlop, *Palaces and Progresses of Elizabeth I* (1962), p. 130.
[41] Sir Sidney Lee, *The Life and Letters of Sir Henry Wotton* (1907), I, p. 156.
[42] J. Wildbloode and P. Wilson, *The Polite World* (1965), p. 185.
[43] Cheyney, *op. cit.*, I, p. 61.
[44] Wildbloode and Wilson, *op. cit.*, p. 171.
[45] Quoted by Neale, *The Elizabethan House of Commons* (1963), p. 303.
[46] Quoted by Rowse, *op. cit.*, p. 38.
[47] C. S. D. Bowen, *Francis Bacon* (1963), p. 138.
[48] C. V. Wedgwood, *The Trial of Charles I* (1964), pp. 33, 72.
[49] Wildbloode and Wilson, *op. cit.*, pp. 102-3.
[50] Stone, *op. cit.*, p. 750.
[51] Cheyney, *op. cit.*, I, pp. 61ff.
[52] C. Roberts, *The Growth of Responsible Government under the Stuarts* (1966), p. 2.
[53] See M. H. Curtis, 'Education and Apprenticeship' in *Shakespeare Survey* No. 17 (1964), p. 53.
[54] Curtis, *op. cit.*, p. 55.
[55] B. L. Joseph, *Elizabethan Acting* (1951), pp. 1ff.
[56] Rowse, *op. cit.*, p. 940.
[57] J. J. Hexter, 'The Education of the Aristocracy in the Renaissance' in *Reappraisals of History* (1961), p. 53.
[58] Sir Humfrey Gilbert, *Queene Elizabethes Achademy* (1572).

3: The Royal Government

THROUGHOUT our period it was normal to regard the government of the country as the personal private concern of the monarch. In practice as well as in words it was the Queen's, and later the King's, government, working in much the same way in 1629 as it had throughout Elizabeth's reign; what we would regard as the central executive was still considered to be part of Court, with little distinction between those who served the monarch as officers of household and those whose service was in government. Decisions were taken and implemented in the name of the monarch; sometimes the King or Queen might actually take the decisions personally, accepting or ignoring the advice of the Privy Council on all matters concerning the life of the nation in peace and war. In two matters only the authority of Parliament was required, in adding to or changing the law by statute as it existed, and in raising taxes 'by subsidy'. But it was constitutionally and legally proper for the royal government to proceed without parliamentary help in the making of peace and war, in levying certain taxes, in administering and regulating the life of the whole country in accordance with law as it existed at any particular moment. If the monarch could finance governmental expenses from personal revenue and from other legal resources there was in theory no need ever to call parliament. The Queen's or King's servants served the monarch no less personally in government than in the royal household, and could legally and constitutionally continue to do so as long as finance was available whether it were provided by Parliament or not.

In talking about Parliament in the age of Shakespeare, we must take care not to think of it in our modern manner as virtually the House of Commons. Parliament as a 'court' or body consisted of Commons, Lords and King-in-Parliament. The monarch's voice was still involved in fact as well as theory as much as those of

Commons and Lords in every Act of Parliament. The Statutes, in accordance with which royal decisions were taken and with which the royal servants governed and regulated the national life, involved the royal will as well as the will of Commons and Lords. But the royal servants were not restricted to acting in accordance with Statute Law. The monarch had the right to make law by Proclamation, provided this did not contravene existing Statute Law. Proclamation could not repeal or change Statute Law.

The scope of the King to make law by proclamation became one of the matters of bitter dispute in the reigns of James I and Charles I. But this particular aspect of the royal prerogative led to no controversy under Elizabeth. There is evidence that by 1535, in the reign of her father, proclamations were held no less valid as law than parliamentary statute. A letter from Thomas Cromwell to the Duke of Norfolk, states that the Lord Chief Justice had declared 'that the King's Highness by the advice of his Council might make proclamations and use all other policies at his pleasure as well in this case as in any other like for the avoiding of any such dangers, and that the said proclamations and policies so devised by the King and his Council for any such purpose should be of as good effect as any law made by Parliament or otherwise.'[1] Four years later came the Act of Proclamations which according to a modern authority, 'deliberately grounded an existing royal prerogative in parliamentary authority'. (Elton, *The Tudor Constitution* [1960], quoted Griffiths, *op. cit.*, p. 536.) The preamble stated that it was difficult to enforce royal proclamations, 'for lack of a direct statute and law to cohart offenders to obey the said proclamations. . . '. In considering the royal powers, the Act declares the necessity for the King with the advice of his Council to 'make and set forth proclamations'. Proclamations were to be obeyed 'as though they were made by Act of Parliament'.[2] Elizabeth, with the advice of her Council, though the decisions were often her own, governed steadily by means of proclamations, sometimes repeating existing Statute Law, sometimes naming offences which were not within the province of that law. The judges and privy councillors at one session of Star Chamber were confident that 'the Queen by her royal prerogative has power to provide remedies for the punishment or otherwise of exorbitant offences as the case and time required, without parliament.' It was declared that the proclamations 'should be a firm and forcible law and of the same force as the common law or an act of parliament'. Cheyney points out (I, pp. 93f.) that the privy councillors 'expressed their preference for prosecuting men for violating a royal proclamation even when there existed a statute prohibiting the same offence'. Burghley's belief as to the scope of the royal power is demonstrated by his suggestion that a special court should be established for the reformation of all abuses in general. The court was not created; but his proposal was for it to proceed 'as well by direct and ordinary course of your laws as also by vertue of your majesty's supreme power, from whom law proceedeth'. (*Lansdowne MSS.*, ciii, 319.)[3] Proclamations were aimed time after time against any increase in the number of lodgings and houses in London, against the sale of grain except in the open market, against the use of fish oil in soap, against duelling, unlicensed books, the practice among country gentlemen of leaving their estates and living in London or other towns. A Proclamation of 1591 against Catholics established commissions in every shire, supported by sub-commissions in every parish, to inquire into the beliefs and attendance at church of the local inhabitants. This so met with the approval of that part of the population represented in the Commons that it was strengthened by an Act of Parliament in 1593.[4]

Elizabeth's proclamations led to no constitutional objections in the Commons. But James issued more in seven years than she had in thirty. Among the many matters included in the Petition of 1610 there was a plea respecting proclamations. 'There is a general fear conceived and spread amongst your Majesty's people that Proclamations will by degrees grow up and increase to the strength and nature of laws.' The Commons declared that the people of the Kingdom of England had 'indubitable right not to be made subject to any punishment that shall extend to their lives, lands, bodies or goods, other than such as are ordained by the common laws of this land or the statutes made by their common consent in Parliament'. Despite Tudor precedent James conceded that proclamations could not claim force equal to Statute Law; but he insisted (and was correct constitutionally) that sometimes proclamations were necessary, particularly in emergencies.[5]

Towards the end of the summer of 1610, Coke, as Lord Chief Justice, was required by the Privy Council to give opinion on the legality of proclamations. He declared 'The King cannot change any part of the common law, nor create any offence by his proclamation, without Parliament, which was not an offence before'. As Bacon pointed out, Coke had in the past given sentence in Star Chamber on offenders against proclamations prohibiting building in the City of London. The Lord Chief Justice evaded this awkward point by replying that all indictments of which he knew end with one of two formulae: *Contra legem et consuetudinem Angliae* (against the law and custom of England) or *Contra leges et statua* (against the laws and statutes). 'But I never heard an indictment to conclude, *Contra regiam proclamationem;* against the king's proclamation.' He was given time to consider the matter more closely and was able to produce evidence of royal proclamations which had not been allowed as law in the past (which evidence has since disappeared). In the end the Privy Council resolved: 'That the King by his proclamation cannot create any offence which was not an offence before, for then he may alter the law of the land by his proclamation in a high point; for if he may create an offence where none is, upon that ensues fine and imprisonment. Also the law of England is divided into three parts: Common Law, Statute Law, and Custom; but the King's Proclamation is none of them'. Despite this resolution, the situation did not change fundamentally. Proclamations were still made as they had been by Elizabeth, and very often concerning the same matters. Just how much could be accomplished by proclamation was never laid down in a hard and fast formulation. It was always a matter of a balance between what the Crown might assume and what the subject did not resent. Practice was accepted as in conformity with theory until somebody saw fit to question it. And if precedent were to be accepted as legal and constitutional justification, we might say that James and Charles continued to conform to the pattern laid down by Elizabeth and accepted by her subjects, even if it was not to be accepted so wholeheartedly by theirs.

Parliament was by no means an important element in this pattern; it sat for no more than thirty-five months out of the forty-four and a half years of Elizabeth's reign, for only about four and a quarter years between 1603 and 1629. Of course what Parliament had once enacted was still taken into account in the governing of the country whether it was freshly consulted or not. But it was usual for the monarch to govern through a number of institutions among which parliament was not included. Working through these institutions the royal servants were able to take and implement decisions, to administer and execute the laws of the country, keep the peace, administer justice, enforce law, collect money, organize army and navy, regulate the religious life of the country and engage in all the various tasks necessary to maintain the national life as that seemed appropriate to the monarch (who might or might not rely upon advisers). When we have seen what these institutions were and how they operated it will be time to consider the place and function of parliament.

Theoretically during the reigns of Elizabeth, James I and Charles I there was no distinction made between the royal Court (virtually the royal household) and those institutions which were 'out of Court', and which we would regard as the central organs of public service. In fact there was still much over-lapping between the two. For instance, Elizabeth and her successors each had a Court consisting of one section, the 'Chamber', concerned with the monarch's personal and domestic life, while another, the 'Household', included all those who were not in the close personal service of the monarch, yet functioned in the workings of the Court establishment as a whole. Officials of the Chamber and Household were 'of Court'; nevertheless, as individuals they might still hold office in the central government 'out of Court'. And high officials of the government were obliged to frequent Court in any case, as there was need for constant attendance on the monarch in whose service they operated. As 'the Prince' was assumed to 'live of his own', no distinction was made between financing the Chamber and Household and what we would regard as the institutions of government. For that reason in order to govern without direct taxation so far as possible Elizabeth strove to keep her expenditure on her Court down to forty thousand pounds annually. But her successors added to their own financial and political embarrassments by allowing the expenses of their Courts to rise. Over 40 per cent of Charles I's peacetime expenditure went on the upkeep of his Court.[6]

Average Elizabethan assumptions are probably represented fairly accurately by Smith's account of the government of the realm. Parliament is 'the whole universal and general consent as well of the prince as of the nobility and commons, that is to say, of the whole head and body of the realm of England'. The nobles and commons together make up the body; the Prince is 'the head, life and governor of this commonwealth' (p. 63). Smith shares the opinion of, but differs slightly in phrase from, Henry VIII on this same subject. In 1543 Henry declared to the House of Commons: 'We be informed of our judges that we at no time stand so highly in our estate royal as in the time of parliament, wherein we as head and you as members are conjoined together into one body politic'.[7] In Henry's view he stood then so highly in his 'estate royal' because in the presence of the Lords and Commons all his subjects stood united in voluntary endeavour to achieve his will. In peace the royal estate was most splendid and powerful in parliament, just as in war when the King was at the head of his army. Smith is quite plain on this:

> For as in war where the king himself in person, the nobility, the rest of the gentility, and the yeomanry are, is the force and power of England: so in peace and consultation where the Prince is to give life, and the last highest commandment. (p. 48)

In the fourth chapter of Book II, Smith tells how "this head doth distribute his authority and power to the rest of the members for the government of his realm'. Government is involved in five main activities; in two of these the Prince is associated with the Lords and Commons in parliament. It is important to note that Smith says that they are 'done by the prince in parliament', not done by the prince and his subjects in parliament. They are 'in making of laws and ordinances for government' and 'providing money for the maintenance' of the realm (p. 59). As we know, the monarch could also make law by proclamation out of parliament. And we shall see how he legally raised funds without direct taxation there.

In two more activities according to Smith the monarch acts out of parliament; that is 'in making of battle and peace with foreign nations' and 'and in choosing and election of the chief officers and magistrates'. These are done 'by the prince himself' (*ibid.*).

The fifth activity of government is 'in the administration of justice'. Smith does not write of this as 'done by the prince himself' because for him parliament is a court. There were three ways 'by the order and usage of England, whereby absolute and definite judgment is given'. One of these, by battle, was still not 'abrogated', but abandoned in practice. The other two are by parliament, and by a normal court, 'by the great assize'. When justice was given by a court outside parliament this was 'done by the prince himself', as Smith says earlier: 'The prince giveth all the chief and highest offices or magistracies of the realm, be it of judgment or dignity. . . . All writs, executions and commandments be done in the prince's name.' Whether it was in or out of parliament, 'the supreme justice is done in the king's name, and by his authority only'. (pp. 61ff.)

Before we consider how these activities occupied the government of the country we need to consider the institutions by means of which they were carried on. The most prominent and active of these institutions was the Privy Council, 'chosen also at the Prince's pleasure out of the nobility or barony, and of the knights, and esquires, such and so many as he shall think good, who doth consult daily or when need is of the weighty matters of the realm, to give thereinto their Prince the best advice they can' (*ibid.*, p. 59). The Council has been described as 'the permanent executive body dealing with government affairs' (Rowse, p. 285). Its members were all very conscious of the fact that they were servants of the monarch. To their personal oath of loyalty they subordinated whatever views they might have, whatever actions they might undertake. They could correspond and converse with all manner of people, even employ their own private intelligence systems, provided they did not compromise the oath of loyalty to the Prince.

Elizabeth's Council varied between eighteen and twenty members, whose meetings she did not attend.[8] James sat in his Council himself from time to time, enlarging it, so that its size varied from twenty-five to thirty members. In 1625 Charles had thirty members in his Council; the number rose to forty-two by 1630; later it was reduced to thirty once more. Under Elizabeth more than eight or ten members rarely attended any one meeting, business often being conducted by only four or five. The monarch could accept or ignore the Council's advice at his own discretion. So tirelessly and devotedly were the Crown's interests served that, as we shall see, there is every justification for the oft-quoted words of Hallam that the realm was supervised, 'as if it had been the household and estate of a nobleman under a strict and prying steward'.[9]

At the centre of government the Council was in immediate touch with the judges of the various courts based in London, with the ecclesiastical authorities and with those in charge of finance. Away from the centre the country was divided and subdivided into administrative units, of which the county and borough were largest. Each unit, large and small, was the responsibility of one or more officials answerable to the Crown. Through them the decisions taken at the centre were able to exert an effect throughout the land.

There were two main links between the Privy Council and local officers. The first was a recently developed office, that of Lord Lieutenant, which was provided for in Statutes of 1550, 1555 and 1558, but is hardly mentioned before the middle of the sixteenth century. The lord lieutenant was usually a peer and often a member of the Privy Council himself. He was responsible for a county or a group of counties, usually in a part of the country where he had interests or estates. In the middle of Elizabeth's reign seventeen out of thirty lords lieutenant were privy councillors; in 1595 twenty-nine counties were supervised by seventeen lords lieutenant of whom nine were councillors.

It was usual for a lord lieutenant to be charged with two counties, but there are cases of the lord lieutenancy of a county being occupied jointly by two or more persons. The lord lieutenant's appointment was held by direct commission from the monarch. Towards the end of Elizabeth's reign it became the custom for each lord lieutenant to have enough deputies to provide each county with at least two. The deputy lieutenants were also appointed by the Crown and named in the commission of their superior, who was also empowered to commission them himself when necessary. The office of lord lieutenant was reserved for men of higher rank or standing, such as Sir Christopher Hatton; the deputies were drawn from the slightly lower class of gentlemen and knights.[10]

The other official link between the Council and local administration was provided by the twelve judges of the London law courts who went on circuit twice a year. In mid-February at the end of Hilary term and in June at the end of Trinity term they were divided into couples (or one was joined by a serjeant-at-law). For these periods of the year the judges did not administer the law in Westminster but covered the counties in the six circuits. After the middle of Elizabeth's reign, Wales was divided into four circuits under special justices. They were called together by the Privy Council before leaving London and were given instructions relating to law enforcement and public administration in addition to their judicial duties. The Council continued to give them instructions, information and advice by messenger once they had left.[11]

Counties with a sea-shore were linked to the Crown by another official, the vice-admiral. He was not appointed directly by the Crown, but by the Lord Admiral, and his commission was under the admiralty. Vice-admirals, too, could act through deputies. Appointments varied, sometimes one official being responsible not for a whole county but a particular stretch of coast. The Privy Council used the vice-admiral, like the lord lieutenant and the judges on circuit, to carry out central decisions, sending them direct orders by messenger and letter.[12]

In the normal hierarchy of royal officials in a county the sheriff stood next in rank to the lord lieutenant. The sheriff was the immediate representative of the Crown in the county, and as such was responsible for hospitality for a royal visit, or for the visit of any distinguished foreigners. He also arranged for the needs of the justices of assize.[13]

In 1588 there were thirty-five sheriffs in England and Wales. The practice was for ministers of state to nominate sheriffs to the monarch for appointment. On November 1 each year a list of some of the leading men of each county was compiled at a meeting in the Exchequer over which the Lord Chancellor or the Lord Treasurer presided, and which judges and councillors attended. The monarch then chose from the list. In London and some other towns sheriffs were elected. A sheriff was bound to remain in his county for the year of his appointment, but could depart if summoned, or licensed, by the Crown. Apart from his responsibilities of hospitality he had administrative, legal and financial duties which will be mentioned later. He was empowered to appoint an under-sheriff to assist him and act as deputy. The sheriff played an important part in the election and assembling of parliament.[14]

The most active local representatives of the central government were the justices of the peace, who also had the greatest variety of duties to perform. Each county of England and Wales had at least twenty justices; in some the number increased to as many as eighty. They were drawn from the gentry, but could include men of higher rank. The justices were appointed by the Lord Chancellor. He would name the list of justices for a whole county, giving them a joint commission under the great seal. This was the 'commission of peace'. Queen Elizabeth herself was not too busy to pay attention to the names, number and behaviour of the justices, in 1595 removing those 'whom she thought not meet'.

Some duties of the justice of peace were performed alone; but some powers could be exercised only by two or more acting together. All the higher judicial and administrative duties were carried out in a general assembly of all those in the county.

Another county official drawn from the gentry was the coroner. The numbers in each county might vary from one to six, elected by freeholders of the county court. This office was filled by gentlemen, but almost certainly below the rank of knight. Its holder had the power to swear in juries, require the attendance of jurors and witnesses, bind over suspects, pronounce judgments of outlawry. The office was mainly concerned with certain aspects of law enforcement, in particular the establishing of causes of death.

The largest administrative division of a county was into hundreds, known in some parts of the country as 'wapentakes'. They varied in size from four or five to as many as eighty in a county; there were between seven and eight thousand in England

and Wales. The hundred was the unit for taxation, for military levy, for levy of equipment, for collection of purveyance and for the enforcing of public order. The official responsible for overseeing the hundred was the constable (or high constable in distinction from the parish official). Sometimes one constable, sometimes two, were responsible for one hundred; it was also possible for one constable to be in charge of two hundreds. According to Francis Bacon, the constable 'ought to be of the ablest freeholders and substantialest sort of yeomen'. Nevertheless, in fact, the constable was almost always a gentleman. Constables were supposed to be appointed annually by the justices of peace at quarter sessions or by the judges at assizes; they were involved in collection of taxes, in military affairs and law enforcement. They also had control of parish constables.

The hundreds were themselves divided into units, variously known as vill, township, tithing, manor, but most frequently referred to in modern times by the name of parishes. The parish was overseen by the parish constable, who was not a gentleman, as we see from Harrison's account of the 'fourth and last sort of people in England', those who 'are to be ruled':

> The fourth and last sort of people in England are day labourers, poor husbandmen and some retailers (which have no free land), copyholders and all artificers, as tailors, shoemakers, carpenters, brickmakers, masons, etc. . . . This fourth and last sort of people therefore have neither voice nor authority in the commonwealth, and are to be ruled and not to rule others; yet they are not altogether neglected, for in villages they are commonly made churchwardens, sidesmen, aleconners, and now and then constables, and many times enjoy the name of head-boroughs'. (*ed. cit.*, Bk. II, chapter 5, p. 118.)

The constable of the parish was usually elected annually by his fellows, to preserve the peace and obey the orders of the justices, to organize hay and corn harvest, the mending of highways, and the raising of hue and cry. It was also his duty to report on strangers, especially suspicious ones, and on local offenders against the law.

Under the constable there were various petty officials concerned with testing and harvesting produce of the fields and protecting agriculture from 'noisome fowl and vermin'; beadles, sidesmen and sextons were involved in church matters.

Each parish also chose churchwardens from the whole population at a vestry meeting in Easter week. Some parishes had two, others three, and others four churchwardens respectively. By the time of James I it became customary, where there were two churchwardens, for one to be chosen by the minister of the parish, and the other by the vestry meeting. Coke ruled that the office was temporal, not ecclesiastical. The churchwardens were responsible for holding in trust all the property belonging to the parish and any money or cattle left to it by bequest. They could levy funds for local and national celebrations. They also co-operated with the new class of overseers of the poor, who, however, levied funds and looked after the poor as well as dealing with vagrants.

A number of towns had developed a different pattern of government by the time of Elizabeth. Most cities and boroughs were subject to the appropriate authority of the sheriff of the county in which they lay, but sixteen had sheriffs of their own; some also had their own coroners. In general the mayor, aldermen and higher officials of the cities and boroughs were the equivalents of the justices of the peace in the counties. Normally there was a mayor or bailiff and two councils; one of these consisted of twelve or twenty-four members (often designated aldermen); the second council, twice as large as the first was known as the Common Council. The Borough was a corporation which co-opted new members. Under it were organized all the activities which took place in the counties, together with such measures as paving, the provision of water and removal of garbage.[15]

Two areas of England and Wales were not connected to the central government in the same way as the counties and towns which we have been considering. These were the North and the Marches of Wales. Each of these areas was governed and administered by a local council, in many ways a miniature Privy Council, appointed by the monarch, and headed by a Lord President. The Council of the North and the Council of the Marches of Wales have been described as 'regional extensions of the English central executive' (Aylmer, p. 23). These councils exercised a jurisdiction which overlapped those of the Queen's (or King's) Bench, the Court of Common Pleas, the Exchequer, Chancery and the Court of Requests. In their procedure these councils were nearer to that of the Star Chamber, however.

As we have already seen, decisions to wage war, make peace, make or break foreign alliances, belonged to the monarch's sole prerogative, in exercising which the advice of the Council could be accepted or ignored. So Smith quite rightly tells us:

> The Prince whom I now call (as I have often before) the Monarch of England, King or Queen, hath absolutely in his power the authority of war and peace, to defy what Prince it shall please him, and to bid him war, and again to reconcile himself and enter into league or truce with him at his pleasure or the advice only of his privy council. His privy council be chosen also at the Prince's pleasure out of the nobility or barony, and of the knights, and esquires, such and so many as he shall think good, who doth consult daily, or when need is of the weighty matters of the realm, to give therein to their Prince the best advice they can. The Prince doth participate to them all, or so many of them as he shall think good, such legations and messages as come from foreign Princes, such letters or occurrences as be sent to himself or to his secretaries, and keepeth so many ambassades and letters sent unto him secret as he will, although these have a particular oath of a councillor touching faith and secrets administered unto them when they be first admitted into that company. So that herein the kingdom of England is far more absolute than either the dukedom of Venice is, or the kingdom of the Lacedemonians was (pp. 58f.).

For day-to-day routine a permanent ambassador in residence was sent to foreign courts; he was usually not a man of first rank. But extraordinary negotiations were entrusted to men of highest rank, to the peers. The prestige of the monarch required ostentation and splendour when negotiations were under way for a military alliance or a royal marriage treaty. The splendid ambassadors had to be sent to represent majesty at a royal christening or in conferring so high a mark of esteem as the Order of the Garter. The ambassador himself was responsible for financing the splendour of his embassy. He paid for transport, servants, the liveries of his gentlemen, his attendants and whatever was required in the way of entertainment and sweeteners to attain his royal master's will. The Crown certainly made some contribution, but nothing very large, to cover these expenses.[16]

Decisions about the Army and Navy also rested solely with the monarch and the Privy Council. The Council organized operations overseas, provided the troops and supplies, and saw to distribution of equipment. In training and raising troops the county was the administrative unit, under the authority of the lord lieutenant or his deputies, or in some cases of the sheriff. The lord lieutenant's commission gave him power to call up the men of the county, to array them, test them, arm them and lead them. Theoretically men could not be called up for service outside their county, but this restriction was ignored in practice by the time of Elizabeth.[17]

Inside the county the administrative unit through which troops were raised and maintained was the hundred. The lord lieutenant could make use of officials right down the hierarchy as far as the constable for mustering, equipping and raising money for military expenses. He himself had to declare his commission to the justices, after which the whole administrative organization was at his disposal to recruit men between the ages of sixteen and sixty into the military service of the monarch.

The monarch and Privy Council might issue authority to raise and organize troops not only to the lords lieutenant, but to deputy lieutenants joined with the sheriff in a commission of musters. As a result one of the qualifications for sheriff's office was an understanding of military matters. On one occasion in 1595 Burghley, meeting with the lord keeper and the justices in London to select sheriffs, deplored the 'great lack of martial men, though otherwise able for wealth and knowledge'. A commission of muster was usually resorted to where no lord lieutenant existed to exercise the necessary powers in a county. Most frequently the vacancy was the result of recent death; but sometimes a new lord lieutenant was not appointed for some considerable time, and the military duties were carried out by the commission. It is possible that in the reign of Elizabeth a decision might have been taken not to make a new appointment in order to prevent the development of a new class of magnates capable of challenging the authority of the Crown. The method of using 'commissioners of musters' was older than the office of lord lieutenant, but was resuscitated in Elizabeth's last years. In 1595 she granted a commission to the members of the Privy Council enabling them to appoint a sheriff and group of county gentry to a commission of muster to exercise all the powers of a lord lieutenant. At the end of the year, in December, the Privy Council's commission was renewed; it was often made use of.

The monarch and Council could delegate authority to raise and train troops a third way, into the hands of the justices of peace of a county acting as commissioners of array. In 1572 a very detailed order to muster and train troops was sent by the Privy Council to the justices of the counties without any special mention of the lord lieutenant as responsible for its enforcement. Smith seems to be referring to this activity of the justices of peace when he says that they 'do meet also at other times by the commandment of the Prince upon suspicion of war, to take order for the safety of the shire, sometimes to take musters of harness and able men' (p. 88).

Whoever held authority from the monarch raised foot-soldiers first by ascertaining by 'muster' (i.e. by actually showing) how many men in a county between the ages of sixteen and sixty were fit for military service of any kind. From the total in a county a 'convenient number' of men were selected, divided into companies and put through military drill, as a result of which they were known as 'trained bands'. The training was conducted by officers known as 'muster masters'. The Council gave the lord lieutenant power to appoint these, but very often took into its own hand the decision to send suitable military men to the counties with letters for them to act as muster masters. Elizabeth and her Council not only dispatched these officials to the counties, but went into considerable detail in instructions for their procedure, how much powder was

I

to be used by men with firearms, how each man was to be trained to handle his piece, the size of the bolts and the length of the range where archers were to practise.

Apart from the trained bands, the rest of the fit men in the county were to be grouped into companies and called out four times a year, supplied temporarily with arms and given a superficial training.

Horse soldiers were raised as the result of lists prepared by the lord lieutenant or the commissioners of musters, showing details of the gentry of the county, who were required to have ready at all times and send to the musters, or provide when needed, at least one horseman mounted and armed. They were also required to have available a certain amount of equipment for the infantry of the shire; more was kept in store in public possession, in armouries or under the care of the constables of hundreds.

For forces overseas the Privy Council sent orders to the county officials to supply appointed officers with special bodies of men, levied, armed and equipped as required. So far as possible the trained bands were not affected, but a levy was made of the correct proportion of different kinds of troops from each parish of a hundred and each hundred of a county. Resisters were conscripted into the forces.

To maintain order among the troops, particularly those returning from foreign service, each county had a provost marshal in command of ten horsemen who each knew the county well. They were paid for with money raised by the justices of the peace, and operated under martial law as proclaimed by the monarch.

In war time, and in the field, the Prince hath also absolute power, so that his word is a law, he may put to death, or to other bodily punishment, whom he shall think so to deserve, without process of law or form of judgment. This hath been sometime used within the Realm before any open war in sudden insurrections and rebellions, but that not allowed of wise and grave men, who in their judgment had consideration of the consequence and example, as much of the present necessity, especially, when by any means the punishment might have been done by order of law. This absolute power is called martial law, and ever was and necessarily must be used in all camps and hosts of men, where the time nor place do suffer the tarryance of pleading and process, be it never so short, and the important necessity requireth speedy execution, that with more awe the soldier might be kept in straight obedience, without which never captain can do anything vaileable in the wars. (Smith, *op. cit.*, pp. 59f.)

When not embodied in a force outside the county, troops were commanded by their local gentry. Supreme command of forces overseas was confined to men of great rank or influence. Such a grandee, who had the right to create knighthoods, was known as the general. He had as second in command a high marshal who was responsible for administration and justice. Next in the chain of command came an inferior general or lieutenant general (or general of horse); beneath came master of ordinance, then sergeant-major general and sergeant-general, followed by colonel. Next came captain, appointed by the supreme general or by the Privy Council; subordinate to the captain were lieutenant and ensign. All these officers were born, or accepted as, of gentle rank.[18]

In theory a distinction ought to have been made between the financing of local troops and raising money by the Crown for national use. But in practice taxes were imposed on counties, hundreds and parishes without any such distinction being made. The lord lieutenant of a county would come to an agreement with its justices of the peace to order a general taxation of the area to pay for arms and the equipment of a given number of soldiers. Alternatively, the nobility and gentry of a shire, together with well-to-do yeomen, might be required to furnish a stated amount of armour, even a piece of armour such as a corselet or steel cap per individual, a weapon or weapons, arrows, bow and pike. At first the Crown had intended to pay the skilled muster masters used to drill the trained bands, but (partly on Sir Walter Raleigh's advice) the cost was shared with the counties. Sometimes the counties alone paid wages as laid down by the Council. Nevertheless, when necessary the Queen was ready to meet the cost of drilling the trained bands; in 1596 she agreed to pay twenty-six captains the sum of six shillings a day for a month to drill these troops. In 1597 the same terms were paid to twenty-seven muster masters. The cost of uniforms and transport for soldiers serving outside their own counties was known as 'coat and conduct money'. From time to time the Crown paid varying contributions towards these expenses, but before the end of the sixteenth century funds levied locally in the shires by local officers paid for soldiers, arms and equipment sent abroad as well as for the home defence forces.[19]

Throughout this period it was possible for the Crown to finance the government of the country out of other sources of income than the extraordinary measure of parliamentary taxation. To begin with, money could be raised from lands owned by the Crown, either in the form of rents or by sale. The great drawback to the second method, of course, lay in the fact that land, once sold, could no longer be a source of revenue. Since the break with Rome the Crown had taken over payments, such as first-fruits and tithes formerly made to the Church; these sources of revenue were administered by two sections of the exchequer, the courts of Augmentations and of First-fruits and Tenths.

Elizabeth, James I and Charles I also benefited from the arrangements made by the earlier Tudors to resuscitate the feudal dues of wardship and first marriage. When any landholder, holding directly from the Crown, was succeeded by a minor, the fact, together with a valuation of the property, was notified to the Master of the Court of Wards and Liveries. He granted the wardship to a relative of the heir, or to any other person at his own discretion. The person granted wardship was responsible for annual payment into the court of whatever amount was decided by the Master in accordance with all special payments due on the land and the profits arising from it. The value of the marriage of the ward was also collected; when the ward came of age, livery of the lands involved more set payments. Cheyney quotes a typical example of the workings of this court. In 1598 Sir Robert Southwell died leaving his widow with a young son. The Master of the Wards placed the boy in his mother's wardship, enjoining her to pay to the court forty pounds a year until he reached the age of ten, fifty pounds from then until fourteen, after which, fifty pounds until he came of age. It was possible to purchase a wardship from the government, which then received not only the purchase price, but an annual payment based on the income of the lands; the income itself went to the purchaser, who was obliged to pay for the upkeep of the estate and the needs of the ward. The Court of Wards and Liveries provided the Crown with an income of several thousand pounds a year; it is known to have been as much as forty-four thousand pounds on one occasion.

Smith has an attitude to wards and liveries which is typical of the Elizabethan reaction to royal prerogatives which seemed onerous to the subjects of Charles and James, and which strike us as scarcely to be tolerated:

This being once granted by act of Parliament (although some inconvenience hath been thought to grow thereof, and with that time hath been thought very unreasonable) yet once annexed to the crown who ought to go about to take the club out of Hercules' hand? And being governed justly and rightly, I see not so much inconvenience in it, as some men would make of it: diverse other rights and pre-eminences the prince hath, which be called prerogatives royals, or the prerogative of the king, which be declared particularly in the books of the common laws of England (p. 62).

Later, Smith goes more fully into this institution, detailing the grievances which arise from it, yet still justifying it:

Many men do esteem this wardship by knight's service very unreasonable and unjust, and contrary to nature, that a Free-man and Gentleman should be bought and sold like an horse or an ox, and so change guardians as masters and lords: at whose government not only his body but his lands and his houses should be, to be wasted and spent without accounts, and then to marry at the will of him, who is his natural lord, or his will who hath bought him to such as he like not peradventure, or else to pay so great a ransome. This is the occasion, they say, why many gentlemen be so evil brought up touching vertue and learning, and but only in daintiness and leisure: and why they be married so very young and before they be wise, and many times do not greatly love their wives. For when the father is dead, who hath the natural care of his child, not the mother, nor the uncle, nor the next of kin, who by all reason would have most natural care to the bringing up of the infant and minor, but the lord of whom he holdeth his land in knight's service, be it the King or Queen, Duke, Marquess, or any other, hath the government of his body and marriage, or else who hath bought him at the first, second or third hand.

Smith gives more details of the abuses of this system and then gives the other point of view:

Other again say, the ward hath no wrong. For either his father purchased the land, or it did descend unto him from his ancestors with this charge. And because he holdeth by knight's service, which is in arms and defence, seeing that by age he cannot do that whereto he is bound by his land, it is reason he answer that profit to the lord, whereby he may have as able a man to do the service.

Another source of income to the Crown came from the fines imposed by the various courts of law. The officer responsible for the collection of this money in each county was the sheriff, who had to account annually for it, either at the Exchequer or in any other manner which the treasury might order. Cheyney (II, p. 349) gives details of the amount collected by the sheriffs of twenty-five counties and thirteen cities and towns in 1592, 1596, 1597 and 1598: in the first of these years it reached £6,100 8s. 3d; it dropped to £3,806 11s. 8d. in 1596; a general pardon in 1597 reduced the total to about £1,500; however, in the next year it rose to £5,124.

Customs brought in larger sums; but the Crown was invariably defrauded of much that was due to it. To prevent this as far as possible Burghley resorted to collection through farming. The best known, and probably the most successful of the 'farmers' was Customer Smythe who negotiated agreements with the government at intervals from 1570 onwards. He paid the sum of thirty thousand pounds a year from 1584 to 1588, still managing to make a profit on what he actually collected from the port of London. A later arrangement, known as the Great Farm of 1605, inaugurated a system of centralization which lasted throughout our period and up to the end of the eighteenth century.[20]

A similar tax, Tunnage and Poundage, was also collected by farming; Smythe had been collector of this tax in the port of London from 1557 onwards. Traditionally these customs duties had been voted by the first Parliament of each reign to successive sovereigns for life. From one point of view it was a parliamentary grant, but once voted it did not have to be renewed. The tax became notorious in the reign of Charles I, who had the misfortune not to have it voted to him by his first Parliament, so that later it could be contested as illegal. Even so he was able to collect it for those years when he governed without Parliament.

Another source of money, again a remnant from feudalism, was purveyance. This was a privilege possessed by the Crown to purchase at a fixed price (which was usually inadequate) provisions for the consumption of the royal household. During the reign of Elizabeth the old practice of each county actually delivering the animals and produce required was gradually abandoned for a money payment negotiated between the justices of the peace and the Privy Council.

Another tax, Ship Money, which was going to cause difficulties for Charles I, was collected in the time of Elizabeth and James from inland, as well as coastal towns, during war or time of warlike emergency to pay for ships for the navy.

The Crown could raise money in addition by making use of its prerogative to issue monopolies, grants of the sole right to manufacture, distribute or sell various goods. Men would pay, not only for these, but for licences and exemptions.

A source of revenue which eventually raised great opposition to Charles I was that of the forced loan. Like so much else in the English constitution of this period, the right to force loans was on the borderline of legality; this was because there was precedent of the monarch's subjects having submitted to it, which could discourage others from resisting it in practice, provided they were not driven too hard. Under Elizabeth the loans were not too unpopular as she gave a receipt for what was loaned and for the most part paid the money back. The money was collected from hundreds and counties, passing through the hands of constables, justices of the peace, deputy lieutenant and lords lieutenants before it went into the royal treasury. Money collected for military expenses usually did not go via the constable. Civil taxation was usually apportioned by the justices among the hundreds of each county; within them there was a further sub-division among the parishes. Collection was by both the high constables and the officers of the parishes.

The money produced from all these sources was dealt with centrally by the Exchequer, which had two departments, the Upper, or Exchequer of Account, and the Lower, or Exchequer of Receipt. As we shall see, to some extent the Exchequer was a court, but it had its purely financial side under the Lord Treasurer, the Chancellor and the Under-treasurer.

The Lord Treasurer appointed all escheators, customs officers, controllers and searchers throughout the kingdom. All officers were under his discipline, directing all searchers throughout the kingdom. He had all the officers involved under his discipline, directing all warrants for Exchequer commissions, granting warrants to the different types of officials. As Lord Treasurer, Burghley sent his serjeant-at-arms into the country summoning sheriffs and collectors to appear when their collections were in arrears through negligence or default.[21]

The Chancellor of the Exchequer was not as important an official as he is today. Burghley handed over to this office the administration of the Court of First Fruits and Tenths, that is of the revenue arising from the first year's value of ecclesiastical benefices and one tenth of the annual revenues. Responsibility for the actual treasure in the Exchequer, chest by chest, lay with the under-treasurer. The institution of the Exchequer was responsible for issuing as well as receiving money. Outside London, in the country, it had a large body of officials. The customs officers in the port of London must be regarded as part of the local not the central organization; according to Rowse there were two customers of 'the small customs' for import and export, three collectors, all five having a clerk each. In addition there were fourteen surveyors and receivers, eighteen waiters, and one searcher. In the rest of the country the ports were treated in fourteen main groups ('head-ports'); each group had a customer and a controller, and some had a clerk and four waiters as well.[22]

In each of the counties money when collected was paid to receivers of Crown revenues appointed by the Exchequer; there were thirty of these receivers in the whole country. Each county had a surveyor of Crown lands; there was one for North and one for South Wales. The Exchequer also supervised the finances of the duchies of Cornwall and Lancaster.

As we have seen, all officers of justice and law-enforcement derived their authority from the Crown; the monarch delegated powers temporarily, and could withdraw them at will. Over the years this royal power had resulted in two supplementary systems developing, an older one of the common law courts, and a newer growing out of the Privy Council. It is important to remember, however, that the judges of the common law courts were as much the royal servants as those in the Privy Council.

Before considering the three common law courts at Westminster we need to know that the law which they administered dealt with real property and written obligations. Common law assumed that all rights (including those of the monarch) are private rights. The law itself rested partly in tradition and custom, partly in parliamentary statutes. There is no written code, but individual cases are decided by recourse to precedent, which is why it is known as case law. This law cannot be altered by judges' decisions, but can be amended and extended by legislation in parliament. It was supreme throughout the land, and differed from all other kinds of law in that decisions as to innocence or guilt are taken by a jury of twelve social equals, while actual sentence in the case of guilt is passed by a judge. Criminal cases proceeded by indictment, civil by writ. Smith comments:

> *Judex* is of us called Judge, but our fashion is so diverse that they which give the deadly stroke, and either condemn or acquit the man for guilty or not guilty, are not called Judges

but the twelve men. And the same order as well is in civil matters and pecuniary, as in matters criminal. (p. 66)

Later he tells us:

And necessarily all the whole twelve must be of the shire and three of them of the hundred where the land lyeth which is in controversy, or where the party dwelleth who is the defendant. (p. 80)

The three courts which gave judgement in accordance with common law at Westminster were the Court of Queen's (or King's) Bench, the Court of Common Pleas and the Court of Exchequer. The two first had each a chief justice and three judges; the Exchequer had as equivalent a chief baron and three associate barons. Baron was merely an alternative title to justice. The position of chief baron was the equal in dignity and importance to that of chief justice in the other two courts, but until fairly late in Elizabeth's reign the associate barons were more expert in finance than law (not that they were at all inexpert in that). Eventually all the barons of the Exchequer were regarded as in every way equal to their equivalents.

At first the King's (or Queen's) Bench was devoted to actions by the Crown and usually criminal actions, but by the end of the sixteenth century many civil actions were also brought there by private persons. Nevertheless the Court of Common Pleas was primarily the court for civil actions between private individuals in our sense of the term (remembering that in Shakespeare's England a Crown action was also brought by the monarch as a private individual). The Court of Exchequer functioned as a court (as distinct from the centre of royal finance) giving particular attention to matters arising out of the Crown's financial rights. It also functioned to some small extent as an equity court.[23]

What is known as 'equity' arose from the inability of the common law, as it existed in statute and recorded decisions, to be flexible enough to avoid injustice in some cases. When common law did not provide a remedy it was possible to petition the Chancellor to exercise discretion on behalf of an individual. The Lord Treasurer and the Chancellor sat in the Exchequer when it treated matters of equity. But such cases were more often taken to another court, Chancery. Here the forms of Roman law were used but with the aim of administering what has been called an 'equitable construction' of common law.

This court was very closely connected with the Queen and the Privy Council, drawing its powers more immediately from the royal source with no defined limits to its jurisdiction and a much more flexible procedure than that of the common law courts. The particularly great authority and distinction possessed by chancery derived also from the fact that it was presided over by the Lord Chancellor, who held a leading position in the royal government, and was prominent in the Privy Council. He sat in the Privy Council's own court of Star Chamber as president, he also presided over the House of Lords, had custody of the Great Seal and was nominal head of the office, also known as Chancery, in which all royal documents were issued. One Lord Chancellor of this period period said of his office and of this court:

> As the chancellor is at this day . . . the mouth, the eare, the eye, and the very heart of the Prince, so is the Court whereof he hath the most particular administration the oracle of equity, the store house of the favour of Justice, of the liberalty Royal, and of the right pretorial, which openeth the way to right, giveth powers and commission to the judges, hath jurisdiction to correct the rigour of law by the judgment and discretion of equity and grace. It is the refuge of the poor and afflicted; it is the altar and sanctuary for such as against the might of rich men and the countenance of great men cannot maintain the goodness of their cause and truth of their Title'.

This Chancellor, Ellesmere, is obviously not unprejudiced, but in fact the court averaged more than one thousand cases per annum in the reign of Elizabeth. It is impossible to talk of a typical case, as so many of different kinds were handled, whenever less flexible courts could not give justice. John Shakespeare, the father of William, mortgaged a piece of land to Edward Lambert for forty pounds, later borrowing more. When Shakespeare senior offered to repay the forty pounds, Lambert refused to return the mortgage until the whole debt was paid, and wanted his son to keep possession of the land. When a debtor paid his debt without asking for return of the bond, and the common law judges would not help him, he turned to Chancery, and the creditor was required to bring the bond into court and cancel it.[24]

Smith approves warmly of this court in which the Chancellor does what his conscience tells him is just in each individual case:

> The chancellor hath the very authority herein as had the *Praetor* in the old civil law before the time of the Emperors. So he that putteth up his bill in the chancery, after that he hath declared the mischief wherein he is, hath relief as in the solemn *forum*. And for so much as in this case he is without remedy in the common law, therefore he requireth the chancellor according to equity and reason to provide for him and to take such order as to good conscience shall appertain. And the court of the chancery is called of the common people the court of conscience, because that the chancellor is not restrained by rigour or form of words of law to judge but *ex aequo* and *bono*, and according to conscience as I have said. (p. 71)

Procedure in Chancery differed from that of the common law courts:

> And in this court the usual and proper form of pleading of England is not used, but the form of pleading by writing, which is used in other countries according to the civil law: and the trial is not by twelve men, but by the examination of witness as in other courts of the civil law. (*ibid*)

Hatton asserted that 'the holy conscience of the Queen for matter of equity is in some sort committed to the chancellor'; and there is evidence that the monarch might give orders for justice and equity to be done in individual cases. There is also evidence that the court really took some pains to care for the poor. The Chancellor was assisted in the manifold cases before the court by twelve 'masters in chancery', of whom the Master of the Rolls was most prominent. There were never more, but might be less, than twelve, none of whom was necessarily given the same powers and duties as the others.

There were other equity courts. That of the Masters of Requests was supported by the Privy Council to deal with irregular civil cases, but the masters themselves were not privy councillors. They held no commission giving them judicial powers, and their court was not set up or regulated by statute. They were appointed by the monarch to a position which involved waiting in attendance in the royal court as well as acting on behalf of the monarch as 'a court of conscience, appointed to mitigate the rigour of proceeding in law', in the words of Walsingham. The masters gave special attention to poor men and to the servants of the Crown, as in this court litigation was cheaper than elsewhere. In particular it dealt with appeals by tenants, evicted or disturbed by their landlords; it ignored territorial divisions into counties, having jurisdiction over the whole country.

Another equity court was the Court of Admiralty, which derived its authority from the Lord Admiral in strict theory, but which by the end of the sixteenth century had become accepted as so necessary that it did not dissolve between the death of one lord admiral and the appointment of a successor. This court dealt with civil cases involving transport of men and goods by water, with piracy, contraband, contracts and personal relations entered into on or beyond the seas or to be performed on or beyond the seas.

The Court of Requests functioned virtually to enable the monarch to use royal power to ameliorate irregularities in civil cases. It had a counterpart dealing with criminal cases in the Court of Star Chamber, whose members, however, were privy councillors. The Court of Star Chamber developed out of the earlier practice of the Council of keeping certain judicial and criminal matters in its own hands. These were dealt with at special meetings reserved for judicial business. By our period they were held on Wednesdays and Fridays during the law terms and usually on the day after each term ended. On these occasions the councillors met in the hall in Westminster known as the Star Chamber. Thus twice a week for sixteen weeks of the year the councillors, who usually met as the Privy Council, sat as a court with a settled procedure and body of legal precedents and practices. They were joined by the chief justices or by others from the law courts. Cheyney (II, pp. 83f.) tells us that on 30 January 1594 the court consisted of Sir John Puckering, Lord Keeper of the Great Seal, Archbishop Whitgift, the Earl of Essex, the Earl of Nottingham, Lord Buckhurst, Sir Thomas Heneage, Sir John Fortescue, Sir Robert Cecil, and Chief Justices Popham and Peryam. These made ten, but the number present could vary from five to fifteen.[25]

The court's jurisdiction was limited only by its own will. It worked according to established precedent, according to its own proclaimed law and according to statute law, and gave all kinds of punishments short of death. Although Star Chamber has been regarded as an instrument of tyranny since the later days of Charles I, in our period it was normally regarded as a beneficial instrument of justice, and its sessions were open to the public. Smith (III, 4, pp. 115ff.) called it the poor man's court, and among other things it certainly dealt with great offenders who might have otherwise escaped justice. Its cases fall roughly into two kinds, breaches of public order, riots and assaults, and treason against the Crown on the one hand, and with direct violations of royal proclamations, grants and commands on the other.

In a matter of what we call public concern, the royal attorney, in one of private relief or satisfaction, the private person's attorney, made a written petition of complaint. Counsel must be regularly admitted to practise in this court, the alleged offences must be properly punishable by the court, and the complainant must hold himself ready to provide proof. Otherwise he could be indicted for bringing a false charge. The person charged received a writ of *sub poena* and must enter into bond to remain within reach. He now had an opportunity to see and take a copy of the charge, being allowed eight days to file an answer in writing, signed by counsel with an oath as to its truth and to the defendant's willingness to answer truthfully further interrogation. Examiners appointed by the court carried out the interrogations, returned a formal written report which the plaintiff was allowed to see so that he could put in a 'replication', to which again the defendant might file a rejoinder. Next, prosecutor and defendant named witnesses, whose testimony was secured in the same manner in writing under oath. The plaintiff then entered his cause and waited for the Lord Chancellor to select it for hearing. Lawyers spoke for prosecution and defence and answered questions put to them by members of the court. Plaintiff, defendant and witnesses did not appear in court in person until the defendant stood at the bar at the close of the case.

Star Chamber's punishments were irregular and usually fitted the nature of the crime. They were of three kinds, imprisonment, fine and, most effectively, the subjection of the criminal to public humiliation, to which physical pains might or might not be added.

One more court was associated with the central government, the Court of High Commission, which regulated ecclesiastical affairs. Until 1625 this was limited to the province of Canterbury, and consisted of the Privy Council, all the judges, the Archbishop, all the bishops, deans, archdeacons of the province, with the addition of several civil lawyers, important peers and gentry. In 1625 a similar court was set up for the province of York, and in 1629 this was extended to cover Scotland. These courts did not administer common law, but functioned in accordance with the principles of civil law (a development of Roman law); the lawyers (known as 'civilians') were organized in an association of doctors of law, or 'Doctors' Commons'. Civil law was taught at Oxford and Cambridge by the two Regius Professors established by Henry VIII.[26]

In the towns and counties justice was administered for the most part by the justices of the peace, in petty matters acting singly or in pairs, but in more important matters as a group in the so-called quarter sessions. Strictly all the justices of a county were enjoined to attend these sessions, but this did not always happen. Each commission to the justices of a county named a shorter list of persons one of whom the Privy Council wished always to be present. Such justices were known as 'of the quorum', from the wording of the commission, *'quorum aliquem vestrum A, B, C, etc., unum esse volumus'* (of whom we wish some one of you, A, B, C, etc., to be one). One man was designated as keeper of records, the *'custos rotulorum'*. After 1590 he was considered to be the personal appointment of the Lord Chancellor. The *custos* had a deputy and usually appointed a lawyer as clerk of the peace. Trial was by jury with the bench of justices deciding the sentence.

In addition to the quarter sessions, justice in the counties was dispensed by the judges, of whom mention has been made, holding their assizes. Often officials and other persons of local importance were associated with the assizes in judging criminals who had been awaiting trial in gaol. The justices also acted without associates as representatives of the monarch and Privy Council in civil cases.

It is not possible to separate the administration of justice from law enforcement in Shakespeare's England. If we start with the Privy Council we find that the two functions were mixed, even apart from the workings of Star Chamber. The Privy Council was constantly concerned with law enforcement, sending orders out into the country, giving individuals special commissions as need arose. It devoted its attention to any occurrence which might lead to a break-down of order, however far distant that might be, searching for agents of sedition everywhere. Among the powers which it exercised in investigation, the Privy Council alone was allowed to use torture, and then only with reluctance, when no other means could obtain a confession of theft as well as treason. The Council served summons and made arrests, using the forty messengers of the monarch's chamber, and lodging prisoners in the Fleet prison.[27]

The justices of assize were used for the enforcement of order on their circuits as well as for the administration of justice. They were required to enforce laws against vagabonds, against breaches of the regulations for dress; they were ordered to stop gentlemen living in towns and cities instead of on their estates, to see that animals were not slaughtered in Lent, to regulate the behaviour of local officials, prevent regrating and forestalling, to keep wine and ale houses in order and to repress slanders and libels.

In the cities and counties the responsibility for keeping the gaols fell to the sheriff, who deputed them a keeper; his responsibilities for the execution of sentences the sheriff could delegate to a deputy. The sheriff was empowered to use his initiative in dealing with any situation likely to cause a breach of the peace, or which contravened the Privy Council's orders designed to keep the peace and to suppress sedition, whether it be against vagabonds or recusants.

He was often ordered to assist the justices of the peace, and some-times to take over their duties when they had been negligent.

Most of the work of law enforcement was done by the justices of peace, who had powers of arrest and petty criminal jurisdiction; from time to time they might find themselves appointed to special commissions by the council. Acting alone, a justice of peace could instigate inquiry into felonies, fine those countrymen who violated the labour, game and enclosure laws, order men and women to be whipped, and send them to gaol or to the workhouse. In the hundreds the justices made use of the high constables to enforce law; in the case of daylight robbery, if the hue and cry were raised without the apprehending of the guilty, the person robbed might sue the hundred for his loss. Sometimes the justices might direct the high constables to lead the officers in a drive against rogues and vagabonds, not only to deal with them, but to investigate any persons who might prove dangerous. In the parishes the parish constables were responsible for law enforcement, arresting crimin-als or raising the hue and cry. The parish constable had the right to arrest the disorderly and carry them before the justice of peace. It was also his duty to search for criminals and to inflict minor punish-ments and collect petty fines imposed by the justices which were not important enough for the notice of the sheriff.[28]

This hierarchy of officials throughout the town and countryside did not only enforce the criminal law and deal with civil matters where appropriate. They were also used to organize such tasks as maintenance of the roads, and the building and repair of bridges. Much legislation which we regard as social was enforced by the justices, the fixing of wages, the care of the poor and infirm, the regulating of trade and apprenticeship. As has often been pointed out, all these local officials served without payment. The system could work only so long as the *élite* in the towns and counties, the richer merchants and the gentry, were prepared to serve the interests of the Crown without feeling that they were sacrificing their own. It could work, also, so long as there was a more than competent Privy Council, whose members did not spare themselves in investi-gating every possible aspect of the processes of administration, making note of everything that went on, forever sending orders,

K

admonishing, aiding, giving special commissions to enable tasks essential to good government to be undertaken as necessary. The system as a whole depended upon the support of the *élite*, and so long as it survived it maintained that *élite* in a position to which the rest of the nation was firmly subordinated.

With or without Parliament, this was the system of government and the way in which it worked. What was added by Parliament? If we are to be guided by the Queen's Speech as delivered by Sir Nicholas Bacon, her Lord Keeper of the Seal, to her first Parliament, which met on 25 January 1559, this Parliament had been summoned to deal mainly with three matters, the 'well making of Laws' for uniformity of religion, the welfare of the Commonwealth and taxation. Neale observes that 'it was almost by convention' that the speech was in three sections.[29] In fact, there were two circumstances in which it was necessary or advantageous to summon Parliament; when direct taxation was necessary to meet extraordinary expenditure, and when it was preferable, if not obligatory, to associate Commons, Lords and King-in-Parliament with special far-reaching measures intended by the royal government.

Direct taxes could be levied only through Parliament and were the special preserve of the Commons. Elizabeth tried to keep taxes low; she sold Crown lands to the value of £876,332 through the course of her reign in order to spare her subjects as much as possible. Nevertheless she found it necessary to ask for money from time to time. Taxation by Parliament was raised in two ways. One was by collecting a fifteenth and tenth of the assessed value of movable property, rural and urban. This came to be accepted in Elizabeth's reign as a sum of £30,000. The second way of raising money in Parliament was by Subsidy, paid at the rate of 5 per cent on the income of any real property worth £20 or more annually. Alternatively, the subsidy could be a payment of 5 per cent of the assessed value of all movable goods, money and valuables owned by all those in the Subsidy Book. No man was obliged to pay both forms of subsidy simultaneously. Something between £80,000 and £100,000 was raised by one subsidy.[30]

Henry VIII's Dissolution with Rome is the best example of the kind of measure with which the royal government felt it was advantageous to associate Parliament as representing the commonwealth as a whole. Smith would describe this as done by the prince in parliament. The King's authority and prerogative as opposed to the claims of Rome were asserted in Acts of Parliament. Elizabeth's first Parliament, apart from dealing with money, recognized her title to the crown, established her as her mother's heir and passed the Acts of Supremacy and Uniformity.[31]

Although Parliament was what has been called an 'occasional' organ of government, when it sat it possessed enormous power, as Sir Thomas Smith observes:

The most high and absolute power of the realm of England, consisteth in the Parliament. For as in war where the king himself in person, the nobility, the rest of the gentility, and the yeomanry are, is the force and power of England: so in peace and consultation where the Prince is to give life, and the last and highest commandment, the Barony for the nobility and higher, the knights, esquires, gentlemen and commons for the lower part of the commonwealth, the bishops for the clergy, be present to advertise, consult and show what is good and necessary for the common wealth, and to consult together, and upon mature deliberation every bill or law being thrice read and disputed upon in either house, the other two parts first each apart, and after the Prince himself in presence of both the parties doth consent unto and alloweth. That is the Prince's and the whole realm's deed: whereupon justly no man can complain, but must accommodate himself to find it good and obey it.

That which is done by this consent is called firm, stable and sanctum, and is taken for law. The Parliament abrogateth old laws, maketh new, giveth orders for things past, and for things hereafter to be followed, changeth rights, and possessions of private men, legitimateth bastards, establisheth forms of religion, altereth weights and measures, giveth forms of succession to the crown, defineth of doubtful rights whereof is no law already made, appointeth subsidies, tailes, taxes, and

impositions, giveth most free pardons and absolutions, restoreth in blood and name as the highest court, condemneth or
absolveth them whom the Prince will put to that trial: And to
be short, all that ever the people of Rome might do either in
Centuriatis comitiis or *tributis*, the same may be done by the
parliament of England, which representeth and hath the
power of the whole realm both the head and the body. For
every Englishman is intended to be there present, either in
person or by procuration and attornies, of what pre-eminence,
state, dignity, or quality soever he be, from the Prince (be he
King or Queen) to the lowest person of England. And the
consent of the Parliament is taken to be every man's consent.
(*op. cit.*, pp. 48f.)

The modern reader of Smith's account must not confuse Parliament with the Commons, as we have already noted. Parliament,
which included the monarch, was summoned and dismissed solely
in accordance with that personage's will. To summon the House of
Lords: 'The Prince sendeth forth his rescripts or writs to every duke,
marquess, baron, and every other Lord temporal or spiritual who
hath voice in the parliament, to be at this great counsel of Parliament such a day, (the space from the date of the writ is commonly
at the least forty days).' The House of Commons consisted of
representatives elected by counties and towns, in each case as the
result of a writ from the royal council to the appropriate officer.
In the counties this was the sheriff, who was enjoined by 'the
Prince' to 'admonish the whole shire to choose two knights of the
parliament in the name of the shire, to hear and reason, and to give
their advice and consent in the name of the shire, and to be present
at that day.' These two representatives were chosen 'by all the
gentlemen and yeomen of the shire, present at the day assigned for
the election: the voice of any absent be counted for none.' Smith
reminds us that yeomen are those 'who may dispend' forty shillings
or more 'of yearly rent of free land of his own.' The same writ
ordered the sheriff to arrange for the election in every town which
had the right to send two representatives (burgesses) to the
Commons; these were elected by 'the plurality of the voices of the

citizens and burgesses.' (pp. 49f.) Smith's account is typical of sixteenth-century assumptions about parliament in that he does not treat the possibility of one element of the institution, the Commons, coming into fundamental conflict with another, the king-in-parliament. We can be almost certain that the very possibility did not occur to him. Similarly he does not mention the fact that, in the view of the Queen and her Council, initiative in introducing matters to be debated in either House belonged to her alone, to be exercised through her servants, the privy councillors in that House. This view was one which they tried fairly successfully to substantiate in practice; it was held equally firmly by James I, Charles I and their counsellors as ideal, although, as we shall see in the fifth chapter, it met with more and more opposition in the Commons. From time to time members of that House found themselves in conflict with the Queen when they opposed her will that certain matters were not to be discussed; yet in principle her prerogative right to prevent discussion and dismiss parliament was not disputed. As with so much else concerning the constitution in Elizabeth's reign, we cannot lay down any hard and fast regulation or indisputable legal definition of the position. For the most part in practice the Queen's assumptions as to her sole right to decide what the Commons should discuss were not contradicted; when they were, this was not developed logically into a consistent assertion as a matter of principle that the Lower House had the right to discuss and initiate whatever seemed to it fit. Elizabeth spoke for her two successors, when she reminded the Speaker in 1593: 'It is in me and my power to call parliaments: it is in my power to end and determine the same: it is in my power to assent or dissent to any thing done in parliaments'.[32] Her statement was not denied by her listeners; it could be interpreted in such a way that her right to assent on occasion to a measure in which private members of the Commons took the initiative in no way weakened her equal right to dissent and prevent them doing any such thing whenever it suited her, which was more often the case. Under Elizabeth, the Commons did not have the right of control over its own elections. Although the Speaker was in theory the House's freely elected spokesman; in fact he was usually nominated by a privy councillor in accordance with the will of the Queen, and was virtually an official of the Crown, by whom he was paid. It was his task to see that there was no encroachment on sovereignty by the House, and to ensure that members concentrated on satisfying the purposes of the Crown as these were set forth in the speech of lord keeper or lord chancellor in the name of the Queen at the opening of parliament. When she stopped debate, or imprisoned members such as Anthony Cope and Peter Wentworth, who insisted on ignoring her commands against discussing religion in the House, she did not appear as an unconstitutional tyrant to her subjects, nor was she denounced as such. The Queen's inability to prevent members of the Commons completely from bringing up matters which she had forbidden will be dealt with in the fifth chapter (see pp. 193ff.). Despite these incidents, however, we can say that she consistently denied parliament any right to take the initiative in proposing what it should concern itself with.

While parliament as an institution was very much the subordinate of the Queen and her Council, the members of the House of Commons had managed to establish for themselves a number of parliamentary privileges which were confirmed throughout the reign of Elizabeth. Between 1515 and 1558 the House had been allowed to share the right to control its own members' attendance. In addition, according to Neale (*Elizabeth I and her Parliaments* [1966], p. 19): 'it had created for itself the right to enforce its privilege of freedom from arrest; it had invented a power to imprison offenders against its privileges and its dignity . . . it had even established precedents for punishing licentious speech by Members.' Although the Commons emphasized their awareness of the fact that it was the right of the Sovereign to administer discipline to offenders, they were actually encroaching on royal privilege. The House had contrived to arrogate to itself 'the functions of a court'.

Four of these privileges or liberties were the subject of petition by the Speaker at the beginning of each Parliament. He asked the Queen in 1559, for instance, for access to her and her nobles to make his reports and have conference, for favourable interpretation of his words in his reports of resolutions made in the House, and for permission to correct any mistakes he might unintentionally make in his reports. A third petition was for the members' freedom from arrest (and for that of their servants) so long as Parliament continued. Probably the most important freedom was the 'liberty of speech for the well debating of matters propounded'. Freedom of speech was granted in the first Parliament of 1559 by a Queen who was content that her Lord Keeper should merely emphasize that the members 'be neither unmindful nor uncareful of their duties, reverence and obedience to their Sovereign'. By this time, according to Gordon Griffiths, 'the petition for freedom of speech was part of the ritual'. However firmly the Queen might insist that it was an act of grace, not to grant it was unthinkable. As time went on it became apparent that Elizabeth regarded this freedom as enabling any member to speak his mind on any matter brought before the House, but she herself retained the sole right to select such matters as were in fact to be spoken about with freedom.[33]

REFERENCES

[1] Cheyney, *op. cit.*, II, pp. 279ff.

[2] See G. Griffiths, *Representative Government in Western Europe in the Sixteenth Century* (1968), p. 536.

[3] Quoted by Cheyney, *op. cit.*, I, p. 139.

[4] J. B. Black, *The Reign of Elizabeth* (1959), p. 408.

[1] W. Petyt, *Jus Parliamentarium* (1739), pp. 321-36; J. R. Tanner, *Constitutional Documents of the Reign of James I* (1930); here and in the following paragraph see also C. S. D. Bowen, *The Lion and the Throne* (1957), pp. 319ff.

[6] Aylmer, *op. cit.*, p. 27.

[7] N. F. Cantor, *The English* (1967), p. 351; G. R. Elton, *The Tudor Constitution* (1960), pp. 330ff.

[8] Cheyney, *op. cit.*, I, pp. 65ff.

[9] Black, *op. cit.*, pp. 108ff; Aylmer, *op. cit.*, pp. 19ff.

[10] Rowse, *op. cit.*, pp. 340f; Cheyney, *op. cit.*, II, pp. 360ff.

[11] *Ibid.*, pp. 381ff.

[12] *Ibid.*, pp. 378ff.

[13] Black, *op. cit.*, p. 214.

[14] For the following paragraphs, see Cheyney, *op. cit.*, II, pp. 343ff., 318, 380ff.

[15] Sir John Neale, 'English Local Government' in *Essays in Elizabethan History* (1958), pp. 214ff.

[16] Stone, *op. cit.*, pp. 459ff.

[17] For the following paragraphs, see Cheyney, *op. cit.*, II, pp. 356-372.

[18] C. G. Cruikshank, *Elizabeth's Army* (1966); Cheyney, *op. cit.*, II, pp. 368ff.

[19] Cheyney, *op. cit.*, II, pp. 373ff; I, pp. 144-147.

[20] Rowse, *op. cit.*, pp. 330ff.

[21] Cheyney, *op. cit.*, II, pp. 346ff; Black, *op. cit.*, p. 214; Rowse, *op. cit.*, pp. 316ff.

[22] Rowse, *op. cit.*, pp. 321ff., 330ff.

[23] Cheyney, *op. cit.*, I, pp. 142f; Aylmer, *op. cit.*, pp. 44ff; Rowse, *op. cit.*, pp. 314ff.

[24] Here and in the following paragraphs, see Cheyney, *op. cit.*, I, pp. 109-131; Aylmer, *op. cit.*, pp. 47, 53.

[25] Cheyney, *op. cit.*, II, pp. 80ff.

[26] Cheyney, *op. cit.*, I, p. 138; Aylmer, *op. cit.*, pp. 51ff; Rowse, *op. cit.*, pp. 365, 381, 405, 424; Elton, *op. cit.*, pp. 313f.

[27] Here and in the following paragraphs, see Cheyney, *op. cit.*, I, pp. 69ff., II, pp. 383; I, pp. 353ff.

[28] G. W. O. Woodward, *Reformation and Resurgence 1485-1603* (1963), pp. 48ff; Cheyney, *op. cit.*, II, pp. 394f., 405f.

[29] Sir John Neale, *Elizabeth I and her Parliaments* (1966), I, p. 42.

[30] Rowse, *op. cit.*, pp. 334-7; Griffiths, *op. cit.*, pp. 535f.

[31] Griffiths, *op. cit.*, pp. 534ff; Black, *op. cit.*, pp. 14ff.

[32] Black, *op. cit.*, p. 217.

[33] Neale, *Elizabeth I and her Parliaments* (1966), I, p. 42; Griffiths, *op. cit.*, p. 533.

4: Degree, High and Base

As we observed in the last chapter, the 'Commonwealth of England' was a society organized in strata and dominated by a small *élite* under its monarch. In theory each rank of society was rigidly separated from the others, but in fact there was mobility. Men went from the lower to the higher, whether it was yeoman, merchant or professional man to gentleman, the lesser gentleman from Master to Esquire, to knighthood or to the hereditary titles of honour. But movement, down as well as up, left society stratified with the *élite* firmly in control.

As Lawrence Stone (p. 65) has remarked, the existence of titles of honour is 'the most immediately distinctive feature of a society dependant upon monarchy'. The hierarchical organization of English society under the Tudors and Stuarts, with degrees of precedence within each section, obviously suited both the controlling *élite* and the monarchy. To maintain the existing state of affairs was obviously to the advantage of both; every member of society should be encouraged to remain in the station into which he was born, should be admonished that the well-being of the commonwealth as a whole was inseparable from the existence of hierarchy. The *élite* and the monarchy benefited from the general acceptance of a doctrine that the inferior should always obey those above him, and that in no circumstances whatsoever should dissatisfaction with a superior be expressed in rebellion. There were obvious practical reasons for the Elizabethan and Stuart preaching of this doctrine.

Those who advocated the preservation of the commonwealth of England as it was were helped enormously by the contemporary philosophic and religious view of the world as a divinely created hierarchy. According to this generally accepted view the divine intention actually expressed itself in hierarchy. Before the creation of the world the angels were ranged in hierarchy beneath God; Satan and those who fell with him were guilty of aspiring for positions to which they were not entitled.

The creation of the world was believed to have been literally an organizing of chaos into order. Milton gives a representative account of the notion of chaos, of unordered matter, in his description of the region traversed by Satan immediately outside the gates of Hell:

> a dark
> Illimitable Ocean without bound,
> Without dimension, where length, bredth, and highth
> And time and place are lost; where eldest *Night*
> And *Chaos*, Ancestors of Nature, hold
> Eternal Anarchie, amidst the noise
> Of endless Warrs, and by confusion stand.

This state of 'Eternal Anarchie', having no bound, length, breadth or height, without time or place existing in it, is literally a perpetual conflict of the four elements in their primeval state, of unformed matter possessing the qualities of heat, coldness, moisture and dryness:

> For, hot, cold, moist, and dry, four Champions fierce
> Strive here for Maistrie, and to Battel bring
> Thir embryon Atoms;

From moment to moment one or the other prevails, but merely by chance, and with an increase rather than decrease of confusion:

> *Chaos* Umpire sits,
> And by decision more embroils the fray
> By which he reigns: next him high Arbiter
> *Chance* governs all.

Milton knows that in 'this wilde Abyss' is the matter out of which the world was made, and wonders if at Doomsday the world will return to this. Although the elements are present in chaos, warring perpetually in their existence as qualities, they do not exist here as actual earth, water, air and fire; for that they must be organized into order by the Divine Word. The poet imagines Satan gazing into this wild abyss:

> The womb of nature and perhaps her Grave,
> Of neither Sea, nor Shore, nor Air, nor Fire,
> But all these in their pregnant causes mixt
> Confus'dly, and which thus must ever fight,
> Unless th' Almighty Maker them or gain
> His dark materials to create more Worlds.
> (Paradise Lost, ed. H. Wright, II, 891–916.)

As they exist in the primeval state of matter, the elements have the qualities mentioned; they are in a state of perpetual transition one into the other, a state of mutability; in addition their mutual conflict means perpetual confusion. In these essentials the elements are unchanged in themselves by the act of Creation; but their activity has been transformed into concord. Thanks to the Fall they do not exist beneath the sphere of the moon in a pure state, but only in impure and mixed forms. Nevertheless, the unformed qualities of chaos have become earth, water, air and fire, each possessing two of the four primary qualities. Earth is cold and dry, water, cold and moist; air, hot and moist; fire, hot and dry.

> Every one of these elements hath two coupled qualities, which constitute the species or nature of it. Yet these qualities by themselves cannot be elements; for qualities are void of body, and of things incorporeal things incorporeal cannot be made. It follows therefore necessarily that every element is a body and a simple-body, and such a one as hath actually in it, in the highest degree, these qualities: heat cold moisture and dryness.
> (Nemesius, *The Nature of Man* [1636], tr. A. Wither.)

Like everything else in creation, the elements have been set in order in hierarchy; earth, at the bottom, is linked to water, next above it, by their sharing the quality of coldness; water shares moisture with air, next above it; and air shares heat with fire, the purest element at the top. Thus organized the elements are in a state of harmony or concord as the result of their perpetual movement of mutual attraction and repulsion. Sir John Davies was not writing fancifully as a poet when he assured his patroness:

> Dancing, bright lady, then began to be,
> When the first seeds whereof the world did spring,
> The Fire, Aire, Earth and water did agree,
> By Love's persuasion, Nature's mighty King
> To leave their first disordred combating,
> And in a daunce such measure to observe,
> As all the world their motion should preserve.
>
> Since when they still are carried in a round,
> And changing come in one another's place,
> Yet do they neither mingle nor confound,
> But every one doth keep the bounded space
> Wherein the dance doth bid it turn or trace.
> This wondrous miracle did Love devise
> For Dancing is Love's proper exercise.
> (*Orchestra, or a Poeme of Dancing* [1596], Stanzas 17, 18.)

In their existence in a state of order, as in their disordered existence in chaos, the elements are perpetually in a state of mutability, ever being transmuted into one another. Nevertheless, despite this mutation nothing is ever lost. I cannot do better than follow Tillyard in quoting as a perfect example of this thinking the speech of Pythagoras in the last book of Ovid's *Metamorphoses* as translated by Sandys in 1626:

> Nor can these elements stand at a stay,
> But by exchanging alter every day.
> Th' eternal world four bodies comprehends
> Ingend'ring all. The heavy earth discends
> So water, clogg'd with weight; two, light, aspire,
> Depress't by none, pure air and purer fire.
> And, though they have their several seats, yet all
> Of these are made, to these again they fall.
> Resolved earth to water rarifies;
> To air extenuated waters rise;

The air, when it itself again refines,
To elemental fire extracted shines.
They in like order back again repair:
The grosser fire condenseth into air;
Air into water; water, thick'ning, then
Grows solid and converts to earth again.
None holds his own: for nature ever joys
In change and with new forms the old supplies.
In all the world not any perish quite,
But only are in various habits dight:
For to begin to be what we before
Were not is to be born; to die, no more
Then ceasing to be such. Although the frame
Be changeable, the substance is the same.

(Bk. XV, 237-58)

In Milton's account of the 'womb of nature' there is an un-planned and unpredictable ever-changing conflict of destructive forces in an enormous variety of hostile combinations. Variety characterizes creation, too; but it is a sustained and sustaining variety of created things in concord. As Sir John Fortescue de-clared in the fifteenth century: 'In this order hot things are in harmony with cold, dry with moist, heavy with light, great with little, high with low'.[2] The divine attribute of God is shown in creating the world in abundance; innumerable kinds are created and innumerable examples of individual created things or creatures of each kind. Spenser's *Hymn of Heavenly Beauty* celebrates 'the endless kinds of creatures' to be found in 'the frame' of 'this wide universe', so many that their 'names' cannot be counted, 'much less their natures' aim'. Hooker refers as a matter of course to God's plenitude in *Of the Laws of Ecclesiastical Polity* (1617–18):

> The general end of God's external working is the exerciseof his most glorious and most abundant virtue. Which abundance doth show itself in variety, and for that cause this variety is oftentimes in Scripture expressed by the name of riches.[3]

The kinds are no longer in conflict; they are organized by the act of creation into a state of order in which they are preserved by the workings of God's Providence. Essentially, order in the universe consists in every creature, animate and inanimate, existing in its appropriate place in relation to every other, under God, in accordance with the intrinsic quality of each. Only in this organization did it seem possible for infinite variety to avoid chaos. Fortescue's account of this ordering explains that God created as many different kinds of inanimate things as he did animate creatures, so that every creature and thing differs in some respects from all others, and is in some respect superior or inferior to all the rest; hierarchy exists among the angels, and from man 'down to the meanest worm'. Apart from Hell and its inhabitants nothing is excluded from the embrace of 'the bond of order'.

It was believed that the universe was literally a structure in which every thing and creature has an appropriate position, from the least important of inanimate things to the most exalted of angels at the foot of God's throne; the name given traditionally to this organization is the 'Chain of Being', though it is more accurately described as a ladder or series of degrees. The image of a chain, however, conveys an essential element of the ordered arrangement, that is, the fact that, while degree is observed, every creature at every stage of the structure is linked to all those above and beneath by the sharing of at least one quality in common. The actual number of individual units thus linked was held to be finite, yet so vast that it could be comprehended by human intelligence no more than if it were infinite.

The top of the ladder or chain reaches to the foot of God's throne. Progress downward goes first through the hierarchies of the angels. These exist in inconceivable numbers but with no trace of confusion, partly because they are arranged in order and partly because their free will is never in conflict with that of God. Angels are purely intellectual, utterly immaterial, in nature. They can apprehend God without any mediation of symbol. God accommodates His nature to the weaknesses of human comprehension, but communicates it immediately to the angels. They exist in such abundance, partly because abundance is the essential characteristic of creation, and partly as an appropriate communication of God's glory. Raymond de Sebonde emphasizes their numbers and their orderliness in *Natural Theology* (1480?):

> We must believe that the angels are there in marvellous and inconceivable numbers, because the honour of a king consists in the great crowd of his vassals, while his disgrace or shame consists in their paucity. Thousands of thousands wait on the divine majesty and tenfold hundreds of millions join in his worship. Further, if in material nature there are numberless kinds of stones, herbs, trees, fishes, birds, four-footed beasts and above these an infinitude of men, it must be said likewise that there are many kinds of angels. But remember that one must not conceive of their multitude as confused; on the contrary, among these spirits a lovely order is exquisitely maintained.

Sebonde remarks that just as there are different degrees on earth so there is a hierarchy among the angels, which he describes as 'unique, artistic, and beyond measure blessed'. He declares them to be ordered in three main divisions, each of which is further divided into three, making nine orders in all.[4]

This belief the Renaissance inherited via Aquinas and Dante from a Christian Neo-Platonist to whom the name Dionysius the Aeropagite is traditionally accorded. Dionysius wrote an account of the angels in his *On the Heavenly Hierarchy* some time in the fifth century A.D. All angels have a natural capacity to apprehend God, but in some it is more powerful than in others. Dionysius declares them to be divided into three main sorts in accordance with their possession of this natural capacity. Those most capable are in the highest order which is contemplative; they are subdivided hierarchically into Seraphs, Cherubs and Thrones; as an order they are nearer the foot of God's throne than any other created things, and the superior Seraph is the nearest of them all. The order immediately below these is more actively contemplative, being active in intention, or willing without action; this hierarchy descends as Dominations, Virtues and Powers. Beneath them comes the order of active spirits, arranged hierarchically as Principalities, Archangels and Angels. Milton refers in the sonnet 'On His Blindness' to the number and activity of the angels, when he imagines

Patience reminding him of the fact that God has no need of his work:

> Thousands at his bidding speed
> And post o'er Land and Ocean without rest.

Each of the angelic orders is perfectly content with the capacity which it has been granted of apprehending God. They are linked one to another by this unique capacity, by the fact that they are all intelligence, that they all love and honour God, and that the superior orders can mediate divine knowledge to those beneath. The lowest order, the Angels, to whom Milton refers in this sonnet, are the link with man, to whom they can manifest themselves, as Donne's *Air and Angels* remarks, in a voice, in some such sight as 'a shapeless flame' or in a 'face and wings / Of air'.

Immediately below the lowest rank of angels comes man. They are linked in sharing the quality of intelligence, and ideally in being moved by a desire to resemble God, to love and worship Him. This sharing of quality by man and angels is mentioned by Hooker in *Of the Laws of Ecclesiastical Polity* (1617-18). He declares the angels to be 'spirits immaterial and intellectual, innumerable and yet ordered'. They not only look upward in adoration but downward, moved to imitate God in benevolence towards men:

> God, which moveth mere natural agents as an efficient only, doth otherwise move intellectual creatures and especially his holy angels: for beholding the face of God, in admiration of so great excellency, they all adore him; and being rapt with the love of his beauty they cleave inseparably for ever unto him. Desire to resemble him in goodness maketh them unweariable and even insatiable in their longing to do by all means all manner good unto all the creatures of God, but especially unto the children of men: in the countenance of whose nature, looking downward, they behold themselves beneath themselves; even as upward in God, beneath whom themselves are, they see that character which is nowhere but in themselves and us resembled.

Man is separated from the orders beneath by his rational soul which he shares with the angels above him; but he shares with creatures beneath him the qualities of feeling, life and existence. Like the ranks of order above and beneath, men are separated in accordance with degree into superiors and inferiors. Sir Walter Raleigh in *The History of the World* (1614) speaks for this whole age when he relates distinctions in human society with those in the world as a whole:

> Shall we therefore value honour and riches at nothing and neglect them as unnecessary and vain? Certainly no. For that infinite wisdom of God, which hath distinguished his angels by degrees, which hath given greater and less light and beauty to heavenly bodies, which hath made differences between beasts and birds, created the eagle and the fly, the cedar and the shrub, and among stones given the fairest tincture to the ruby and the quickest light to the diamond, hath also ordained kings, dukes or leaders of the people, magistrates, judges and other degrees among men.[5]

Over half a century earlier in 1549, Cranmer was quite certain that 'the good order of the whole world, that is everywhere and has ever been' consisted in 'commoners' being governed 'by the nobles and the servants by their masters'.[6] In a yet earlier work, Sir Thomas Elyot declared that the inequality of men was the reason why 'God hath ordained a diversity of pre-eminence in degrees to be among men for the necessary direction and preservation of them in conformity of living.'[7] It was no more than natural that when Henry Peacham celebrated his ideal in the *Compleat Gentleman* (1622), the very virtue of nobility which distinguishes the gentleman is related to all other instances of degree in the universe as a whole:

> If we consider arightly the frame of the whole universe and method of the all-excellent wisdom in her work as creating the forms of things infinitely divers, so according to dignity of essence and virtue in effect, we must acknowledge the same to hold a sovereignty and transcendent predominance as well of rule as place each over either. Among the heavenly bodies we see the nobler orbs and of greatest influence to be raised aloft,

L

the less effectual depressed. Of elements the fire, the most pure and operative, to hold the highest place. The lion we say is king of beasts, the eagle chief of birds, the whale and whirlpool among fishes, Jupiter's oak the forest's king. Among flowers we most admire and esteem the rose, among fruit the pomeroy and queen-apple; among stone we value above all the diamond, metals gold and silver. And since we know to transfer their inward excellence and virtues to their species successively, shall we not acknowledge a nobility in man of greater perfection, of nobler form, and prince of these?

Like the angels, men are organized in a hierarchy, in a society of various estates, all satisfied and not aspiring to move from their station, with wife and children obeying the father in the family, and all obeying the superior in the state.

Beneath man in the Chain of Being come the beasts, which do not possess reason, but share with him feeling as well as life and existence. Animals are divided into three major ranks: first are those which have all the senses, memory and the ability to move, the higher animals such as dogs, horses, apes, cattle, lions, tigers, elephants and so on. The class of animals beneath these consists of animals (or insects) which have memory and movement but not all the senses. The third and lowest rank of animals have the sense of touch but are devoid of hearing, memory or movement; here we find shell-fish and creatures such as various parasites. As we have seen, there is further division into kinds according to excellence within the three main grades.

Beneath animals which have feeling come plants or vegetable life, sharing only life and existence with the major category immediately above. They cannot reason, are without sense and cannot move, but they can grow, nourish and reproduce themselves. In this they are superior to the class of things which merely exist, such as stones, metals, liquids.

This organization of all that has been created is simultaneously a separation in accordance with differences and a linking in accordance with qualities shared in common. Every class has a primate, as we have seen, the lion among beasts, the eagle among birds, the oak among plants, the diamond among stones. Excellence and durability among individuals and kinds is related to the balance or proportion in which the elements are mixed in each case; the more perfect the balance, that is the closer it is to an equal mixture of all four elements, the more perfect the kind or individual example, and as a result the more durable. Gold was considered the most perfect, most durable, of metals because, according to the alchemists, it was made up of the four elements in equal proportions. It is to this quality of gold that Shakespeare refers in the conceit in which he tells the person whom he addresses in his sonnet:

> Sometime too hot the eye of heaven shines,
> And often is his gold complexion dimm'd.
>
> (Sonnet 18.)

The implication is that the subject's complexion (colour, appearance, character and physique) is made of a perfectly proportioned mixture which is constant in every way.

Although every class is inferior to those above it, yet it excels all others, above and below, in one single quality. Stones are more durable than plants; plants are able to assimilate nourishment more completely than animals. Animals surpass man in desires and in physical energy. Man excels the angels in his ability to learn; they already possess all the knowledge they are capable of. And in adoration they excel all beneath them, but obviously excel in no particular their superior, God.

I have deliberately treated the mediaeval and renaissance conception of universal order as a descending scale from angel to stone. But Shakespeare's contemporaries more usually concerned themselves with the scale as one of ascent towards God. Each class from stones to man contributes to that above it. The elements feed plants, which nourish animals; the flesh of animals is eaten by men. Milton's Raphael tells Adam how everything that comes from God returns up to him in this progression:

> One Almightie is, from whom
> All things proceed, and up to him return,
> If not deprav'd from good, created all
> Such to perfection, one first matter all

Indu'd with various forms, various degrees
Of substance, and in things that live, of life:
But more refin'd, more spiritous, and pure,
As nearer to him plac't or nearer tending
Each in their several Spheare assignd,
Till body up to spirit work, in bounds
Porportion'd to each kind. So from the root
Springs lighter the green stalk, from thence the leaves
More aerie, last the bright consummate floure
Spirits odorous breathes: flours and thir fruit
Mans nourishment, by gradual scale sublim'd
To vital Spirits aspire, to animal,
To intellectual, give both life and sense,
Fansie and understanding, whence the soul
Reason receives, and reason is her being,
Discursive, or Intuitive; discourse
Is oftest yours, the latter most is ours,
Differing but in degree, of kind the same.

(*Paradise Lost*, V, 469–90.)

Here is one version of the ascent; another, as we find it in such works as Higden's *Polychronicon* and the *Natural Theology* of Raymond de Sebonde remarks on the fact that the topmost example of each inferior class is linked to the bottom example of the class immediately above. The topmost plants share their immobility with the lowest beings which have feelings, such as shell fish. Earth is below water, but its uppermost part touches the lowest of the superior. Water's highest part is in contact with the lowest part of air. Similarly, when the humours of the human body are perfectly blended it is in contact with the human soul which is spiritual and immaterial, and therefore shares a quality with the spiritual order of angels above.[8]

Had it not been for the Fall every part of the structure, each individual member of each class, would exist in undisturbed order. But the sin of Adam was rebellion; an aspiring out of his place, an ignoring of degree. It was the result of the temptation by Satan, who with his fallen angels had aspired earlier in conflict with degree and had thus been excluded from the ordered universe. Nevertheless, there were some people who believed that evil spirits (i.e. devils, evil angels) were organized in their own hierarchy of evil. Burton in *The Anatomy of Melancholy* is quite sure as a Christian that 'Lucifer, the chief of them, with his associates, fell from heaven for his pride and ambition; created of God, placed in heaven, and sometimes an angel of light, now cast down into the lower aerial sublunary parts, or into Hell, and delivered into chains of darkness to be kept unto damnation.' Burton mentions the belief of Girolamo Cardano that evil spirits involve themselves in the Chain of Being in a perverted malignant way: 'they feed on men's souls, the elements are food to the plants, plants to animals, animals to man, man to other beings,—not the gods, for their nature is far removed from ours,—wherefore to the Daemoni: and so, belike, that we have so many battles fought in all ages, countries, is to make them a feast, and their sole delight.[9] There were various suppositions as to the number or ranks of evil spirits. Burton remarks: 'Gregorius Thosolanus makes seven kinds of aetherial Spirits or Angels, according to the number of the seven Planets.' Nevertheless, some authorities insisted that there were nine kinds of bad as of good angels:

> Yet thus much I find, that our School-men and other Divines make nine kinds of bad Spirits, as Dionysius hath done of Angels. In the first rank are those false Gods of the Gentiles, which were adored heretofore in several Idols, and gave Oracles at Delphi and elsewhere; whose Prince is Beelzebub. The second rank is of Liars, and Equivocators, as Apollo Pythius, and the like. The third are those vessels of anger, inventors of all mischief; as that Theuth in Plato; Esay (*Isaiah*) calls them vessels of fury; their Prince is Belial. The fourth are malicious revenging Devils; and their Prince is Asmodeus. The fifth kind are cozeners, such as belong to Magicians and Witches; their Prince is Satan. The sixth are those aerial devils that corrupt the air, and cause plagues, thunders, fires, &c., spoken of in the Apocalypse, and Paul to the Ephesians names them the Princes of the Air; Meresin is their Prince. The

seventh is a destroyer, Captain of the Furies, causing wars, tumults, combustions, uproars, mentioned in the Apocalypse, and called Abaddon. The eighth is that accusing or calumniating Devil, whom the Greeks call Diabolos, that drives men to despair. The ninth are those tempters in several kinds, and their Prince is Mammon. (Burton, *op. cit.*, ed. Dell and Jordan-Smith [1948], pp. 163f.)

Speculation about the names, primates and hierarchies of devils, however, was esoteric and not widespread. On the other hand there was widespread belief in the ordering of the universe as described in a Chain of Being from the meanest of inanimate things to the foot of God's throne, even if it is unlikely that many who shared the belief would be able to give an accurate account of the hierarchies and qualities of the angels. That they existed, were immaterial and were linked directly to men was enough. So was the knowledge, as widespread as Christianity, of the fact that since man's fall, Satan and his servants have strained every effort to destroy God's handiwork, which is triumphantly maintained in its existence as order thanks to His Providence.

Man's transgression has left the universe capable of disintegrating into chaos; for he has rebelled once and is prone to rebellion again. As every link in the chain is involved with every other, any break, however small in itself, can lead eventually to enormous repercussions. And man is far from being the least important of the links. On the contrary, inferior only to God and the angels, combining the spiritual and the material, his actions can affect everything inferior to him, the planets, the weather, imperilling or destroying the harmony maintained by Providence among sources of discord since the Fall. Hooker asks:

Is it possible that man, being not only the noblest creature in the world but even a very world himself, his transgressing the law of his nature should draw no manner of harm after it?

Hooker is quite sure it will:

For we see the whole world and each part thereof so compacted that as long as each thing performeth only that work which is natural unto it, it thereby preserveth both other things and also it self. Contrariwise let any principall thing, as the Sun, the Moon, or any one of the heavens or elements, but once cease or faile, or swerve; and who doth not easily conceive that the sequel thereof would be ruin both to itself and whatsoever dependeth on it?[10]

It follows that man must organize himself in such a way that the conflicting wills of individuals work in harmony, with the inferior willingly subjecting himself to his superiors. As Providence has organized the universe in a ladder or chain of degree, so man's political, or rather, social life has been providentially organized in a commonwealth of hierarchies. In this way, as Forest puts it in *A Comparative Discourse of the Bodies Natural and Politic* (1606), 'God hath knit together a passive subjection to an active superior'.[11]

Pierre de La Primaudaye was writing in *The French Academy* primarily with France in mind, but he treats of what he regards as fundamental facts common to all orderly societies:

Every civil society must be kept in order by some policy, which is a necessary help to cause a man to walk in his vocation. But as the elements cannot be intermingled one with another, except it be by an unequal proportion and temperature; so I think that civil policies cannot well be preserved but by a certain inequality which is to be seen in all countries by diverse sorts of governments.[12]

He proceeds to repeat the doctrine which we have already become familiar with; in the whole world, inferiors obey superiors, this being true of the heavenly bodies, the elements, forms of life, man ruling over all.

We have also seen by proceeding from one particular man to a family made of many persons, how the head commandeth diversely over the parts of his house. Even so it is necessary that every civil society, which is made one of many families tending to a general good, should be kept in by some policy consisting in commanding and obeying.

It is not surprising that Spenser, a poet (and one tinged with

Neo-Platonism), should see in the act of Creation the organizing force of Love resolving discord into harmony; his *Hymn in Honour of Love* exults because:

> The earth, the air, the water, and the fire,
> Then gan to range themselves in huge array,
> And with contrary forces to conspire
> Each against other, by all means they may,
> Threat'ning their own confusion and decay:
> Air hated earth, and water hated fire,
> Till Love relented their rebellious ire.
>
> He then them took, and tempering goodly well,
> Their contrary dislikes with loved means,
> Did place them all in order, and compel
> To keep themselves within their sundry reigns,
> Together linkt with adamantine chains;
> Yet so, as that in every living wight
> They mix themselves, and show their kindly might.
>
> So ever since they firmly have remained,
> And duly well observed his behest;
> Through which now all these things that are contained
> Within this goodly cope, both most and least,
> Their being have.

It is, to our modern minds, much more surprising to find a hard-headed member of the ruling class admonishing delinquent inferiors in the same vein. When Sir John Cheke denounced rebellion in *The True Subject and the Rebel* (1549), he expressed basically the same doctrine as Spenser:

> Love is not the knot only of the Commonwealth, whereby diverse parts be perfectly joined together in one politic body, but also the strength and might of the same, gathering together into a small room with order, which, scattered, would else breed confusion and debate.[13]

We find the same assurance in Thomas Starkey's *Dialogue between Cardinal Pole and Thomas Lupset* (written 1536-38). The true commonwealth exists where all the parts are 'knit together in perfect love and unity; every man of every degree does what he should, contributing his share to the whole, generously, without envy or resentment. And when every member of society fulfils his proper function 'with perfect love and amity one to another', then when this life is over they will all enter the perfect commonwealth maintained by God in heaven.[14]

Shakespeare gives an explicit account of the importance of every member of the commonwealth co-operating in the Archbishop of Canterbury's counsel to Henry V. Exeter has just remarked that:

> government, though high and low, and lower,
> Put into parts, doth keep in one consent,
> Congreeing in a full and natural close,
> Like music.

Canterbury agrees:

> Therefore doth heaven divide
> The state of man in divers functions,
> Setting endeavour in continual motion;
> To which is fixed as an aim or butt
> Obedience.

He goes on with the account of order among the honey bees, analogous to that among men, ending:

> I this infer,
> That many things, having full reference
> To one consent, may work contrariously.
> (*Henry V*, I, ii. 180–206.)

Here Shakespeare states explicitly that men of different degrees and vocations can all contribute to the commonwealth's unity when they aim at obedience. In *Richard III* he implies what we have seen explicit in Starkey and Cheke, as well as in Spenser, that Love knits together the commonwealth of England. For Richard declares himself from the first the enemy of Love. So long as the 'winter of our discontent' continued, Richard could advance his own interests, but now all activity centres itself on love; those who were enemies have now become friends. Richard speaks of love in the sense of courtly love. He talks of a world full of proportion and harmony by insisting that he, lacking them, is fundamentally opposed to these 'fair well-spoken days'. His 'since I cannot prove a lover' should be taken in two senses; he cannot thrive (prove) as a lover because he appears 'rudely stamp'd' and not delightful to look upon; and, second, so long as around him those who once fought bury their enmity in love, he will have no opportunity to advance towards his goal, the Crown.

Richard is determined to 'prove a villain'—to reveal himself eventually a villain, and to thrive by being a villain. 'Villain' has two senses; first the normal one, an evil, malicious person; but it has a special sense of being as ignoble as a mediaeval serf, a rough, churlish, uncivilized person, quite unredeemed by the qualities of polite society, the very opposite of a nobleman dedicated to the service of courtly love. In the allegory of *The Romance of the Rose* the personification of the lady's uncivilized barbarian tendency to behave harshly appears as Daunger, a rude, coarse, beetle-browed peasant, a villain. Villainy and love are fundamentally opposed to one another. So is Richard opposed to every effort made by Edward IV to save his dynasty and the peace of the realm by prevailing on enemies to be reconciled to one another.

This is the kind of insight into problems of order and society which we expect to meet in the work of a balanced personality in which religious idealism is integrated with understanding of the world as it is. But it does not reduce the quality of his personal artistic sensitivity if we recognize that people who were not artists also viewed society as held together by a force which they called Love, and saw disorder and disintegration of the universe as a real consequence of civil discord. That is why Elyot's first chapter of *The Book Named the Governor* (1531) declares that a magistrate functions as part of a universal order, the only alternative to which is a return to chaos, to the state of primeval matter before creation, a transition scarcely to be imagined in its full horror:

Take away order from all things, what should then remain? Certes nothing finally, except some man would imagine eftsoons chaos. Also where there is any lack of order needs must be perpetual conflict. And in things subject to nature nothing of himself only may be nourished; but, when he hath destroyed that wherewith he doth participate by the order of his creator, he himself of necessity must then perish; whereof ensueth universal dissolution.[15]

If we return to consider some of the essential elements of the existing social and political order in England we see that it was not difficult to find justification for the *status quo* in the dominating assumptions as to the actual nature and structure of the ordered universe; on the contrary, it must have been extremely difficult not to relate the existing hierarchical society of England to the rest of the Chain of Being; one did not have to be a subtle or original thinker to justify the demand for absolute obedience to duly constituted authority by reminding Englishmen that everything from the meanest to the highest beneath God in the Chain of Being was subject to another. It was only natural that those who preached obedience and being contented with one's rank in society invoked these dominating assumptions.

Upholders of government in Tudor and Stuart England concentrated on three main points. They insisted that the commonwealth of England was virtually a divinely constructed society. Differences of degree, being divinely ordained, should not be obscured or ignored. The inferior must yield obedience to superiors in all things not contrary to God's law; and even in such matters there was no excuse for rebellion, the cause of more harm than good. We read this doctrine in a homily of 1547:

Every degree of people in their vocation, calling and office hath appointed to them their duty and order. Some are in high degree, some in low; some kings and princes, some inferiors and subjects; priest and laymen, masters and servants, fathers and children, husbands and wives, rich and poor and every one hath need of other so that in all things is to be lauded and praised the goodly order of God without the which no house, no city, no commonwealth, can continue and endure.[16]

In theory we can distinguish between a conception of the commonwealth as a divinely ordained arrangement for the wellbeing of all men, and a conception of degree as essential to the preservation of order in the universe. The latter does not necessarily imply the former; but the men of Shakespeare's age were virtually incapable of conceiving of the commonwealth except in terms of degree. How else could men of differing qualities combine for the common good, except in hierarchy? Elyot insists, as something that goes without saying, that taking into account natural and unavoidable differences and inequalities between men, God has avoided disorder by ordaining 'a diversity or pre-eminence in degrees'. His belief in the Chain of Being gives him the assurance that rank has an appropriate fitness to rule. The same belief gave Cranmer equal confidence to assert that the *élite* were more fitted to bear authority than those who were not of gentle birth: 'Take away gentlemen and rulers and straightway all other falleth clearly away and followeth barbarical confusion.' This is in his *Sermon on Rebellion* (1549); in his answer to the demands made by the rebels of 1549, he reminded those whom he addressed that it was illogical to expect to undo in one country what was fundamental everywhere else in the universe: 'Standeth it with any reason to turn upside down the good order of the whole world, that is everywhere and has ever been, that is to say the commoners to be governed by the nobles and the servants by their masters?' (p. 185).[17]

The rebels might have replied in the words in which Sir Thomas More denounced the deviations of actual commonwealths, as they existed, from the ideal which was always invoked in their justification:

> When I consider and weigh in my mind all these commonwealths, which nowadays everywhere do flourish, so God help me, I can perceive nothing but a certain conspiracy of rich men, procuring their own commodities under the name and title of the commonwealth.
>
> (*Utopia* [1515–16], tr. R. Robinson, Bk. II.)

Obviously there is much truth in this: it was convenient for those few members of society who ruled and enjoyed luxury to justify their good fortune by calling it divine ordinance. Nevertheless, we must not dismiss the ruling class's conception of the commonwealth as nothing more than expediency. Human beings are so illogical and so prone to confusion as to their own motives that it was possible for those who wished to maintain the existing state of hierarchy in England to believe genuinely that it was for the best for all men. Starkey's *Dialogue* has one speaker fear that abolition of the law of primogeniture might lead to civil disorder as a consequence of depriving the people of natural leaders. In 1549 Sir John Cheke was confident that, in the commonwealth, superiors and inferiors had need of one another, but the rulers conferred a real benefit in maintaining order among those whom they ruled: 'one kind hath need of another and yet a great sort of you more need of one gentleman than one gentleman of a great sort of you'.[18] Our modern disinclination to admire such breath-taking arrogance should not prevent our recognizing its source as more than self-interest.

As we have already seen in Chapter 2, Englishmen and women of Shakespeare's age were acutely conscious of the importance of degree and precedence in their social life. The College of Heralds not only conferred arms on those whom it recognized as gentle, but carried out visitations about once a generation after 1530 to ensure that coat armour had not been assumed without warrant. Changes in the ownership of land resulted in more than two thousand successful claims for arms being made between 1560 and 1589; another seventeen hundred and sixty grants were made in the next fifty years. Professor Stone (pp. 66ff.) gives a contemporary account of what happened at Stafford in 1583. The names of those whose assumption of arms was disallowed were publicly displayed, causing much humiliation.

Elizabeth was much concerned to restrict the numbers of all degrees of gentility. Not only did she demand scrutiny of those who claimed to be Master or Esquire; she created comparatively few knights, so that the numbers fell by about half from six hundred between her accession and her death. She objected to the generosity of her commanders, Essex and Lord Howard of Effingham, in creating sixty-eight knights on the Cadiz expedition of 1596. In 1599 she was so annoyed by Essex's creating eighty-one knights in Ireland that but for Cecil's persuasion she would have deprived these creations of their precedence as knights at public gatherings. Elizabeth was equally parsimonious in creating peers. She was concerned, however, for the dignity of the peerage, as witness her reprimand to Sidney for quarrelling with Oxford as an equal. We cannot be certain, however, that her concern with rank was the result simply of her sharing the conception of an ordered universe which we have been considering. It may have been as much the outcome of a conservative nature and a practical awareness that titles should not be cheapened. For James I, who certainly believed in hierarchy in principle, was not deterred thereby from creating the new hereditary title of baronet as well as numerous knighthoods and different ranks of the peerage. In fact his creations actually gave rise to conflict of a kind which the Act of Precedence of 1539 had been designed to prevent, although it confined itself to establishing precedence at Court. Below the Court it was normal to give precedence at public meetings in accordance with degree of nobility as regulated by the Heralds. At the best of times there were conflicts and jealousies. For instance, Sir William Drury, father of Donne's patron, died from a wound received in a duel over precedence. Drury had rashly claimed precedence over Sir John Borough, the son of a Baron, 'contrary to the Method settled in the ranking of English Nobility'.[19]

The inflation of honours by James I led to much tension between the new and the old. Nevertheless, the Stuarts, who cheapened the reputation of the peerage as a whole, were quite convinced that order in the state was bound up inseparably with the recognition of degree. It is not surprising that an aristocratic society which valued rank and precedence should justify its selfishness as being in accordance with divine intention whenever there was need. It was even possible to defend duelling as a means of preserving precedence without which there would be no degree:

> Take away honour, where is our reverence? take away reverence, what are our laws? And take away law, and man is nothing but a gross mass of all impiety. (Gervase Markham, *Honour in his Perfection* [1624], p. 4.)

The Tudors, without a standing army and an adequate professional civil service, required an *élite* through whom they could govern. The existence of that *élite* and that method of government could be justified by the contemporary belief that degree was essential to the divine intention for the world. The same belief justified another need, the need to avoid civil disorder, whether that degenerated into open rebellion or not. Not unnaturally supporters of the existing social order took advantage of the fact that there already was a doctrine of the duty of obedience and of the wickedness of rebellion. In facing actual disorder and in a successful effort to forestall it before it occurred, the monarchy and its servants emphasized this doctrine, not as something new but as something generally admitted, of which men had merely to be reminded. In fact there are times when government supporters are almost saying that if the discontented had realized just what they were doing they would have abandoned their ways as against the ordinance of God. The governor, whether he be magistrate or monarch, is the representative of God and should be obeyed as such. In the words of Hooper: 'The office of a magistrate is the ordinance of God.' Gardiner declares that a king 'representeth the image of God upon earth'; and this is true even if an individual king were an infidel.[20]

At first there is no distinction between monarchs and other heads of government. English writers may speak of kings rather than magistrates simply because they are thinking of their own country in particular. But when they thought of it they were emphatic that obedience was owing to all holders of public office, royal or not. In his *Annotations in the Thirteenth Chapter to the Romans* (1551) Hooper insists that Paul's statements apply not only to 'kings and emperors, but all such as be appointed to any public office and common regiment, either for a king, where as in a kingdom, or in the place of a king, where as in the state of the commonwealth is no monarchy'. The celebrated homily of 1571, *Against Disobedience and Wilful Rebellion*, likewise does not restrict divine support to monarchs: 'All kings, queens and other governors are specially appointed by the ordinance of God.' Nevertheless, this homily warns subjects specifically of the spiritual result of disobeying princes: 'Such subjects as are disobedient or rebellious against their princes, disobey God and procure their own damnation.'

Twenty-two years earlier in his *Notes for a Sermon on the Rebellion of 1549*, Cranmer makes an important qualification, which was generally conceded; obedience was only to be given in 'worldly things', not in cases of false doctrine. 'Though the magistrates be evil and very tyrants against the commonwealth, yet the subjects must obey in all worldly things.' The book of homilies printed under Edward VI in 1547 contains *An Exhortation concerning Good Order and Obedience to Rulers and Magistrates*, which agrees that no subject is constrained to obey commands contrary to God's law, but there must be no active rebellion:

It is intolerable ignorance, madness and wickedness for subjects to make any murmuring, rebellion or insurrection against their most dear and most dread sovereign Lord and King, ordained and appointed by God's goodness for their commodity, peace and quietness.

Once this has been emphasized, the *Exhortation* admits that obedience need not be given to superiors, 'be they kings, magistrates or any other' when their demands are 'contrary to God's commandments'.

Even in such circumstances, however, it was better to suffer the tyranny of an unjust monarch than to rebel. God in his own way will deal with the monarch; by rebellion the subject will be exposing the whole world to the repercussions of his act of disobedience. This is said emphatically by Latimer in a *Sermon on the Lord's Prayer* in 1552:

Be ye subject to all the common laws made by men of authority; by the king's majesty and by his most honourable council or by a common parliament: be subject unto them, obey them, saith God. And here is but one exception, that is, against God. When laws are made against God and his word, then I ought more to obey God than man. Then I may refuse to obey with a good conscience, yet for all that I may not rise up against the magistrates nor make any uproar; for if I do so, I sin damnably. I must be content to suffer whatsoever God shall lay upon me. (*Sermons*, ed. G. E. Corrie [1844], IV, p. 371.)

In practice the commonwealth could not function if individual selfish interests were allowed to express themselves unchecked. Discontent could easily lead to a breakdown of government; the country could be exposed to foreign invasion, to riots, to civil war. All these are horrible enough in themselves to make men want to avoid them, especially men in control. Even without any religious justification supporters of the *status quo* in the England of Shakespeare's age would have needed to insist on the duty of the subject never to rebel. History showed what happened when the subject rebelled. There was the recent history of England in the Wars of the Roses, as well as the calamities which befell rebellious nations mentioned in the Bible. They could all be used to prove that God had never allowed ultimate success to any rebellion against a legal monarch. And in the face of external foes, dissension at home was criminal folly; the dumbshow of *Gorboduc* merely repeats a common assumption already expressed verbally by Cranmer in a *Sermon on Rebellion:* 'It is an easy thing to break a whole fagot when every stick is loosed from another.' In his Preface to the 1576 edition of his *Acts and Monuments*, John Foxe uses the image of a ship at sea to represent the situation of Englishmen in 'one commonwealth' and in 'one church'. If the ship is divided it is wrecked. 'No storm so dangerous to a ship on the sea, as is discord and disorder in a weal public.' Partly because unity was needed in what was genuinely conceived of as the national interest, partly as a result of what we might call the interest of the dominant class, and partly from devout religious conviction, there were few voices to disagree with the homily of 1571 *Against Disobedience and Wilful Rebellion:*

> He that nameth rebellion, nameth not a singular and only sin, as is theft, robbery, murder and such like; but he nameth the whole puddle and sink of all sins against God and man, against his prince, his country, his countrymen, his parents, his children, his kinsfolks, his friends and against all men universally; all sins, I say, against God and all men heaped together, nameth he that nameth rebellion.

It is often stated that a theory of the Divine Right of Kings was an essential part of the more comprehensive belief in an ordered

M

universe, in degree and the subject's duty of not rebelling in any circumstances whatsoever. This is not entirely accurate; the two beliefs make sense together, but belief in the Chain of Being did not necessarily entail belief that alone of all rulers the monarch derives his authority from God, or that monarchy is necessarily the best form of government. Our knowledge of Shakespeare's historical plays (in particular of *Richard II*) may lead us to assume without justification that such terms as 'God's vicar' and 'Gods on earth' were used only of annointed monarchs; but these terms could be used of any 'magistrates', including justices of the peace of Stuart England. Christopher Hill refers to an occasion when a privy councillor disapproved in Star Chamber of a suit brought by a gentleman against the lowest officer in the hierarchy, a village constable: 'Let all men hereby take heed how they complain in words against any magistrate for they are gods'.[21] The constable owed his 'godlike' quality not to any share of royalty or to having been sealed in his office sacramentally, but obviously to the fact that he was a duly appointed officer to whom obedience should be given as such.

Even belief in the Chain of Being did not necessarily imply acceptance of a subject's duty to obey without rebellion. For Augustan England, as late as the time of Alexander Pope, contained people who could reconcile the notion of the Chain of Being with the oligarchical rule of the House of Hanover, despite the claims of the Stuarts. As late as 1732, Pope could write:

> See, through this air, this ocean and this earth,
> All matter quick, and bursting into birth.
> Above, how high, progressive life may go!
> Around, how wide! how deep extend below!
> Vast chain of being! which from God began,
> Nature's ethereal, human, angel, man,
> Beast, bird, fish, insect, what no eye can see,
> No glass can reach; from infinite to thee,
> On thee to nothing.—On superior powers
> Were we to press, inferior might on ours;
> Or in the full creation leave a void,

Where, one step broken, the great scale's destroy'd:
From Nature's chain whatever link you strike,
Tenth, or ten thousandth, breaks the chain alike.
(Essay on Man, Epistle I, 233–46.)

Not till late in Elizabeth's reign was there any talk of the Divine Right of Kings in the sense that monarchy is the best form of government, that only kings owe their authority simply to God, that royal power is absolute, unrestricted by human law or institution, that obedience to the monarch is due to his having experienced the sacrament of anointing, rather than to him as one among other holders of authority and to the fact that he is superior in the Chain of Being.

To some extent the view of kingship which we receive as 'the theory of the Divine Right of Kings' developed in England as a result of the repeated insistence that Church and State are but two aspects of the commonwealth, with the monarch supreme; this insistence was made from the days of Henry VIII on. On it depended the royal claim to supremacy in ecclesiastical affairs. This supremacy was regarded more strictly as belonging to the monarch in parliament, but it led to argument as to the power of the Crown in spiritual affairs. Common law limited this in civil causes; but there was no history of precedents to act as guide in defining the limits of ecclesiastical jurisdiction. Nevertheless, by the last twenty years of Elizabeth's reign the civil sovereign had in fact acquired the power of deciding vital matters of prayer, ritual and church organization. It became a test of loyalty to attend authorized church services and to recognize royal supremacy. Moreover, the monarch issued a commission to bishops, as to lords lieutenant, officers in the army and justices of peace. They were all servants of the Crown.

The strongest claim for anything approaching a Divine Right of Kings was made by William Tyndale (the translator of the New Testament) in his *Obedience of a Christian Man* as early as 1528: 'He that judgeth the king resisteth God and damneth God's law and ordinance.' So far he is not very extreme; it is only when he considers the limits which are proper to obedience that he makes a claim which closely resembles what was often to be said some hundred years later: 'The king is, in this world, without law, and may at his lust do right or wrong and shall give accounts but to God only'.[22] J. W. Allen (*op. cit.*, pp. 33f.) points out that Tyndale himself attacked Henry VIII in the matter of the divorce, and suggests that in sixteenth-century usage the king-in-parliament is envisaged.

Nevertheless, even if political theorists and the Queen herself did not formulate hard and fast claims, Elizabethan readers of Sir Thomas Elyot's very popular *Governor* (1531) found there a certainty that monarchy is the best form of government. Moreover, he thought it relevant to remind them that hierarchy exists in nature. He thought the arrangement of the angels in hierarchy and what he considered to be true of the organisation of the honey-bees supported the institution of monarchy among men. Fifty years later, Charles Merbury committed himself in *A Brief Discourse of Royal Monarchy as of the best Common Weal*. He prefers monarchy to the joint rule of 'a number of good men and men of reasonable wealth' and to the rule of aristocracy. He regards the king as accountable for his government only to God and his conscience. But 'full and perpetual' as Merbury declares the royal power to be, he does not give the king the right to make law. The English Crown 'is subject unto laws, both civil and common', but these must be agreeable to 'the law of God'. It was not until the last decade of Elizabeth's reign that definite claims were made for the rights of a sovereign monarch unlimited by any human law or institution.

These claims may have been provoked by the book published by the Jesuit, Father Parsons, in 1594, under the pseudonym of Doleman. This *Conference About the Next Succession to the Crown of England* declares that monarchy is the best form of government, but argues that a king who does not govern equitably according to the laws of God ought to be deposed. He follows with the assertion that as nobody has an absolute right to rule, so nobody has an absolute right to inherit the crown. Doleman may well have been reacting to the tendencies of the time to claim absolute power for kings as authorities deriving their power from God; but in any case his aim would be to deny the supremacy of Elizabeth as Queen, and to deplore the possibility of her being succeeded by a monarch with equal pretensions.

We find a radical claim for the powers of monarchy in Sir John Hayward's answer to Doleman's *Conference*. This *Answer to the First Part of a certain Conference concerning Succession* did not appear until 1603. Hayward insists that monarchy is the form of government most 'natural' to mankind as also the most efficient. It is impossible for obedience to be given to more than one commanding will; a union of many governing wills is virtually impossible of attainment. In a book written in Latin in 1603 (tr. into English, 1703) Sir Thomas Craig wrote: 'Reason which governs in men aims always at monarchy, as the most certain form of government.'

Hayward also insisted that hereditary monarchy is the best of all monarchical forms of government; the right of the heir to succeed is absolute. The most notorious of monarchies in which the ruler's heir had no right to the succession was Poland, a country whose history has amply justified the *Answer's* argument. Shakespeare treats monarchies of this kind in two plays, *Macbeth* and *Hamlet*. Because the throne of Scotland is elective, Macbeth has grounds for hoping that he might become King without 'my stir', without any action on his part. Duncan has the right to name his successor, who is then normally confirmed as such by election. After Duncan's death, Macbeth is 'named'. In *Hamlet* the assumption is that had Hamlet's father not been poisoned, he would have named his son to succeed him. In the absence of the Prince, Claudius has contrived to be named and elected. He has 'popp'd in' between what Hamlet has expected and the actual confirmation of the hopes in election. In the first act Claudius names Hamlet as his successor; and in the last Hamlet declares that Fortinbras 'has my dying voice'.

Hamlet touches an issue which is treated more fully by Hayward. This is the relation of the former subjects of one dynasty or ruler to a new monarch who has usurped his throne. 'The successors of a usurper by course and compass of time may prescribe a right, if they who have received wrong discontinue both pursuit and claim'. The fact that Claudius is secretly a usurper might give Hamlet the right to claim back the throne, once his father's murder is known, but there are no grounds to justify a rebel like Laertes, knowing nothing of the truth, attempting to seize the throne for himself. Even if the Gentleman had known the truth he would still have been able to describe the rabble in the same words:

> And, as the world were not but to begin,
> Antiquity forgot, custom not known,
> The ratifiers and props of every word,
> They cry, 'Choose we; Laertes shall be king'.
>
> (IV, v. 100–103.)

Laertes and his supporters are rebels; they are not trying to redress a wrong done to Hamlet and his father; they do not even suspect any such wrong. As a result Claudius is not disillusioned in his confidence that he is protected by 'such divinity' as 'doth hedge a king'. Had Hamlet been his opponent the situation would have been different. Only if Hamlet does not dispute his succession is Claudius invulnerable to his subjects; and Hamlet has not branded him a usurper in public.

One of the ironies of *Hamlet* lies in the fact that the Prince, at a time when he does not suspect his uncle of murder, regrets that the throne has come to Claudius for the want of any opposition to his taking possession of it. This is in the first soliloquy, in the regret that the world is an unweeded garden, that 'things rank and gross in nature / Possess it merely'. To 'possess merely' means more than to possess it completely; the term 'mere possession' is used in law to denote possession acquired by squatters' rights, for want of a counter-claim by a rightful owner. Shakespeare and Hayward are in agreement. Only the persons who have 'received wrong' can oppose a usurper; failing their protest he is secure in his subjects' obedience. Nobody but the wronged persons are justified in displacing the usurper. Hamlet is permitted to do it; Laertes is not.

It goes without saying that Hayward insisted that in no circumstances whatsoever is rebellion justified. To be sovereign a 'prince' acknowledges himself subject to God alone; but there is no unequivocal assertion of the monarch's right to abolish parliament or to make law as a prerogative.

Modern historians are rightly cautious in their treatment of the notion of the Divine Right of Kings in the age of Shakespeare. They point out that in this period all right was from God, and that in fact there existed in most men's minds a compromise between acceptance of the facts that the monarch in England had definite prerogatives, that he made law only in parliament, that he was supreme in ecclesiastical affairs, that rebellion was never justified. In different minds these beliefs existed simultaneously, their respective strengths differing from individual to individual and in different circumstances. The Queen was quite certain that she held her throne from God, to Whom alone she was accountable; but she did not insist that her power was absolute; and while she might assert that parliamentary privileges depended on her will, she had too much common sense to make it her will to abolish them.

To say with Shakespeare's Richard II:

> Not all the water in the rough rude sea
> Can wash the balm off from an anointed king,
>
> (III, ii, 54–5.)

was still not a claim that the anointed king had absolute power. The monarch was not bound, as Elizabeth proclaimed in 1585, 'to yield account or to render the reasons of their actions to any others but to God'; but that does not mean his power was absolute in the modern sense of the word. When she thought it necessary, Elizabeth was quick enough to remind her subjects that she was their anointed Queen. She behaved as if she regarded herself as involved in a sacramental function for the good of her people, a function which did not limit itself simply to governing them for their own good. She carried out the traditional right of touching for the King's Evil, actually placing her hands on the sores of the afflicted who sought her aid. There were moments when in practice it was necessary to refuse 'to have every man, according to his own censure, to make a doom of the validity and privity of his prince's government, with a common veil and cover of God's word, whose followers must not be judged but by private men's exposition'.[23] This is no more extreme in practice than James' insistence in 1605 that Kings are God's 'vice-regents on earth and so adorned and furnished with some sparkles of his divinity'.[24] But where James delighted in proclaiming a consistent theory, Elizabeth contented herself with an exercise of princely power which maintained her authority according to differing circumstances. She did not claim the right to make law (neither did James, for that matter); in practice she could virtually have made law by the adroit use of proclamation. Nevertheless, she neither took advantage of this possibility in practice nor claimed it as a prerogative in theory. But we see how delicate was the balance between absolute power and power subject to limitation when we note that without ever claiming the right to set aside law, she actually issued licences to enable law to be evaded in such special cases as the export of unfinished cloth. Nevertheless it appeared to her and her subjects that England, in the words of William Lambarde, had 'such a prince as is well pleased not only to rule others but also to suffer herself to be ruled by the laws of her land'.[25] The Queen did not regard the fact that she could be described as suffering herself to be ruled by the laws of the land in any way a diminution of her royal power. Her subjects did not find any invasion of their liberties in the fact that her observance of law was an act of free will.

It is impossible to convey by verbal description or analysis the essential reality of any compromise in which men and women refuse to be inhibited by fundamentally conflicting principles; so many things are known and left unsaid; so much is achieved by shared knowledge and experience, by look and intonation. We should remember this whenever we try to decide exactly what was meant on any particular occasion when people spoke about monarchy, its limitations, its scope in Elizabethan and Stuart England. The same words can so easily communicate different meanings according to individual speaker or listener and the circumstances of speaking and hearing. James' relationship with his subjects in the Commons was less successful than that of Elizabeth with hers, not because his conception of monarchy was different from hers, or because he claimed anything fundamental that she had not, but rather because he constantly proclaimed principles in order to resist encroachment. Yet there was still the same basic compromise, with the monarch avoiding the practice of what he declared he had the right to do in principle. Perhaps it is more accurate to say that he argued that his powers were limited only because in his absolute authority he had chosen of his own free will to grant privileges to his subjects. A limitation of power which existed in fact could be presented as no limitation in principle, because in limiting himself the monarch had exercised his absolute power for the good of his subjects; they had not forced him to do so.

Unlike the Queen, James published his views on kingship in *The Trew Law of Free Monarchies* (1598). Here, and later when he sat on the throne of England, he argued, or rather declared, that royal authority cannot be limited. He is fighting to conserve, however, not extend. This becomes plain, for instance, when we examine his insistence in the notorious speech in parliament of 1610: 'the state of monarchy is the supremest thing upon earth', with its claims that a king resembles God. Nevertheless, despite what looks like an extreme assertion of absolute power to modern eyes, James scolds, 'I would not have you meddle with such ancient rights of mine as I have received from my predecessors'. He does not simply state with irresistible confidence that his rights have come from God, but argues that they have come from predecessors, and that is why he should be allowed to enjoy them unchanged. 'All novelties are dangerous' in the state as in human bodies. He wants no contention about his ancient rights and possessions, for that is tantamount to declaring him unworthy of inheriting what his predecessors enjoyed and left to him. To argue thus in practice is not to assert the absolute power of kingship in the sense that we understand that today.[26]

Neither James nor those with whom he argued acted consistently in accordance with logical theories of royal powei respectively held. We see this in the dispute between King and Commons in 1604, after the royal proclamation that all election returns for the new Parliament should be made in chancery, in which office any which were contrary to the terms of the proclamation would be rejected. Subsequently, the court of chancery declared void the election of one Godwin, an outlaw, who had defeated Fortescue in Buckinghamshire. A second election went to Fortescue, but the house summoned Godwin and ordered him to take his seat after he had made a statement of his case.

James intervened; he told the Commons that their privileges derived from him and should not be used against him. When the Commons stood firm, James upbraided them for withstanding 'an absolute king', ordered them to confer with the judges in chancery, and then gave way and admitted that they had the right to decide about their own returns. Strange conduct for an absolute king, as we understand that office. Equally illogical was the response of the Commons. What the King no longer demanded as of right, they gave him willingly as subjects, issuing a new writ for Buckinghamshire.[27]

Modern historians regard this matter of deciding about election returns as a first minor battle against the royal prerogative. But there is no certainty that the Commons or the King necessarily shared this view. They conceded his point, he theirs. This is not so much compromise as an inability to perceive that disagreement derived from two fundamentally conflicting principles. The compromise is in the minds of the two parties: the king sees himself as bound by his own free will, with his power still absolute in that he has freely granted his subjects privileges. The subjects do not regard insistence on their privileges as an infraction of his; his giving way does not limit his royal authority; they immediately comply with his wishes, because the prevailing conception of the commonwealth assumes that (in the words of Canterbury in *Henry V*):

> many things, having full reference
> To one consent, may work contrariously.
>
> (I, ii. 205–6.)

James insisted that he was absolute but gave way; the Commons insisted on their privileges but actually made the same decision as that which they had rejected from chancery.

In the period which we are considering as the age of Shakespeare, theories of monarchy, its powers and limitations, were not being thought out consistently in England; but from time to time, as the need arose in practice, attempts would be made to rationalize what seemed possible or convenient as if it derived from a logical and consistent theory covering all cases. When a merchant named

John Bate refused in 1605 to pay duty on currants imported from the Levant, explaining to the Privy Council that he believed the import duty to be illegal, the government, despite all the claims that might be made for royal power as coming from God, sought the opinion of the court of exchequer. Chief Baron Fleming gave a decision which illustrates perfectly how contemporary theory relates to a detailed knowledge of law and precedent, a fundamental certainty about royal power as somehow absolute and some how limited simultaneously, and the need to solve a problem in practice. Fleming declared that a king's power is ordinary in some circumstances and absolute in others. When it concerns individuals, rights of property and the execution of civil justice, the king's power is 'ordinary' being exercised in the ordinary courts of law in accordance with common law; moreover the ordinary power of the king is subject to parliament, that is to the combination of Lords, Commons and king. But the king has absolute power to be used for the general benefit of his subjects as a whole as he in his wisdom sees fit. All foreign affairs, including trade from abroad, are controlled by the king's absolute power. The imposition on currants, like any other imposition on imports, is therefore rightly levied by the absolute power of the monarch, an opinion supported by precedent, for no case existed previously of an Act of Parliament or a petition against the imposition of duties on foreign goods. Fleming was not laying down a fundamental theory of royal power; he combined his knowledge of law with his acceptance of the fact that in some real but undescribed way the king had absolute power, while in other respects past and present experience showed it to be limited. The result was an explanation of the reason for the legality of the imposition on currants, which he was at pains to insist extended to the regulation of foreign trade but no further.[28]

An extreme claim for the absolute powers of royalty was made by John Cowell in his dictionary of legal terms, *The Interpreter* (1607). His treatment of such terms as 'King', 'Prerogative', 'Parliament', 'Subsidy' seems to assert that the king is above law, 'by his absolute power'. James hastily sent a message to both Lords and Commons, disavowing Cowell's claims for his prerogative, declaring that he had no powers to make law or levy taxation internally without parliamentary consent. He also ordered that *The Interpreter* be suppressed.

It is clear that with all his talk of free monarchy, of the Divine Right of Kings, of a king's absolute power, James did not think he could exercise power in the despotic manner which his words suggest to our minds. And in the notorious book itself, Cowell admits that absolute as royal power may be in essence, in practice the king consults the three estates of the realm, 'for the better and equal course in making laws'. This he does, not by any outward compulsion, but either of his own free will, 'or by reason of his promise made upon oath at the time of his coronation'. Here, again, we have the peculiar reasoning which asserts that a limitation freely accepted does not affect the absolute nature of royal power. That the limitation exists, however, is not denied.

Those who opposed James and Charles on specific points did not challenge the principle of monarchy, did not deny that kings ruled by divine right. They merely did not see that divine right meant power to ignore, make or change law. Opposition in Parliament, refusal to pay forced loans, did not derive from any basic theory against monarchy. The kings and their protesting subjects were equally inconsistent. Royal insistence on divine right did not mean that the speaker claimed despotic right to ignore law and make it as he pleased. In June 1628 Charles declared, 'I must avow that I owe the account of my actions to God alone'. But this was a belief shared by his predecessor, Queen Elizabeth. Charles was more rigid in practice, however, than either his father or his royal kinswoman. And circumstances had so changed since Elizabeth's time that a refusal to call Parliament or a threat to dissolve it, if sitting, seemed a greater menace to protesting subjects who were still far from having made up their minds to rebel. During the agitation against his favourite, Buckingham, Charles reminded Parliament, 'Remember that parliaments are altogether in my power for their calling, sitting and dissolution; therefore, as I find the fruits good or evil, they are to continue, or not to be'. Here is what everybody had accepted as valid in the days of Elizabeth. In itself this is no claim to arbitrary power. Elizabeth rarely proclaimed her power to be absolute, but managed to act with great

freedom in a manner which did not appear to deny the rights of
her subjects; James proclaimed the nature of his powers more often
and with greater consistency, but also showed himself flexible in
practice; Charles said little about his conception of royal power
but was rigid in behaving consistently in accordance with it.[29]

Eventually, of course, bitter conflict developed between those
who supported the king's prerogative and those who insisted upon
the subject's liberties. But even those members of parliament
responsible for the Petition of Right in 1629 did not deny the
validity of monarchy or of acknowledged prerogatives. They
merely attempted a definitive declaration of what the law was and
asked for it not to be broken; they insisted that they did not intend
to 'intrench upon' the royal prerogative. Both sides insisted that
the King was only confirming ancient liberties and granting nothing
new; but neither side agreed as to the extent of what was actually
confirmed. Nevertheless, the most tenacious opponent of royal
power, Sir John Eliot, declared that any liberty which a king grants
to his subjects does not prejudice his sovereignty. He was imprisoned in the Tower after the dissolution of Parliament in 1629,
and refusing to yield to the King, eventually died there of persist-
ent ill health. In his prison Eliot wrote a work on the rights of
sovereignty, *De Jure Majestatis*. He had joined with other members
of parliament in refusing to include in the Petition of Right any
recognition of the claim that royal power was absolute, even when
the monarch willingly limited it. When Eliot attempted to develop
a theory of government he found himself stating like any Tudor
propagandist that in extraordinary necessity the king has power
to tax arbitrarily, and that even bad kings are to be obeyed to avoid
the possibility of greater evils. He was certain that subjects cannot
share sovereignty, and that in England the king is sovereign as he
alone can summon parliament. He obviously did not regard his
own actions and intentions as any attempt to share sovereignty or
to make the authority of parliament prevail over that of the king.
It seems that opponents and supporters of James and Charles each
regarded the king's power as sovereign despite liberties granted to
subjects. Where the monarchs' supporters (and they themselves)
insisted that the granting of these privileges did not subtract from

absolute power under God, so their opponents insisted that in petitioning for their privileges to be confirmed they were not encroaching in any way on the sovereign power properly belonging to a king. Eliot did not see himself as trying to assert the authority of parliament over the king. As Christopher Hill has pointed out, many members of the parliamentary opposition to Charles resorted to legal antiquarianism because they were incapable of admitting to themselves that they were infringing on the royal sovereignty. Mr Hill suggests that 'they had to pretend they were exercising immemorial rights of the Commons, and that those who advised the king otherwise were the innovators'.[30] I believe this to be substantially true, but would suggest that these parliamentarians were probably not aware of their pretence, but genuinely persuaded themselves that they were not innovators because otherwise they would have had to think out for themselves a consistent theory of sovereignty in place of that of the Divine Right of Kings whose validity they assumed as something taken for granted.

To sum up, it seems inaccurate to speak of a theory of the Divine Right of Kings as deriving from a belief in the Great Chain of Being. This belief existed both before and after the period in which the Divine Right of Kings was proclaimed. There is no doubt that people in Tudor and Stuart England believed that the institution of monarchy was peculiarly suited to function as part of the ordered universe. Their notions of order also helped to justify the established stratification of the commonwealth as it existed. But mere belief in the Chain of Being, the duty of subjects to obey, the Divine Right of Kings or the fact that monarchs are answerable only to God, did not mean a belief in the right of a king to rule arbitrarily without conforming to existing law. Few people, if any, knew exactly what they meant by absolute power; in practice they were none the less certain when they thought it was being infringed upon or exercised. It appears safe to suggest that belief in the Chain of Being helped to prevent the subjects of Charles and James from resorting to rebellion, helped also to prevent them from recognizing that they were innovators, that in fact they were encroaching on royal prerogative according to law. Thus it was that a man like Sir John Eliot could agree with Shakespeare's Richard II about the impossibility of undoing the act of anointing of a king, with Claudius about the divinity hedging kingship, and still engage in opposition to royal power in his parliamentary campaign for the liberties of the subject. In demanding liberties he did not deny the fact that he was a subject, just as in confirming liberties Charles did not regard himself as limiting his absolute power.

REFERENCES

[1] Quoted by Tillyard, *op. cit.*, pp. 61f.
[2] Sir John Fortescue, *Works*, ed. Lord Clermont (1869), I, p. 322.
[3] Quoted by Tillyard, *op. cit.*, p. 25.
[4] Here and in the following paragraphs, see Tillyard, *op. cit.*, pp. 40ff.
[5] Quoted by Tillyard, *op. cit.*, p. 11.
[6] Cranmer, *Writings*, etc., ed. J. E. Cox (1844), II, p. 185.
[7] Elyot, *The Book Named the Governor* (1531), ed. H. H. Croft (1833), I, p. 209, quoted by Allen, *op. cit.*, pp. 135f.
[8] See Tillyard, *op. cit.*,
[9] W. Burton, *The Anatomy of Melancholy* (1621), ed. Dell and Jordan-Smith (1948), pp. 158, 163.
[10] Quoted by Tillyard, *op. cit.*, pp. 93f.
[11] Quoted by Winny, *The Frame of Order* (1957), p. 90.
[12] Trans. T. Bowes (1586), quoted by Winny, *op. cit.*, pp. 105ff.
[13] Quoted by Allen, *op. cit.*, p. 141.
[14] *Starkey's Life and Letters*, ed. S. J. Herrtage (1878), pp. 45ff., 54-6, quoted by Allen, *op. cit.*, p. 141.
[15] Quoted by Tillyard, *op. cit.*, pp. 11f.
[16] Quoted by C. Read, *The Government of England under Elizabeth* (1960), p. 2.
[17] Here and in the following paragraphs, see Allen, *op. cit.*, pp. 135ff.
[18] Sir John Cheke, *The True Subject and the Rebel* (1549)
[19] R. C. Bald, *Donne and the Druries* (1959), p. 159.
[20] J. Hooper, *Annotations in the Thirteenth Chapter to the Romans* (1551); S. Gardiner, *De Vera Obedientia* (1555), both quoted by Allen, *op. cit.*, p. 126. Also see Allen, *ibid.*, for the following paragraphs.
[21] Hill, *The Century of Revolution 1603-1714* (1966), p. 64.
[22] Tyndale, *Obedience of Christian Man* (1528), edition of 1582, p. 22.
[23] D'Ewes *Journal*, see G. W. Prothero, *Select Statutes and other Constitutional Documents Illustrative of the Reigns of Elizabeth and James I* (1964), p. 222.
[24] See Davies, *op. cit.*, p. 5.
[25] 'Charge to the Quarter Sessions at Maidstone after Easter, 1586' in *William Lambarde and Local Government*, ed. C. Read (1962), p. 83.
[26] Quoted by C. Hill and E. Dell, *The Good Old Cause* (1949), pp. 118f.
[27] See G. R. Davies, *The Early Stuarts 1603-1660* (1937), pp. 1ff; J. R. Kenyon, *The Stuart Constitution* (1966), pp. 27, 37-8.
[28] Davies, *op. cit.*, p. 10; Kenyon, *op. cit.*, pp. 8, 12.
[29] Davies, *op. cit.*, p. 22-5.
[30] Hill, *op. cit.*, pp. 62ff.

5: Events and Explanations

THE last two chapters have dealt with the government of England by a small *élite* between 1558 and 1630, and with a philosophy which divided humanity, like the rest of creation, into hierarchies, the existence of which under the monarch, God's deputy, were essential for the preservation of order and, literally, the prevention of chaos. This philosophy leads to a theory of government which subordinates the *élite* consistently to the Crown, just as the rest of the country is subordinated to that *élite*.

At the beginning of our period for the most part what was demanded by theory happened in practice; but as time went on more and more issues evoked among various members of the *élite* a disinclination to concede that utter unresisting co-operation which the Crown might regard as ideal. In the absence of a standing army and of a competent and large enough bureaucracy the royal government could not be carried on without the co-operation of the *élite*. As a result, wherever the gentlemen or nobility of England saw any kind of threat to their interests (which they might sincerely regard as the best interests of the country as a whole), their utter unquestioning preparedness to carry out the wishes of the Crown was exposed to a strain.

For the Crown the ideal state of affairs would have been one in which the gentle classes were completely co-operative, ready to carry out the royal wishes, carrying out existing statute law, not contesting royal proclamation of law, confirming it by statute whenever that might seem convenient. This state of affairs would include the royal prerogative to raise funds for all normal purposes without summoning parliament. That institution would function only in states of emergency to vote extraordinary taxes, or to associate the whole political nation with the royal policy expressed by the King in Parliament. And then the Crown would be the arbiter of what matters were to be considered in the Commons. The equivocal nature of some key aspects of the English constitution was such that there appeared to be legal justification for the insistence of the Crown, in the persons of Elizabeth, James and Charles, that this was how England should be governed. Elizabeth did not come so near a consistent formulation of the rights of prerogative as James, or even Charles; but in practice she showed that fundamentally she shared their views (though the consensus of modern opinion is that she was more tactful and more realistic in her actions).

Despite Elizabeth's assumptions, despite religio-political assertion of the duty of the subject to obey, from the very beginning of her reign she did not receive from the *élite* that ideal subordination of their actions to her decisions as to what was in their best interests. From her accession onwards she was involved in two issues which seemed to various of her gentle subjects to be of such vast importance to the well-being of the nation that they insisted on considering them in the Commons despite her commands to the contrary; these issues concerned religion and the succession to the throne, which for the first years of the reign were inseparable from the problem of her marriage. The determination of some members of parliament to consider these matters was not intended primarily as an encroachment on the royal prerogative as a matter of principle, yet that principle was involved fundamentally. Under Elizabeth the anxiety of Protestants for the future of their faith in this country led to what were tantamount to attempts at encroachment on the prerogative of the Crown to arrange royal marriages and alliances; under James and Charles there was conflict over the monarch's sole right to determine foreign policy. In all three reigns religion led some members of the *élite* in and out of parliament to oppose the monarch. In all three reigns there was conflict over finance; and in all three, discontent with officials or ministers brought some of the monarch's gentle subjects into conflict with the royal prerogative.

When members of the *élite* found themselves discontented with what was demanded of them by Elizabeth, James or Charles, or with the manner in which the royal servants carried out their

N

monarch's policy, there were four ways, short of rebellion, in which the discontent could have some practical results. The first was what we might call a sort of mild but effective sabotage, as when local justices of the peace and greater magnates might mitigate penalties against recusants or Puritans, or not assess themselves and their neighbours strictly in accordance with regulations when it came to taxation. The subject might also be driven to a breach of the law respecting trade. A second way open to subjects to avoid carrying out royal policy was by resort to the common law courts; this was a practical expedient rather than a consistent attack on the prerogative as such. The third method of airing a grievance and of trying to have it redressed was through parliament, but obviously only when it was sitting. A fourth method open to private individuals was by petition to the monarch for redress of a grievance. By 1642, a large part of the *élite* found itself adopting the first method, with refusal to carry out the contested law or the sovereign's wishes being converted into active rebellion. In our period, however, apart from abortive attempts at rebellion by a minority, the majority of the *élite* preferred to turn to the courts or to parliament; the fact that such action could be justified as legal and constitutional enabled the hard-pressed subject to evade admitting to himself that he had set his feet on a road, which as James and Charles rightly insisted, would lead to a weakening of royal power which was supported by the constitution. If we take a survey of all three reigns we find that what was at first a loyal wish of members of the *élite* to act in what they saw as the best interests of the nation led to years of bickering and of out and out conflict. And as a result such members of the *élite* gradually developed an interpretation of the constitution which differed radically from that held by the Crown.

Religion was a source of active if unostentatious opposition to the royal commands from 1559 onwards. Influential people succeeded in evading the oath of supremacy; in addition to those who were not in one of the specified categories which must take it, there were others who should have taken it but had not been required to by officials lax in their duty. Moreover, the sheriffs had contrived to give insufficient support to the bishops when they wished to enforce the secular penalties of excommunication. As a result, when the second Parliament of the reign met in 1563 the law was amended. An Act increased the penalties for upholding papal authority, and named new classes of subjects who must take the oath of supremacy—members of parliament, schoolteachers, lawyers, barristers, sheriffs—and included 'all persons whatsoever who have or shall be admitted to any ministry or office belonging to the common law or any other law within the realm'.[1] The administration of the oath was handed to archbishops and bishops, with the Lord Chancellor authorised to issue such powers to anyone he regarded fit; the supervision of the whole proceeding was entrusted to the Court of Queen's Bench.

Another Act named penalties for officials who did not aid the ecclesiastical authorities in implementing excommunication. Nevertheless the justices of the peace in the north continued to be hostile or unhelpful. An official enquiry in 1564 discovered that this was true of half of the justices in the whole country, with a much higher proportion in the north.

Obstruction by justices was certainly present in 1571, if we are to take notice of the remarks of the Lord Keeper, Sir Nicholas Bacon, in reply to the Speaker of the House of Commons at the end of the session of Parliament, a session which had given the Queen much displeasure. In her name he denounced those who did not execute the laws well. The Queen, he said, did all she could, giving her royal assent to laws, proclaiming and publishing them, granting her commission of peace to men throughout the realm who were sworn to carry them out. She went further, summoning individuals to Star Chamber every year to exhort them to do their duty. 'Is it not, trow you', demanded Bacon, 'a monstrous disguising' when a man did not do what his oath demanded, stirring up discontent instead of keeping the peace, 'leading and swaying of juries according to his will, acquitting some for gain, indicting others for malice, bearing him for his servant or friend, overthrowing the other for his enemy, procuring all questmongers to be of his livery', and directing all enquiries to his own satisfaction by 'his winks, frownings and countenances'?[2] There were similar complaints as late as 1578.

Many of the Queen's subjects who differed from her over religion were Protestants who would have liked reform to have gone further. When it was clear that this could not be done by Parliament, the clergy in the south-eastern dioceses resorted to a habit of holding meetings every week or fortnight to study the Scriptures and improve morals. These 'prophesyings' or 'exercises' were intended to supplement the canons of the Church and to deepen the religious life of the community without contravening or subverting the doctrines of the Church of England. The fact that the laity might be present without taking part added to the possibility that these meetings might lead to open or covert opposition to those doctrines. Archbishop Grindal therefore issued regulations in 1576 to prevent such dangers. But the Queen regarded the whole movement as an attempt to defy law and the royal prerogative and secretly continue a reformation of the Church. In 1577 she ordered Grindal to suppress the meetings and to report the names of any who disobeyed for the council to deal with them. Grindal refused to obey her, comparing her command to 'the anti-christian voice of the Pope', he was deprived of his office and was unable to exercise his temporal jurisdiction for five years.[3]

The Puritans were more deeply involved in conflict with the Crown after Whitgift became Archbishop of Canterbury in 1583. His six articles of that year compelled the clergy to subscribe to the ecclesiastical supremacy of the Crown, the book of common prayer and the ordinal as totally in agreement with Scripture, the whole of the Thirty-nine Articles as consonant with the word of God. Very soon over two hundred ministers were suspended in East Anglia, Essex and Kent. Whitgift used the High Commission as an inquisitorial court in which suspects and witnesses were asked to take an oath (known as *ex officio*) obliging them to answer what they were asked. Anyone refusing to take the oath was handed to Star Chamber to be punished. Only in this way could the Crown overcome the attitude of local officials who favoured Puritan ministers.[4]

Not long after Whitgift's appointment, the Puritans developed a new method of circumventing the Crown in ecclesiastical matters. All the clergy of a district who were prepared to follow a new Book of Discipline were organised in a 'classis', a secret synod. These men tried to keep within the letter of the law, but omitted offending passages in the Prayer Book whenever they could; they preached Puritan interpretations of the Bible; congregations elected their ministers and recommended them through the 'classis' to the bishop for consecration. Churchwarden and collector for the poor were called elder and deacon respectively. These Puritans worked in such secrecy, and so much within the letter of the law that it was very difficult for church officials to obtain enough evidence to convict them of an open infringement of it.[5]

Some Puritans decided to break away. In 1567 one attempt at Plumbers' Hall had failed with imprisonment of the leaders. But in 1580 Robert Browne and Henry Barrow led a group preaching congregationalism; they declared the close connection of Church and state to be unscriptural, denied the need for a learned ministry, emphasized inspiration, and advocated a form of public worship without hierarchy or ritual. They were determined on immediate reform and continuously clashed with the ecclesiastical policy of the Crown.

Between the end of 1587 and that of 1589, Puritan oppositi   to the Crown showed itself in the Marprelate pamphlets, but eventually the anonymous authors had to stop to avoid discovery. One of the chief writers, John Penry, escaped to Scotland, but was lured back and executed in 1593.[6]

The government treated extreme Puritans as if they were Anabaptists, dedicated in the imaginations of the ruling circles and of the populace to the subversion of church, state and public morals. In 1589 a group of Presbyterian leaders, including Cartwright, were summoned by the commission, refused to take the oath and were sent to prison until 1592, when they were released because no open infringement of the law could be proved against them. But the more extreme Puritans suffered much more. John Udall, suspected of being a Martinist, was sentenced to death but died in prison before execution in 1590. One, Hackett, accused of plotting against the Queen's life, was executed in 1592. In 1593, Barrow and Greenwood, the separatists, were executed for seditious speeches. This same year the Conventicle Act threatened exile or death to all who persisted in absence from the Anglican Church or in attending conventicles. By the end of the reign the Puritan movement was kept firmly under. They had been defeated, but not destroyed, and continued to oppose the ecclesiastical power of the Crown by preaching and teaching while apparently obeying the letter of the law in the reigns of James and Charles. After the Hampton Court conference, James issued a proclamation on 16 July giving clergymen until 30 November to conform. James hoped to exclude as few as possible and to that end he therefore declared:

> that this our admonition may have equal force in all men's hearts to work a universal conformity, so we do require all archbishops, bishops, and other ecclesiastical persons to do their utmost endeavours, by conferences, arguments, persuasions, and by all other ways of love and gentleness, to reclaim all that be in the ministry in obedience of our church laws, for which purpose only we have enlarged the time formerly prefixed for their remove or reformation, to the end that if it be possible that uniformity which we desire may be wrought by clemency and by weight of reason, and not by rigour of law. And the like advertisement do we give to all civil magistrates, gentlemen, and others of understanding, as well abroad in the counties as in cities and towns, requiring them also not in any sort to support, favour or countenance any such factious ministers in their obstinacy, of whose endeavours we doubt not but so good success may follow, as this our admonition, with their endeavours, may prevent the use of any other means to retain our people in their due obedience to us, and in unity of mind to the service of Almighty God. (Cardwell, *Documentary Annals*, II, 80–4.)

In September the King licensed the canons drawn up by Convocation which put the same demands to candidates for holy orders as those of Whitgift in 1583. Many of the gentry petitioned on behalf of the clergy. At the most three hundred were silenced; the figure may be as low as one hundred and fifty, of whom no more than eighty or ninety lost their benefices. Many conformed but did everything they could within the established Church to communicate to others their ideals of godly living. One way round the demand for conformity was for preachers not to present themselves for benefices but to concentrate on sermons, both delivered and published. As a result the Crown ordered the universities to treat all graduands as if they were clergymen presenting themselves for benefices. Cambridge did not comply until 1613. By the sixteen-twenties there were so many preachers, usually giving 'lectures' on Sunday afternoons that the government gradually began to obstruct and then control them. In 1623 a proclamation revived a Star Chamber decree of 1586 against unlicensed printing, and in 1624 another proclamation decreed that no work on religion or church government was to be published without the imprimatur of an archbishop, the bishop of London or a vice-chancellor of one of the universities. From 1625 on wealthy laymen, known as 'lay feoffees', started to buy up impropriations as they became available, using the income either to support incumbents of whom they approved or to pay lecturers. In the second half of this decade the sects so firmly handled by Whitgift began to increase again.[7]

Members of the *élite* were moved to resist, either openly or covertly, measures taken by James and Charles to raise money. After the dissolution of the Parliament of 1614 James issued a general appeal for a benevolence. When not enough genuinely free gifts were forthcoming, the Privy Council instructed sheriffs and justices of the peace to inform people with wealth in their counties that the Crown would be gratified by free gifts and would remember them gratefully. We are told that the justices of Devonshire were typical of their counterparts in the rest of the country; they refused to establish this precedent. They insisted that they would always be ready to give according to the ancient and lawful customs of the country, but would not exhort others to do so in this manner. They were summoned before the Council, where proof was given them that free gifts had often been made without coercion in the past. James received twenty thousand pounds from the City and Court, but no more than another forty thousand pounds from the rest of the country.

In similar circumstances Charles tried to finance his government with a free gift, which also failed, in 1626. He then resorted to a general loan, which was to be forced at a much higher rate than those of the past. Parliament had just refused to grant the King the taxes which this loan was to replace; moreover, there was little possibility of Charles ever being able to repay the money, assuming that he intended to. When the judges declared the loan illegal, the Chief Justice, Sir Randal Crew, was dismissed. Many of the King's subjects refused to pay, and a small proportion, seventy-six in number, were imprisoned. The majority of the *élite* paid what they were asked, the total coming to between £240,000 and £250,000; the five subsidies refused by Parliament would have amounted to about £300,000.[8]

In the time of Elizabeth there had been a certain amount of individual resistance to monopolies by people not normally lawbreakers. Sir Edward Coke defined monopolies as 'an institution or allowance by the King by his grant, commission or otherwise, to any person or persons, bodies politic or corporate, of or for the sole buying, selling, making, working or using of anything whereby any person or persons, bodies politic or corporate are sought to be restrained of any freedom or liberty that they had before, or hindered in their lawful trade'.[9] As these grants were usually secured by letters patent under the Great Seal they were also known as patents. They fell into three categories: grants giving sole rights to supervise some trade or activity, those giving sole rights to use a process of manufacture either new or revived from disuse and, third, those giving the exclusive rights to trade in some commodity or with certain foreign countries or places. These grants were made to allow a form of trade to the privileged, even when the law did not permit it. For example, despite the law forbidding the export of unfinished cloth, the Merchant Venturers and individual courtiers were given grants permitting them to do so. Monopoly grants could be outside common law and statute law; these privileges were drawn from the reserve powers of the Crown, the prerogative. They were not restricted to great courtiers, but went to fairly humble servants of the monarch at Court.

There was little, if any, resistance to the first kind of monopoly. When a private individual made a stand it was in such cases as when Charles Snead, a gentleman of Kent, declared his intention of ignoring the monopoly of starch manufacture possessed by John

1 The presentation of the Speaker, November 1584 (an illustration from Robert Glover's *Nobilitas politica vel civilis*, 1608)

2 Westminster Hall in the early seventeenth century

3 The Spanish Treaty Commissioners at Somerset House. The conclusion of peace with Spain in 1614 was the first English historical event to be recorded in this direct manner. On the right, from the window, are the Earls of Dorset, Nottingham, Devonshire, Northampton and Salisbury

4 A bachelor dinner party (illustration from *The Roxburghe Ballads*)

5 An illustration from Caspar Rutz' *Habitus variarum orbis gentium* (1581), showing various contemporary English costumes

6 Elizabeth supervises the kill at a hunt (illustration from C. Turberville's *Book of Faulconrie and Venerie*, 1575)

7 Elizabeth and courtiers at a hunt picnic (also from Turberville)

8 James I and Charles entertaining the Spanish ambassadors, 18 November 1623 (illustration from W. B. Rye, *England as Seen by Foreigners*)

9 Charles I dining in public

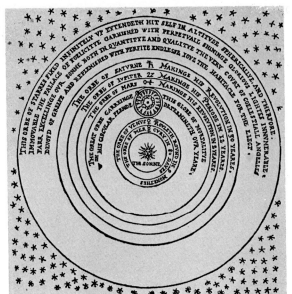

10 The earliest English diagram of the Copernican Universe, from Thomas Digges' *A Perfect Description of the Celestial Orbs* (1576)

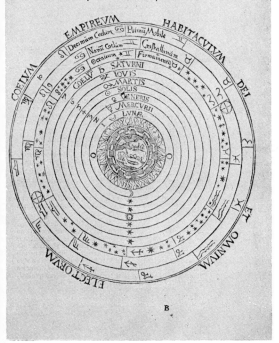

11 Another diagram of the Universe, from Peter Apian's *Cosmographia* (1539)

Pakington. Information was laid against him to the Privy Council. One Osmund Withers of Taunton was suspected of breaking the monopoly and manufacturing starch. When Captain Moffatt and William Lyons went to investigate the alleged offence, Withers and his family resisted the search of their house. Withers was arrested, but was rescued by his friends and the bailiff of Taunton seems to have turned a blind eye. The offender was again arrested by the constable and brought before the Chief Justice and remanded. Nevertheless he was not prevented from escaping again.[10]

Sometimes subjects with grievances attempted to gain redress in the common law courts, but with comparatively little success, except in ecclesiastical matters, in the reign of James I. The plea that a monopoly or patent was 'contrary to law' was of no avail when the royal prerogative of Elizabeth was involved. Cheyney quotes the case of a citizen of London who brought suit in the Court of Common Pleas against the holder of a patent. The Privy Council sent a letter in the Queen's name to Chief Justice Anderson and the other judges telling them that she would not let her prerogative come into question in a court of law and ordering a stay of the suit. In January and February of 1596 six merchants in succession were summoned before the Privy Council for selling a commodity without permission of patentees. The punishment consisted of having to attend the court daily until dismissed. Indignation against monopolies continued to grow in the second half of the fifteen-nineties. After agitation in Parliament in 1601, Elizabeth issued a proclamation 'for the reformation of many abuses and misdemeanours committed by patentees of certain privileges and licences to the general good of all her Majesty's loving subjects'. One class of monopolies was abolished; the rest were to be tested in the common law courts. In 1603 in the famous case of Darcy v. Allen the judges decided unanimously that a monopoly was illegal by both common and statute law, that it was justifiable only when a new invention was made or introduced, or when it was needed in the interests of the country. But, despite this judgment, monopolies and patents continued to be granted and enforced right up to the great outburst against them in Parliament in 1624.[11]

Subjects who turned to the courts for defence against the monarch's displeasure at the refusal of a loan did not succeed. As we have seen, Charles I continued with his demand for a forced loan in 1626 even when the Chief Justice had declared it illegal. Five of the knights who had been imprisoned for their refusal to contribute applied for a writ of habeas corpus in order to bring their case before the common law Court of the King's Bench. When the return to the writ gave no reason for their imprisonment, merely stating that it was by command of the King, one of the five, Darnell, withdrew. The other four argued that they should be released on bail, having been committed to prison without cause shown. The judges found for the Crown, the attorney general having contended that by precedent the Crown need not give a reason for imprisoning subjects. The court had apparently intended only to postpone a decision until the King had been consulted; the four knights could have applied for another writ the next day. But they and the public assumed that the verdict implied that the loan was legal, and that so was imprisonment for refusing to contribute. Even more important, the verdict was taken to support the claim of the Crown to have the right to imprison for any period without the prisoner having any redress at law.[12]

A subject might resist what he regarded as an illegal demand of the Crown only to find himself imprisoned and then sued himself in a common law court. This is what happened to John Bate, the merchant, who in 1606 refused to pay a duty of five shillings and six pence, imposed on imported currants. It has been said that Chief Baron Fleming's judgment seemed to give the monarch the power to place impositions on any commodity whenever he wished.[13]

The King's power is double, ordinary and absolute, and they have several laws and ends:

> That of the ordinary is for the profit of particular subjects, for the execution of civil justice, the determining of *meum;* and this is exercised by equity and justice in ordinary courts, and by the Civilians is nominated *jus privatum*, and with us Common Law: and these laws cannot be changed without Parliament, and although that their form and course may be changed and interrupted, yet they can never be changed in substance. The

absolute power of the King is not that which is converted or executed to private use, to the benefit of any particular person, but is only that which is applied to the general benefit of the people and is *salus populi;* as the people is the body and the King the head. (J. P. Kenyon, *The Stuart Constitution* [1966], p. 62.)

This absolute power is not governed by common law, but varies in accordance with what the monarch considers necessary to the public good. Fleming said that the impositions and the King's imprisoning of Bate 'ought to be ruled by the rules of policy' according to which the King had used his extraordinary power well:

All customs, be they old or new, are no other but the effect and issue of trade and commerce with foreign nations; but all commerce and affairs with foreigners, all wars and peace, all acceptance and admitting for current, foreign coin, all parties and treaties whatsoever, are made by the absolute power of the King; and he who hath power of causes likewise hath power of effects. No exportation or importation can be but at the King's ports, they are the gates of the King, and he hath absolute power by them to include or exclude whom he shall please; and ports to merchants are their harbours and repose, and for their better security he is compelled to provide bulwarks and fortresses, and to maintain for the collection of his customs and duties collectors and customers; and for that charge it is reason that he should have this benefit. (Kenyon, *op. cit.*, p. 63.)

Fleming's judgment was really upon the Crown's power to control trade rather than to raise revenue; but James took it as giving him the right to raise money by impositions; he and his councillors took advantage of this case to do so, as did Charles I. In 1628 merchants who tried to evade impositions had their goods seized and were unable to recover them by recourse to law.[14]

When it was a matter of opposing the ecclesiastical High Commission, members of the *élite* had more success with the common law courts, which had their own private reasons for obstructing the churchmen. As we have seen, from 1583 on, Whitgift used the High Commission as an inquisitorial court to wage war against the Puritans. In Cawdry's case in 1592 the common law judges ruled that the commission was a valid court. Early in the reign of James I it came to refer to itself as the Court of High Commission, and, after the Hampton Court conference and the Canons of 1604, was used against ministers who would not conform. As a result Puritan ministers and patrons of livings began to appeal to the Court of Common Pleas to transfer to its lists cases on those of the High Commission, and even to re-try some cases. From this year on the common law judges took to issuing writs prohibiting the commission to proceed in cases which they said should properly fall within common law court jurisdiction. In 1605 Archbishop Bancroft was alarmed by the tendency to limit the scope of the commission to the offences enumerated in section VIII of the Act of Supremacy, and to punishments awarded by the other ecclesiastical courts, of excommunication, deprivation and penance. He drew up twenty-five leading questions on the relation of lay and ecclesiastical jurisdiction, asking the King to submit them to the judges. They insisted that prohibitions could be issued against the Church courts and denied that they were weakening the power of the Crown.[15] As a result of attacks on the High Commission in Parliament, in 1606 the Chief Justices of King's Bench and Common Pleas were asked by the Privy Council about the legality of the *ex officio* oath. Coke and Popham answered that the accused should be provided with a list of headings under which he was to be examined; and that, with or without the list, no layman could be cross-examined on personal belief and theology. Coke gave the following opinion: 'No man ecclesiastical or temporal shall be examined upon secret thoughts of his heart or of his secret opinion. And the defendant must have, as in Star Chamber and Chancery, the bill delivered unto him, or otherwise he need not answer to it. Laymen for the most part are not lettered, wherefore they may easily be inveigled and intrapped and principally in heresy and errors of faith.'[16]

In June 1607, Nicholas Fuller introduced a bill in the Commons to restrict the High Commission to the powers given to it under the Act of Supremacy. He had earlier criticized the commission scurrilously in public, with the result that when Parliament rose he was imprisoned for contempt. Coke at King's Bench answered Fuller's appeal with a writ of prohibition, whereupon the commission changed the charge to schism, slander, heresy, impious error, and the holding of pernicious opinions, all ecclesiastical offences. The judges declared their opinion that the interpretation of the Act of Supremacy (which decided the commission's powers) lay with them.

Then the King intervened, declaring that as he was supreme judge under God, he could arbitrate between the commission and the common law courts. But Coke did not agree and for two years continued to issue prohibitions, seriously damaging the efficiency of the commission. Again the judges referred to the Act of Supremacy, denying the right of the commission to imprison, and rejecting the canons of 1604 wherever they were in conflict with common law or statute. Eventually James imposed a truce. Doubt of the commission's right to imprison left defendants free to refuse the oath with no fear of imprisonment; the proceedings could not go forward until they took it. In 1611 the Crown issued new letters patent, making the commission a court, defining its jurisdiction and giving it power to imprison and insist on the *ex officio* oath. After 1611, the High Commission was used less and less to procure conformity in the Church. Between 1611 and 1640, only twenty per cent of its cases were instigated by the commissioners and were not always of any real importance. The other eighty per cent were brought by private litigants, often to remove drunken or immoral clergymen, or those unsatisfactory for some eccentricity. By the sixteen-thirties much of its business concerned marriage troubles. In these, with the power to fine and imprison it was very effective; Sir Giles Allington was successfully prosecuted for incest and Viscountess Purbeck for adultery.[17]

Parliament was certainly the most effective method by which grievances could be brought to the notice of the Crown; nevertheless, even with the right to refuse subsidies, the Commons could do little in fact to persuade the monarch to give redress in the years between 1559 and 1630. In the matter of monopolies there were some apparent successes; yet, even after the Statute against these patents in 1624, they continued, owing to the failure to provide against granting them to companies. As early as 1571 some members of the Commons pointed out that it would be hard to collect the subsidies owing to the existence of monopolies by which 'a few are enriched' and 'the multitude impoverished'. A committee was formed to meet in Temple Church the following Monday. But, before that, the Speaker read the House a message from the Queen admonishing them for wasting time and referring to one Bell's speech on licences, as seeming to 'speak of her prerogative, but quietly and orderly'. The subject did not come up again in Parliament for over twenty years. In 1597 a bill was introduced against monopolies. After much discussion it was referred to a committee; Sir Thomas Cecil moved that instead of the bill a petition to the Queen to take action should be drawn up; this was referred to the same committee. On December 14 the chairman of the committee did not report on the bill or the petition, but presented a form of humble thanks to Elizabeth for redressing the grievance. This was included verbatim in the Speaker's speech to her at the end of the session and she accepted it; apparently she had already promised some action. She certainly made this promise when accepting the thanks.[14]

When Parliament met again in 1601, attack after attack was delivered on monopolies, with members insisting that they had no intention of touching the Queen's prerogative. Apart from dealing with the evils of monopolies, the debate concerned itself with the respective merits of two alternative procedures, whether to introduce a bill to redress the grievances or to petition the Queen. The member who introduced the bill emphasized the fact that he was not attempting to call the royal prerogative in question: 'Far be it from this Heart of mine to Think; this Tongue to speak or this Hand to write any Thing in Prejudice or Derogation of Her Majesty's Prerogative Royal and the State.' Advising against the bill Francis Bacon had reminded the House: 'the Queen, as she is our sovereign, hath both an enlarging and restraining power. For by her prerogative she may first set at liberty things restrained by statute law or otherwise; and secondly, by her prerogative she may restrain things that be at liberty.' He concluded, 'I say and I say again, that we ought not to deal, to judge or meddle with her majesty's prerogative.' After a week of almost continuous debate on the subject, the Commons suddenly received a message from the Queen independently removing the grievance, before the bill had been passed or the petition drawn up to be forwarded to her. She now exercised her prerogative to declare void all letters patent concerning salt, vinegar, alcohol and liquids containing it, salt fish, train oil, fish livers, pots, brushes and starch. A second group of monopolies could now for the first time be considered by the courts of law, with no special protection or privilege being reserved for the monopoly holder. As Cecil warned the house, Elizabeth did not intend to let herself be 'swept out of her Prerogative'. Her proclamation threatened punishment for any of her subjects who 'shall seditiously or contemptuously presume to call in question the power or validity of her prerogative royal annexed to her imperial crown'. Her action constituted an insistence that it was not the place of Parliament to try to redress such grievances by legislation; the sole method lay with the royal prerogative.[19]

As we have seen, despite the judgment that monopolies were illegal, given in the Darcy v. Allen case of 1603, they continued, with the result that in 1604 a bill was passed in the Commons (only forty members dissenting) giving all merchants full liberty to trade with all countries. This bill was dropped after a conference with the Lords; but in 1605 a more limited measure was passed allowing all subjects to trade with Spain, Portugal and France. Parliamentary objection was expressed concerning certain individual monopolies in 1606, and the King took measures (again as part of the royal prerogative) to redress the grievances. Parliament took up monopolies again among all the other financial grievances in 1610. As a result, James issued his Book of Bounty, a proclamation affirming the illegality of these grants. He promised he would issue no more, but they continued, owing to his financial difficulties. Again the Commons attacked monopolies in 1614. Seven years later the Commons denounced them once again, but now going so far as to investigate grievances and to require holders of patents to appear and present them for inspection. The bill which the Lower

House passed against monopolies was rejected by the Lords. In 1624 the attack was renewed and the Statute of Monopolies became law. This was a declaratory Act, establishing the proper interpretation of common law; it was not an introduction of new law. Even this was not a real attack on the prerogative. Nevertheless this statute has been correctly described as 'the first statutory invasion of the prerogative'; it gave 'a statutory definition to the subject's interest in royal grants, and thus set a statutory limit to the area in which the prerogative operated'.[20]

The House of Commons was also the scene of attempts to redress grievances caused by impositions, but the matter was not taken very far, largely because the *élite* represented there was not much concerned with the interests of merchants, base men, more involved with their private profit than the common good. In 1610, however, the feeling against impositions was much stronger and an inquiry was called for. Opposed by James' command not to discuss the matter, and by his assertion that his prerogative was not to be called in question, the Commons drew up a petition which was entered in the journal of the House; they asserted that Parliament (i.e. Commons, Lords and King) enjoyed the ancient undisputed right to debate freely anything concerning the subject; they asked permission to examine the new impositions thoroughly. The King now admitted that they could properly be investigated by Parliament. One member, William Hakewill, gave a noteworthy description of the nature of the debate: 'The question now in debate amongst us is, whether his Majesty may, by his prerogative royal, without assent of parliament, at his own will and pleasure, lay a new charge or imposition upon merchandises, to be brought into, or out of this kingdom of England, and enforce merchants to pay the same?' He insisted that taxation was vested in England in the sovereign authority, which was the King in Parliament.[21] Impositions were first in the list of grievances in a new Petition of Grievances presented to James on 7 July. His Majesty's 'most humble Commons assembled in Parliament' carrying out their function as such, 'and out of a duty to those for whom we serve, finding that your Majesty, without advice or consent of parliament, hath lately in time of peace set both greater impositions, and far more in number, than any of your noble ancestors did ever in time of war'. In such terms and 'with all humility' they presented 'this most just and necessary petition' to the King: 'that all impositions set without the assent of Parliament may be quite abolished and taken away, and that your Majesty, in imitation likewise of your noble progenitors, will be pleased that a law may be made during this session of parliament, to declare that all impositions set or to be set upon your people, their goods and merchandises, save only by common assent in parliament, are and shall be void.'[22] As James' reply to the petition as a whole was unsatisfactory, Cecil found it impossible to complete the negotiation of what was known as the 'Great Contract', in accordance with which the King would give up his right to levy impositions in return for a guarantee of sufficient income from the Commons to make his prerogative action unnecessary. He adjourned the House on 24 November and dissolved Parliament the following January. No more was done to abolish impositions in our period.

But there were other, more famous, customs dues which gave rise to fierce conflict in Parliament; these were known as 'tunnage and poundage', duties on wine and wool, usually bestowed upon each monarch for life by the first Parliament of each reign. In 1625 the Commons granted tunnage and poundage to Charles for only one year. This was not done vindictively, but simply because the intention was to review the whole field of customs duties. The restricted grant was a temporary measure, pending full discussion. But the bill designed to effect this discussion was not accepted by the Lords, and when the session had ended Charles had not been authorized to collect tunnage and poundage for a longer period. The Parliament of 1626 declared that collection was illegal, but a bill to indemnify him did not pass. After this Parliament was dissolved, the Privy Council declared that tunnage and poundage was an inseparable part of the royal revenue, had been so since the reign of Henry VI and was now to be enjoyed by the monarch independently of any parliamentary grant. The Commons did not dispute the fact that the King ought to collect these duties in 1628, and ways and means were still being discussed when the Petition of Right was passed. This was followed by strong attacks on Bucking-

o

ham and the conduct of the war; before long the subject of tunnage and poundage was taken up again, with a renewal of the proposal to include these taxes in a review of all duties on import and export. It was suggested that the review might be left until the next session, and that an enabling bill should now be passed authorizing collection in the meantime. Charles now repudiated the claims of the Commons to any control over tunnage and poundage; they replied with a remonstrance ending with what they described as a 'humble declaration' to the following effect:

> That the receiving of tunnage and poundage, and other impositions not granted by parliament, is a breach of the fundamental liberties of this kingdom, and contrary to your Majesty's royal answer to the said Petition of Right; and therefore do they most humbly beseech your Majesty to forbear any receiving of the same, and not to take it in ill part from those of your Majesty's loving subjects who shall refuse to make payment of any such charges.

The next day the King prorogued Parliament, repeating a statement of his intention of abiding by the Petition of Right; nevertheless, he insisted that it was not generally interpreted as including tunnage and poundage.

By this action the Commons were virtually encouraging their fellow subjects to refuse to pay a tax. The result was that some merchants did as was suggested, but lost their goods by order of the Privy Council ratified by the court of Exchequer. When Parliament assembled again in 1629 the group of members led by Eliot went even further, on 2 March, holding the Speaker in the chair to prevent an adjournment until they had pushed through three resolutions, two of which concerned tunnage and poundage:

> 2. Whosoever shall counsel or advise the taking and levying of the subsidies of tonnage and poundage, not being granted by Parliament, or shall be an actor or instrument therein, shall likewise be reputed an innovator in the Government, and a capital enemy to the Kingdom and Commonwealth.
> 3. If any merchant or person whatsoever shall voluntarily yield,

or pay the subsidies of tonnage and poundage, not being granted by Parliament, he shall likewise be reputed a betrayer of the liberties of England, and an enemy to the same.

Not long after dissolving Parliament, the King issued a proclamation declaring that he would continue to levy tunnage and poundage, 'not purposing to overcharge our subjects by any new burdens, but to satisfy ourselves with those duties that were received by the King, our father, of blessed memory, which we neither can nor will dispense withal'. With the failure of Parliament to prevent the levying of these duties, many London merchants tried to organize a stop in trade, but the results were so bad economically that it was preferable to pay despite the lack of parliamentary authority.

Parliament had no more success in its opposition to the various feudal payments to the Crown which had been revived by the Tudors. In 1583 Elizabeth vetoed a bill to deal with purveyance, a matter which did not come up again until 1589, still with no success for her subjects.[23] In 1604 the Commons petitioned James to abolish this payment, of which Bacon assured him: 'There is no grievance in your kingdom so general, so continual, so sensible, and so bitter unto the common subject' (*Works*, X, 83). The petition declared the number of grievances which persisted despite at least thirty-six laws prohibiting the various abuses. When they conferred with the Lords, the Commons found that there the opinion was that the Crown should receive fifty thousand pounds per annum as compensation. The view of the Lower House was that in principle it was wrong to give compensation for the loss of what was in any case an abuse of privilege, and to which the Crown was therefore not in any case entitled. The resulting stalemate left the Crown continuing to collect purveyance, much to the discontent of the subjects, who included it in their list of grievances in 1606 and again in 1610. Had the Great Contract been negotiated purveyance would have been abolished.[24]

This would also have happened to that other feudal due, wardship, which had been suffered without much discontent until Cecil succeeded his father as Master of the Wards in 1598. The Commons recognized the legal right of the Crown to these dues when the issue was raised in 1604, and offered to provide a larger revenue annually than had ever been obtained from the Court of Wards. James upbraided them for their proposal, and they replied in the Apology of the House of Commons. As the Lords had not supported the Commons, wardship continued, and was among the grievances listed in 1610, again without avail.[25]

Landowners in parliament, and those whom they represented outside, objected to measures taken by the Crown in respect of its tenants whose titles to land were defective, or did not exist. A commission to arrange a composition payment by tenants was appointed in 1599, renewed in 1603, 1605, 1606, 1608, 1609, 1611 and 1613. But opposition grew. In 1606 the Commons called William Tipper, secretary of the commission, to the bar. Little was done by the Crown to redress grievances. In 1618 a new commission was issued. Three years later its secretary and his son were strongly criticized by the House, which was dealing so sharply with Mompesson. Sir Edward Coke introduced a bill 'for the general quiet of the subjects against all pretences of concealment.' It was not passed until 1624, however, and gave protection only to those who could prove continuous possession for over sixty years. In 1628 Charles appointed another commission, applying also to those who occupied reclaimed land, those who had encroached on the royal forests, those who had enclosed common land and wastes despite the many proclamations forbidding it. In fact there was virtually nothing which Parliament was able to do on behalf of landowners affected.[26]

Henry VIII had deliberately associated himself with the Commons and the Lords in his breach with Rome, and Elizabeth followed his example in her plans for a Church settlement and declaration of her supremacy when she called the Parliament of 1559. It is not surprising, therefore, that from then onwards English Protestants looked to Parliament for redress in what they regarded as religious grievances. Once the legislation of 1559 had been passed, members of the House of Commons assumed that they had the right to amend it if necessary. Their assumption was strengthened by the fact that the legislation of 1559 itself was the result of a compromise between the Queen's plans and the demands of the Protestants for greater change. The bill to secure uniformity in the Church gave rise to prolonged argument, and eventually passed with a majority of no more than three. Three suggested bills to establish the supremacy of the Crown in the English Church were abandoned before the final shape was reached which could win approval of both houses, and there is evidence that the bill which was finally passed was much argued over and changed. The Commons were encouraged in their assumptions as to their function in religious issues by the fact that Elizabeth deliberately ignored Convocation, which she saw as a body empowered only to handle Church discipline, not matters affecting the law of the land as a whole. She also insisted that the Commons, on the other hand, had no business discussing doctrine. Nevertheless, discuss it they did, and succeeded in making the government change its policy. In the end Elizabeth gave way to the Protestant divines, but one result in the opinion of Sir John Neale was her stern refusal to compromise with the Puritans later in her reign, and her determination not to yield on the vestment controversy when that developed.[27]

The first Parliament of Elizabeth's reign vested in the Crown the supreme power over the national Church for ever; in all essential points Henry VIII's anti-papal legislation was revived, and that of Mary in favour of the papacy was nullified. The Act of Uniformity brought back the Edwardian Prayer Book with slight changes. Penalties were also imposed on any offenders against the Act of Supremacy and the Act of Uniformity. As we have noted, these penalties were not imposed satisfactorily, with the result that the government introduced stronger measures into Parliament in 1563. Nevertheless, the Queen refused to allow this same Parliament to have any voice in the Thirty-Nine Articles newly drawn up by Convocation. As a result these did not really have any binding force in law. The Parliament of 1566 was similarly not asked, or rather was not allowed, to introduce a bill touching religion, which in the Queen's view could be dealt with only by the royal prerogative. Some of the clauses of the Thirty-Nine Articles (not treating doctrine) were unacceptable to the Puritans in Parliament, who succeeded in having them expunged in 1571 when the articles were given all the authority belonging to statute. The Parliament of 1566 saw much wrangling between the Commons and the government over ecclesiastical, among other, matters. The Parliament of 1571 brought to a head the conflict between members of parliament, who wanted to carry on the reformation, and the determination of the Queen to defend her prerogative. Among the reform measures was a bill introduced by Walter Strickland for reform of the Prayer Book. He was summoned before the Privy Council and temporarily forbidden to take his seat in the House 'for the exhibiting of a bill into the house against the prerogative of the Queen'. In 1572 Elizabeth instructed the Speaker to tell the House that in future 'no bills concerning religion shall be preferred or received into this house' unless their provisions had already received the approval of the clergy. Her attitude was that she and Convocation were concerned with matters of doctrine (to the exclusion of Parliament), and that she, the Lords and Commons were concerned with the making of law involving that doctrine (to the exclusion of Convocation). To that end on this occasion she impounded two bills which had been introduced to regulate 'rites and ceremonies'.[28]

Elizabeth was able to maintain her prerogative right to regulate the Church, without having to contend with really concerted attempts by reformers to do it themselves in Parliament. She thoroughly approved of the petition of the Commons in 1576 that she might reform some of the practical defects which prevented individual clergymen ministering satisfactorily to their charges; she was prepared to do something about abuses such as pluralities and uneducated clergy, provided the Commons recognized her prerogative and petitioned her without asserting how they thought the abuses ought to be corrected. This for Elizabeth was thoroughly constitutional. But in 1580 she objected to the initiative shown by the Commons, at the suggestion of Paul Wentworth, in deciding independently on holding a day of public fast and a daily preaching so that they might be better blessed of God 'in all their consultations and actions'. When the Queen sent a message of disapproval the House made 'humble submission unto her majesty, acknowledging the said offence and contempt'. The next day the Queen sent her answer, that she did not object to their fasting and praying, but to their manner 'in presuming to indict a public fast without order and without her privity, which was to intrude upon her authority ecclesiastical'.

On various occasions Elizabeth intervened to moderate or prohibit savage measures taken against non-conformists, mainly recusants, for what they thought rather than for what they did. In 1587, however, her prerogative was directly challenged when Anthony Cope introduced into the Commons a bill which petitioned for the annulling of the Acts of Supremacy and Uniformity and of the Prayer Book. Cope actually asked for the repeal of all laws governing ecclesiastical affairs, and for the authorizing of a new book with a new form of public prayer and giving and taking of the sacraments. The Queen easily quashed this move, with Cope, Peter Wentworth and others in support going to the Tower. She informed the Commons that she regarded the petition as being 'against the prerogative of her crown'. The Commons had already in 1559 given their consent, confirming and enacting as law that 'the full power, authority, jurisdiction, and supremacy in church causes' was inseparable from 'the Imperial Crown of this Realm'.

At the opening of the session of 1589, the Queen sent the usual admonition against dealing with ecclesiastical causes. Nevertheless, on 25 February a member named Davenport called attention to grievances of some of the Queen's subjects caused by certain parts of the ecclesiastical law, and suggesting changes. Wooley, Secretary to the Privy Council, immediately stated that he believed the House incompetent to deal with such matters, and reminded his listeners of the Queen's instructions. The Speaker kept Davenport's manuscript statement for three weeks, returning it without bringing up the matter in the House. Elizabeth had so firm a grip now that there was no need to take punitive action.

We have already noticed that many of the English ruling class objected to the practice of the High Commission in forcing defendants to take the *ex officio* oath. In particular the lay lawyers denounced this, and it was more than a coincidence that in 1593 two bills against the practice were introduced into Parliament by a civil lawyer, James Morice, an attorney of the Court of Wards. One of the privy councillors in the Commons warned the House that the Queen would be displeased at this ignoring of her prohibition against discussing ecclesiastical matters. Coke, the Speaker, took the bills home with him before laying them before the House. When the Queen heard what was happening Morice was taken into custody, remaining in prison until the end of the session. Elizabeth asked Coke what was in the bills, allowing him to keep his promise not to let anyone see them, and insisted vigorously that Church matters were not to be discussed any more that session.[29]

The Queen allowed the Commons to discuss some matters, such as pluralities in 1589, when they passed a bill which was stopped in the Lords. But in 1597 a similar measure was withdrawn, apparently by royal command. When the same matter came up yet again in 1601 she did not object, but one of the Queen's serjeants in the House declared that the debate was a violation of the prerogative; this time the bill got no further than the second reading. Elizabeth was more permissive when the Commons discussed the habit of the bishops of giving long leases on their lands, when there were objections against absence from church, profane swearing and neglect to observe the sabbath.

In May 1604, after the failure of the Hampton Court conference, and with Convocation drafting new canons to discipline the Church, a group of members of the Commons drew up a list of articles to be discussed in conference with the Lords, repeating much of the millenary petition. As the Lords were unco-operative, a number of bills were introduced into the Lower House to translate a substantial part of this petition into law. Little in fact was achieved because the session was so far advanced. Nevertheless, James responded like Elizabeth to this breach of the royal prerogative when he prorogued Parliament in July. He was particularly incensed by the assertions in the Apology of the House of Commons, which was never formally delivered to him; the Commons denied that the King could make religious changes (including laws) without the consent of Parliament. Denying any intention of upsetting the *status quo* of the English Church, they wanted the abandoning of 'some few ceremonies of small importance'.[30]

Early in the session of 1606 the Commons denied the right of Convocation to legislate independently, brought in a bill 'for the more sure establishing and assuring of true religion'. For this it was essential that 'no alteration should be of any substantial point of religion but by parliament with the advice and consent of the clergy in convocation'. Their own attempts to reform the ministry were defeated in the Lords. In the same year the Commons passed a bill to allow clergymen to appeal against disabilities which they suffered as a result of the King's proclamation on conformity in 1604. This bill failed in the Lords, as did another to modify or establish more accurately the exact meaning of the Subscription Act of 1571. Very early in 1606 a bill for observation of the sabbath failed when sent to the Lords.

The active Parliament of 1610, not unnaturally, actually passed a bill to modify the Subscription Act, and the Petition on Religion which was submitted to James in July again referred to the plight of dispossessed Puritan ministers. It should be noted that the petition was made to the King as crowned by God 'with supreme power, as well in the Church as in the Commonwealth'. The second article pleads on behalf of the dispossessed clergy who were 'ever ready to perform the legal subscription appointed by the statute of the 13th of Elizabeth' concerning doctrine, but did not conform 'in points of ceremonies, and refusing the subscription directed by the late Canons'. In the most docile style the Commons continued as follows:

> We therefore most humbly beseech your Majesty would be graciously pleased that such deprived and silent Ministers may, by licence or permission of the Reverend Fathers in their several dioceses, instruct and preach unto the people, in such parishes and places where they may be employed, so as they apply themselves in their Ministry to wholesome doctrine and exhortation, and live quietly and peacably in their callings, and shall not by writing or preaching impugn things established by public authority. (Kenyon, 144.)

For the rest of the reign of James I, Puritans in the Commons did little more than attempt to preserve the sabbath from profanation. A bill for this purpose was read on the first day of the session of 1614, but did not become law. In 1618 James issued his Declaration of Sports in which he blamed over-strict enforcement of the observance of the Lord's Day for the increase of Papists in Lancashire. After his subjects had attended church each Sunday, they should be permitted to take part in a list of sports and recreations. He forbade 'bear and bull baitings, interludes and, at all times in the meaner sort of people by law prohibited, bowling'. The Parliament of 1621 saw the debate of a bill for punishing 'abuses of the Sabbath day', but the King prohibited the House from legislating against those recreations which his Declaration permitted. In 1624 he vetoed a bill to punish various activities on the Lord's Day. In 1626 and 1628 Parliament passed Acts reinforcing the Declaration of Sports.

The first Parliament of Charles I's reign saw a clash between the Commons and Laud, whose sermon before them in June 1625 exalted the royal power. They were particularly outraged by the writings of a clergyman, Richard Montague, rejecting the doctrine of predestination, advocating auricular confession in some circumstances, declaring points of agreement between Catholics and Protestants, and insisting that the Pope was not always in error. Laud supported Montague, to the annoyance of the Parliament of 1626. At the end of this session Charles issued a proclamation for peace in the Church expressing his disagreement with both sides. But the Puritans in the Commons were increasingly disturbed by the growth of the number of supporters of the doctrine of Arminianism which claimed apostolic succession for the Anglican bishops. Puritan fears and anger came to a head in 1628 over Roger Manwaring, who had preached a sermon before the King in July 1627 declaring among other things, that Parliaments 'though such assemblies as are the highest and greatest representatives of a kingdom be most sacred and honourable, and necessary also for those ends to which they were first instituted, yet know we must that ordained they were not to this end, to contribute any right to kings, whereby to challenge tributary aids and subsidiary helps, but for the more equal imposing, and more easy exacting of that which unto kings doth appertain by natural and original law and justice, as their proper inheritance annexed to their imperial crowns from their very births.' Although from one point of view this was political or constitutional, rather than doctrinal, inasmuch as it expressed opinions held by a number of churchmen opposed to further protestant reform, Manwaring's sermon and the repercussions to it were involved in the ecclesiastical controversy. In 1628, the Commons impeached him and forced him to retract. On 11 June of that year they sent up a remonstrance against innovation in religion, the growth of Arminianism and the activities of Laud, saying that he was responsible for the fact that preferment lay open only to those clergy who embraced the new errors.[31]

In the second half of 1628 there was a great reorganization of the dioceses with a number of Laud's supporters installed, especially in the wealthy South. The Commons, alarmed, started an investigation into the state of the Church in January, 1629, criticizing two of the bishops, Neile and Montague, violently. A sub-committee prepared resolutions on religion declaring that the Thirty-Nine Articles had been modified by the Lambeth Articles of 1595, by the Articles of the Irish Church (very anti-Arminian) in 1615 and by the Synod of Doort of 1619. In the debate before the remonstrance was drawn up, Pym asserted that Parliament was the only power in the land competent to protect it from Arminianism. The Arminians were represented by most speakers as hardly different from Jesuits who would themselves triumph with the success of Laud and his followers. Eliot asserted openly that the bishops were not to be trusted with interpreting the Thirty-Nine Articles.

There was now no possibility of compromise on matters ecclesiastical, for the Commons were asserting their right to determine the religion of the country. Charles, like James and Elizabeth in such a situation, decided to adjourn the House to prevent the Commons interfering in matters concerning his prerogative. When the Speaker tried to obey the royal command, he was held in his chair while three resolutions were passed, the first of which stating:

Whosoever shall bring in innovation of religion, or by favour or countenance seek to extend or introduce Popery or Arminianism, or other opinion disagreeing from the true and orthodox Church, shall be reputed a capital enemy to this Kingdom and Commonwealth.[32]

A week later Charles dissolved Parliament. His rule for the next eleven years without calling a parliament was fundamentally in agreement with the constitution, even if it could be argued that for some of his activities he required the assent of the Commons and Lords to his will as King. What is of enormous importance for us is the fact that the Commons could do little to change matters which fell within the royal prerogative when the monarch was determined that they should stay as they were, or when he intended innovations. Ultimately there was only one way of stopping a monarch who would not compromise; that was by rebellion. And in 1629 the Commons were not ready for that.

Everything combined to make the questions of succession and royal marriage of great concern to the subjects of Elizabeth, and, despite the fact that they involved the prerogative, they were debated over and over again in the Commons. In 1559, even before the Act of Supremacy was treated, a draft petition was considered on 4 February begging her to marry and provide the realm with an heir. Eventually the petition was carried to the Queen by the Speaker, the members of the Privy Council in the House and thirty other members of parliament. Elizabeth's answer evaded the request, but she approved of the deputation for not suggesting a possible husband, 'for that were most unworthy the Majesty of an absolute princess, and unbeseeming your wisdom who are subjects born'.[33]

Her 'subjects born' were plunged into fear when Elizabeth fell seriously ill of smallpox in October 1562. When Parliament met in 1563 both Houses were anxious to have the succession established by law, both presenting petitions. The Lords stressed the need for marriage, the Commons, the necessity for delimiting the succession. The Queen again evaded her subjects' demands, but did not reprimand them for an invasion of her prerogative. Once Parliament had been prorogued, however, she allowed herself the satisfaction of imprisoning a chancery lawyer, John Hales, who had written a pamphlet against the Stuart claim, defending that of Lady Catherine Grey to the succession.

By 1566, international events had shown the danger to England if the Queen were to die unmarried with the succession not established. When Parliament met in October, a member named Molineux moved that the Commons take up again their petition to the Queen on marriage and the succession from the session of 1562-3. Before this could be done she summoned a deputation from both Houses, insisting that whatever she might do would come of her own free will out of consideration for her subjects, and not because they tried to make her do it, it being monstrous 'that the feet should direct the head'. After some weeks of conflict she commanded the Commons directly 'that they should no further proceed in their suit, but to satisfy themselves with her highness' promise of marriage'. This provoked from Paul Wentworth three questions to the House as he moved 'whether the Queen's commandment was not against the liberties'. First he asked whether the command to the Commons not to concern itself any more with the succession was a breach of the liberty of free speech, or not; the second question was whether the fact that a privy councillor pronounced the commandment in the Queen's name in the House carried enough authority to silence the members or to bind them to acknowledge the commandment or not? Last he asked whether, if the commandment was not a breach of the liberties, or if the message from the Queen carried authority, 'then what offence is it for any of the House to err in declaring his opinion to be otherwise?' Two days later, on 11 November, Elizabeth summoned the Speaker, sending him back to the House with a repetition of her command not to treat of the succession, telling any person who might object and had further reasons, to 'come before the Privy Council, there to show them'. A month later, after a compromise had been reached to some extent, with the Queen promising, but allowing her subjects no right by which they might demand a promise from her, to marry to secure the succession. But they offended her by incorporating into the preamble to the subsidy bill their joy at the promises to marry and to determine the succession as soon as circumstances made it possible. She wrote her comments on the final text of this preamble to the effect that 'I know no reason why my private answers to the realm should serve for prologue to a subsidies-book. At the end of the session, after some weeks of wrangling which we noted over religion, she herself addressed the Lords and Commons saying, among other things:

> As to liberties, who is so simple that doubts whether a Prince that is head of all the body may not command the feet not to stray when they would slip? God forbid that your liberty should make my bondage, or that your lawful liberties should anyways have been infringed.

Her commandments, she declared, were no infringement of their liberties, as indeed, had she been minded, she could have shown those who doubted her.

The succession did not cause any conflict in Parliament until February 1593, when Peter Wentworth and Sir Henry Bromley presented a petition to the Lord Keeper, urging the Lords to join the Commons in asking the Queen to 'entail' the succession, they having drawn up a bill to that end. They and their supporters were imprisoned. When the question was raised in the Commons with a member moving that the Queen be petitioned for their release, on the grounds that their presence in the House was needed in debates on the subsidy or their constituents would not be represented, the privy councillors pointed out that she had her own reasons for the imprisonment and was not likely to be more lenient if petitioned, rather the reverse. In fact the Queen was putting into action the attitude expressed on her behalf by the Lord Keeper in reply to the Speaker's petition for the 'traditional' liberties of the House:

> For liberty of speech her majesty commandeth me to tell you that to say yea or nay to bills, God forbid that any man should be restrained or afraid to answer according to his best liking, with some short declaration of his reason therein, and therein to have a free voice, which is the very true liberty of this house; not as some suppose to speak there of all causes as him listeth and to frame a form of religion or a state of government as to their idle brains shall seem meetest.

The nearest Parliament came to raising the subject of the succession for the rest of Elizabeth's reign was when a bill was drawn up (it is presumed by a privy councillor) to forbid the writing or publishing of any book on the matter. There is no record that this bill was ever introduced.[34]

It has already been observed that succession to the throne is inseparable from the subject of royal marriage in certain circumstances. This was true not only of the possible marriage of Elizabeth, but of that of James' son, Charles. Foreign policy was also involved in the latter's marriage, as in the marriage of his sister to Frederick, Duke of Palatine. Although no royal marriage was involved in the proposed peace with Spain, which was very unpopular in the country as a whole, Parliament was asked to redress grievances arising from it. In 1607 London merchants complained to the Commons of Spanish seizure of their ships with the torture, imprisonment and death of their crews. A suggestion by the Commons that letters of marque should be issued in reprisal drew from Salisbury the reply that to make war or peace was a prerogative of the Crown (he had a great list of precedents) and that the Commons should not attempt to meddle in matters which were constitutionally not their concern. Nevertheless, they became involved in foreign policy, in the question of a royal marriage and of the succession, in 1618 when Gondomar arrived as Spanish ambassador to detach England from a Protestant alliance, with the offer of a possible marriage of the Infanta to the Prince of Wales. The Spaniards insisted that a marriage treaty must be sanctioned by the English Parliament, and that the marriage should not take place until three years had passed to test whether freedom of worship for English Catholics was really allowed. James delayed calling a Parliament; but by November 1620 his son-in-law was in danger of losing his lands in the Palatinate and the King needed money to try to save him.

When Parliament met in January 1621 James was in a difficult position because, while the members supported his intention of saving the Palatinate, they opposed his equally strong wish to marry his son to the Infanta. He despised the interest of his subjects in foreign affairs, which he saw as no concern of theirs, and therefore alienated members of parliament by saying no more than that he would not allow religion to be endangered by the match with

Spain, and that he planned to send an army to Germany in the summer to preserve Frederick and Elizabeth. As he gave no indication of his intended relations with foreign powers, or of the possible expenses of the war, Parliament merely granted two subsidies.

Foreign policy did not come up again until the monopolists had been dealt with and the Parliament had been adjourned. After the adjournment the Commons were given no clear account of royal policy, but merely told that their business was restricted to granting supplies for the army in the Palatinate. They voted a subsidy for immediate support of that force and then drew up a petition giving their view of the situation in Europe. They saw the causes of the trouble as the Roman Catholic league abroad, headed by the King of Spain, encouraging popery in England. They asked for war against the head of the Catholic league, and for the Prince of Wales to marry a Protestant. James now forbade any member of the Commons to attempt to discuss or involve himself with 'anything concerning our government or matters of state'. In particular the marriage to the Infanta was not to be discussed. The King threatened punishment for any member who ignored his command, whether Parliament were sitting or not.

Another petition came from the Commons acknowledging that peace, war and the marriage of the Prince of Wales could be decided solely by the royal prerogative, giving as their reason for petition the need to make sure that certain facts came to the King's attention. James pointed out that whatever they might say to the contrary, their advice did in fact entrench on his prerogative. On 18 December 1621 the Commons drafted the famous Protestation denying the King's right to imprison members at his will, asserting that their lives and privileges were 'the ancient and undoubted birthright and inheritance of the subjects of England'. As for the King's prohibiting their discussion of foreign policy, they insisted that it was proper to debate and advise on what concerned the King, state, defence of the realm and the Church of England, and that they had every right to discuss and make resolution on these matters.

James, like Elizabeth, adjourned and dissolved Parliament, imprisoning two members and confining a third to his house for their share in defying him. Tearing the Protestation from the journal of the Commons at a Privy Council meeting, he condemned it as framed so generally and ambiguously as to serve as precedent for invasion of most of the Crown's prerogatives, in which he was justified. Nevertheless, three years later when his negotiations with Spain had failed, he summoned Parliament. This time he completely reversed his attitude, confiding in the Commons, promising to give them full particulars of his negotiations, so that they would be in a position to give him their counsel. His speech at the opening of Parliament on 19 February 1624 assured his hearers:

> The properties and causes of calling a parliament (and so go the writs) are to confer with the king and give him their advice in matters of greatest weight and importance. For this cause have I now called you together, that ye may have proof of my love, and of my trust; I have now called you to give me your advice in the greatest matters that ever could concern a king; a greater declaration of my confidence in you I cannot give.

He then referred to his negotiations, adding that when they had been given all the details, 'I shall then entreat your good and sound advice, for the glory of God, the peace of the kingdom, and the weal of my children. Never king gave more trust to his subjects than to desire their advice in matters of this weight, for I assure you, ye may freely advise me, seeing, of my princely fidelity, ye are entreated thereunto'. It seems that James' new attitude derived from the wish of Charles and Buckingham to reverse foreign policy after their rebuff in Spain.[35]

Charles, when King, reverted at once to the traditional refusal to let the Commons have any say in foreign policy, with the result that his first Parliament voted him no more than two subsidies as an interim grant, much less than he needed for the war. So long as Buckingham continued to mismanage military and naval affairs, and so long as the Commons were obstructed in their attempts to establish responsibility for the disaster which overtook the army commanded by Count Mansfeld in Germany, they refused to vote supplies. Apart from that one occasion when James took Parliament into his confidence on foreign affairs in 1624, the Crown and

P

its supporters resolutely asserted in practice and theory that these were solely the concern of the royal prerogative and were not to be debated by either House. The fact that James had turned to Parliament in 1624 by no means implied the right of that body to be consulted. It merely showed that the King had the right to consult whom he wished, in or outside the Privy Council and that nobody had the right to be consulted.[36]

We saw in the last chapter that the Tudors refused to allow their subjects to have any say in the appointment or removal of royal servants. Nevertheless, there was grumbling in 1536 against new *parvenu* counsellors surrounding the throne, and again in 1569. The fact that Parliament had been asked to vote Acts of Attainder could be taken as precedence for the two Houses claiming to have been associated with condemnation of a minister of state. If any section of the *élite* were to be dissatisfied and strong or bold enough, it was also possible to put forward mediaeval precedents for refusing to allow royal servants to plead the royal command as an excuse for wrong-doing, for demanding that the monarch ought to act on the advice of counsellors acceptable to Parliament, and for Parliament's power of impeachment.[37]

These issues did not come to the fore in the reign of Elizabeth, not even in the attempts made by the Commons to mitigate the burdens of purveyance and monopolies. But James' failure to remove the grievances caused by these practices led to attacks in 1610 by some of the Commons against two of his lesser servants, one of whom they imprisoned while investigating the other. This Parliament also saw an oblique attack on the privy councillors and a complaint that the King should not rely on the advice of irresponsible advisers. As the Great Contract was in process of being drafted, the Commons inserted a clause to permit the royal servants to be used and imprisoned no less freely than other men. Before this was presented to James it went to the Lords who gave their approval. On 17 July 1610, it was humbly presented by four privy councillors to James at Theobalds. The King at once refused the petition, which he found applicable only to times in which either the monarch was unjust and his servants were instruments of tyranny, or when the Crown was weak and must subordinate itself to wanton and insolent behaviour from its subjects. When this reply was transmitted to the Commons, they were ready 'to 1est satisfied with the answer'. Their unruliness subsided as surely as that of their predecessors who had been told in 1589 that the Queen would herself punish her servants if they did wrong.

But another grievance of the Commons, against impositions, led to attacks on the counsellors responsible for advising the King to establish them. On 2 July 1610, James Whitelocke and William Hakewill both declared impositions illegal, reminding the House that in 1376 Parliament had condemned Lord Latimer and Richard Lyons for 'procuring impositions to be set without assent of parliament'. Another member compared Salisbury, the Lord Treasurer, to Empson and Dudley, who had suffered attainder by the House. In November, when it was clear that the Great Contract would not go through, there were attacks in the Commons against any who might advise the King to extend the prerogative 'beyond the bounds'. These were not likely to be privy councillors, but various of the clergy who preached every day against the fundamental laws of the kingdom, urging that 'Kings are not bound by their laws', and that the monarch 'may of right take things without parliament that are granted in parliament'. As these men were happy to flout the common law in order to curry favour and win preferment in the Church, it was proposed to pass a bill against them to prevent their enjoying the rewards of their behaviour. A proposal was also made to inquire into the behaviour of the Scots at Court. But James prorogued Parliament.[38]

In the Parliament of 1614 the Commons voted that the King had not been correctly informed about the rights of his subjects concerning impositions, that the Barons of the Exchequer should not have ruled on impositions until they had asked the advice of Parliament. The House declared that precedents existed for a parliamentary censure of judges who did not seek advice from the Lords and Commons in matters touching the liberty of the subject. And again attacks were made upon the Scots and Papists at Court. As a result James dissolved Parliament.[39]

When they met again in 1621 the Commons arrested seven of the King's servants, questioned another fourteen, expelled three and prevented another from sitting in the House. During the spring the members of the Commons impeached Sir John Bennet, Dr Theophilus Field, Sir Giles Mompesson, Sir Francis Bacon and Sir Francis Mitchell, despite the fact that some of those affected were servants of the monarch in the contemporary view. The King and his supporters insisted that the Commons' actions derived from private malice, and from an intention of beginning with smaller persons and progressing to their superiors, until finally the royal prerogative itself would be seriously limited. But the active party in the Commons (numbering less than thirty) asserted that they wanted merely to pass laws which would reform abuses, and to punish wrong-doers. This small group could have done very little if the rest of the members had not agreed with them that the King was unable to remedy the abuses practised not only in his administration but in his Court. As there were no precedents for the Commons alone passing judgment on those whom they found delinquent, the Lords were consulted. The Upper House then found precedents which allowed them to examine, judge and condemn Sir Giles Mompesson.

When James intervened to prevent action against others of his servants less directly involved than Mompesson, the Commons were satisfied with passing a law to prevent similar mistakes or abuses in the future. But at this moment it was revealed that Bacon had accepted gifts from suitors in the court of chancery. When the Commons decided to send the evidence against him to the Lords there was an attempt by the King to save his servant by proposing that Parliament should name commissioners to investigate the matter and report to him for him to pronounce judgment. But the Commons decided that royal servants should answer for their crimes not to the king's commissioners, but to the High Court of Parliament. The Lords supported the Commons, without a single voice being raised, in a chamber containing Prince Charles and Buckingham, to deny the right of the Upper House to try and to judge the monarch's Lord Chancellor.

James warned the Commons that they should not proceed against men who may have erred, but who had advised him as well as they could and in good faith. The House accepted this principle and impeached only those royal servants in whose favour the king could not interpose his prerogative; where the delinquent had perpetrated a personal crime, such as accepting bribes, the King was not involved and the Commons acted. There was an attempt to trap Buckingham by persuading Sir Henry Yelverton to confess that he had imprisoned men breaking alleged monopolies under duress from Buckingham; but Yelverton discredited himself by asserting that his offence was to have served the King too well; his allegations could not be proved before the Lords owing to a lack of witnesses and to his not possessing the stamina to go through with his story.

Despite all setbacks, however, Parliament as a whole emerged from the disputes of 1621 with three definite rights; the Commons could inquire into the actions of the King's servants, the right of inquiry; they could also present men for crimes in which the King's personal authority was not involved, the right of presentment; this presentment was to the Lords, who established their right to judge men who had come under their jurisdiction, the right of judgment.[40]

As a result of these gains by Parliament, four new constitutional issues were raised: what was the responsibility of a counsellor whose advice proved to be unsuccessful? Must a counsellor answer for having given advice which Parliament later declared to have been unlawful? Could a counsellor plead that his advice was given with the agreement and support of other counsellors? Could a counsellor plead that he had obeyed the monarch's commands?

Looking back today we are conscious chiefly of the principles involved in these issues, but in 1621 and the next few years these principles were for the most part obscured by the personalities and feuds which give rise to parliamentary action. Buckingham's power was still so enormous that much that happened was either directed by or against him, rather than the result of an attempt to put clear principles into action. In 1624 he used Parliament against his personal enemy, the Earl of Middlesex. Indeed, the Court factions tried with greater or less success to use the Lords and Commons. Middlesex fell not merely because he had offended the Commons and Lords, but because Prince Charles objected to him. He was presented by the Lower House and judged by the Upper, not for carrying out the King's commands, but for abuses of his office, such as doubling a fee, accepting bribes, failing to keep accounts in the Wardrobe, for mismanagement and extortion in the Ordnance. The King's right to protect those who gave him advice and who carried out his commands was not challenged. Parliament merely insisted on, and demonstrated, its right to deal with law-breakers whose crime was not inseparable from the office of a servant of the Crown, when they happened also to be holders of such office.

The Parliament of 1624 attacked the royal prerogative in another way; the Subsidy Bill provided that the Commons should name the treasurers responsible for spending the money raised; they and the council of war were made accountable to that House for the expenditure of the money. This clause had been inserted at the suggestion of the King, on the advice of Buckingham, who is considered to have wanted money for war against Spain, even at this cost. The peers objected to the bill as increasing the privileges of the Commons; but when the judges were asked for advice they declared there was no breach of law, as the privileges were not claimed by right, but in an Act of Parliament, to which the assent of King and Lords might or might not be given.

The last words which James addressed to Parliament objected to attacks on his servants. He forbade the two Houses to examine and judge his servants, 'from the greatest ministers of state to the scullion in the kitchen'. Nevertheless, when he died the Commons had gained the right to impeach a minister of state, and arrest, question and censure him, if he were not a peer. The Lords now had the right to judge and sentence those presented to them by the Commons. The minister before the House of Lords would find himself defenceless if he had accepted bribes or extorted money by abuse of his office; if he had done none of these things the King's intervention and nothing else was sure to save him; he could not rely on the plea of having made errors, or that other ministers had agreed with his advice, or that he had consulted legal authorities or obeyed the royal command. A man who had given wicked advice to the King or obeyed a royal command which was illegal, would be dealt with for any crimes which did not involve the King, even if his advice and obedience were his real crimes. Up to the end of the reign of James I, Parliament did not formally assert that his advice and obedience were themselves criminal.[41]

With the accession of Charles I, Buckingham's power increased to such an extent that members of the Oxford Parliament of 1625 objected to the fact that the King was not taking his Privy Council into his confidence, but governing through his favourite. Again, it is uncertain how far the Commons were inspired by faith in a fundamental principle of the constitution or by hatred and fear of Buckingham; and this is true of the Lords as well. It is certain, however, that the two houses co-operated out of enmity for this one man, rather than out of united reverence for a principle. From 1612 onwards both James and Charles made a practice of ignoring the Privy Council and taking the advice of individual favourites. Constitutionally they had a right to do this. In practice, however, they unintentionally encouraged the Commons to search for precedents justifying parliamentary demands for the removal of incompetent ministers. As a result, in 1625 they begged the King to choose 'a wise, religious, and worthy council' and consult it for every important act of state. When Buckingham denied that the King had ever done anything but this, his opponents in the Commons found themselves unable to proceed far, because any inquiries they made into the giving and taking of advice inevitably failed in the face of the refusal of witnesses to break the oath of secrecy to the Crown sworn by all privy councillors on taking office. It was therefore impossible to establish responsibility for the incompetence with which the war was being conducted, and for the decision to loan ships of war to the French to be used against the Huguenots of La Rochelle.[42]

This Parliament, which protested against intervention by foreign ambassadors in the government of England, is memorable on three counts: in it the Commons for the first time attacked a minister whom they did not accuse of having broken the law; for the first time they witheld supplies on the grounds that the King was not taking the advice of worthy counsellors; and for the first time they challenged the King's right to forbid them to proceed against one of his servants. One member, named Alford, pointed out that all justices of the peace and deputy-lieutenants were the King's servants, 'and indeed no man can commit a public offence but by colour and opportunity of public employment and service to the king', so that to accept the royal command was virtually to destroy Parliaments.[45]

When Parliament met again in 1626 Buckingham was becoming a general object of dislike to those who saw him as a bad counsellor and incompetent statesman, as well as to the older nobility hating a *parvenu*, and to many disappointed courtiers. As Charles accepted responsibility for everything his favourite had done, the Commons found that they could do little against Buckingham until they had established who was responsible for the misgovernment of the last few years. They also had to discover how they could absolve the King from all blame despite his protestations to the contrary. And finally they had to solve the problem of forcing the King to dismiss the guilty, once guilt had been proved. As the councillor's oath of secrecy still obstructed the Commons, they decided to take common fame as strong enough to allow them to accuse, but not to condemn. On the basis of common fame a complaint against delinquents could be transmitted to the Lords or to the King. When Charles tried to stop the House questioning Buckingham they sent him a remonstrance declaring the undoubted right of Parliament to question and complain of all persons of any degree who were the origin of grievances to the commonwealth. The Commons refused to grant supplies until the end of the session and voted for the impeachment of Buckingham. The King's support of the Duke and a threat to dissolve Parliament if the Subsidy bill were not passed within a week brought from the Commons another remonstrance in which the removal of Buckingham was a condition for the voting of supplies. It was also declared that it was possible for an adviser to be removed for faults which were not criminal, but which showed his unsatisfactoriness for his office. Charles dissolved Parliament before the remonstrance could be presented.

Charles continued to govern through his favourite until the need for money led to the Parliament of 1628. This time the Commons refused to agree that a servant of the King surrendered all independent responsibility and conscience. They did not attack Buckingham but turned to lesser people. After the Duke's death Parliament attacked other ministers in 1629. The dispute over tunnage and poundage led the House once again to resort to common fame, to asserting that as the King can do no wrong, his servants cannot plead his commands, and to voting remonstrances against those regarded as evil counsellors. Charles then dissolved Parliament.

For the next eleven years the King followed the Tudor example of government by a Privy Council. As a result, when Parliament met again in 1640 it was not the form of the government but its policies which were the subject of conflict. Nothing which had been asserted as a right in 1629 was relinquished eleven years later; the Commons went further, declaring that the rights had now become duties to interrogate the King's servants and search his state papers, to accuse ministers on common fame. They suggested it was the duty of ministers to protest formally and even resign if the King followed illegal advice. They asserted that not the King but his ministers must be held responsible for government, good and bad. Ministers who persisted in illegal, dishonourable, unsuccessful policies could be impeached or removed; if the demands of the Commons were not met they had the right, they declared, to withold supplies.

The demands which were to be made in 1640 had not been successful up to 1629. When Charles decided to rule without Parliament the House of Commons had been successful in asserting only one privilege with such certainty that it was never called in question; this was the right to determine the validity of the election of its own members. Through the whole of our period the Speaker of the House of Commons was in fact a royal servant, though he began eventually to behave as if he were subordinate to the wishes of that House. The position of the House of Commons at the beginning of Elizabeth's reign has been well described by Sir John Neale:

Thus between 1515 and 1558 the House of Commons had acquired the right—not the exclusive right—to control the attendance of its Members; it had created for itself the right to enforce its privilege of freedom from arrest; it had invented a power to imprison offenders against its privileges and its dignity; it had converted an uncertain prescriptive enjoyment of free speech into a formal privilege possessing revolutionary possibilities; it had even established precedents for punishing licentious speech by Members, thus covertly encroaching on the jurisdiction of the Crown, though on each occasion it took care to recognize that discipline in such matters belonged to the Sovereign. In brief it had arrogated to itself the functions of a court. (Neale, *Elizabeth I and her Parliaments* [1966], p. 19.)

Elizabeth never retreated from her position that the freedom of speech of the Commons was limited to discussion of whatever issues she and her councillors had decided to lay before them; members did not have freedom to initiate matters independently. When members ignored her commands not to discuss certain matters or deliberately called her prerogative in question, she imprisoned them without her actions being questioned by the House. The Commons did not dispute that she possessed the lawful power to make their actions nugatory if she so wished.

In principle the situation was unchanged when James called his first Parliament. But he did not ensure that his privy councillors continued to dominate the Commons, with the result that private members had an opportunity to emphasize grievances such as purveyance and monopolies. In the past, privy councillors had dominated individual committees. In this Parliament members began to enlarge committees into committees of the whole House, thus avoiding the control of the councillors and of the Speaker. This Parliament of 1604 finally secured to members of the Commons freedom from arrest, except for treason, felony, or breach of the peace. The right to decide the validity of the election of members was also acquired by this Parliament.

The Apology of the House of Commons, which was drawn up in 1604, was not presented to the King, but it expresses clearly what the Commons had now come to believe about their privileges and proceedings. They declared that their privileges were the general liberties of England, which consisted chiefly in free election, freedom from arrest during parliamentary sessions, freedom of speech. All these, the Commons contended, were their rights. They complained that these rights or privileges had recently been more threatened 'than ever (as we suppose) since the beginning of parliaments'. They saw it as necessary to point out that it was easy for the 'prerogatives of princes' to grow, but 'the privileges of the subject are for the most part at an everlasting stand'. The Apology even declared that 'the voice of the people, in the things of their knowledge, is said to be as the voice of God'.[44]

A substantial number of members of the Commons continued to hold these views right up to 1629. Their interpretation of the constitution was just as steadily and consistently rejected by the upholders of the royal prerogative who were theoretically no less justified in their own interpretation. As we have seen, it was possible for the two interpretations to be held and to clash during the reign of Elizabeth. Historians usually account in a number of ways for the fact that the clash did not take place. Differences of character and ability between Elizabeth and James, the former having more tact and more understanding of her subjects who were fellow-countrymen, are often cited. It is a fact, moreover, that once the boroughs sent gentlemen rather than citizens as their representatives, the self-confidence and independence of members of the Commons increased. There was little they could do, however, unless they had the co-operation of the Lords. This was witheld in 1629, as a result of what was regarded as the rash and offensive behaviour and views of some members of the Commons, notably of Eliot. When Charles dissolved Parliament and embarked on his eleven years of rule by Council he had by no means alienated so many of the *élite* to such an extent that they would take up arms against him. But unless he was able to remove the grievances which we have been considering, the recall of Parliament would inevitably lead to a repetition of the conflict between the two interpretations of the constitution which existed from 1604 to 1629. And this is what in fact happened when Parliament met after eleven years.

We have been dealing with a number of elements of conflict which existed in the body politic between 1558 and 1629, and which led to a conflict between the Commons (joined occasionally

by the Lords) and the royal prerogative over the redress of grievances. In some respects the political and social structure of the
commonwealth lent itself to this discord. For instance, the fact
that it was not possible for the royal treasury to pay a bureaucracy
adequately meant that officials relied for payment on fees which
they charged those who benefited from the performance of their
duties. This system had obvious opportunities for bribery, corruption and extortion. The servants of the monarch tended to be
rewarded by offices from which they could extract such fees, and
by patents and monopolies which became so resented by their
fellow-subjects.

Sir John Neale has given a full account of Elizabethan methods
of rewarding royal officials and civil servants.[45] Minor officials
very often had a servant-master relationship with the more important officials who appointed them, and who paid them, or allowed
them to be paid out of fees and gratuities. Great magnates were
besieged by younger sons of the gentry, eager to take up 'the
gentlemanly profession of serving men', not adequately paid, if
paid at all by their patrons, but dependent on gratuities. The
greater men were able to bestow offices upon, or sell them to, the
lesser. Both prestige and fortune depended upon wielding enough
influence at Court, where competition was intense for power as
well as wealth. Faction developed automatically in this state of
affairs, with the great competitors working to place their supporters in positions of influence. Things became worse in the reign of
James I, but even in Elizabeth's time voices were heard denouncing
the self-seeking corruption of the Court. In *Mother Hubberd's
Tale*, Spenser spoke for many a disappointed and disillusioned
seeker of honour and wealth at Court:

> Full little knowest thou that hast not tried
> What Hell it is in suing long to bide;
> To lose good days that might be better spent;
> To waste long nights in pensive discontent;
> To speed today, to be put back tomorrow;
> To feed on hope, to pine with fear and sorrow;
> To have thy Prince's grace, yet want her Peer's;

To have thy asking, yet wait many years;
To fret thy soul with crosses and with cares;
To eat thy heart through comfortless despairs;
To fawn, to crouch, to wait, to ride, to run,
To spend, to give, to want, to be undone

(*op. cit.*, 895–906.)

Self-seeking rivalry increased at Court in Elizabeth's last years, but it grew much worse in the days of her successor, accompanied by much worse corruption and even greater bitterness between factions. As orthodox theory and practice exalted the monarchy, making it the centre of the state, so its defects as well as its virtues came into prominent view. Corruption, self-seeking and extravagance at Court disgusted old-fashioned moralists and disappointed self-seekers alike.

At the beginning of James' reign, Samuel Daniel wrote hopefully of the new Court:

What a great check will this chast Court be now
To wanton courts debauch'd with Luxury . . .

When James had been on the throne for some ten years, Webster put into the mouth of Antonio in *The Duchess of Malfi* praise of the French king:

In seeking to reduce both State, and People
To a fix'd Order, their juditious King
Begins at home: Quits first his Royall Palace
Of flattring Sicophants, of dissolute,
And infamous persons—which he sweetly termes
His Masters Master-peece (the worke of Heaven)
Considring duely, that a Princes Court
Is like a common Fountaine, whence should flow
Pure silver-droppes in generall:

This is the ideal Court which can keep the whole land sound; but corruption of the Court is attended no less certainly by infection of the country, a fact which Antonio deplores:

> But if't chance
> Some curs'd example poyson't neere the head,
> Death and diseases through the whole land spread.
> And what is't makes this blessed government,
> But a most provident Councill, who dare freely
> Informe him the corruption of the times?
>
> (I. i. 6–19.)

As we have seen, by this time James was no longer relying on a 'most provident Councell', and his Court was poisoned rather than wholesome 'neere the head'. It is most unlikely that James' subjects read Webster's lines as a condemnation of their monarch, for the scene of the play is set in the past and in Italy. Indeed, had there been any likelihood of its being so construed the play would never have been licensed by the Master of the Revels. But what Antonio deplores in theory of a corrupt Court was being said in fact of the Court of James I not many years after his coronation. Not only was there much extravagance, peculation and financial corruption, but drunkenness, lust and debauchery were rife. The Court was frequented by prostitutes, pimps, procuresses; and the King's attraction towards the young men who were his favourites did not add to the respect which his Court was gradually losing throughout the land. Although Charles I did not countenance the licentiousness which his father permitted, his dependence on Buckingham exposed him to the disapproval which that personage deservedly attracted.

Apart from the moral failings of courtiers, they attracted the envy and hatred of all those members of the *élite* who were at a disadvantage in respect to them. The courtiers reaped the greatest harvest of monopolies, patents, sinecures, offices carrying fees, and received what seemed much too large a portion of the profits which might have been more evenly distributed to the gentle classes throughout the country. Pride of family was often offended by a new creation; a knight whose family had long been gentle would find himself forced to give precedence to an upstart who had purchased a baronetcy; members of the older nobility found themselves eclipsed by parvenus of greater rank who had the ear of the

King. From such dissatisfaction among other causes there developed the split between the peers and the monarch. The older peerage despised the new; the gentry as a whole despised any whom they they could accuse of 'base blood'. By the sixteen-twenties, according to Stone (p. 123f.) there was a large group of peers actively opposed to royal policies and royal favourites. Jealousies of one kind and another accounted for the hostility.

This chapter has given a survey of some of the more important issues over which there was conflict between the Crown and various sections of the *élite*, despite their acceptance of the theory of subordination of subject to monarch in accordance with the doctrine of hierarchy. We have been concerned with what the subjects declared their grievances to be and the reasons which they gave for their behaviour. Both inside and outside parliament these members of the *élite* were in fact defending or promoting their individual and class interests, which they also regarded as the interests of the people of England as a whole; in this assumption they may have been sincerely confused; nevertheless, whatever their motives, the people of England in succeeding centuries have certainly enjoyed rights and liberties which derive from the opposition of members of the *élite* to the prerogative claims of the Crown when it was worn by James I and Charles I.

For the first twenty years of this century it was usual to accept at their face value the claims of the opponents of the Crown between 1603 and 1629; the Civil War was seen as a split between freedom-loving subjects, fighting for liberty of conscience and modern democracy against an incompetent, corrupt, bigoted tyranny. The conflict was regarded as wholly concerned with religious and constitutional issues. But Marx and Freud, among others, have convinced the twentieth century that nothing is ever so simple as it seems, that men invariably give the wrong motive for their actions; as a result historians have been led to reject the motives which the opponents of the prerogative in the seventeenth century assumed as theirs, and to find economic, rather than religious or constitutional, reasons for the Civil War. The name of Tawney has been incorrectly coupled with a view that puritanism and capitalism were virtually interchangeable terms, that with the development of capitalism the grievances of the *élite* were really more economic than religious. In fact Tawney's argument in *Religion and the Rise of Capitalism* (1926) was not that puritanism produced capitalism, but that capitalism made use of protestantism in general and of the English Puritans in particular. In this work he sees Charles I, Laud and Strafford conscious that the troubles of this and of the last reign came from an aggressively capitalist gentry intent on seizing control of the government. Without accepting the whole of Tawney's thesis (to which nothing like justice has been done here) we can see that opposition to the ecclesiastical policy of the High Commission derived to some large extent from the individual selfishness of landowners who did not want to lose what they had acquired of the property of the Church since the breach with Rome, and of lawyers anxious to preserve the prestige of their own court and the size of their fees.

Later (in the *Economic History Review* in 1940) Tawney put forward the argument that the Civil War was caused by the rise of one section of the *élite*, an aggressive new middle class, determined to combine political with economic power. This view has been countered by those such as J. H. Hexter who point out that in fact the middle class as it has been known since the nineteenth century did not exist in the age of Shakespeare.[46] Another opponent of Tawney's, Professor Trevor-Roper, has declared that owing to inflation and the rise of capitalism it was possible for the gentry to thrive most easily by gaining favour at Court. As we have seen, fortunes could be made by those who were successful there, to the envy and disapproval of the unsuccessful; and this disapproval was intensified by the moral laxity of the Court of James I. It is certain that the *élite* developed two parties, one of the Court, the other of the Country, though in our period it is not true to say that every gentle Englishman belonged to one party or the other. Lawrence Stone differs from both Tawney and Trevor-Roper, finding that in our period there were certainly shifts of power and wealth within the strata of the *élite*, seeing the peerage losing power and prestige, but not economic power or wealth, relative to the rest of the gentry.[47]

This short and superficial survey of opposing views on the conflict between the *élite* and the Crown in no way does justice to the knowledge and skill of the historians involved. Nevertheless we need not be afraid to reject any individual explanation of the complexities underlying the conflict between the monarchy and its subjects. At the moment of writing, historians are emphasizing more and more the truth that past explanations are based on insufficient evidence, and that until much more is known for certain about many aspects of life in our period it will be impossible to develop a satisfactory comprehensive explanation for the split between a large part of the *élite* and its 'Prince'.

Economic changes were certainly of importance, though not the only cause. Too much weight has been given in the past to the effects of enclosure, for instance; in fact land was enclosed only in certain areas of the country, and it was still possible to win arable land from the forests and the waste. There was undoubtedly a shift in the relative proportions of the national income in the hands of different elements in society. Inflation also undoubtedly played a part in the developing discontents. It was possible to rise into and to fall from the gentry; and inside that *élite* itself there were risings and fallings of groups; the peerage lost ground until the sixteen-twenties, but then gained financially once more, even if their prestige and power did not also recover. Again, there was undoubtedly a split between those who sought their fortune at Court and those who stayed at home on their estates and did their duty in the countryside and as members of parliament. However complex the causes of discontent may have been, Englishmen of the early seventeenth century voiced them in terms of religion, in terms of conviction about the rights of the Commons, the role of Parliament, the scope of the royal prerogative and the proper function and powers of the judiciary. So long as the Crown relied on the goodwill and co-operation of a substantial part of the *élite* for the processes of government away from the centre, the gentlemen of England were in a position to make themselves felt—once enough of them shared the same grievances. Taking into account the possibilities of conflict inherent in the unformulated assumptions concerning parliament and prerogative, and the weaknesses of the central government in the face of a substantially disaffected *élite*, we must

Q

conclude that whatever the causes of open conflict in 1642, the gentlemen and peers paid more than lip-service throughout our period to the notion that subjects ought to obey, that they owed this duty to the monarch, to the commonwealth and to themselves.

REFERENCES

[1] See J. Black, *The Reign of Elizabeth*, p. 24.

[2] Sir John Neale, *Elizabeth I and her Parliaments*, I, pp. 238f.

[3] Black, *op. cit.*, pp. 193-4, 197f.

[4] *Ibid.*, pp. 198f; C. R. Elton, *The Tudor Constitution* (1960), pp. 217ff., 444ff.

[5] Black, *op. cit.*, pp. 20ff.

[6] J. W. Allen, *A History of Political Thought in Sixteenth-Century England* (1960), pp. 215ff.

[7] J. P. Kenyon, *The Stuart Constitution* (1966), pp. 136f., 126ff.

[8] G. P. Davies, *The Early Stuarts* (1937), pp. 17f.; H. Hulme, 'Charles I and the Constitution' in *Conflict in Stuart England*, ed. B. D. Henning (1960), pp. 97f.

[9] *The Third Part of the Institutes of the Laws of England* (1660), chap. LXXXV, 181, quoted by E. R. Foster, 'The Procedure of the House of Commons Against Patents and Monopolies, 1621-4', in *Conflict in Stuart England*, p. 59.

[10] E. R. Cheyney, *op. cit.*, II, pp. 290ff.

[11] *Ibid.*, pp. 297ff.; Elton, *op. cit.*, pp. 314ff.; Black, *op. cit.*, pp. 231ff.; G. Davies, *op. cit.*, pp. 23ff.; Kenyon, *op. cit.*, pp. 38, 57f., 65f., 201, 307; Foster, *op. cit.*, pp. 59ff.

[12] Black, *op. cit.*, pp. 37f.; H. Hulme, *op. cit.*, pp. 59ff.

[13] Black, *op. cit.*, pp. 10f.

[14] Kenyon, *op. cit.*, pp. 61ff.

[15] Elton, *op. cit.*, pp. 220f., 226f.; Kenyon, *op. cit.*, pp. 176ff.

[16] Quoted by C. S. D. Bowen, *The Lion and the Throne* (1957), p. 298.

[17] Kenyon, *op. cit.*, pp. 176ff.

[18] Cheyney, *op. cit.*, II, p. 295ff.

[19] Cheyney, *op. cit.*, II, pp. 301-4; Black, *op. cit.*, p. 232.

[20] Davies, *op. cit.*, pp. 328ff.; Kenyon, *op. cit.*, pp. 64ff.; Foster, *op. cit.*, p. 76f.

[21] Davies, *op. cit.*, pp. 13f.

[22] Here and for the following paragraphs, see Kenyon, *op. cit.*, pp. 71ff., 60f., 50, 85.

[23] Neale, *Elizabeth I and her Parliaments*, I, pp. 122f.

[24] Black, *op. cit.*, p. 4; Kenyon, *op. cit.*, pp. 54, 68f.; Clayton Roberts, *The Growth of Responsible Government in Stuart England* (1966), pp. 13f.

[25] Kenyon, *op. cit.*, pp. 38ff., 54ff.,61-2; Black, *op. cit.*, p. 13.

[26] Kenyon, *op. cit.*, pp. 87f.

[27] Neale, *Elizabeth I and her Parliaments*, I, p. 82.

[28] Here and in the following paragraphs, see Black, *op. cit.*, pp. 14ff., 24ff., 196f., 204, 219ff; Cheyney, *op. cit.*, II, pp. 282f.

[29] Cheyney, *op. cit.*, pp. 283f.

[30] Here and in the following paragraphs, see Davies, *op. cit.*, p. 5f; Kenyon, *op. cit.*, p. 126ff., 144.

[31] *Ibid.*, 9ff., 14ff; Davies, *op. cit.*, pp. 6ff., 66ff., 42f.

[32] H. Hulme, *op. cit.*, p. 104.

[33] Here and for the following paragraphs, see Black, *op. cit.*, pp. 18f., 95ff., 219ff; Neale, *op. cit.*, I, pp. 125ff., 137f., 142, 152, 161, 172ff.

[34] Here and in the following paragraphs, see Black, *op. cit.*, p. 219; Cheyney, *op. cit.*, II, p. 280; Davies, *op. cit.*, 48f., 26ff., 53ff.

[35] Kenyon, *op. cit.*, p. 48; Hulme, *op. cit.*, pp. 94ff.

[36] Davies, *op. cit.*, p. 58.

[37] Here and in the following paragraphs, see C. Roberts, *op. cit.*, pp. 21f.

[38] Kenyon, *op. cit.*, 70f., 72f., 56ff; Davies, *op. cit.*, pp. 12f.

[39] Roberts, *op. cit.*, 21f.

[40] Foster, *op. cit.*, pp. 60ff; Davies, *op. cit.*, pp. 24f; Kenyon, *op. cit.*, pp. 57, 98; Roberts, *op. cit.*, pp. 22ff.

[41] Foster, *op. cit.*, pp. 76ff; Roberts, *op. cit.*, pp. 35ff., 43ff.

[42] *Ibid.*, p. 47; Davies, *op. cit.*, pp. 33f; Hulme, *op. cit.*, pp. 95ff.

[43] Here and for the following paragraphs, see Roberts, *op. cit.*, pp. 51ff., 60ff., 72ff.

[44] Davies, *op. cit.*, pp. 5ff; Kenyon, *op. cit.*, pp. 24f., 27f., 39ff.

[45] See 'The Elizabethan Political Scene' in *Essays in Elizabethan History* (1958), p. 59ff.

[46] J. H. Hexter, *Reappraisals in History* (1961), chap. 2, 'Storm over the Gentry?'

[47] H. R. Trevor-Roper, 'The Elizabethan Aristocracy', in *Economic History Review*, 2nd series III (1951), pp. 279-98; 'The Gentry 1540-1640', *ibid.* supplement (1953); *Historical Essays* (1957), chaps. 27, 29. See also W. H. Coates, 'An Analysis of Major Conflicts in Seventeenth-Century England' in *Conflict in Stuart England*, ed. Henning (1960), pp. 17-39. Stone, *op. cit.*; see also *Social Change and Revolution in England 1540-1640* (1965).

6: Man, the Cosmos and Providence Divine

In this chapter we shall be concerned with what was generally accepted as true of the universe and all it contained, including man, at the beginning of Elizabeth's reign. We shall treat the planets and the 'fixed stars', the constitution of matter, the nature of man, his psychology, anatomy and physiology, his relation to the natural forces and phenomena through which Providence controls the universe according to the dominant belief of the sixteenth century. Obviously, we cannot be sure that everybody shared this knowledge and these beliefs to the same extent; but large numbers of Elizabethans thought and lived in terms of them. With the above proviso, it is therefore justifiable to attempt a summary, yet comprehensive, account of the essential details of what an informed contemporary of Shakespeare could have thought about the world, what it is and how it functions.

We have already treated the normal view of the world as created out of Chaos after the Fall of the Angels, of the nature of the need for order and hierarchy in every aspect of creation. We have seen how the elements were believed to be organized in a harmony transcending their mutually conflicting natures. We have also noted that Elizabethan Englishmen, who accepted this account of man and the universe, also believed that as a result of Adam's Fall there is a perpetual danger of creation disintegrating into chaos once more, a danger averted only by the Providence of God.

During the period covered by this book some elements of the account of the world inherited from the Greeks and medieval Christianity were shown to be untenable, chiefly in the fields of astronomy and medicine. But those Englishmen who rejected details of the natural science of the past did not abandon their certainties about the creation of the world, about the Fall and God, as derived from the Scriptures and theological tradition. Such men still regarded as historical facts the Fall of the Angels, the Creation and the Fall of Man with its consequences for the world beneath the moon. It was possible to accept Copernicus and still fear the great enemy, Satan, while putting one's trust in the shaping power of Providence Divine.

The doctrine of Providence asserts that when God created the world He did not withdraw His control and leave it to develop independently, but continued and continues to govern it and will do so up to its dissolution on the Day of Judgment. Providence is the way in which this divine power of control manifests itself. It is of two kinds: General Providence is concerned with the larger matters, but Special Providence takes into account the most insignificant of creatures and actions, involving them in the divine plan for the world and for man. Providence is that aspect of God's omnipotence which is aware of all that will happen in time as a swift single moment in His consciousness. In a world which has suffered a fall and is exposed to the onslaught of Satan and his evil spirits the ends of Providence are achieved not only through the actions of men, but through Fortune inter-acting with them. Before we can understand this doctrine we need to know more about what was held to be true of man and the world in which he lives; for Providence works through man and this world, making use of them, taking the smallest detail of each into account. Nevertheless, at this point we may notice that the doctrine was held by Queen Elizabeth and her counsellors, by James I and his, as by Charles I and his. It was held by Raleigh and Bacon and later by Sir Thomas Browne. When Browne looked back on the course of his own life he was convinced that to some extent God's Providence is to be seen clearly and obviously in the natural world as it exists and functions. This is the 'ordinary and open way of his providence'. But there is another way 'full of meanders and labyrinths'. This more 'particular and obscure method' of the workings of Providence concerned with individuals is 'that serpentine and crooked line, whereby he draws those actions his wisdom intends, in a more unknown and secret way'. This is called fortune, but in fact these 'rubs, doublings and wrenches pass a while, under the effects of chance' and eventually when they are carefully examined they 'prove the mere hand of God' (purely, nothing else than, the hand of God).[1]

This is the doctrine which we find in Baldwin's popular work *A Treatise of Moral Philosophy* (1547):

> This term of Fortune or chance, used of man, proceeded first out of ignorance and want of true knowledge, not considering what God is, and by whose only foresight and providence, all things in the world are seen of him before they come to pass. (6th ed., 1640, Folio 157r°.)

We find it again in the official homily, the *Sermon for Rogation Week*:

> The paynims' philosophers and poets did err, which took Fortune, and made her a goddess, to be honoured for such things. . . . Epicures they be that imagine he (God) walketh about the coasts of the heavens, and hath no respect for these inferior things, but that all these things should proceed either by chance or at adventure, or else by disposition of fortune, and God to have no stroke in them. (*Certain Sermons and Homilies* [1623], II. p. 223.)

Not surprisingly Lancelot Andrewes, preaching on the cause of the plague in 1603, declared:

> Sure, if a sparrow fall not to the ground without the providence of God, of which two are sold for a farthing; much less doth any man, or woman, which are more worth than many sparrows. (*XCVI Sermons* [1629], p. 160, sig. Oooo4V°)

The problem for modern minds is to reconcile Elizabethan pronouncements on Providence with freedom of will for human beings. Before we can do this, however, we must understand Elizabethan assumptions about man and the world which Providence controlled, through which it worked.

As we have seen, the world system was created by a divine ordering and organizing of the elements out of the chaos in which they existed in a state of incessant conflict. What is usually called the Ptolemaic-Aristotelian account, merged with Christian teaching, assumes a perfect world before the Fall, consisting of an enclosed sphere at the centre of which is the earth; between the earth and the outermost sphere there are a number of other spheres, each with the same centre; composed of crystal, the spheres support and move the planets and what are regarded as the fixed stars. Since the Fall, as a result of the relationship between man and his earth, the heavens are divided into two separate regions. One is enclosed by the sphere of the moon, the sphere nearest to the earth; matter in these regions is composed of the four elements and is subject to decay. The moon, its sphere and everything outside it is made of an incorruptible substance, sometimes called the quintessence and sometimes ether. In each case the substance is incorruptible and pure. The quintessence is formed of a different mixing of the four elements from that which existed beneath the moon; those who regarded the heavens as made of ether conceived of it as an ultra-pure sort of air:

> This air shineth night and day of resplendor perpetual and is so clear and shining that if a man were abiding in that part he should see all, one thing and another and all that is, from one end to the other, all so lightly or more as a man should do here beneath upon the earth the only length of a foot or less. (Vincent of Beauvais, *The Mirror of the World*, tr. W. Caxton [1481, 1490], ed. O. Prior [1913], p. 49)

Thomas Hill tells us of the difference between the two regions in *The School of Skill* (1599):

> The parts or regions of the world are two, as the Ethereal and Elementary. The Ethereal region is the higher and upper part of the world, which encloseth the Elementary region. The elementary region is the nether part of the world which is contained within the hollow upper face of the Moon's orb and sphere, in which are all corruptible bodies and things harmed by diverse alterations, except the mind of man. (Sig. A4v°)

The centre of the earth is the centre of this universe. Here is the element earth, cold and dry. It is surrounded by the element water, cold and moist. This is surrounded on the surface of the earth by the element air, which is moist and hot; and air is itself surrounded by the element fire, which is hot and dry. It was believed that meteors and fiery exhalations occurred and died away in the region of fire immediately beneath, or within, the sphere of the moon.

There were three slightly different accounts of the spheres postulating nine, ten or eleven in number. Thomas Blundeville in *M. Blundeville His Exercise* (1594), ignoring Copernicus, declared that there were eleven:

> In ascending orderly upwards from the elements they be these. The first is the sphere of the Moon; the second, the sphere of Mercury; the third, the sphere of Venus; the fourth, the sphere of the Sun; the fifth, the sphere of Mars; the sixth, the sphere of Jupiter; the seventh, the sphere of Saturn; the eighth, the sphere of the fixed stars, commonly called the firmament; the ninth is called the Second Movable or Crystal Heaven; the tenth is called the First Movable; and the eleventh is called the Imperial Heaven, where God and his angels are said to dwell. (Folios 135r°–136r°.)

Other astronomers asserted that there was only one 'movable' sphere, the Primum Mobile, which moves from east to west, causing all the spheres within to go in the opposite direction. But both schools agreed as to the composition of the spheres and stars:

> The Imperial Heaven, as our ancient divines affirm, is unmovable, and this heaven, being the foundation of the world, is most fine and pure in substance, most round of shape, most great in quantity, most clear in quality and most high in place. (*ibid.*)

The Primum Mobile, whether as ninth or as tenth sphere, is thus described:

> . . . called in Latin *primum mobile*, is also of a most pure and clear substance, and without stars; and it continually moveth with an equal gate from east to west, making his revolution in twenty-four hours. (*ibid.*)

This is true of the substance of the eighth sphere:

The eighth heaven, otherwise called the firmament, is a most glorious heaven adorned with all the Fixed Stars, called Fixed because they are fixed in this heaven like knots in a knotty board, having no moving of themselves, but are moved according to the moving of this eighth sphere or heaven wherein they are fixed. (*ibid.*, Folio 156r°).

The seven planets were not regarded as fixed stars because each has its own sphere, moving independently of one another; the fixed stars, however, all move in the same sphere.

Popularly the stars are often spoken of as made of fire, but not of the impurity of sublunary fire, the purest of the elements of that region. The more professional view declared:

The stars be of the same substance that the heavens are wherein they are placed, differing only from the same in thickness; and therefore some, defining a star, do say that it is a bright and shining body and the thickest part of his (*i.e. its*) heaven, apt both to receive and retain the light of the Sun and thereby is visible and object to the sight; for the heaven itself, being most pure, thin, transparent and without colour, is not visible. (*ibid.*)

The world which is thus described is inhabited by created beings, of which man and all beneath him in the Chain of Being inhabit the sublunary, corruptible region. There are also two kinds of spirits; those which did not fall with Satan, popularly called angels, inhabit the imperial heaven, and come and go in the service of God through the whole world. The fallen angels, now evil spirits or devils (yet strictly also to be described as angels), are confined to the sublunary region, emerging from hell to carry out their evil intentions and dwelling in the earth or the air. Angels are pure spirit of a substance too pure and ethereal to be perceived by human sight. To manifest themselves to human beings they take on a shape of pure air (ether) which is still grosser than their own substance. Evil spirits manifest themselves similarly, as we see from Banquo's remark to Macbeth that the 'earth has bubbles as the water hath' and that the witches are 'of them', and can disappear back into the ground as a result.

We have noted in an earlier chapter the fact that in this mediaeval-Elizabethan picture of the world the angels are organized in nine hierarchies, each of which has a function in the operations of the heavens. Each order of angels performs the task of regulating the appropriate sphere. To the Primum Mobile are allocated Seraphs, to the eighth heaven, the firmament, 'adorned with all the fixed stars' are the Cherubs. Thrones look after the sphere of Saturn; that of Jupiter is regulated by Dominions, that of Mars by Vertues. The sphere of the Sun is under the care of Powers; Principalities regulate that of Venus; Archangels attend to Mercury, and Angels (the lowest of the nine orders) serve the sphere of the moon.

On earth, man's body, like everything else there, is composed of the four elements. Nicholas Breton tells us:

I find by my reading that man was compounded of the four Elements of Fire, Water, Earth and Air. I thus understand the four Elements—choler, phlegm, blood and melancholy. (*Wits Trenchmour* [1597], sig. C3v°.)

The elements are seen in human beings in the form of secretions, known as humours. Each humour corresponds to the appropriate element, choler to fire, blood to air, phlegm to water, and melancholy to earth. Each humour is either moist or dry, and each (hot or cold) is of a certain temperature. The result of the blending could could be described in two terms, either as 'complexion' (literally a blending together) or as 'temperament' (literally a temperature). The terms apply both to the dominant humour in the individual mixture and to the inner psychological and the exterior physical results. A sanguine complexion or temperament is one in which the sanguine humour (blood) dominates, with a light, optimistic, spritely psychological attitude and a clear, light ruddy pinkness of face.

It was believed that in good health a man lived through four periods, each of which was dominated by the appropriate humour. Thus the third phase was that of melancholy, but this was not a state of illness. The term melancholy was used to denote a malady only when it was applied to the results of a rise in temperature which affected one of the healthy secretions, turning it black. Even healthy melancholy was black. Unhealthy melancholy was produced when the sanguine, choleric or phlegmatic humours went 'adust', were burned up and turned black. When healthy melancholy went adust, the result was a very dangerous state of ill-health. Modern commentators do not always realize that they are liable to take an Elizabethan's account of a symptom of one of the states of melancholy 'adust' and assume indiscriminately that it belongs to the kind of melancholy which was natural. It is clear, for instance, that commentators have made this mistake with Hamlet, who is described by Ophelia as having been of a sanguine temperament before he fell ill. His melancholy is not constitutional; it is a consequence, not the cause, of his reaction to his father's death, his mother's remarriage and the behaviour of his fellow Danes.

In this world before Descartes had put forward his conception of man as a dualism, a physical machine controlled by a rational mind, a living human being was believed to be a 'single state' of body-soul, fused together inseparably until the body dies. The Elizabethan speaks of the soul as being 'three-fold', as having three aspects or faculties. With two of these man is linked to beings below him in the Chain of Being; with the third he is linked to those above. With plant life he shares a vegetable soul which has life but no feeling; this soul is responsible for growth, procreation and nourishment. With beasts, birds, reptiles and fishes man shares a sensible soul, through which feeling functions, in addition to life. Above man in the chain are the Angels; and with them he shares a rational soul which permits thinking and a direct knowledge of God. A typical account at the beginning of our period declares:

> The soul of man hath three powers. One is called the life vegetable, in the which man is partner with trees and with plants. The second power is the life sensible, in the which a man is partner with beasts, for why all beasts have lives sensible. The third is called soul reasonable, by the which a man differeth from all other things, for there is none reasonable but man.
> (J. Wilkinson, *The Ethics of Aristotle* [1547], sigs. A6r°, A6v°.)

This statement confines itself to a comparison of man to other life on earth. The same comparison occurs in the following:

In diverse bodies the soul is said to be threefold, that is to say, *Vegetabilis*, that giveth life and no feeling, and that is in plants and roots, *Sensibilis*, that giveth life and feeling, and not reason, that is in unskilful beasts, *Racionalis*, that giveth life, feeling and reason, and this is in men. (*Bartolomeus de proprietatibus rerum*, ed. S. Batman, *Batman upon Bartolome his Book* [1582], Folio 14r°.)

The threefold soul carries out its actions with and in the body, as what is known as function, through the media of three substances known as spirits. Each of these is simultaneously a state of body and of soul, being the most ethereal form of body or the grossest form of soul. Vegetable, or natural, spirits are produced in the liver, with blood and the humours. They are described as follows:

they are a substance subtle and aerious of our body, bred of the part most pure and thin of the blood, sent through all the body, to the| effect, the members may do their proper actions. (P. Lowe, *A Discourse of the Whole Act of Chyrurgerie* [1597], sig. D2v°.)

Vegetable or natural spirits are produced in the liver, the dominant organ of the lower belly, together with blood and the humours. This organ is the seat of the vegetable functions. Vegetable spirits leave the liver through the veins with the blood, rising to the region of the middle belly, where the heart is the seat of the vital functions of the sensible soul. In the heart, vegetable spirits are refined into vital spirits. The blood from the liver is received in the right ventricle of the heart, which sends some of it to the lungs. A thinner and more 'subtle' part of the remainder filters through into the left ventricle where it is mixed with air from the lungs and the resulting vital spirits are expelled on contraction of the organ, accompanied by blood, air, and 'sooty excrements'. The spirits go with the blood through the arteries, maintaining the vital heat of the body. Some part of spirits and blood rise to the brain, the only organ in the head, the seat of the rational soul. Here there is another refinement of vital into animal spirits, by means of which rational soul and body function as one inseparably.

Beasts have only vegetable and vital spirits, wanting a rational soul, and therefore devoid of the physiological apparatus to refine vital spirits further. This is the basis of Polixenes' conceit in *The Winter's Tale*, when he tells Hermione how he and her husband played together in their youth as innocently as lambs, unstained by the inherited guilt from Adam's sin borne by all human beings:

> We were as twinn'd lambs that did frisk i' th' sun
> And bleat the one at th' other. What we chang'd
> Was innocence for innocence; we knew not
> The doctrine of ill-doing, nor dream'd
> That any did. Had we pursued that life,
> And our weak spirits ne'er been higher rear'd
> With stronger blood, we should have answer'd heaven
> Boldly 'Not guilty', the imposition clear'd
> Hereditary ours. (I. ii. 67–75.)

As lambs they would have no rational soul; their weak spirits would never go from the heart to the brain to be refined into animal spirits. If they had never grown into maturity their blood would not have been strong enough to carry the spirits to the brain, they would not share the guilt of all men, remaining 'twinn'd lambs'.

Macbeth is speaking in terms of the traditional account of the inseparable function of body-soul in an inseparable single state, when he imagines the murdered Duncan so powerfully as to make the vision seem more real than the reality of the heath and companions.

> My thought, whose murder yet is but phantastical,
> Shakes so my single state of man
> That function is smother'd in surmise,
> And nothing is but what is not. (I, iv. 138–41.)

[My thought which is of a murder as yet only imaginary, so shakes the single indivisible state of body-soul in which I am a man, that the ability of body-soul to work as an entity is smothered in imagining, and nothing exists for me but what does not really exist (i.e. what I am imagining).]

And Hamlet describes the player's acting in the same terms of soul and body functioning in an inseparable single state:

> this player here,
> But in a fiction, in a dream of passion,
> Could force his soul so to his own conceit
> That from her working all his visage wann'd;
> Tears in his eyes, distraction in's aspect,
> A broken voice, and his whole function suiting
> With forms to his conceit.
>
> (II, ii. 579–85.)

What the player is imagining affects the single seat of body-soul, and 'his whole function' responds appropriately.

Man in his 'natural' life (that is mortal life, supported by the physiological processes described) is a fusion of corruptible, mortal, physical body and incorruptible, perfect, immortal, spiritual soul. The fusion is the result of that 'subtle' substance, at once body and soul, called spirit. 'Subtle and serious' is the description of spirit in a serious medical work; and 'that subtle knot' is John Donne's term for it in *The Extasy*, 'That subtle knot which makes us man.' This is not poetic metaphor but literal Elizabethan physiology. He is no less literal when he declares:

> our blood labours to beget
> Spirits as like souls as it can.

Man maintains this fusion of body-soul throughout mortal or natural life. Separation comes with death; but during life the imperfection of the body, a direct result of the Fall, can have repercussions on the soul. The rational soul itself is considered by Elizabethans to have two aspects, 'wit', which is passive, and 'will,' which is active. Wit is also called 'reason', 'judgment' and 'understanding'. In mortal life both wit and will can function only through the senses. To wit falls the task of taking decisions in respect to the information received from them, and thanks to that same Fall they are very prone to error. Before their information is available to wit it passes through the faculties of 'common sense' and 'imagination'. As its name suggests, common sense is a combining and selecting of the reports of the senses and also a perceiving of such qualities as size, shape, duration, movement (which Aristotle calls 'common sensibles') involving more than one sense, and qualities associated with, but not directly apprehended by, sense impressions. The resulting composite pictures are perceived as mental images by imagination, by which faculty they should be referred to wit for a decision as to their truth or falsehood or to memory for retention. Unfortunately another result of the Fall is the tendency of imagination to rebel against the control of reason, by stimulating the heart into arousing the passions. Imagination attempts to embrace sensual pleasure and avoid sensual pain. It and the passions it provokes to achieve its end are no less mortal, corruptible and animal or bestial than the rest of human physiology and anatomy.

To prevent the errors of imagination and the senses doing harm they should ideally be firmly controlled by reason. For wit has the power to distinguish between truth and falsehood, so that will (the active part) shall embrace good and avoid evil. Unfortunately again, the Fall has left will imperfect and open to being misled by the passions, the result of wanting pleasure and fearing pain as perceived and apprehended by the senses and imagination. It is not surprising, therefore, that for centuries before Thomas Hobbes, Christian moralists taught that imagination should be controlled by reason both in life and art.

In the Chain of Being man is unique in combining substance proper to the sublunary world (his body) with substance proper to the region outside the circle of the element, fire, bounded by the sphere of the moon (his soul). There is uncertainty as to the substance of the soul, but none as to its comparatively perfect, incorruptible nature:

If the body be so fearfully and wonderfully made, what may we say, what may we not say, of the Soul for whom it was made —the quickener and mover of this engine, inhabitant of this house, life of this earth, light of this orb, and may it be soberly construed) a little God in this little World? The Soul and not the body is the man. God the efficient framed it, not of earth, of elements, of heavenly, of any matter, but, to show His infinite power, made his greatest woɪks, this greatest work of nothing, and vouchsafed himself to be the samplar and prototype—that, as the body is an express image and brief compendium of the world, so the soul is a vive representation and model of the glorious Trinity in incomprehensible unity, made—not the image, which is Christ's prerogative, and to be made had made it not the image of the eternal, but—*ad imaginem*, in or after that image whose perfections it doth, not without imperfection, resemble. (S. Purchas, *Purchas his Pilgrimage* [1619], p. 117.)

This was published by Samuel Purchas in 1619. He does not think the soul is made 'of earth, of elements, of heavenly, or any matter'. But some contemporaries believed it to be of the quintessence (heavenly matter), others a refinement of the spirits or of the humours, or air, or fire, or blood, or a combination of these three latter. And when it comes to deciding how the three faculties of the soul are separate and connected, Burton probably speaks for most people with his admission that this 'is beyond human capacity'.[2]

In speaking of the human body as 'this little world', Purchas was hardly using metaphor. Man is regarded literally by Shakespeare's contemporaries as a little world, a microcosm, because he combines within himself so much that is common to both regions of the macrocosm, that beneath and that above the moon. In *The Courtier's Academy* (?1598), Romei agrees: 'the body of man is no other but a little model of the sensible world, and his soul an image of the world intelligible.' (p. 17.) Helkiah Crooke's textbook on human anatomy finds it necessary to expand this information:

The ancient Magicians (for so natural philosophers were of old termed), as also the great wise priests of the Egyptians, did make of this whole universe, three parts. (*Microcosmographia* [1618], p. 6.)

The lowest, the sublunary, is commanded by the inhabitants of the uppermost, who are intellectual and angelical, 'the *Intelligentiae*'. Between these two worlds is the middle, or heavenly, world, where the Sun rules the rest of the stars. So the human body has three corresponding parts. Uppermost is the head, 'castle and tower of the soul', where reside reason, wisdom, memory, judgment and discourse, 'wherein mankind is most like to the angels or intelligencies'. The middle part is 'the breast or middle venter', where the heart is seated, 'whose likeness and proportion to the sun, is such and so great, as the ancient writers have been so bold as to call the sun the heart of the world, and the heart the sun of man's body'. Crooke points out that the sublunary part of the world is 'expressed in the inferior venter or lower belly'. He is assured, 'that all things are found in the body of man, which this universal world doth embrace and comprehend'. The brain corresponds to the moon, the liver to Jupiter, the gall-bladder to Mars, the spleen to Saturn. The angry glare from human eyes is the lightning, intestinal noises represent all kinds of thunder, bones the rocks, and hair the woods, and so on.[3] Shakespeare writes in this tradition when the Gentleman tells Kent how in Lear's rage in 'his little world of man' the King strives to outdo the violence of the storm outside him.

So far as the Elizabethan was concerned God made the world solely for man, and since the Fall Divine Providence has been in control of every detail, again, solely in the interests of man. Providence works through the natural sublunary world, through human beings and through the world above the moon to overcome the assaults of Satan and his servants. Often the cost in human suffering may be great, but the end is always the triumph of good and the defeat of evil; and this will be the course of things until the Day of Judgment. The ends of Providence are attained in an interaction between human Free Will and all those chance happenings over which human beings have no control, many of which cannot be anticipated. These happenings are thought of as the symbolic figure Fortune, no goddess in her own right, but essentially the servant of Providence. Although everything that will happen is known to Providence, this knowledge does not impose restrictions on human will, which is left free to respond to circumstances as they occur. The Elizabethans owed their clarity on this point to a tradition stemming from Boethius, whose *Consolations of Philosophy* ends with the demonstration by the personification, Philosophy, that will is indeed free:

R

And so the freedom of men's will remains inviolate, and the laws are not unjust which assign rewards and punishments for wills unbound by any necessity. Moreover, God who has knowledge of all things remains looking down from on high, and the ever-present eternity of His vision agrees with the future character of our acts, dispensing to the good rewards, to the evil punishment. (*The Consolations of Philosophy*, with English translation by the Rev. H. F. Stewart [1918], p. 411.)

As I have pointed out elsewhere, it was hardly possible for an educated person (or many uneducated) not to have been influenced by thinking basically Boethian. In 1593 this work was translated by the Queen herself. A translation by 'I. T.' which appeared in 1609 is still the foundation for a standard modern edition.[4]

According to Elizabethan belief the stars play an important part in the actions whereby Fortune, the servant of Providence, helps to bring about the divinely planned ends. The stars exert an influence not only on the weather, on plant and animal life, but on human beings. The rational soul, however, is immune to stellar influence; that affects only what is mortal and irrational, composed of sublunary matter, that is, all that is physical in man, his body, imagination and passions, his senses. A representative account is given by John Frampton in *The Art of Navigation* (1595):

these seven planets are called stars, which are movable not because they err, but because their movings be not uniform nor agreeable; these do move the elements, and do corrupt the things that are corruptible, they bring cloudy weather, and raiseth up the waves of the sea, they move tempests, and causeth flowers to grow, and the heavens and planets have natural vertue to cause these effects; the works of these planets are diverse, according to the variations of the countries and regions, and thereby their impressions are printed in beasts, birds and plants, and in men, they incline more to one than to other: but although they do so incline and move, they do not constrain nor bind by force, but rather as Ptolemy saith: the wise man is lord over the stars, he is wise that followeth not sensuality, but reason. (Sig. B6r°.)

As the stars cannot affect what is rational they do not bind or determine human behaviour. But their influence on the physical part of the 'little world', on such secretions as the humours, can incline a person towards actions. A man or woman inclined by the stars to good can easily strengthen the tendency by the use of reason. But when stellar influences incline men to evil, then they must exercise reason to evade or overcome the inclination. Sir Walter Raleigh deals fully with this topic in section eleven of the first chapter of Book One of his *History of the World* (1614):

Of fate: and that the stars have great influence: and that their operations may diversely be prevented or furthered.

And, as of nature, such is the dispute and contention concerning fate or destiny; of which the opinions of these learned men that have written thereof may be safely received, had they not thereunto annexed and fastened an inevitable necessity, and made it more general, and universally powerful than it is by giving it dominion over the mind of man, and over his will. . . . Plotinus out of the astronomers calleth it a disposition out of the celestial orbs, unchangeably working in inferior bodies, the same being also true enough, in respect of all those things which a rational mind doth not order nor direct. Ptolemy, Seneca, Democritus, Epicurus, Chrysippus, Empedocles, and the Stoics, some of them more largely, others more strictly, ascribe to fate a binding and inevitable necessity. . . . And certainly it cannot be doubted, but the stars are instruments of far greater use, than to give an obscure light, and for men to gaze on after sunset; it being manifest, that the diversity of seasons, the winters and summers, more hot and cold, are not so uncertained by the sun and moon alone, who always keep one and the same course, but that the stars have also their working therein.

And if we cannot deny, but that God hath given virtues to springs and fountains, to cold earth, to plants and stones, minerals, and to the excremental parts of the basest living creatures, why should we rob the beautiful stars of their working powers? For seeing they are many in number, and of eminent beauty and magnitude, we may not think, that in the treasury of his wisdom who is infinite, there can be wanting (even for a star) a peculiar virtue and operation; as every herb, plant, fruit, and flower adorning the face of the earth hath the like. For as these were not created to beautify the earth alone, and to cover and shadow her dusty face, but otherwise for the use of man and beast, to feed them and cure them; so were not those uncountable glorious bodies set in the firmament, to no other end than to adorn it; but for instruments and organs of his divine providence, so far as it pleased his just will to determine. (*Op. cit.*, ed. Oxford [1829], II, pp. 27ff.)

Raleigh insists that although the stars exert influences God has not 'constrained the mind and will of man by any celestial enforcements'. But he is sure that 'the stars and other celestial bodies incline the will by mediation of the sensitive appetite (i.e. of the sensible soul), which is also stirred by the constitution and complexion'. This 'cannot be doubted'. He is also sure that 'all those which were created mortal, as birds, beasts, and the like, are left to their natural appetites; over all which, celestial bodies (as instruments and executioners of God's Providence) have absolute dominion. What we should judge of men, who little differ from beasts, I cannot easily tell; for as he that contendeth against those enforcements may easily master or resist them.' He is quite sure that it is 'absurd to think' that 'either the stars or the sun have any power over the minds of men immediately . . . other than as aforesaid, as the same by the body's temper may be affected.' He insists that 'superior bodies' do not 'have rule over men's minds, which are incorporal'.

Raleigh accepts the normal Elizabethan belief that the stars affect men's 'conditions' but not our minds. 'Conditions' is the term applied to the physical part of man, everything involved in the body, but not to the rational soul, which is incorporal. One result of stellar influences is the difference between parent and child, or between individual children of the same parents. The dominant constellation at conception and birth can incline one child of virtuous parents towards vice; a different constellation can incline another child of the same parents to virtue. In each case the child has the power to counteract the 'celestial inclination'. It is to this power of the stars over physical conditions that Kent refers in *King Lear*, when he comments on the difference between Cordelia on the one hand and her sisters on the other. All three are born to the same parents; Cordelia's virtue and her sisters' vice are due to the inclination of 'the stars above' which 'govern our conditions'. Note that Kent does not say 'our souls', but 'our conditions'. As Raleigh says: 'And it is diverse times seen, that paternal virtue and vice hath its counter-working to these inclinations . . . the sons of virtuous men, by an ill constellation, become inclinable to vice; and of vicious men to virtue' (*ibid.*, pp. 30f.). In *King Lear*, Edmund insists (in agreement with orthodox doctrine on the stars) that his perverted will can resist any stellar inclination to virtue.

The stars not only affect human beings themselves, but events in which they are or might be involved. In each case the purpose and justification of the astrologers' study of the heavens is to enable human beings to avoid harm by the exercise of reason. The ideal defence against Fortune in every form, stellar or otherwise, is patience. A man can survive evil influences if he can control himself and postpone an undertaking at an inauspicious moment. Similarly, when he suffers set-backs, or is exposed to the temptation of an opportunity to thrive by wrong-doing, patience, giving him a determination to wait and suffer if necessary, can save him from harm. In *Endimion and Phoebe* (1595), Michael Drayton sings:

> Our lives' effects and fortunes are
> As is that happy or unlucky star
> Which, reigning in our frail nativity,
> Seals up the secrets of our destiny,
> With friendly planets in conjunction set
> Or else with others merely [utterly] opposite.
>
> (Sigs. E3v°—E4r°.)

John Dee, both famous and notorious as an astrologer, defends his science as follows:

Astrology is an art mathematical, which reasonably demonstrateth the operations and effects of the natural beams of light and secret influence of the stars and planets in every element and elemental body at all times in any horizon assigned. (*The Elements of Geometry* [1570], Sig. biiir°.)

Astrology was frowned upon during Shakespeare's lifetime only in its perversions. Astrologers who duped themselves, or their victims, by claiming to be able to foretell the future in detail by reading the heavens were deservedly in ill-repute. But those who restricted themselves to 'general predictions' (that is to the kind of events which would take place, rather than claiming to know exactly what would happen to individuals) were attended to with respect. In *The Advancement of Learning* (tr. Wats, 1640), although he denounces individual predictions, Francis Bacon justifies astrology as a worthy branch of learning and accurate in its general pronouncements.

The Elizabethans believed that God's Providence makes use of phenomena in the heavens and on earth in another way in order to save mankind from evil. In this case the phenomena do not exert an influence like that of the stars on the body. Instead, Providence aims at stimulating man's exercise of reason to save himself. When men are in any particular danger of suffering from divine anger for misdeeds, Providence provides a warning in the shape of a portent. The portent does not cause the harm which might ensue, but simply portends or is an advance warning of it. According to the old view of the world and the heavens, a portent is a Divine interference with the natural world, an earthquake, a comet, or eclipse of the sun or moon, or both. The frightening phenomena seen in the sky the night before Caesar's murder are a warning to Rome of a monstrous event which will bring disaster to the state. If Caesar and his supporters were warned or his enemies deterred by the portents, Rome would be spared years of civil war and slaughter. We should note that Gloucester in *King Lear* does not make the 'late eclipses' responsible for the troubles of the kingdom. He says that they 'portend no good'. They are intended as a warning to the King and his people. Presumably if Lear had heeded the warning and changed his ways, he and his people would have been spared much physical and mental agony.

The classic example of the head of a state and advisers heeding the warning of a portent occurred with the earthquake of 6 April 1580. The Queen and her Council accepted the earthquake as a portent of imminent divine punishment for their sins and those of the people. They instituted special fast days and days of prayer by proclamation. A special form of prayer was drawn up for the use of heads of households when the 'family' gathered together before retiring to bed.[5] Later, when England had successfully withstood the attack of the Armada, Elizabethans could convince themselves that the good sense and piety of their government had been acceptable to heaven.

It is now a commonplace of the history of science and thought that the age of Shakespeare saw great increases in true knowledge of the heavens and earth, in craft and technology, in medicine and anatomy, as a result of which the old account discussed above was displaced and the authority of Aristotle in particular was discredited. To some extent this commonplace is justified, but we must remind ourselves that by 1630 radical change had taken place only in astronomy, anatomy and technology. The physiology of Galen and the received account of the four elements were not yet discredited. More important, however radical the changes might be in astronomy, especially after Galileo's announcements of 1610, they did not lead to a crisis of faith. Men still believed in Providence, in the influence of the stars, in the Fall and the Day of Judgment. It is true that the new knowledge initiated a development leading logically and inevitably to the enlightened rationalism of the eighteenth century and to the clash between science and religion which disturbed so many people in the nineteenth. But men who accepted the new knowledge in the seventeenth century did not realise that they ought to fear for their faith. On the contrary, they were often delighted to find that God was no less omnipotent and no less a source of awe and of love when contemplated in His works as they were now to be recognized. So far as churchmen, Protestant or Catholic, were disturbed by the new astronomy, it was in three respects. Copernicus' hypothesis seemed to contradict biblical passages traditionally interpreted as assuming the earth's immobility with the sun normally in motion, except when as with Joshua it was described as standing still as a result of Divine intervention. The Aristotelian-Ptolemaic universe had given emotional and intellectual satisfaction in that it seemed to answer commonsense observation, and showed a mutually confirming inter-relationship of space and God's declared intention respecting man. In one detail Christianity had always been in conflict with Aristotle, over the nature of the heavens, which he declares incorruptible and eternal, while Christian doctrine declares that the whole system will disappear with the Day of Judgment. The new astronomy as it developed disturbed men's minds with the notion of infinite space, inured as they were to one of infinite time. Until Galileo's announcements of 1610 there seemed no over-riding reason for adopting the views of Copernicus. To many people the compromise of Tycho Brahe seemed preferable, with the sun moving round the earth, and the rest of the planets moving round the sun.

By 1630, thanks to Galileo and, to some extent, to Kepler's mathematics, most important astronomers had in fact accepted Copernicus, but no completely satisfactory theoretical explanation existed, and universities taught the three main competing theories side by side.

In England there had been a prevailing opposition to Aristotle in general, which encouraged opposition to his astronomy. An important part in this discrediting of the Stagirite was played by Barnaby Googe's translation of the *Zodiacus Vitae* of Marcellus Palingenius. The first three books appeared in 1560, the first six in 1561. In 1565 the whole work appeared under the title of *The Zodiac of Life*. It was read in a large number of grammar schools and attacked the infallibility of Aristotle, put reason before authority as a guide in natural philosophy, gave an account of cosmology differing from the accepted system, was influenced by neo-Platonism and suggested that the stars are inhabited by creatures of a higher order than the mortals on our earth.

The important results of the new astronomy stemming from Copernicus may be summed up for our purposes as the rejection of the notion that the heavens are divine, the ousting of the Primum Mobile as of any importance in the motions of the heavens, the insistence that the sun and not the earth is at the centre of the world. The first thorough-going Copernican in England was Thomas Digges, who published in 1576 *A Perfit Description of the Coelestial Orbes, according to the most ancient doctrine of the Pythagoreans: lately revived by Copernicus, and by Geometrical Demonstration approved.* This was after the discovery of the new star in the constellation of Cassiopeia (1572). And despite the fact that, as we have seen, the Copernican argument was to disprove the theory that new stars were miraculous, both Digges and Tycho Brahe regarded this *nova* as a miracle.[6]

In our period gradual acceptance of the new astronomy and of other new elements of 'scientific thinking' did not alter men's faith in Providence, nor lead them to deny that the stars influence human beings, as we have seen from that 'advanced' thinker, Raleigh. Bacon did not accept Copernicus, but in so many respects he has been taken as typical of the new attitude to knowledge that it is relevant to note that he did not deny stellar influence; and the eleventh chapter of Book II of *The Advancement of Learning* treats the history of Providence, which concerns itself with

'late and unlooked for judgments; unhoped for deliverances suddenly shining forth; the divine counsels passing through such serpentine windings and wonderful mazes of things; at length manifestly disentangling and clearing themselves. Which serve not only for the consolation of the minds of the faithful; but for the astonishment and conviction of the consciences of the wicked.'

As we have seen (in the Introduction) Donne's knowledge of the new astronomy did not disturb him; he still believed in Providence; his despair was over his own feared damnation for personal sin, not for the disintegration of a familiar universe. Whatever effects new astronomy exerted on men's minds in general, it is certain that many still believed in a world peopled by good and evil spirits as well as men and creatures without reason. And with this belief went another, in witchcraft, which, as is well known, persisted for some decades after 1630. It is true that James I weakened in his suspicions of witches among his subjects, and Reginald Scot was sceptical of the very existence of such people. Yet Sir Thomas Browne still believed in witches in the sixteen-thirties, and the belief crossed the Atlantic to cause much misery before the end of the century.

We should not think that new explanations of such phenomena as earthquakes, eclipses, comets and new stars meant an end to the old belief in portents. These were still interpreted as portending 'no good' to human beings, and sent by God as a warning. According to the old school of thought the portents were the result of a divine interference with the normal processes of the natural world. The new 'wisdom of nature' might insist that the phenomena had natural causes, but regarded them nonetheless as valid portents. Instead of arguing that God interferes with nature miraculously to warn mankind of sin and punishment, the new thinkers declare that Providence has known from the first that natural causes will result in the comet, earthquake or eclipse, at the exact time when it can act as a warning to erring human beings. The opinion of the common man was that whatever the cause, natural or miraculous, the portent should be treated as such. Indeed, the earthquake of 1580, which resulted in fast days and special prayers in England at the order of the Privy Council, caused great alarm in Rouen. According to a letter written by an Englishman visiting that city, some people were of the opinion that the phenomenon was due to natural causes and not to a miraculous intervention by God; nevertheless, they regarded it as a portent and awaited with trepidation the actual occurrences which would follow it, and of which it was a warning.[7]

This is the attitude of Gloucester in *King Lear* to the recent eclipses. He does not claim to be able to explain what caused them; whatever cause or explanation can be given by 'the wisdom of nature', yet the actual things that have happened afterwards, 'the sequent effects' have been a scourging, a punishing of nature. That the eclipses were portents has been proved by later events; the King has abdicated and disowned his daughter; he has banished Kent; and Gloucester fears that there is more to come, 'we have seen the best of our days'. How right he is, as the play shows. Presumably, if Lear had examined himself for sin and changed his ways these harms would have been avoided.

The other radical discovery which heralded the rejection of much that was accepted from Galen and Aristotle is that concerning the circulation of the blood and the function of the heart. Galen declares that the blood flows from the right chamber through the septum into the left chamber of the heart. In 1543, when Vesalius published at Padua the results of his own anatomical research based on dissection, he said that the septum was very thick muscle. In 1555, in the second edition of *Concerning the Fabric of the Human Body*, he rejected Galen's account, insisting that blood could not pass through the septum.[8] So long as men believed that the three souls involved virtually different fluids respectively it was difficult to imagine that blood could circulate through the heart from the arteries to the veins and back. The heresy of Michael Servetus, who was burnt by Calvin in 1552, involved the assertion that the soul of man is blood. He was therefore able to suggest the lesser circulation of the blood through the lungs from the right chamber of the heart to the left. Work on the circulation of the blood was carried forward by Realdus Columbus, his pupil, Cesalpino, and by Giordano Bruno, before William Harvey finally established his theory in 1628. The three latter all found the old notion of man as a microcosm a help rather than a hindrance in their work; for if motion were circular in celestial matter according to Aristotle, and in the sphere of the earth, according to the new astronomers, why should there not be circular motion in the body? Moreover, it was not too hard to think of the heart as dominant in human physiology with the ancient assertion of Aristotle to fall back on, that this organ controlled the body, rather than sharing with the liver and brain. Harvey's own words show how it was possible for an innovator to continue to hold valid much that his own discovery was to discredit:

> I began to think whether there might not be a motion as it were in a circle in the same way as Aristotle says that the air and the rain emulate the circular motion of the superior bodies: for the moist earth warmed by the sun evaporates; the vapours drawn upwards are condensed, and descending in the form of rain moisten the earth again; and by this arrangement are generations of living things produced; and in like manner too

are tempests and meteors engendered by the circular motion, and by the approach and recession of the sun. And so in all likelihood does it come to pass in the body, through the motion of the blood. (Quoted by S. F. Mason, *A History of the Sciences* [1966], pp. 216f.)

In his *Anatomical Disquisition On the Motion of the Heart and the Blood* (1628), Harvey showed that the heart is a pump, responsible for the motion of the blood, through itself and the arteries and veins. Nevertheless, despite the fact that he disproved so much of Galen, Harvey still believed that this organ also charged the blood with vital spirits.

The Englishman of this period who has most caught the imagination of twentieth-century English scientists is Francis Bacon. Nevertheless, it is impossible to demonstrate that Bacon was an inspiration to the scientists and technologists of his own day. He was hardly capable of putting his own programme into practice and much that he advocated had already been called for by others, notably by Robert Recorde and John Dee. In 1570, Dee hurriedly wrote a preface to Henry Billingsley's translation of Euclid. This preface anticipated much that Bacon wrote in the *Advancement of Learning* (1605) and the Latin version of 1623. Dee gives an outline of the branches of mathematical learning, their nature, relation to one another, their present state and his suggestions for their better development. The method and attitude are the same as Bacon's, except for the important fact that this latter denigrated mathematics in favour of inductive reasoning, that is, collecting enough particulars to justify generalization.

In the event the great changes of the seventeenth century were to be the result of mathematical thinking, not of inductive reasoning. One result of the Copernican hypothesis was to make men feel, not that they were insignificant, but that they could no longer clearly find God in His creation. According to the doctrine of accommodation, human beings are incapable of knowing God in the way that the angels know Him. He has therefore accommodated Himself to humanity who can glimpse His quality in His works. When the old cosmography was exploded without another taking its place coherently and satisfactorily, it was as if God were not letting himself be apprehended by mankind. But when Newton employed mathematics to explain the universe coherently once more, he was hailed with delight by the religious. His feat was to support faith not undermine it. Once more God was accommodated to mankind; His work could be comprehended and in it something essential of Him.

Bacon has been hailed in the twentieth century as a forerunner of modern determination to control the forces of nature in the material interests of mankind; he has also been seen as a modern sceptic. But Bacon was neither materialist nor sceptic. He certainly wanted to improve the lot of his fellow-men by making use of the abilities given them by God and the resources of the earth, created for them by God. But for him there was no assumption that men could contrive much alone independently of their Creator. He was one of those thinkers, like Milton, who believed that man ought to do all that he could to realize his potential in this life, but only by the grace of God could much be achieved.[9] Bacon's optimism was different from that of scientists of the last two hundred years. He accepted the Fall as a fact, but thought that Providence intended men to overcome some of the consequences. In this belief, it is true, he differed from those of his contemporaries who held that since the Fall mankind had deteriorated progressively and that the lost ground could not be regained. Such thinkers were convinced that the deterioration would continue until the end of the world which was not far distant. Another view saw mankind as incapable of any real knowledge. This is exemplified by Cornelius Agrippa's *Of the Vanity and Uncertainty of Arts and Sciences* (1575). Bacon, obviously, disagreed with this counsel of despair, but his optimism, if that is the right word for it, was cautious and restricted.

Bacon has also been seen by some in the twentieth century as responsible for protecting scientific inquiry from the charge of atheism or scepticism by declaring that its pursuit is nothing more than getting to know God in His works. It is true that this was his view; but it had existed for centuries before his birth. He was not responsible for dissipating bigoted opposition to science as forbidden knowledge.

While modern minds have hailed Bacon as an inspiration it is doubtful if any scientist of the last hundred years has been stimulated initially by him. It is true, however, that a modern scientist will be delighted to find in this seventeenth-century writer an attitude of mind with which he agrees and which confirms him in his own assumptions about knowledge and the organization of human and natural resources. Bacon was certainly something of an inspiration to the generation immediately following his own. Wats, who translated the *De Augmentis Scientiarum* in 1640, wrote of his author:

> the first that ever joined rational and experimental philosophy in a regular correspondence; which before was either a subtlety of words, or a confusion of matter. He, after he had surveyed all the records of antiquity, after the volumes of men, betook himself to the study of the volume of the world; and having conquered whatever books possessed (his spacious spirit not thus bounded) set upon the kingdom of nature, left such laws behind him, as may suffice to subdue the rest. (Preface, sig.* 2v°.)

As we have seen, Bacon was not the first to do all this, though Wats' praise shows how early his prestige as a statesman led to his being hailed as the man who left 'such laws behind him' as would allow others to obtain his objectives. Wats' own dedication to the new science did not prevent him from believing in the influence of the stars. He declares that Bacon's attempt 'was favoured by the stars of his nativity'. Bacon certainly inspired John Bulwer to collect all that he could on the use of the body in the past and present in 'rhetorical delivery'. His two works *Chironomia* and *Chirologia*, published together in 1644, have been a valuable source of information on the stage playing of Shakespeare's day. To sum up, there is no doubt that Bacon's logic and confidence, and his ability to understand and demonstrate the need for inductive reasoning encouraged the next generation in part of their work. But he cannot be given credit for the vast mathematical progress of the age of Newton. In Bacon we can find much that was typical of the old and new thinking of Shakespeare's time.

Within a few decades after 1630 there would be vast changes in human thought and in technology and science. The seeds of these changes had already germinated in Shakespeare's lifetime. Nevertheless, there had been little disturbance of traditional thought associated with the old picture of the world by the end of the third decade of the seventeenth century. Great changes had taken place and were near to winning general acceptance in astronomy; other changes were taking place in other branches of learning. Nevertheless, the traditional Christian belief in the Fall and its consequences was not weakened. Men still believed in a world ruled by Providence, working, among other things, through the influences of the stars. Despite the much quoted line from John Donne, 'all coherence' had not gone.

Notwithstanding his individual inability to perceive coherence in his own life or in the course of the world, the contemporary of Shakespeare was confident that this was due to his human weakness; he was confident that in some way which he could not perceive Providence was always in control. He knew as well that his duty and his only defence lay in patience. Thus when Queen Elizabeth wrote to console Lady Drury on the death of her husband, Sir William, she said:

Be well ware, my Bess, you strive not with divine ordinance, nor grudge at irremediable harms, lest you offend the highest Lord, and no whit amend your married hap. (*The Letters of Queen Elizabeth*, ed. G. B. Harrison [1935], p. 199.)

When Sir John Norris died in the service of the Queen in Ireland in 1597, she wrote to his mother, Lady Norris. Starting with condolence the Queen added:

But now that Nature's common work is done, and he that was born to die hath paid his tribute, let that Christian discretion stay the flux of your immoderate grieving, which hath instructed you both by example and knowledge, that nothing of this kind hath happened but by God's divine Providence. (*ibid.*, pp. 250f.)

The Queen continues graciously and with real sympathy, but ends with the hope, 'that the world may see, that what time cureth in weak minds, that discretion and moderation helpeth you in this accident, where there is so just cause to demonstrate true patience and moderation.'

In 1599, the fourth of the five sons of Lady Norris died also in the Queen's service in Ireland. Elizabeth had the fifth recalled to comfort his parents. She wrote to them that she was reluctant to write because to offer comfort is merely to reawaken sorrow. But she sent the letter, having seen enough to rely on their constant resolution, 'as well as on the experience of other like mishaps, which your years have seen as also chiefly upon your religious obedience to the work of His hands, Whose strokes are unavoidable' (ibid., p. 268).

Elizabeth was sincere in her condolences, was not hypocritical in her submission to Providence. When the Armada had been scattered by gales, Elizabethans delighted to remark that Providence intervened in their favour; they saw the intervention as no comment on their own prowess, but as a recommendation that they had been favoured by Heaven. And Protestant Europe was quick to see in this a sign that Catholics were destroyed, not protected, by Providence. This exultation was made more permanent in the memorial medal struck outside England which declared, 'God blew and they were scattered'. The belief in Providence of Elizabeth and her subjects was retained by her successors, James I and Charles I, and their subjects.

REFERENCES

[1] Sir Thomas Browne, Religio Medici (1635), ed. G. Keynes (1928), I, p. 23.
[2] R. Burton, The Anatomy of Melancholy, ed. Shilleto (1893), I, p. 177.
[3] Ibid., pp. 6ff.
[4] See B. L. Joseph, Conscience and the King; A Study of Hamlet (1953), pp. 133f.
[5] Public Record Office, Calendar of State Papers, 1579-80, ed. A. J. Butler (1904), pp. 227ff.
[6] See J. Dillenberger, Protestant Thought and Natural Science (1960), p. 70.
[7] Public Record Office, loc. cit.
[8] S. F. Mason, A History of the Sciences (1966), pp. 216f.
[9] Bacon, De Augmentis, tr. Wats (1640), pp. 19ff.

7: Literature in the Age of Shakespeare

It is not unusual for accounts of literature in this age to proceed chronologically. To some extent it lends itself to this treatment inasmuch as new poets appear, fashions change, creative individuality insists on something more than continuing in exactly the same way as predecessors and contemporaries who have a different individual vision of life and appropriate manner of communicating it. But the danger of a chronological approach lies in the ease with which we can find ourselves neatly describing how beginnings flower into maturity, followed by a conventional decadent aridity, from which literature is rescued by a new school. The danger with the literature of Shakespeare's age lies in the temptation to find a fine flowering in the years of the Armada and immediately after, followed by a conventional decadence, from which emerges the utterly praiseworthy verse of the Metaphysicals, after which the New Philosophy and Neo-Classicism between them drain life, inspiration and wholeness of vision out of English literature.

We have seen already that the so-called New Philosophy of literary historians was not exactly what they describe. This should warn us that in our approach to the literature, as to every other aspect of this age, we must beware of accepting a neat generalized account which seems to offer us a key to the enormous variety which in fact existed. A useful understanding of the literature of this age can come only from having read with understanding enough actual writing, enough particulars, to warrant every generalization which we are tempted to make.

Failing that wide and detailed reading, the best, but still inadequate, substitute which I can suggest is to call attention to some aspects of the literature which seem to me of importance and which enable me to indicate how the verse and prose of Shakespeare's contemporaries might be read with understanding and experienced as art and what qualities of writings and attitudes to the subject and to life itself we should learn to recognize and appreciate. But it must be stressed that one man's response to Elizabethan and Jacobean literature is not intended as an infallible guide. It is certainly in no way a satisfactory substitute for the right kind of detailed and imaginative concentration on enough individual examples of smaller and greater pieces of verse and prose. For that detailed and imaginative concentration will not only allow us to respond to the individual works of art, but will also permit us to recognize style and qualities which persist long after Shakespeare's death throughout the whole so-called Augustan period. There is much continuity of style, content and inspiration.

One of the few statements which may be made with a fair degree of confidence is that what we usually have in mind when we talk of the literature of this age is the product of an aristocratic culture. What was not written by aristocrats was usually written for them, assuming their tastes, their interests, their ideals. This is not surprising when we consider where the wealth of England tended to be found, where writers were to look for patrons. This period saw so great an increase in the number of writers that the competition for a patron became intense. Great magnates and great ladies, such as Sir Philip Sidney's sister, the Countess of Pembroke, could afford to maintain protegés; but there were few patrons who could, or cared to, afford to pay for more than one or two individual dedications. As a result most professional writers were obliged to change patrons, even in some cases dedicating the same work to more than one. But in each case, with the major or the more insignificant patron, the result was writing attuned to an aristocratic culture. There was some middle-class culture, but, as will be seen below, that hardly differed in the essence of its ideals and assumptions from what was intended for the *élite* above. Twentieth-century writers on the culture of middle-class Elizabethan England often describe as middle-class works and aspects of education which were in fact directed at the *élite* or coloured by its tastes and demands.

English humanist education aimed at blending with Christianity all that could be accepted from classical paganism. And, as we have seen, by the middle of the sixteenth century, schools and their curricula had been harnessed in a drive to produce an educated *élite* of soldiers and lesser and greater administrators. Just as Roman and Greek ideals of honour, friendship, patriotism, patience, integrity and valour blended with their Christian equivalents, so the classical example to illustrate an ideal, embody a theme, springs into view even more often than the Christian. It should not surprise us, therefore, to find that when Shakespeare brings Lear face to face with Edgar disguised as the Bedlam, the King finds some consolation in the presence of 'unaccommodated man' who suggests to him the thought that there was once a Theban, Epaminondas, who, like Socrates, triumphed over fortune and poverty to perfect himself in learning and patience and who became an inspiration to his own and later times. No wonder, then, that Lear calls the Bedlam, 'learned Theban' (III, iv. 161).[1] One of the paradoxes of the aristocratic education and literature of the time is that it could communicate accurately and sensitively the splendour of humility, to the delight of aristocrats whose arrogance in their personal life would strike us as outrageous. Christianity and paganism are blended in the imagining of a king rising to real splendour of spirit by way of the companionship and example of one seemingly reduced as low as man can go on the way to being no more than an animal.

Elizabethan love poetry, especially in the sonnet, is the expression of an aristocratic culture. Though John Donne might make fun of some of its conventionality, he himself belonged to an aristocratic circle, and wrote to be read by the *élite*, not by merchants, yeomen, peasants or apprentices.

The humanist attitude to the classics permeates Elizabethan literature; it is commonplace to acknowledge the relationship between the two cultures. With the humanist respect for Greece and Rome the Elizabethans inherited the fallacious view of a barbarous time stretching from the break-up of the Roman Empire virtually down to their own age, certainly in England, if not south of the Alps. 'Monkish' and 'dark' were the words to be applied to English culture of the Middle Ages. This is why Sir Philip Sidney regarded Chaucer's achievement in *Troilus and Criseyde* with such awe; the Elizabethan said of his great predecessor: 'of whom, truly, I know not, whether to marvel more, either that he in that misty [*dark*] time, could see so clearly, or that we in this clear age walk so stumblingly after him. Yet had he great wants, fit to be forgiven, in so reverent antiquity.' (*An Apology for Poetry* [c. 1583, pub. 1595], ed. G. Gregory Smith in *Elizabethan Critical Essays* [1931], I, p. 196.)

Sidney's humanist education is responsible for the writing early in the fifteen-eighties of both 'we walk so stumblingly after him' and 'Yet had he great wants'. Sidney's own ignorance of Middle English, like that of almost all his contemporaries, meant that he could not master Chaucer's versification and often misunderstood his sense. Yet the aristocratic notion of service to a lady in love had survived. And the aristocratic mind, which had steeped itself in the sensitive appreciation of minute technicalities of the poet's art, was capable of a vivid response to the immensity of superb poetic imagining and recognized enough of Chaucer's superiority to the poets of Sidney's own short lifetime. However far Chaucer was from the classical ideal in some respects, yet in essentials he expressed it.

The humanists who moulded Elizabethan education were in many ways responsible for the nature of the literature of Shakespeare's age. They saw the mediaeval past as barbarous, and while aiming at a resurgence of Greek and Roman writings, were actually the instigators of an outpouring of mature work in the vernacular. A new Christian culture equal to the classics in art and superior to them in morality, was the humanist goal. One result was the new spate of studying the classics and of imitating them in the classical languages. With this activity in itself we are not concerned; but we are very much concerned with many of its by-products.

Not the least of these by-products in importance was the emphasis placed on literature as both teaching and delighting. This underlying theory of the nature and function of imaginative literature goes back to Aristotle's answer to Plato on poets, but has merged with some Christian notions of the relation between humanity and the rest of the world since the Fall. We find the theory stated magnificently in Sidney's repudiation of the calumny that poets are liars who ask us to mistake their stories for truth. Like Lodge,[2] but much more elegantly and fluently, Sidney asserts that the poet does not lie, but that he imagines. That is why this apologist insists that poetry is not a matter of writing verse, but of using the imagination, 'verse being but an ornament and no cause to Poetry, sith there have been many most excellent Poets that never versified, and now swarm many versifiers that need never answer to the name of Poets . . . it is not rhyming and versing that maketh a Poet. . . . But it is that feigning notable images of virtues, vices, or what else, with that delightful teaching, which must be the right describing note to know a Poet by.' (*op. cit.*, pp. 159ff.) It is the poet's ability to create which has led to his being called Poet in Greek, 'wherein I know not, whether by luck or wisdom, we Englishmen have met with the Greeks in calling him a maker'. Sidney insists that Plato was himself a poet, in that he imagined dialogues spoken by citizens of Athens, who in actual life would never have thought of the words which he put into their mouths: 'And truly, even Plato, whosoever well considereth, shall find that in the body of his work, though the inside and strength were Philosophy, the skin as it were and beauty depended most of Poetry: for all standeth upon Dialogues, wherein he feigneth many honest Burgesses of Athens to speak of such matters, that, if they had been set on the rack, they would never have confessed them.' (*ibid.*, pp. 155, 152.)

Sir Francis Bacon agreed that poetry is not a matter of verse or rhyme, but of imagining.[3] He certainly does not deny (as we shall see below) the claim of men like Sidney and Puttenham, that in his creativity the poet shows a human equivalent of the divine. 'A Poet is as much to say as a maker,' these are Puttenham's opening words: 'Such as (by way of resemblance and reverently) we may say of God; who without any travail to his divine imagination made all the world of nought. . . . Even so the very Poet makes and contrives out of his own brain both the verse and matter of his poem, and not by any foreign copy or example.' (*The Art of English Poesy*, ed. G. Smith, *op. cit.*, II, p. 3.) So Sidney exults: 'Onely the Poet . . . lifted up with the vigour of his own invention, doth grow in effect another nature, in making things either better than Nature

bringeth forth, or, quite a new, forms such as never were in Nature.'
(*op. cit.*, p. 156.)

To understand the nature of poetry is to realize that poets do not
lie:

> of all Writers under the sun the Poet is the least liar, and,
> though he would, as a Poet can scarcely be a liar . . . for the
> Poet, he nothing affirms, and therefore never lyeth. For, as I
> take it, to lie is to affirm that to be true which is false. . . . But
> the Poet (as I said before) never affirmeth. The Poet never
> maketh any circles about your imagination, to conjure you to
> believe for true what he writes. (*ibid.*, pp. 184f.)

Moreover, in his imagining the poet does not waste his time or
ours; he teaches. Sidney refers to this function of the poet in his
discussion of what he calls 'the right poets'; they are those who
'most properly do imitate to teach and delight, and to imitate
borrow nothing of what is, hath been, or shall be: but range, only
reined with learned discretion, into the divine consideration of what
may be, and should be . . . for these indeed do merely make to
imitate, and imitate both to delight and teach, and delight to move
men to take that goodness in hand, which without delight they
would fly as from a stranger; and teach, to make them know that
goodness whereunto they are moved, which being the noblest
scope to which ever any learning was directed.' It is in this respect
that poetry is the greatest form of human intellectual activity.
Sidney asserts the commonplace of his age: 'the ending end of all
earthly learning being vertuous action'. An imagined example has
as much power to move men to virtue as a real one. As a result the
poet achieves the 'ending end' of learning most completely: 'For
he doth not only show the way, but giveth so sweet a prospect into
the way, as will entice any man to enter into it.' (*ibid.*, pp. 159, 161,
172.)

For the purposes of his argument Sidney points out that an
imagined example is as efficient as a real one in the moving of men
to virtuous action. But he and the viewpoint which he represents
go even further than this. It is observed that since the Fall the
physical world which we know from our senses is imperfect; real

examples have suffered from the divine reaction to the sin of Adam. As a result, to study the natural world as it has existed since the Fall is to be increasingly aware of imperfection due to that Fall. Moral philosophy can teach what ought to happen, but this is not what happens in the fallen world; human beings may know perfection intellectually, but they cannot experience it in reality. Similarly natural philosophy can bring a knowledge and experience of details of the world which has suffered a fall. So it is with history; it gives an account not of what ought to have happened, but of what has actually happened in the past, of the triumphs of evil-doers and the sufferings of the virtuous and just, for it recounts the deeds of fallen humanity.

All this Sidney tells us clearly: 'The Natural Philosopher thereon hath his name, and the Moral Philosopher standeth upon the natural virtues, vices and passions of man; . . . The Lawyer saith what men have determined. The Historian what men have done. . . . And the Metaphysick, though it be in the second and abstract notions, and therefore be counted supernatural, yet doth he indeed build upon the depth of Nature.' (*ibid.*, p. 156.) Later Sidney adds:

> The Philosopher therefore and the Historian are they which would win the goal, the one by precept, the other by example. But both not having both, do both halt. For the Philosopher, setting down with thorny argument the bare rule, is so hard of utterance, and so misty to be conceived, that one that hath no other guide but him shall wade in him till he be old before he shall find sufficient cause to be honest: . . . On the other side, the Historian, wanting the precept, is so tied, not to what should be but to what is, to the particular truth of things and not to the general reason of things, that his example draweth no necessary consequence, and therefore a less fruitful doctrine.
>
> Now doth the peerless Poet perform both: for whatsoever the Philosopher saith should be done, he giveth a perfect picture of it in some one, by whom he presupposeth [*imagines*] it was done. So as he coupleth the general notion with the particular example. A perfect picture I say, for he yieldeth to

the powers of the mind an image of that whereof the Philosopher bestoweth but a wordish description: which doth neither strike, pierce, nor possess the sight of the soul so much as that other doth. (*ibid.*, p. 164.)

The difference between the function of history and philosophy in giving a knowledge of the fallen world, and that of poetry in enabling the human mind to experience perfection through the imagination is stressed in the 1605 version of Bacon's *Advancement of Learning*. Again we find an Elizabethan (in this case one who, like Shakespeare and Jonson, was a Jacobean) asserting that history and philosophy can only bring the mind, by way of the senses, down into contact with 'the nature of things'. But many of his modern readers overlook the fact that for him the 'nature of things' was fallen and imperfect, which was why the mind of man does not enjoy it. First he points out that what he is discussing (one of the principal Portions of learning) is 'nothing else but Feigned History'; he then declares:

The use of this Feigned History hath been to give some shadow of satisfaction to the mind of Man in those points wherein the Nature of things doth deny it, the world being in proportion inferior to the soul.

Here again is the assertion that the reality of a fallen world is not satisfying to a mind which intuits perfection. The human mind therefore prefers a 'shadow', an image, of what cannot be had in substance; in this case the shadow is preferable to the substance. Bacon continues with the same account of poetry as Sidney; it serves and benefits in giving magnanimity, morality and delight. That is why it has always been regarded as having 'some participation of diviness, because it doth raise and erect the mind', instead of buckling and making the mind stoop to 'the Nature of things', to imperfection in a fallen world.[4]

The mind of man, coming from God and intuiting perfection, is satisfied with the close contemplation of nothing less. As Sidney puts it: 'sith our erected wit (*i.e.*, *our reason*) maketh us know what perfection is, and yet our infected will keepeth us from reaching unto it.' This comes after a passage insisting that it is not 'too saucy a comparison' to compare the 'highest point of man's wit with the efficacy of Nature'. Instead honour should be paid 'to the heavenly Maker of that maker, who, having made man to his own likeness, set him beyond and over all the works of that second nature, which is nothing he showeth so much as in Poetry, when with the force of a divine breath he bringeth things forth far surpassing her doings, with no small argument to the incredulous of that first accursed fall of *Adam*'. (Sidney, *op. cit.*, p. 159.)

The great point is that despite the Fall the poet can still imagine an unfallen world:

> Nature never set forth the earth in so rich tapestry as diverse poets have done, neither with pleasant rivers, fruitful trees, sweet smelling flowers, not whatsoever else may make the loved earth more lovely. Her world is brazen, the Poets only deliver a golden. (*ibid.*, p. 56.)

The second edition of *The Advancement of Learning* (in Latin, entitled *De Augmentis Scientiarum etc.*), in its English versions by Wats in 1640 and Stebbings in 1857, says explicitly what we have seen was implied by the version in English of 1605. Bacon calls poetry 'The Second Principal Part of Human learning':

> Now let us proceed to *Poesy*. *Poesy is a kind of learning in words restrained; in matter loose and licens'd;* so that it is referred, as we said at first, to the *Imagination*; which useth to devise, and contrive, unequall and unlawfull Matches and divorces of things. And *Poesy*, as hath been noted, is taken in a double sense; *as it respects Words: or as it respects Matter.* In the *first sense*, it is a kind of Style and Form of Elocution, and pertains not to *Matter*; for a *true Narration* may be composed in *Verse*; and a *Feigned, in Prose*. In the *latter sense*, we have already determined it, *Principal member* of Learning, and have placed it next unto *History*; seeing it is nothing else than *Imitation of History at pleasure*. (*op. cit.*, tr. Wats [1640], p. 108.)

He says that most other kinds of poetry will be considered as philosophy and relevant to the treatment of arts of speech. 'Under the name of *Poesy*, we treat only of *History Feigned at Pleasure*.' Like Sidney, Bacon sees the heroic poem as an imagining of a perfect world:

> As for *Narrative Poesy*, or if you please *Heroical* (so you understand it of the *Matter*, not of the *Verse*) it seems to be raised altogether from a noble foundation; which makes much for the Dignity of man's Nature. For seeing this sensible world, is in dignity inferior to the soul of Man; *Poesy* seems to endow Human Nature with that which History denies; and to give satisfaction to the Mind, with, at least, the shadow of things where the substance cannot be had. For if the matter be thoroughly considered; a strong Argument may be drawn from *Poesy*, that a more stately greatness of things; a more Perfect Order; and a more beautiful variety delights the soul of Man, than any way can be found in Nature, since the Fall. Wherefore seeing the Acts and events, which are the subject of true *History*, are not of that amplitude, as to content the mind of Man; *Poesy* is ready at hand to feign *Acts* more *Heroical*. Because *true History*, through the frequent satiety and similitude of Things, works a distaste and misprision in the mind of Man; *Poesy* serveth and conferreth to Delectation, Magnanimity, and Morality; and therefore it may seem deservedly to have some Participation of Divineness; because it doth raise the mind, and exalt the spirit with high raptures, by proportioning the shows of things to the desire of the mind; and not submitting the mind to things, as *Reason* and *History* do. And by these allurements, and congruities, whereby it cherisheth the soul of man. (*ibid.*, p. 109.)

Bacon is talking really only of what he describes as imagined history, that is the heroic poem, or epic (and of tragedy). Inasmuch as it is an imagining of knowledge, poetry is a principal part of learning. In the 1605 version he called it an imagining out of the stuff of knowledge. The world which we know through our senses, in the shape of history or natural, or moral, philosophy, is fallen, and does not therefore satisfy the human mind which intuits perfection. Where other parts of learning make the mind stoop and respond to the fallen world, poetry enables the mind of man to experience through the imagination that unfallen perfection no longer existing in reality—the shadow (imagining or image) of things is given where they no longer exist in substance. It is important to note that Bacon understands why the mind of man prefers the imagining of perfection to the reality of the world since the Fall, and he finds this right. Sidney also finds in poetry an inspiration toward magnanimity, delight and morality. He and Bacon agree that this part of learning 'cherisheth the soul of man'.

That Milton held this view of poetry, in particular of epic, is obvious enough. But it is not so often realized that Thomas Hobbes also saw the heroic poem as a more delightful and powerful form of instilling morality than moral philosophy. He asserts: 'But so far forth as the Fancy of man has traced the ways of true Philosophy, so far it hath produced very marvellous effects to the benefit of mankind.' And he proceeds to list the achievements of civilized men as 'the workmanship of Fancy but guided by the Precepts of true Philosophy'. At this point he follows Sidney and Bacon in ascribing to Fancy, the poetic imagination, the power to teach and delight where philosophy fails.

'But where these precepts fail [*the precepts of true Philosophy*] as they have hitherto failed in the doctrine of Moral virtue, there the architect, Fancy, must take the Philosopher's part upon herself. He therefore that undertakes an Heroic Poem, which is to exhibit a venerable [*worthy of reverence*] and amiable Image of Heroic virtue,' must be both poet and philosopher, must imagine, in Bacon's language, 'a dream of learning'.[5] In 1675 in his preface to his translation of the *Odyssey*, Hobbes implies a belief that heroic images may delight but will not necessarily move us to virtue: 'For all men love to behold, though not to practise, Virtue.'[6] Nevertheless, in his earlier work he shares the view of poetry which was usual in Shakespeare's lifetime. This view of poetry, moreover, is fundamental to the development of the neo-classical conception of poetic justice. If a poem is to allow us to imagine a world more perfect than anyone has experienced since the Fall, then vice must be punished, virtue triumphant. This is what would happen in a perfect state of affairs. As a result critics, poets and the public came to believe that misery and happiness in epic and tragedy (particularly in tragedy) must never be undeserved. Thus it was that the death of Cordelia in *King Lear* appeared to some of the public after the middle of the seventeenth century as an outrageous denial of the assumption that a poet communicates to us his imagined experience of perfection.

This account of poetry applies most accurately to epic, tragedy and comedy (to other kinds of narrative, and to tragi-comedy, as well); but it could be used to justify the psalms and various other forms mentioned by Sidney. Nevertheless, much of the verse which we regard today as most representative of Shakespeare's age can hardly be defended as teaching, though it certainly delights. This fact must not surprise us in view of our admission that in the Elizabethan age, as in others, human beings are inconsistent and illogical. Sidney, who wrote the *Apology*, also wrote sonnets which elude his defence. This he admitted in the sonnet whose first lines run:

> Leave me, O love which reachest but to dust
> And thou, my mind, aspire to higher things.

This sonnet ends:

> And think how evil becometh him to slide
> Who seeketh heaven and comes of heavenly breath.
> Then farewell, world! thy uttermost I see:
> Eternal Love, maintain thy life in me.

And in the *Apology* he admits 'man's wit may make Poesy', which, instead of teaching morality, 'doth, contrariwise, infect the Fancy with unworthy objects' (p. 186). Before his death Sidney regretted having done this in his *Arcadia*. Although some parts of this were deservedly seen as inspiring Christian fortitude by later generations, the work as a whole is permeated with a pagan quality; the characters communicate an un-Christian obduracy to events. Sidney knew his own work.

Humanist education was also responsible for assumptions about the nature of different kinds of literature, assumptions which mingle elements of social doctrine with those of aesthetics. The view, which had existed since the Greeks, was warmly championed that an essential element of an audience's response to tragedy lay in the fact that it is asked to imagine the downfall of a heroic or potentially heroic personage to misery and death. For the most part renaissance tragedy in England concerns itself with persons belonging to the aristocracy in the society imagined by the dramatist. Strict neo-classical doctrine (conforming to the practice of medieval poets) insisted that an aristocratic society can be painted only in a high literary style. As we shall see in a later chapter, even popular Elizabethan tragedy for the most part conforms to this requirement, even if the playwright or his audience might be unable to distinguish between a high-flown and a genuine high style.

What was true of tragedy held good for epic. Here the aim was to communicate in imagined 'history' the poet's apprehension of the highest ideals which ought to inspire the morality and conduct of his contemporaries. These, the morality and conduct, may have changed, but the conception of epic is still that which we can find in Homer, in Virgil, in *Beowulf*, in *Troilus and Criseyde*. Spenser went to Italian romantic epic for his model; his allegory communicates his ideal of human conduct through his imagining of episodes such as we find in Ariosto. Treating a different virtue in operation in each book of *The Faerie Queene*, he aimed at inducing his readers to experience imaginatively what unfallen magnificence is. The famous letter to Raleigh has led to some confusion, largely, I suspect, owing to our tendency to misread his reference to Aristotle as a model. Spenser does not say that he will deal with the various virtues exactly as Aristotle did, or that he will treat the same number, but that he will follow the Greek's example in treating the public virtues as a whole separately from those of private life. His aim was what we have heard from Sidney and Bacon, to provide an ideal of civilized conduct, and to move his readers to attempt to embody that ideal in themselves.

Milton tried to communicate to his contemporaries (and he seems to have succeeded) his certainty that the most heroic human conduct ever known in the past and ever to be known in the future took place on the Cross. The Atonement and the Crucifixion meant a truer heroism than could be imagined in terms of conventional epic, of deeds of arms, even if the writer tried to use these allegorically. When Milton sang that his aim was 'to justify the ways of God' he did not mean that he was going to prove that the divine actions were just. In seventeenth-century English he was asserting his delight in bearing witness to the fact that the course of God's Providence treats men better than they deserve. Thanks to that 'more heroic martyrdom unsung' the 'anger and just rebuke' of Heaven allows mercy as well as justice to men. What is important for us to realize is that Milton's celebration of an act of humility and sacrifice is a celebration of the most heroic conduct that he can imagine. In his aim, if not in his example, he conforms to humanist tradition; the same is true of his style. It is high to suit the dignity of his theme.

Humanist education actually influenced the style of English verse and prose, not only in larger matters but down to quite small details. To some extent this was what we might regard as an impact made in the normal course of things by Greek and Latin culture on an existing literature. But the influence was also the result of a systematic employment of classical models, of analysis of classical style in practice and theory, in order to produce a new classical literature in Latin and Greek. Literature and composition as taught under the name of Rhetoric in the education developed for the renaissance *élite* meant that pupils learnt to identify, define and produce examples of every element of style to be found in their classical models. They were guided to develop their own ability to write by the method known as Imitation which we find expounded in detail in theory and practice in the second book of Roger Ascham's *The Schoolmaster* (1570).[7] At first intelligent and controlled imitation of an existing model develops the pupil's ability, giving him experience of other men's imagining and writing, until at last he imagines his own 'matter' and has formed his own style.

Although men like Ascham aimed at promoting writing in the classical languages, one result of their work was that English writing in the vernacular put into practice what had been learned from the classical models. In addition the Elizabethans applied to their reading of other vernacular languages, in particular French, Italian and Spanish, the methods acquired in the study of the classics. An excellent example of the method and its results is Abraham Fraunce's *The Arcadian Rhetoric* (1588).[8] Fraunce gives examples from contemporary French and Italian, as well as from Latin and Greek, of the various elements of style which he defines and discusses. His work is really an English treatment of that part of Rhetoric, which was named *Elocutio*. The fact that in any treatment of this subject we find each rhetorical figure defined and illustrated has often led modern readers mistakenly to assume that here is a purely superficial and mechanical art. In fact systematic study of the figures, whatever it might do to us today, certainly enabled the great poets of the age of Shakespeare to communicate to us in a manner which has never been eclipsed.

Fraunce and Puttenham, whose *Art of English Poesy* (1589) treats the same ground more fully, enable us to see more easily than the Latin works and the more down-to-earth English treatments, the beneficial results of this study. Where most writings on *Elocutio* (or 'Elocution' in Elizabethan English) are concerned merely to give a systematic account of something to be learnt and understood intellectually, Fraunce and Puttenham are more interested in showing what happens to the poetic mind which has grasped the intellectual understanding and converted it into creative imaginative activity. Thus Fraunce goes to Sidney's first sonnet for his example of the figure of *Climax*:

Loving in truth, and fain in verse my love to show,
That the dear she might take some *pleasure* of my *pain*,
Pleasure might cause her *read, reading* might make her *know*,
Knowledge might *pity* win, and *pity grace* obtain.

(*op. cit.*, pp. 38ff.)

Sidney recounts how he hoped that his 'show' of unhappiness might take him step by step through his lady's pleasure until he experienced her 'grace'. This particular figure Fraunce defines as 'a reduplication continued by diverse degrees and steps, as it were, of the same word or sound'. In addition to the figure of climax, however, Sidney expresses himself through that of rhyme, and through the repetition of *might* and the internal rhyming of *make—take*, apart from alliteration. Here, in one single quatrain, we have a complexity of sound patterns expressing a complexity of meaning. The patterns are there for the delight and aesthetic gratification they give in themselves, yet even more for what they enable the poet to express as a poet. This should always be remembered when we read such statements as that by Fraunce that figures of words 'altogether consist in sweet repetitions and dimensions' (*ibid.*, p. 167); it is true that they are formed by the repetitions in 'dimensions', but at the same time they communicate meaning.

We might notice that in his first line Sidney is playing with the idea that verse is a 'feigning', when he says he is 'fain' to show truth; a similar conceit involves the thought that verse is often accused of merely showing what is not true because the poet is by nature a liar. Sidney 'feigns' in verse to show sincerely that he loves 'in truth'. This is the kind of statement to be expected of love poetry in an aristocratic tradition in which the lover assumes the role of vassal to an overlord.

It is impossible to give here anything like a comprehensive account of English verse of the age of Shakespeare. But the greater our knowledge and experience of a variety of poems, the more we are in a position to realize that in their sound patterns the competent poets were able to express complexity of meaning with compression and clarity of surface sense.

The figure which we found in the first stanza of Sidney's sonnet, climax (or 'the ladder'), both lends organization to, and derives from the organization of, Spenser's thoughts in this passage from Book Two of *The Faerie Queene* (1596):

> all that pleasing is to living ear,
> Was there consorted in one harmony
> Birds, voices, instruments, winds, waters, all agree.
> The joyous *birds* shrouded in cheerful shade,
> Their notes unto the *voice* attemper'd sweet;
> Th' angelical soft trembling *voices* made
> To th' *instruments* divine respondence meet:
> The silver sounding *instruments* did meet
> With the base murmur of the *water's fall*:
> The *water's fall* with difference discreet,

Now soft, now loud, unto the *wind* did call:
The gentle warbling *wind* low answered to all.
(Ed. J. C. Smith [1961], I, p. 337, Canto XII, lxx, lxxi.)

A well-known and much misunderstood passage in Hobbes'
Answer to Davenant (1650) contains this same figure of climax:

> *Time* and *Education* begets *experience*; *Experience* begets
> *memory*; *Memory* begets *Judgement* and *Fancy*: *Judgement*
> begets the *strength* and *structure*, and *Fancy* begets the
> *ornaments* of a Poem.   (*op. cit.*, ed. Spingarn, p. 59.)

This passage has been misunderstood when it has been read out of
context; as we have seen, Hobbes agreed with Sidney in the belief
that in teaching moral philosophy 'Fancy, the architect' enables
the poet to imagine the perfect, unfallen world. By 'the ornaments
of a poem' Hobbes does not mean superficial, external decoration
or style. He makes that clear later in a passage which many modern
commentators do not appear to have read:

> the descriptions of worthy circumstances are necessary acces-
> sions to a Poem, and being well performed are the Jewels and
> most precious ornaments of Poesy. Such in *Virgil* are the
> Funeral games of *Anchises*, The duel of *Aeneas* and *Turnus*,
> &c.   (*ibid.*, p. 62.)

Hobbes sees Fancy as involved in imagining episodes; it is the
faculty which transforms the source material into the completely
imagined poem, not a skittish, superficial power of empty decoration.

To some extent the Englishman of Shakespeare's time is developing what is natural to his native tongue, what exists in native tradition, and an English counterpart to what he finds in Italian and
French as well as in the classics. This is true of stanza forms
especially as seen in Spenser. Perhaps no better examples could be
found to illustrate the impact of humanist teaching, native tradition and French and Italian example than in the writing of the
sonneteers. In the sonnet, whichever formal variant rhyme-scheme
may be adopted, we have aristocratic spirit and subject-matter

T

expressed in an intricacy of thought and sound pattern deriving from the discipline and interests of an *élite* culture. In the sonnet we find melody, beauty and colour of imagery and complexity of thought and imagining fused to a verbal dexterity which is not content with mechanical patterning but demands precision of language.

Although blank verse became the staple of the dramatic poets there are probably no more than a dozen non-dramatic poems in blank verse before 1642 in English. Like the French and Italians, the Elizabethans tended to evolve a vernacular equivalent for the classical hexameter outside drama in rhyming lines rather than in blank verse. Gradually in our period rhyming couplets ousted more complicated arrangements, but it took some time before the English poet could write sustained passages in heroic couplets, maintaining the clarity, precision, smoothness and complexity which he could attain with comparative ease in the final couplet of a sonnet, in isolated couplets in drama or in shorter pieces of non-dramatic verse. In the gradual development of the non-dramatic heroic couplet the discipline of figures played a large part. This is true also of its part in the development of blank verse in drama; but this we leave for a later chapter. In both kinds of verse, in and outside drama, one figure soon becomes dominant; that is antithesis, a figure in which the relationship of sound comes when we communicate vocally a relationship of contrasting ideas. The first line of an example from Puttenham's *The Art of English Poesy* runs as follows:[9]

Good have I done you, much, *harm* did I never none.

Here, in addition to the antithesis, *good—harm,* we have an implied contrast of *much—never none,* [and a similar relationship of meaning which produces an equivalence of sound: *have I done —did I.* We may also notice in passing the internal rhyme of *done—none.*

Of course, there is an enormous difference in subtlety and smoothness of thinking and of rhythm between this and the sureness of touch with which Dryden begins his poem:

> In pious times, ere priestcraft did begin,
> Before polygamy was made a sin.
> (Absalom and Achitophel [1681], 1–2.)

Here the contrast is between one fact that polygamy has become a sin, and the other that it has not always been one. Yet, here, too, we find the obvious equivalence of *ere—before*. Much time might be spent to advantage analysing the relationship between the clarity and complexity of thought and the rhythm which it produces owing to the mastery with which Dryden chooses his words and expresses himself in their ordering. But our main concern is with the presence of antithesis and of that conjoining of words and ideas, which are not necessarily in contrast but which are related to one another and which produce a similar sound pattern, to that of antithesis, chiefly by change of pitch and length of vowel when spoken with meaning.

This characteristic element of Augustan verse is present, as is to be expected, in Pope. The opening lines of *The Rape of the Lock* (1712) express smoothly with varied harmony the contrasting ideas with which the poet contemplates this heroic storm in a tea-cup:

> What *dire offence* from *am'rous causes* springs,
> What *mighty* contests rise from *trivial* things.

And again the rhythm of antithesis is supported by that deriving from the equivalence, *contests—things*.

A similar organization of thought and words gives us the complexity as well as the clarity of:

> *Slight* is the subject, but *not so* the praise
> If she inspire and he approve my lays.
> (The Rape of The Lock, Canto 1, 5–6.)

The first line has the linking of *subject—praise*; the second links *he—she*, and then, combining them in an implied 'they', relates them jointly to *my*. And *inspire* is related vocally and in meaning to *approve*.

Polished antithetical writing was no new thing in English. It faces us in the first couplet of Chaucer's *Prologue*:

> Whan that Aprille with his shoures soote
> The droghte of March hath perced to the rote.

Modern readers more often than not miss the antithesis of *Aprille—March*; the two months are contrasted in their qualities, and April is undoing the work of its predecessor, just as *shoures* are in contrast to *droghte*. But there is an implied antithesis between the ability of sweet showers to pierce and what has been hardened by bitter drought.

To provide one of the best examples of this kind of writing in early seventeenth-century England we must turn to a passage from drama.

> This world is not for aye; nor 'tis not strange
> That even our loves should with our fortunes change;
> For 'tis a question left us yet to prove,
> Whether love lead fortune or else fortune love.
> The great man down, you mark his favourite flies;
> The poor advanc'd makes friends of enemies.
> And hitherto doth love on fortune tend;
> For who not needs shall never lack a friend.
>
> *(Hamlet,* III, ii. 195–202.)

The last four lines of this extract from one of the speeches of the Player King show Shakespeare's ability to turn his training in figures of words to poetic (which is in this case also dramatic) advantage. We have three examples of open antithesis in *great man—poor*, *down—advanc'd* (literally 'raised up'), *friends—enemies*; but *great man* and *poor* are antithetical ideas, as are *down* and *advanc'd*. The last couplet has examples of equivalence rather than antithesis, but the organization of the related words produces a rhythm coming from clear explicit sense with complex implications; the related words are *love—fortune*, *not—never*, *needs—shall . . . lack*.

When Nicholas Grimald lamented the death of his mother (?1555) he contrasted the clamour of some who grieved at her passing with his father's self-control:

> But my good sire gave, with soft words, relief,
> And cloaks with *outward cheer* his *inward grief,*
> Lest by *his care your sickness* should augment,
> And on *his case your thoughtful heart* be bent.

(*A Funeral Song, upon the decease of Annes, his mother,* ed. J. W. Hebel and H. H. Hudson, *Tudor Poetry and Prose* [1953], p. 52.)

When we speak the lines to communicate the relationship of word to word as meaning, changes of intonation give rise to this characteristic rhythm. We have it (probably earlier) in Wyatt's well-known first line:

> They *flee* from me that sometime *did* me *seek.*
>
> (Hebel and Hudson, *op. cit.,* p. 18.)

I have italicized only the antithesis, *flee—did seek*: but Wyatt organizes his meaning in two more: *they—that, from me—me.* In this way he can express his bitterness that the very people who used to take trouble to join his company are now concerned to shun him.

The emergence of the heroic couplet as a dominant form in the seventeenth century should not surprise anyone with hindsight who has read enough sonnets which achieve a resolution of meaning in a final couplet. Let us read the end of one of Richard Lynche's, *Diella* (1596):

> *Anger the one,* and *envy* mov'd *the other,*
> To see *my love* more fair than *Love's fair mother.*
>
> (*ibid.,* p. 221.)

Or from another, Griffin's *Fidessa* (1596):

> But after all my comfort rests in this,
> That for *thy sake my youth* decayed is.
>
> (*ibid.,* p. 225.)

Greater sophistication produces Daniel's:

> Men do not weigh the flower for what it was
> When once they find her flower, her glory pass.
>
> (S. Daniel, *Delia* [1594], *ibid.,* p. 244.)

And what we find later in the Augustan couplet is already present in Shakespeare's last lines to Sonnet Thirty-Two:

> But since he died, and poets better prove,
> Theirs for their style I'll read, his for his love.

The underlying discipline came from teachers, in school and out; those in school are exemplified by Stanyhurst's praise of Virgil, the 'surpassing poet', for 'words so fitly couched, with verses so smoothly slickt, (*i.e. polished*) with orations so neatly burnisht, with similitudes so aptly applied, with each decorum so duly observed'. Outside school the poets developed for themselves or learned from other poets how to express complexities without losing the qualities of style which Stanyhurst admired so much in his great Roman original. And so we have the superb clear and complex landscape of Book Four of *Paradise Lost*, in which Milton's mastery of sound and meaning relies on a more subtle form of antithesis than that which we can expect to meet in any rhetoric book—however much such a book might have been responsible at some point of the poet's development before he was capable of what he has written:

> Both where the morning Sun first warmly smote
> The open field, and where th' unpierc't shade
> Imbrownd the noontide Bowers.   (244–6.)

We can start by noticing the repetition of *where*, and the contrast, *morning–noontide*; also that of, *open field—Bowers*. But complexity comes from the implied contrast of the sun like a sword hitting the open field (but with a morning weakness) with that same sword, driven now with all the strength and possessing all the cutting edge and point of midday, and yet unable to penetrate the shade of the woods. The result is to intensify the antithesis between the exposure of the open field and the impenetrable thickness of the woods.

One more quotation from Milton will serve to emphasize the fact that the Augustan couplet grows quite accountably out of English literature as it was written in Shakespeare's age. When Adam regrets the over-confidence which led Eve to her (and his) downfall, he says how she left him unimpressed by warnings:

> Either to meet no danger or to find
> Matter of glorious trial.   (Bk. IX, 1176–7.)

Here our related words are *to meet—to find, no danger—Matter of glorious trial.* And Milton's subtlety of writing makes us aware of Adam's anguished sarcasm as he regrets the fact of Eve's insistence that any 'trial' she might encounter would be no danger, whereas in truth her greatest danger lay in the unfounded confidence which found shame when expecting glory.

Much has been said about the deliberate avoidance of easy clarity by the Metaphysical poets, and in particular of Donne and of his 'rough' rather than 'smooth' rhythms, in his own days as well as later. Nevertheless, he shared the inheritance from humanism which we have observed in the verbal organization of more melodious and smooth poets. It is to be said, moreover, that very often later readers have found Donne and other Metaphysicals difficult largely owing to ignorance of the surface sense of Elizabethan words, and in half-ignorance or confusion over Elizabethan ideas. For instance the 'subtle knot' of *The Extasy* which 'makes us man', is a simple reference to generally understood renaissance physiology, which regarded 'spirit' as the physical substance, at once body and soul, in which the two are inextricably one in 'natural life'. Donne wrote when he cared to in a way more obviously akin to what we have been examining:

> And thou the subject of this well-born thought,
> Thrice noble maid, couldst not have found nor sought
> A fitter time to yield to thy sad Fate,
> Then whiles this spirit lives; that can relate
> Thy worth so well to our last nephews' eyne
> That they shall wonder both at his and thine:
> Admired match! where strives in mutual grace
> The cunning pencil and the comely face.
>   (*The Anniversaries*, ed. Manley [1963], 11–18.)

Again we glimpse the antithetical organization of the *Break of Day*:

> Why should we rise because 'tis light?
> Did we lie down because 'twas night?
> Love which in spite of darkness brought us hither
> Should in despite of light keep us together.

The felicitous clarity of the last couplet is the result of the dexterity with which the following relationships are organized: *in spite of darkness—in despite of light, brought us—keep us; hither* and *together* are related less obviously, in that one implies movement to this place and the other being without motion in this place.

The entrancing rhythms of *Air and Angels* arise from this kind of organization of meaning and words:

> So in a voice, so in a shapeless flame,
> Angels affect us oft . . .
>
> .   .   .   .   .   .
>
> Whilst thus to ballast love *I thought*,
> And so more steadily to have gone,
> With wares which would sink admiration,
> *I saw* I had love's pinnace overfraught.

I thought is what he intended; *I saw* tells what he accomplished. Apart from the direct antithesis *ballast—overfraught*, there is another, less direct, between *ballast* and *wares which would sink admiration*.

The sure sincerity of the hymn *At the author's last going into Germany* is communicated by a mastery of verbal structure which owes much to the same tradition as produced the most sugary of Elizabethan love poems:

> In what torn ship soever I embark,
> That ship shall be *my emblem* of *thy ark*;
> What sea soever swallow me, that flood
> Shall be *to me an emblem* of *thy blood*;
> Though thou with clouds of anger do disguise
> Thy face, yet through that mask I know those eyes,
> Which, though they turn away sometimes,
> They never will despise.

There are subtle changes in the positions of repeated words, or of similar sounds—*what*—*ship*—*soever*—*that*—*emblem*; the italics have already called attention to *my*—*thy, emblem*—*ark, to me*—*thy, emblem*—*blood.*

It is obvious that Donne does not strive for melody and harmony with the single-mindedness of an ordinary sonneteer. He concentrates on what Samuel Johnson later called 'strength', that is, on complexity and meaning; but his ear was alert for music and sinuous rhythm, which he produces naturally from his meaning. Much has been written in this century to the effect that some renaissance poets, notably Donne, evoke with their verse the colloquial rhythms of their times, but that others, notably Milton, ignore or distort these same rhythms. This criticism is as ill-advised as it is founded on ignorance. Guesses may be made about the colloquial rhythms of the sixteenth and seventeenth centuries (they may be dignified in academic jargon as 'conjectures'), but little is known for certain about the rhythms of daily speech in those times. Rhythm is basically physical, arising from everything that a human being does, not only vocally, when communicating meaning for any particular purpose. Until we know much more about the intonation of the past and the psycho-physical communication of meaning we are in no position to talk with authority on this subject. This is not a popular view; but popularity is no test of truth. If we are ill-informed on the matter of colloquial intonation, we must submit to being equally, if not more, ill-informed about the rhythm of the verse of the age for the speakers of that age. When the modern reader concentrates on the sense of each word, relating it to the others to produce meaning, and then uses his voice and body to communicate that meaning in those words, he will find himself producing the tones natural for him in which to communicate that meaning. While his tones will be natural, they will make an artificial pattern as the result of the poet's verbal organization. The result will sound like a fusion of the colloquial with the artificial to the modern ear. This I find as true of Milton as of Donne and Shakespeare; but only, and this must be stressed, when the reader takes the trouble to ascertain the sense of each word, to grasp the complete meaning, to communicate it.

Not a little of what has been said about the verse of our period pertains to its prose. Again we have the results of native tradition combining with foreign models and humanist imitation. There is no place here for anything like a full treatment of prose, but we can notice the tendency of prose, like verse, to be organized in antithesis and equivalence. Here is Ascham, tutor to Queen Elizabeth:

> Mean men have eyes to see, and cause to lament, and occasion to complain of these miseries; but other have authority to remedy them, and will do so too, when God shall think time fit. (*The Schoolmaster* [1570], see Hebel and Hudson, *op. cit.*, p. 637.)

Mean men stands in antithesis to *other*; similarly *have eyes, cause, occasion* are related to *have authority*; and *to see, to lament,* and *to complain* are related to *to remedy them.*

Those famous, or notorious, works, *Euphues* and the *Arcadia*, exhibit the same fundamental organization. I call them notorious, because they are so often misrepresented as merely absurdly artificial or over-ornate. Here is a passage from *Euphues*:

> Aye, but Euphues, hath she not heard also that the dry touch-wood is kindled with lime, that the greatest mushroom groweth in one night? That the fire quickly burneth the flax? That love easily entreth into the sharp wit without resistance, and is harboured there without repentance? If therefore the Gods have endowed her with *as much bounty as beauty*; if she have no less *wit* than she hath *comeliness*, certes she will *neither conceive sinisterly of my sudden suit, neither be coy* to *receive me* into her service, neither suspect me of lightness in yielding so lightly, neither reject me disdainfully, for loving so hastily.
> (J. Lyly, *Euphues: The Anatomy of Wit* [2nd ed. 1579], see Hebel and Hudson, *op. cit.*, p. 762.)

I have indicated the barest minimum by italics; a meaningful reading of this passage will of itself reveal the relationship of word to word, which is idea to idea communicated in articulate sound patterns.

And here is a passage from the *Arcadia*:

> *They* perceived *he* was *not willing to open* himself *further*, and

therefore, *without further questioning*, brought him to the house, about which they might see (with fit consideration both of the air, the prospect, and the nature of the ground) all such necessary additions to a great house as might well show Kalander knew that *provision* is the *foundation of hospitality*, and *thrift* the *fuel of magnificence.* The house itself was built of fair and strong stone, *not affecting* so much *any extraordinary kind of fineness* as *an honorable representing* of *a firm stateliness.* The lights doors and stairs rather directed *to the use of the guest* than *to the eye of the artificer*, and yet as *the one chiefly heeded* so *the other not neglected*; each place *handsome without curiosity* [i.e. *over-meticulousness*], and *homely without loathsomeness*; not *so dainty* as *not to be trod on*, not yet *slubbered up* with *good fellowship*; all more *lasting* than *beautiful*, but that *the consideration* of the *exceeding lastingness* made *the eye believe* that it was *exceeding beautiful.*
(Sidney, *The Countess of Pembroke's Arcadia* [1590], see Hebel and Hudson, *op. cit.*, p. 847.)

So few examples whether of verse or prose cannot be taken as a cross-section of what was produced in this age. Nevertheless they serve to illustrate the point that, like many other elements of the life of the time, they anticipate what developed in the later seventeenth century. I have deliberately called attention to aspects of Elizabethan and Jacobean writing which are shared by that of the Restoration and Augustan periods, and I frankly emphasize this so as not to mislead anyone into thinking that the two ages agreed more than they differed. There were many differences between the writing of the two ages; nevertheless the earlier shows us much that helps to explain the characteristics of the later. Before 1642, even before 1605, and certainly before the Court in exile was steeped in French culture, English literature contained seeds of what was to come, and many of them had already germinated. This need cause no surprise; the Elizabethan glories of English literature, no less than the neo-classic glories of France, derived from humanism. Each country sought to achieve in its native tongue what it valued in the classics. And from one point of view it is not inaccurate to say that what is often regarded as typically Augustan in English was merely a natural development of something already present in the lifetime of Shakespeare.

So far we have proceeded as if nothing at all was written for the middle class and for the peasants and 'base mechanicals'. Indeed, as has been said above, that literature in which we usually glory as Elizabethan was written for the *élite*, or dominated by its concerns and attitudes. The only other section of society which was in any way articulate, or rather whose articulateness has been preserved in print, was the middle class. This does not mean, however, that there was a separate middle-class culture, whose literature differed in essential respects from that of the *élite*. Most of the evidence usually put forward to suggest that this separate culture existed is in fact proof to the contrary. It is true, for instance, that many middle-class writers had shared the education intended for their betters; but this very sharing led them to adopt, consciously or not, the ideals and practices of the *élite* in their writing. We may place Shakespeare in the middle class (if we are disposed to ignore the grant of arms to his father which put him technically among the gentry); but Shakespeare's plays and poems are essentially an expression of an aristocratic culture. The same is true of Marlowe and the other 'Cambridge wits'; whatever their origins, they absorbed and transmitted much that was aristocratic in origin.

In our treatment of the Elizabethan middle class we must beware of being misled by views put forward some decades ago respecting Elizabethan and Jacobean economics and sociology which are no longer completely accepted by historians. We must also be careful not to accept middle-class imitation of *élite* ideals and behaviour as evidence of middle-class as distinct from upper-class culture. Dekker and Deloney are unusual in their attempts to express essentially middle-class ideals and attitudes. Even so, Deloney affords us evidence of the pervading force of aristocratic attitudes and practices when, in *Jack of Newbury*, he defends Jack's lavish entertainment of the King as showing the magnanimity of weavers. In other words, what Deloney puts forward as admirable in the middle class is exactly what was to be found in aristocracy.

Only too often the heroes of middle-class romances and plays are not asserting the importance of an element of middle-class culture essentially different from that of the aristocracy; far from it, they usually ape the heroic deeds of noble champions, to prove that apprentices can shine in the same areas as their betters. And in our period there is no conscious insistence that, because middle-class virtues may be valid, therefore the whole principle of hierarchic subordination should be subverted. Jack of Newbury actually supports rather than subverts this principle when he refuses to leave the station in life into which he was born and elects to remain a weaver. So-called 'Puritan' attitudes (which are very difficult to isolate) are not necessarily merely middle-class; we must not therefore assume that simply because middle-class literature shows pride in that class, it is a sign of a growing repudiation of the upper as a better class, one which is to lead and to be obeyed. It is true that we can find in this literature seeds which flowered in middle-class life in the centuries that followed. But very little is to be found which is of fundamental importance and which differs from what we find in the literature of and for the *élite*. Even the middle-class insistence on the corrupting effect of idleness has its counterpart in aristocratic literature, and the image of men, like swords, rusting when unused, is itself aristocratic and has a long aristocratic history.

In treating this matter, it is again necessary to state frankly that this may be an erroneous view, but it is based on the evidence as I read it. How easily the evidence may be read another way is exemplified by a play, Heywood's *A Woman Killed with Kindness* (1607). I am referring to it in this chapter on non-dramatic literature, however, because its theme and plot concern the problem with which we are dealing. Ostensibly it is a middle-class play by that middle-class playwright who was called 'a prose Shakespeare'. Master Frankford may seem to us to be middle-class, but the title sets him among the gentry; so do his way of life, his estates, his friends, with knights among them. He is betrayed by his steward, not an officer of a middle-class household. Yet in his behaviour to the wife who has betrayed him with his trusted subordinate, Heywood makes Frankford flout obvious aristocratic principle and practice. The wronged husband does not kill; he does not avenge his honour on his wife or her paramour. Instead he sends her from his presence, from her children, to an outlying manor; there she tactfully wastes away, punishing herself in her consciousness of guilt, and most complaisantly dying, so that he may forgive her in a touching repentance and reconciliation at her death-bed. In so far as bloodshed is not resorted to for punishment and to avenge stained honour, we are in a middle-class world; but in so far as Frankford's honour is seen as stained, and his wife has to die, we are in the world of aristocracy, even if the death is natural technically (yet he drives her to it, as certainly as if he stabbed her). We must not argue that death-bed reconciliation is essentially middle-class rather than aristocratic, or we shall have to label Hamlet, Prince of Denmark, as having lost caste in that, when both are dying, he forgives Laertes for murdering him. Here the reader will, I hope, find why I look upon this play as fundamentally deriving from aristocratic not middle-class culture; here, too, he may see better than I do, and recognize my bias.

It is worth stating again, and with emphasis, that the foregoing account of the literature of the age of Shakespeare makes no claim to being exhaustive, and even less to providing any kind of a key which will unlock doors to knowledge and understanding which can be gained only by wide and deep reading. Those elements of English literature to which I have called attention have been selected as of greatest importance in relation to the picture of the age given in this book as a whole; they have not been selected, however, as evidence that this picture alone is valid. Today we are likely to discount the Elizabethan ideal of poetry as teaching and delighting with an imagined experience of the unfallen world and as a sophisticated mastery of technique, as well as an effort to reproduce in English civilisation what was admired in the classics. Because we believe (to my mind mistakenly) that the Augustans subordinated imagination to rational intellect, we commit the opposite error and ignore the fusion of rational intellect with imagination in the literature of the earlier period. Nevertheless, no theory or history of literature is as important as the individual response to individual works of art. The reader is advised to use this account and others only to help him to respond; whatever places itself between the reader and the work of art, assuring him that it is worthless because it is not something else, is to be viewed with great caution lest more bad criticism drive out good art from our civilization.

REFERENCES

[1] See *King Lear*, ed. B. L. Joseph (1966), pp. 38f., 155f.

[2] *A Defence of Poetry* (1599), ed. G. Gregory Smith, *Elizabethan Critical Essays* (1937), I, pp. 61ff.

[3] *Op. cit.*, tr. Wats, II, xiii, pp. 108f.

[4] *The Advancement of Learning* (1605), ed. J. E. Spingarn, *Critical Essays of the Seventeenth Century* (1908), I, p. 6.

[5] *An Answer to Davenant's Preface to Gondibert* (1650), ed. Spingarn, *op. cit.*, II, p. 60.

[6] *Ibid.*, p. 68.

[7] Ed. G. Gregory Smith, *op. cit.*, I, pp. 5ff.

[8] Ed. E. Seaton (1950).

[9] Ed. G. D. Willcock and A. Walker (1936), p. 210.

8: Drama in the Age of Shakespeare

THE drama of this age lends itself to a number of different treatments; we could consider it chronologically, divide it into categories in accordance with the themes, or into tragedy, comedy, tragicomedy, or treat individual dramatists separately. Instead of adopting any of these methods we shall give our first attention to considering what kind of an art Shakespeare and his contemporaries assumed drama to be, and whether, in fact, they were right. From time to time individual plays or playwrights will receive treatment, as will some of the more popular themes; but the main object is to discover what the dramatists and their audiences assumed about the art itself, what they thought was done in drama which is not done in non-dramatic literature, what theatre-goers expected from a performance which could not be obtained elsewhere.

In criticism, playwrighting and staging, English drama shows no sign of having been influenced by the development of European Neo-Classicism which saw the art as essentially one of deception; the artist is seen as seeking a compromise between his art as a poet and his need as a dramatist to present an audience with what they will accept as hardly distinguishable from what can be found in life outside art. After Castelvetro's commentary on Aristotle's *Poetics* in 1570 Neo-Classicism in Europe gradually succumbed to this view, with the result that while earlier critics demanded the unities of time, place and action as aesthetic necessities hallowed by Aristotle, after Castelvetro they were seen as essential to the dramatist's deception of his audience.

Castelvetro used a false logic and a misinterpretation of Aristotle to establish to his own satisfaction that tragedy is a greater form than epic. His argument runs that, as poetry is an imitation of life, its method must be one of verisimilitude, of fashioning the artistic medium into a close semblance of what is being imitated. The better the verisimilitude the better the poem.

He points out quite truthfully that in life we find not only insubstantial thoughts and words (spoken and unspoken) but such substantial things as men, women and children, houses, clothes, animals, boats and so on. In his terminology, 'Life consists of words and things'. The poet has to imitate both words and things with verisimilitude. The epic poet uses only words as his medium; he must imitate both words and things with words. A verbal imitation of words can have verisimilitude; but it is impossible with verisimilitude to imitate things by means of words.

The tragic poet, however, has not only words with which to imitate the words of life; he uses things, his actors, the stage, the properties to imitate the things of life. His imitation can be verisimilar; it follows, therefore, that a tragedy is a better (that is, more verisimilar) imitation of life, and is therefore a better poem.[1]

In his proof of the superiority of tragedy (which is, in fact, no real proof at all) Castelvetro seemed to have given a definitive account of drama as an art involving the theatre, an art, essentially, of deception by means of verisimilitude. Ideally, words should never be used to imitate things; only things can imitate things with verisimilitude. It is not necessarily true to claim that all later demands for a consistently realistic theatre derived from Castelvetro; but he was the first to make what appeared to be a logical case for this view of drama. It was a view which resulted, in France, Spain and Italy, in dramatists virtually accepting rules which aimed at achieving as much verisimilitude as contemporary taste held desirable. And deception of the audience was always the explicitly declared goal.

In England during this period, however, the view of drama which we have just examined gained no foothold, to judge by what was written by critics and playwrights, and, so far as the evidence suggests, by what was done in performance in the play-houses. Englishmen do not seem to have regarded drama as an art in which the audience is deceived, but as one in which it is stimulated into imagining. The performance is acknowledged as a work of art; there is no need to try to deceive anyone into believing that it is not.

v

Sidney's defence of the poet as a person who does not deceive applies to the playwright. Of all poets, dramatic and non-dramatic, Sidney declared (it will be remembered): 'The Poet never maketh any circles about your imagination, to conjure you to believe for true what he writes.' (*An Apology for Poetry*, ed. G. Smith, I, p. 185.) And to come more specifically to drama: 'What child is there that, coming to a play, and seeing *Thebes* written in great letters upon an old door, doth believe that it is Thebes?' (*ibid.*) That being so, what man is deceived? So his argument runs.

Sidney demands the unities in drama, but not as being essential to the creating of illusion by consistent realism. The unities are necessary to art, to art which does not try to deceive. This appears to be the view of Ben Jonson, if we are to take his practice as indicative of his conception of drama.

After 1660, when Howard and Dryden argue for and against rhyme and blank verse in drama, Howard's denunciation of rhyme insists that it is a breach of verisimilitude. People do not speak in rhyme outside art. Dryden's answer assumes Sidney's argument to some extent; he says it is not a matter of whether rhyme exists in dialogue outside drama, but whether it is used with satisfactory art to communicate the dramatist's imagining of a relationship between characters in dialogue.[2] Over sixty years earlier a dispute over the superiority of blank verse to rhyme in tragedy between Thomas Campion and Samuel Daniel did not even take verisimilitude into account. What mattered to both was the suitability or not of rhyme to the dignity of style essential for tragedy.[3]

Sir Richard Baker (who died in 1645) insisted that actors do not try to deceive the audience in the theatre, but to make them imagine: 'not to deceive, but to make others conceive.' (*Theatrum Triumphans* [1670], pp. 21ff.) I have not found before 1642 in England any explicit or implicit assertion that the aim and method of drama is to deceive by verisimilitude; rather that the dramatist asks other men 'to conceive', to imagine, as in any other form of art. But from Davenant's *Declamations at Rutland House* (1657) onwards we can find the admission or insistence that drama deceives. In these dialogues Aristophanes is made to defend dramatists from the charge of lying, not by Sidney's true account of what the art is, but by agreeing that deception takes place, but that it is harmless.[4] In this chapter we are dealing with the time between 1558 and 1629, when drama was regarded as harmless and as involving, not deception, but imagining.

What is known of Elizabethan stages confirms rather than conflicts with the conclusion drawn from the evidence just considered, that the Elizabethans did not attempt to deceive, but regarded drama like any other art as a communication of an imagining by the artist which stimulates other people into an equivalent imagining. There is much controversy as to the exact details of the architecture of Elizabethan stages; the theatres most often treated by modern historians of the stage are the Globe, the Swan, the Fortune, the Red Bull and the Blackfriars. All but this last named were outdoor theatres, with no roof over the auditorium which surrounded a large platform, jutting out from a structure built into the walls and known as the tiring-house. The audience's side of this wall formed a background against which the plays were performed. The other side of the wall were the changing rooms, hence the name tiring-house, for which another term was 'the players' vestry'.

Scholars still argue about the details of the wall of the tiring-house facing the audience; some interpret Elizabethan accounts as evidence for two or more doors, arranged symmetrically each side of a central inner stage (the 'study') above which was a gallery, or tarras (the 'chamber'). Some theatre historians, basing their case on the only contemporary drawing of a popular theatre, the Swan (by the Dutchman, De Witt, in 1596), reject the possibility of an inner stage, and claim that the upper gallery was used for spectators. Even when we have certain details of the dimensions of a theatre, such as the Fortune, there is still no certainty about the construction of the tiring-house façade, about the number of doors and windows, the existence of an inner stage, the use of the gallery. Some theatres had more than two levels for performance, that is, as many as three above the platform, and all seem to have had trapdoors, with access to and from a basement under it. The outdoor, or un-roofed, theatres had a penthouse above a portion of the platform near the tiring-house wall; performance necessarily took place in daylight. An indoor theatre such as the Blackfriars was lit artificially, and could be used at night. Again, details of such theatres are largely a matter of conjecture, which is itself no more than a dignified name for a guess.

There is evidence that three-dimensional structures (such as a small castle to represent a city), tents and booths were placed on the stage, though there is no certainty as to their positioning, or whether they remained in place throughout a performance, even in scenes in which they were not used. Artificial trees, fountains, arbours, were also used; but it does not seem that any of these structures or properties were intended to create illusion by means of consistent realism. The stage, with or without such helps, was primarily a playing space, on which the actors behaved as if they were in the place and conditions mentioned by or implied by the dialogue. The playing space was related to the three-dimensional structures and to the tiring-house wall with its doors, windows (of whatever number), inner and upper stages (if any). A stage door might represent the door of a palace at one moment, as in *King John* (I, i); the same stage door might later represent nothing at all, but merely provide access for the actors onto the stage, as in the same play (II, i) when the King of France with his army comes on stage through one door, and the King of England with his forces through the other. And, possibly, the gallery, or some elevated structure on the platform represented the walls of the city on which the citizens stand. Here we have an example of a fundamental principle of Elizabethan popular staging; the stage, or any part of it, or any structure on it, could represent anything which the action required, provided the actors behaved as if it were what it represented. Actors moving on the stage as if on the deck of a violently rocking boat at sea make us imagine it to be the deck of the imaginary boat in which the characters they represent are travelling. We imagine that they are the characters and the stage is the boat. Sometimes what was used resembled the represented feature as that is to be found outside art, sometimes it did not; but it could be treated by the players as if it did. For instance, the stage in bright sunlight could be treated by the actors as if it were a platform before a castle at dead of night. The actor with a lantern who behaved as if he required its light in the dark made the audience, who knew it was daylight, imagine a scene taking place in the dark in the imagined Elsinore of *Hamlet*.

What scenic effects the Elizabethan created were not intended to deceive, but, in Sir Richard Baker's words, 'to make others conceive'. There was plenty of noise, music, thunder, wind, cheering crowds, rain, cannon (alarums), as required; colour and pageantry were provided by hangings, banners, costumes. But the stage, and everything on it, was there for the use of the actors, who behaved as if they were the persons whom they represented in the appropriate places mentioned or implied in the text.

We have already noticed that one element of the life of noble households and of the Court was the staging of costly and luxurious masques. There is evidence that these were staged in specially converted halls, sometimes, at Court, in a hall built specially for the purpose. The methods of staging owed much to Inigo Jones after his return from Italy in 1605. He applied to the masque all that he had learned of staging in general in Italy. As a result, although the performance of regular drama was hardly affected, we can find that those who staged masques took advantage of Italian methods which had developed up to 1605; there was a raked stage to allow perspective scenery to function, the scenery itself consisting at first of three-dimensional wings, ranged in pairs between the downstage area and the back-drop or shutters. Also, the scene was enclosed in a perspective frame approximating to the proscenium arch; borders were used above the wings. In addition to scenery for perspective, masques took advantage of what could be done for spectacle by means of scenes which opened, moving clouds and glories, that is, a cloud or chair on which a supernatural personage could descend and ascend. By 1640 it seems clear that Court performance of some kinds of drama, like that of masques, made use of most of the machinery and methods of constructing and changing sets which were usual in the English theatre from the Restoration through the eighteenth century. Certainly the scenes could be changed by the same system, that is, by using pairs of flat-painted wings running in grooves in the stage floor parallel to the proscenium frame. Other grooves were used to move the borders which completed the perspective above the wings. And the wings themselves could be angled to prevent the size of the actors destroying the perspective. There was even a front curtain. As the stage was raked, that is, sloped upwards away from the audience, it was necessary to have a flat portion downstage on which the masquers could move; this, too, became normal practice in the performing of plays after 1660. It is fairly certain, however, that these methods did not spread to the popular theatres, private or public, before 1642.

Much confusion has occurred on the subject of Elizabethan acting, often the result of uncertainty among those who are not actors as to what, in fact, an actor does. Acting is behaving as if you were an imaginary person whom you represent. To say this is by no means to say what you have to do in order to act, but what you are doing when acting. To assess the evidence which survives as to the nature of Elizabethan acting it is necessary to understand not only what acting is, but what is demanded of the person training to become an actor, and then how he puts his acquired skills into effect when playing a role.

Evidence suggests that in the history of the Western world, at least, an actor plays a role competently when he is identified. That means that he has decided what it is that the role thinks, wants as an objective, and feels as a result in certain specific circumstances. The actor uses his imagination to know what it would be like to be the person he represents; he then uses his own body, voice, thoughts, wants and emotions in order to behave as if he were that person and, simultaneously, to communicate to his audience all that that means. The identified actor always knows that he is an actor using himself to communicate for an imagined character; nevertheless, while knowing that he is not, he behaves as if he were that person.

Extant evidence suggests that in the past and present there have been some few actors who prepare a role by achieving the identification just described; when it comes to actual performance, however, they do not repeat the experience; instead they are able to reproduce the external details of voice, movement, expression and so on, which were produced during preparation by being identified. But the sum of the evidence leads to the conclusion that the actors of the age of Shakespeare not only aimed at identification in rehearsal, but re-created the experience in every performance in order to appear 'the very man'.

A commendatory poem by Arthur Hopton, inserted before Heywood's *Apology for Actors* (1612), praises players because they 'appear to you to be the self-same men' whom they represent. In the book itself, Heywood says that in performance the audience responded 'as being wrapt in contemplation' (could a better description be found?) for it was 'as if the personator were the man personated, so bewitching a thing is lively and well-spirited action'. (Sigs. A1v°, B4r°.)

Elizabethan accounts assume that good acting approximates to 'doing it to the life', and is to be praised as 'lively' and 'natural'. In the play of the same name (1623) Nero asks: 'Did I not do it to the life?'; the reply comes:

> The very doing never was so lively
> As was this counterfeiting.
> (Anon., ed. Horne [1888], III, ii, pp. 41f.)

In the Prologue to *Ram Alley* (1609) the actor's art is described as:

> to show
> Things never done with that true life,
> That thoughts and wits should stand at strife,
> Whether the things now shown be true,
> Or whether we ourselves now do
> The things we but present.
> (W. C. Hazlitt, *Dodsley* [1875], X, p. 269.)

Coriolanus in Shakespeare's play does not object to deceiving the Romans; he merely doubts his ability to play the part well enough to deceive them because he detests them so much:

> You have put me now to such a part which never
> I shall discharge to th'life   (III, ii. 105–6.)

And it is in accordance with the same view of acting that Randolph praised Thomas Riley's performance in *The Jealous Lovers* (1632):

> When thou dost act, men think it not a play
> But all they see is real.

('To his friend, Thomas Riley' [1632], in *Poetical and Dramatic Works of Thomas Randolph*, ed. W. C. Hazlitt [1875], I, p. 60.)

And a character of *An Excellent Actor* (attributed to John Webster) declares in 1615: 'What we see him personate, we think truly done before us.' (*New and Choice Characters of Several Authors*, 6th ed. [1615], p. 147.)

Just after the Restoration, Flecknoe praised the power of identification shown by Shakespeare's actor, Burbage: 'a delightful Proteus, so wholly transforming himself into his part, and putting off himself with his clothes, as he never (not so much as in the tiring-house) assumed himself until the play was done'. It is not surprising to be told that he went on acting the role fully, 'never falling in his part when he had done speaking, but with his looks and gesture maintaining it still unto the height'. (*A Short Discourse of the English Stage* [1664], Sig. G7r°.)

Contemporary accounts of both Burbage and Riley bear witness to their ability to identify closely with each individual role. The elegy on Burbage says:

> He's gone, and with him what a world are dead,
> Which he reviv'd to be revived so.
> No more young Hamlet, old Hieronymo.
> King Lear, the grieved Moor, and more beside,
> That liv'd in him, have now for ever died.
> Oft have I seen him leap into the grave,
> Suiting the person which he seem'd to have
> Of a sad lover with so true an eye,
> That there I would have sworn he meant to die.
> Oft have I seen him play this part in jest,
> So lively that spectators and the rest
> Of his sad crew, whilst he but seem'd to bleed,
> Amaz'd, thought even then he died indeed.

(Repr. Sir Edmund Chambers, *The Elizabethan Stage* [1923], II, p. 309.)

Flecknoe talks of Burbage as 'Proteus'; Randolph praised the same ability to 'change shape' in Riley:

I have seen a Proteus, that can take
What shape he please, and in an instant make
Himself to anything: be that or this
By voluntary metamorphosis . . .
. . . O, that day
(When I had cause to blush that this poor thing
Did kiss a Queen's hand, and salute a King)
How often had I lost thee! I could find
One of thy stature, but in every kind
Alter'd from him I knew; nay, I in thee
Could all professions and all passions see.
When thou art pleas'd to act an angry part,
Thou fright'st the audience; and with nimble art
Turn'd lover, thou dost that so lively too,
Men think that Cupid taught thee how to woo.

(op. cit., I, p. 60.)

The playwrights, actors and audiences of Shakespeare's age all seem agreed that the player should appear to be the person whom he represents as if come to life. Whatever the actor did, in fact, the result was that he sounded and looked to the audience as if he were a particular human being behaving as such a person would behave. The fact that he spoke blank verse or rhyme or unrealistic prose meant that he communicated their qualities as language; but it did not mean that he used tones or stood or moved or sat in a way that seemed unnatural.

Human beings communicate with one another outside art not merely by verbalising, by articulating words with specific senses all relating to one another to make up meaning; we find that what we want to communicate results in stresses, in changes in pitch, in volume, in intensity, in length of syllables, in the pace of the voice; simultaneously, expression, movement of speakers, glance of the eyes, poise of head, of the whole body, quite apart from hands and arms; all these non-verbal expressions of meaning are fused with what we say verbally. In art the actor uses all these elements which are natural to human beings outside art; but he uses them to communicate as if he were an imaginary character in a relationship with others in a particular situation. The evidence is that this was true of Elizabethan actors, as it was true of Elizabethans living their lives outside art.

When all this is known, however, we still cannot be certain what the Elizabethan actor did when he appeared on stage as if he were the very man. We do not know if he did exactly what he would have done offstage. He apparently conformed to real-life behaviour in such things as bowing, kneeling to superiors, covering and uncovering his head. We can find in *Chironomia* and *Chirologia* by John Bulwer (1644) and in other similar works quite a number of descriptions of the ways in which people in this period actually communicated non-verbally offstage. Often what is described is so natural to human beings that it is still found on and off the stage today. And some 'actions' (as non-verbal communication was called) can be found described explicitly or implied in the texts of individual plays as well as in books on the art of acting. Bulwer gives an account of 'biting the thumb' which is confirmed by the opening scene of *Romeo and Juliet*. He also tells how many of the Covenanters on the Scottish border in 1639 took the oath with two hands, not one, held up to heaven, as a sincere communication of the intensity of their determination. Beaumont and Fletcher's *The Maid's Tragedy* has a scene in which Melantius tells his sister, Evadne, to swear, raising both her hands to heaven, that she will not yield to the king again.[5] (IV, i. 164–5.)

But to know such things is still not to know exactly what Elizabethans did on the stage. When we try to imagine how an actor succeeded in behaving as if he were the character whom he represented to the satisfaction of his contemporaries, we have to take into account what they expected in the theatre, what relation it bore to what they expected from such a person in similar situations in life outside the theatre. We also need to remember that the actor may well have been acting lines which would not be spoken by such a person in real life.

Elsewhere[6] I have called attention to the demands made by such lines as Romeo's when he wants to make Juliet realize that it is the dawn and he must go:

> Look, love, what envious streaks
> Do lace the severing clouds in yonder east
>
> (III, v. 7–8.)

Nevertheless, this passage will serve most conveniently to illustrate the points to be made here. The first two words, 'Look, love', are realistic; that is to say, they closely resemble what might actually be said by such a person outside art in such a situation. But the rest of the statement is not what such a man would really speak outside a play. Romeo's image describes what he sees and communicates his reaction to it, all as something he does to obtain his objective, to persuade her to recognize that the time has come to part. He sees a split in the darkness, with streaks of light, looking like lacing, criss-crossing from one side of darkness to the other. But he implies that, whereas lacing normally holds severing parts together, this lacing of light will push the splitting fragments of darkness further apart; they derive from the same source as the line of light which severs the clouds. The adjective 'envious' communicates Romeo's bitterness that the light in the east virtually begrudges him and his wife any longer time together. This as a whole is a complex poetic statement; nevertheless it communicates what such a man would think, want and feel, even if not in the words which he would actually use, outside a play. The Elizabethan actor (like the modern) satisfied the demands of this poetic statement by communicating through it what goes on within Romeo. His tones were those natural to him to communicate this meaning, his movement, his 'action' as a whole achieving the same end. Every sound was natural; but the pattern of natural sounds derived from the verbal pattern of the lines. The result was an artificial pattern of utterly natural sounds. He seemed 'the self-same man', and he did justice to his lines as a poetic statement.

The actor became identified as the result of knowing the senses of the individual words and why they are used by the character; his 'action' consists of using them as if he were the character. The process of preparation makes him very much aware of the relationship of word to word both as a pattern of articulate sound and as a communication of meaning. The physical rhythm of his performance is produced partly by the verbal arrangement of his lines, partly by what he thinks, feels, wants as he behaves as if he were the imaginary character. His emphasis, his changes of pitch, stress, length of vowel, embody the verbal patternings of his lines. The Elizabethan achieved all this in performance as the result of appropriate training of voice, body and imagination. He was on a stage, which was not consistently realistic, acting in a play which was not consistently realistic. But thanks to this training he satisfied his audiences by appearing to them as if he were the very man.

That Elizabethan actors received the necessary training is the conclusion suggested by such evidence as survives.[7] This is to be found in two separate kinds of sources: first in the comparatively few Elizabethan accounts of stage-playing itself; and second in much fuller accounts of the art of verbal and non-verbal communication, known variously as the 'action' or 'pronunciation' of the orator or the rhetorician. In this, boys and men were trained as in stage-playing to use all those changes of voice, body and expression which are normal to human beings to communicate their meaning, but as perfectly as possible, and taking into account what is to be communicated, where and to whom.

The connection between the verbal and non-verbal communication of the orator and that of the player has been misconceived by some modern writers as one in which the latter learned from the former. Just the opposite is true; the orator was advised to watch and study with the player to learn the ultimate perfection of his art. That is why we should not be surprised to read in one of Shakespeare's contemporaries: 'In the substance of external action for most part orators and stage-players agree.' (Thomas Wright, *The Passions of the Mind in General* [1604], p. 179.) The great difference lies in the fact that the orator speaks in his own person, or uses his voice and body, his 'action', to communicate what he wants, while the actor puts all his physical and mental resources into communicating what is wanted by the role he is playing. Differences also derive from the respective differences of place, occasion, audience, of orator and actor.

Training in acting stage plays was considered one of the essential ways of developing one's powers as an orator. This was partly because the actual process of communicating verbally and non-verbally was the same in each, and partly because the discipline of appearing on a stage in performance gave a self-confidence and competence to the individual. In school and university, training was given in this way; and from accounts of what was done we can read that schoolboy and undergraduate were instructed to become identified with the role, to behave 'as if' they themselves needed to speak the lines, not only lines in a play but lines which they might be given to 'pronounce' as part of a dialogue in the learning of Latin.[8]

Descriptions of Elizabethan stage-players say that the excellent actor did to perfection what was managed no more than satis-factorily by the orator. We find in the teaching of 'action' to orators an insistence on the need to relate the individual words of a passage of the text to the inner needs of the character speaking. Boys were told to notice the key-words of the rhetorical figures, these being the ones which needed emphasis in speaking. In actual fact, however, in order to recognize the key-words of the figures you have to understand them as a communication of meaning as well as a verbal pattern. So that recognition of verbal arrangement and of what is being communicated by the words in the arrange-ment is one and the same thing. Emphasis, moreover, was not a matter of mechanically depressing or elevating pitch, alternating stress, changing length, intensity and volume. These elements of 'action' were the result of articulating the words to communicate meaning. To be told that the Elizabethan actor 'had all the parts of' an excellent orator is to learn, not that acting was mechanical and without identification, but that the identified actor did to perfection everything which we know the orator was striving for; and the actor, inasmuch as he acted a role, did much not within the orator's scope. From the teaching of the orator's 'action' at school, how-ever, we can find out much about that common ground, that 'most part' in which actors and orators agreed. In particular we learn to understand the way in which the actor performed what was de-manded by his lines both as expression of character and as poetic statement.

Writing on the acting of Shakespeare's age is sometimes misunderstood today as a result in changes in psychological theory. The Elizabethans talk of 'external action', a term which is anathema to modern minds, convinced that 'external' acting is superficial, false, mechanical. Among modern psychologists the view that the human body, all that is 'external', obeys the prompting or guidance of an inner 'reality', 'soul', 'mind', has become outmoded. But writers on acting rarely avail themselves of modern psychology; they still try to interpret the processes of acting in accordance with the notion deriving from Descartes that body is ruled by mind. To such thinking 'external action' must seem bad acting.[9]

But Elizabethan psychology viewed the relationship of 'body'/ 'mind' in human beings in a manner which approximates very closely to that of modern psychologists, though without the support of factual experimental evidence. For Shakespeare's age, we remember, a living person is an inextricable fusion of body/soul. Death separates the two, but in life they are one. What the body did was also done by the soul. Reason, imagination, wanting, emotion, voice, body, all were seen as inextricably linked; that is why external action was seen as a mirror of an internal emotion, thought, desire. The 'inner reality' and its 'outer show' were the same thing. And it was emphasized that in oratory, as in stage-playing, to make others feel, you must feel yourself.

Hamlet's account of the Player's response to his own imagining of the fall of Troy sums up the Elizabethan view of acting; it is a process in which the 'whole function' suits 'with forms' to what the actor is imagining. 'Function' is the word used by Elizabethans of the single operation of body-soul as one entity:

> Tears in his eyes, distraction in's aspect,
> A broken voice, and his whole function suiting
> With forms to his conceit.   (II, ii. 548–50.)

And it is all for an imaginary person who means nothing at all to the Player as a person. But the Player as an actor has imagined what it is like to care about Hecuba, to have seen the last hours of Troy. He behaves as if it had all happened to him, using his own mental and imaginative powers, his trained voice, body, face, to communicate as if he were the very man.

Hamlet's words to the Players have been responsible for modern misunderstanding. Here is nothing on acting that Shakespeare would have cared to claim as his own. Hamlet says what everybody else said; the direction not to saw the air comes from Quintilian, the Roman orator who was studied in the Elizabethan grammar school. And so far as I can ascertain there was no stiff, unnatural, exaggerated contemporary fashion of acting (its chief exponent was certainly not Alleyn) to be attacked by these words.

Hamlet has a different reason for speaking about acting. He relies on the First Player performing correctly one speech which has been put into the play to catch Claudius off guard. Hamlet says 'Speak the speech', and he means 'the speech', the speech which he has himself just written. The Player has not yet rehearsed it, has merely heard Hamlet 'pronounce' it. Hamlet cannot tell the Players of the importance of this speech, and the play as a whole, to him in ending his uncertainty about his uncle and the Ghost. A badly performed speech will not help; if Claudius does not betray himself it might be because the speech is not played well enough. The Prince therefore stresses the importance of the speech as part of a general statement about the 'purpose of playing', which is to make people recognize themselves in the characters of the play. He wants Claudius to recognize himself in the murdering usurper on stage. So we need not be surprised to find that the so-called 'directions to the Players' are a collection of generally accepted tags which everyone had heard on the subject of acting. They tell us nothing which is not to be found elsewhere.

We see that what is known about acting, staging, theatre-structure in this period conforms to the Elizabethan assumption that drama is an art which does not lose its force as such by the admission that it is art. What the audience heard and saw in performance was not designed to deceive them into the belief that this was not a work of art. They imagined and knew that they were imagining, in the words of Thomas Heywood, 'as if wrapt in contemplation'. They responded as if 'the personator were the man personated'. And they responded also to the dramatist's art as an imaginer of relationships in action, which was also an art of verbal felicity. To write a good play, which staged well, there was no need to abandon all that you had acquired of the art of a poet, as that exists outside drama; you put your mastery of that art at your own disposal (and that of player and audience) in your imagining of drama.

The difference between drama and non-drama lies in what is being imagined. The dramatist always imagines in terms of characters in action. The words he gives them tell us what he has imagined them doing to attain an objective. The difference between non-dramatic and dramatic imagining is easily illustrated by Plutarch's account of Cleopatra at Cydnus in contrast to Shakespeare's imagining of the scene; his Enobarbus recalls it for a specific reason, to communicate to the Romans who have questioned him just what kind of a woman she is, the spell she exerts, the improbability of a woman like Octavia having the power to oust her from Antony's life. Plutarch gives us a lively account simply to let us know what happened; he speaks to us directly in his own person as writer. But Shakespeare does not speak in his own person directly; he imagines an occasion in which for a specific reason Enobarbus re-experiences what happened in the past as if it were happening again, his objective being to let the Romans know. His attitudes to them, to Cleopatra, Antony, Octavius and Octavia are all involved in the imagining. And Shakespeare does not tell us any of these non-dramatically by narration; they are implied by the words of Enobarbus in the situation, in relation to other imaginary persons and to the forces which he assumes in the world. The words are good writing in their own right; but they also let us know what is done by Enobarbus, what he thinks, wants and feels; that is what makes them dramatic.

The Elizabethan dramatist was at liberty to use his art as a poet, an art which he shared with the non-dramatic poet, provided what he communicated by this art was a dramatic imagining, that is of relationship of character to character in action. We must therefore expect to find in Elizabethan drama many of those characteristics of writing which we also find in the non-dramatic writing of the age. Thus Lyly gives us in his plays the same kind of prose as he gives us in *Euphues*, with this great difference, that the patterning of *Endymion*, for instance, communicates the inner life of the speaker in action. Shakespeare's Doctor in *Macbeth* speaks in prose in the patterning of balance and antithesis which we have observed in non-dramatic writing:

> A great perturbation in nature, to receive at once the benefit of
> sleep and do the effects of watching! (V, i. 9–11.)

'Perturbation in nature' means upsetting of the physiological processes; 'watching' means staying awake. Here we have a linking of *receive—do*; *benefit—effects*; *of sleep—of watching*. The same play gives us a more intricate example of this balancing in verse running through lines of dialogue:

> *Macbeth*   My dearest love,
>   Duncan comes here tonight.
> *Lady Macbeth*   And when goes hence?
>
>   (I, v. 55–6.)

The balance is between *comes—goes*; *here—hence*; *tonight—when*.[10]

The Elizabethan and Jacobean dramatists employ the techniques of non-dramatic writing in their dramatic imagining. We may find any figure of words mentioned in the books on rhetoric, similarly tropes and figures of sentence (expressions of emotion). Modern criticism is particularly aware of the dramatist's imagery as expressive of implication and theme. We do not, however, pay enough attention to the imagery as a communication of what the character does in action. We noticed that Romeo's image of the dawn splitting and lacing the darkness communicates what he wants, feels and thinks. This is true of all dramatic imagery. It always communicates in action what is going on within the speaker. Imagery of darkness communicates Shakespeare's imagining of meaning in *Macbeth* involving conflict between evil and good; but Macbeth's own needs, his own objective, not to be exposed, are communicated in his imagery; his wife's objective, to be given the strength to kill Duncan herself, is communicated in hers; and Juliet's natural longing for protection for her married love for Romeo is communicated in the images which she uses of darkness and night.

When imagery paints for us a scene which cannot be or is not

w

shown on the stage, again the inner life of the character is communicated in action. And it is only when the imagery expresses what the character thinks, wants and feels as an action in a relationship of characters that the actor can enable his audience to respond at least as fully as when reading the lines in the book.

According to one Elizabethan who enjoyed the performances of Burbage and Alleyn, the greatest pleasure of a play lay in performance, simply because then he could respond to the author's imagining of character in action, an imagining communicated by means of words suited to the person, and acting deriving from the words. For him 'action' was the greatest pleasure of a play; and by 'action' he meant what happened when an actor responded to the verbal text, perceiving relationship of word to word not only as relationship of sound, but as meaning for the imagined character. The acting made all this apparent to the audience in a relationship in space on the stage between actors behaving as if they were the men and women whom the author has imagined in action; he explains in what lies the essential pleasure of a good performance:

> It is the ingeniousness of the speech, when it is fitted to the person; and the gracefulness of the action when it is fitted to the speech; and therefore a play read hath not half the pleasure of a play acted: for though it have the pleasure of ingenious speeches, yet it wants the pleasure of graceful action.
>
> (Sir Richard Baker, *op. cit.*, pp. 34f.)

The dialogue is appropriate to the characters; and the acting, inasmuch as it is appropriate to the dialogue, is also appropriate to the characters.

In yet more respects than these which we have already noticed, humanistic education exerted an influence on the popular drama of England. The strict rules of Neo-Classicism insisted upon the preservation of the unities of place, action and time. These obviously were flouted, except when a dramatist deliberately wrote in accordance with them, as Shakespeare did in *The Tempest* and Jonson in *Volpone*; but popular dramatists learned in school something about plotting which enabled them to maintain coherence of action even when there was more than one plot. Neo-classic demands that tragedy and comedy, high and low persons and styles, must not be mixed were not binding on the popular dramatists; yet these writers tended to write tragedies concerning persons of high social standing. No tragedy by Shakespeare has a person of less than noble birth for a protagonist; Marlowe's Faustus and Tamburlaine develop the characteristics of noblemen, do not behave in accordance with their lowly origin. The style of popular tragedy, despite comic episodes, is predominantly high, aspiring after dignity if not achieving it. Conversely, most Elizabethan comedy treats of low persons in a low style. Moreover, Jonson's care to keep his style low enough, even in *Volpone*, did not make his comedy unpopular.

Neo-Classicism probably influenced Elizabethan dramatic plotting much more than is usually realized today. The schoolmasters were often what we would call 'practical critics' now; they analysed not only the verbal but the dramatic techniques of plays in Latin (classical and renaissance) and, to a lesser extent, in Greek. By the late sixteenth century much critical attention to Roman comedy had resulted in an ideal dramatic structure being put forward as suitable for contemporary drama, including tragedy. Elsewhere I have called attention to the fact that several of Shakespeare's tragedies are constructed in accordance with the notion of dramatic structure associated with Scaliger. It is mentioned in *Roman Antiquities* by Thomas Godwin (1614), by Dryden in his analysis of Jonson's *Silent Woman* after the Restoration, and was taught in Elizabethan grammar schools in Shakespeare's lifetime.[11]

Popular dramatists did not conform strictly to neo-classical demands, but in their own ways made use of what they cared to. The ideals of good writing in drama were those of good writing outside, provided every word was needed by the speaker in his imagined relationship. What made Shakespeare's non-dramatic sonnets good writing also made his dramatic sonnets good as writing; but their dramatic quality lies in their communication of, for instance, the relationship of Romeo and Juliet, each with a specific objective in that first meeting during the festivity at her house.

Many of the essential elements demanded by the humanists were in fact supplied by the popular dramatists but in a less rigid way.

The neo-classic and the popular view of drama agreed in England during this period (as distinct from the neo-classic view in Europe) that it is an art of imagining character relationships in action; it is not an attempt to deceive an audience with more or less consistent realism, but a communication of an imagining by an artist, or in other words, a work of art. John Webster really speaks for the popular dramatists as a whole when he writes in his Preface to *The White Devil* (1612) that his mistakes (including deviations from neo-classic demands) were not ignorantly, but willingly committed. In fact the defects of this play, like those of *The Duchess of Malfi* (1623), are due, not to breaking neo-classical rules, but to sloppy imagining, weak construction, incomplete characterization. As he himself admitted, his actors were able to overcome his defects in the theatre by imagining more consistently and communicating their imagining in their performance.

In one modern view Webster wrote a special kind of 'satiric' tragedy, communicating in an orderly artistic manner his awareness of a chaotic universe. It is equally possible, however, (and to my mind more accurate) to see in his tragedies an artistically chaotic communication of a vision of an ordered universe; the chaos comes not from his vision, but from his artistic defects, defects which he did not deny.

It is necessary to state emphatically a point of view rarely encountered today; that is, that apart from Shakespeare and Jonson, with the possible exception of Marlowe and Webster, most of the popular drama of this age is artistically weak. We should also exclude much of the middle-class comedy from this judgment; but Marston, Massinger, Beaumont and Fletcher in their would-be serious writing are hardly ever more than second-rate, and often much worse. The fact that they have written in verse seems to have dazzled our eyes to their defects. Their plays are for the most part to be compared with the average undistinguished modern television play, dependent on the actors and on the acquiescence of an audience expecting nothing better. Jonson's contemporaries laughed at him, not because they rejected Neo-Classicism in principle, but because they could not relate what they accepted in principle to the practice of entertaining popular or Court audiences. He seemed ludicrously pedantic in his determination to maintain in his writing for the popular stage the principles which were regarded as ideal.

The dramatists of this age wrote histories, pastorals, romances, comedies, tragedies and tragi-comedies. Some plays were written merely for entertainment. Others communicate to us the artists' response to life, part of which response can be abstracted and expressed as an intellectual statement. But as in every age there were far fewer men who made a play an artistic fusion of imagining and meaning because they needed to, and far more men who touched superficially on a matter which they were not gifted enough to treat satisfactorily. Nevertheless, the drama as a whole shows us much that we have seen as historical fact in earlier chapters. It remains to be said, however, that the quality of a dramatist does not lie in his accuracy or the copiousness of his information on some aspect of society or thought; his quality lies in his ability as an artist to imagine and communicate to us an integrated coherent statement in the form of a work of art.

REFERENCES

[1] L. Castelvetro, *Poetica d 'Aristotele* (1570), p. 16. See also H. B. Charlton, *Castelvetro's Theory of Poetry* (1913), p. 84; A. H. Gilbert, *Literary Theory from Plato to Dryden* (1940), pp. 305f. I have discussed the importance of Castekvetro's *Poetica d'Aristotele* in these respects in *Elizabethan Acting* (1951), p. 113f., and in 'The Elizabethan Stage and Acting' in *The Age of Shakespeare*, ed. B. Ford (1955), pp. 147ff.

[2] J. Dryden, *An Essay of Dramatic Poesy* (1668), ed. W. H. Hudson (1931), pp. 61ff.

[3] T. Campion, *Observations in the Art of English Poesy* (1602) and S. Daniel, *A Defence of Rhyme* (?1603), both ed. G. Gregory Smith, *op. cit.*, II, pp. 351, 382.

[4] Sir William Davenant, *Works* (1673), sigs. Uu4 (p. 341), Xx 2 (p. 345).

[5] *Chirologia*, p. 160, *Romeo and Juliet*, I, i. 41-2 and *Chirologia*, pp. 51f.

[6] Joseph, *Elizabethan Acting* (2nd ed., 1964), pp. 25ff, 83f.

[7] See Joseph, *op. cit.*

[8] *Ibid.*, pp. 7ff.

[9] B. L. Joseph, *Acting Shakespeare* (2nd Ed. 1969), p. xiii.

[10] B. L. Joseph, *The Artistry of Shakespeare. The Drama and Language of Macbeth* (1968), 5ff.

[11] Godwin, *op. cit.*, pp. 70ff; Dryden, *Essay of Dramatic Poesy*, ed. cit., pp. 16, 42ff.

9: Shakespeare in His Age

To read Shakespeare is to find much to which we become accustomed when we study the age in which he lived; but there is hardly a trace that he was aware of any of the changes which were taking place in scientific thinking and practice. Parliament hardly enters the world of his work; if we relied on his plays we would not suspect the changes taking place in English society. We can learn of such personages as the Queen and Essex; he knows about the exploration of new lands and seas. His world is obviously the world which we noticed in Chapter Two, a world in which a small *élite* dominates, in which hierarchy differentiates all in their appropriate steps from lowest up to highest, in which the subject has a duty always to obey, in which the monarch rules by divine right and the magistrate governs in accordance with divine intention. He knows about the governing of the kingdom through the various courts, the justices of peace, the local officials, such as the watch, constables and beadles. But he shows little, if any, sign of an awareness of a failure of nerve among his contemporaries; which is not surprising, in that we have found little evidence for any such failure in the appropriate sections of this book.

Nevertheless, it must be recognized that one characteristic of the greater writers of all times has often been an insight into the significance of contemporary events and thoughts, an articulate awareness of what is developing towards a future climax. Such artists see more clearly and powerfully than the rest of us; they observe signs which we ignore, they interpret more accurately the meaning of what they see. I myself do not find this particular sort of insight in Shakespeare; but many people find it in him, particularly in *King Lear*. Later in this chapter we shall consider the possibility that in that play he is communicating his awareness of the passing of an age of certainties, of order and tenderness between man and man, an age which is giving way to a harsh neo-barbarism, in which man's relation to man is that of predator to his prey, in which faith with its consolations will disappear, as if he had gazed like Thomas Hardy at an unrelenting deterministic universe in which human beings are the playthings of indifferent forces. Allowing for the possibility that Shakespeare is indeed contemplating such a world in *King Lear*, a world for him of both present and future, his work gives little hint of the enormous changes going on around him. We might rejoice in the fact that for him the world had a stability which is expressed in his art. We cannot prove what he believed or disbelieved; but we can certainly say that he wrote in terms of many contemporary certainties, and as if he shared them. He seems to have been responding to the world around him as if the human beings in it were much as they have always been since the Fall, and much as they are likely to continue to be until the Day of Judgment.

I must insist that I am not trying to prove that Shakespeare was a Christian (of any particular denomination), an atheist or a sceptic. But he writes as if he accepted broadly the doctrines of the Elizabethan Anglican Church (though there are traces of Catholic thought in some places). The fact that an artist seems to write in accordance with a religious faith by no means proves that he held this faith; the very fact that he is an artist allows him to use his imagination to write as if he believed. On the other hand the consistency of Shakespeare's imagining in terms of what might be called the 'Old Philosophy' must make us wonder why he chose to exercise his creative imagination in this way, if in truth he was personally detached from the religion and *Weltanschauung* of his writings. As has been noted above, he lives imaginatively in a world which began with Creation, which has suffered a Fall, and which will continue to be much as it is until Doomsday. He seems to accept the Redemption as a fact. For him the time between the Fall and the Day of Judgment is something without substance; it will all pass away, and only life in eternity will endure. We find this in Macbeth's reference to his life on this earth before death as on 'this bank and shoal of time' (I, viii. 6). The sea of time is ever in motion, has no stability; compared with it a sandbank is solid; but compared with dry land the sand bank is insubstantial. Even so human life compared with the ceaseless flux of time has an illusory stability; but compared with eternity human life is insubstantial.

Shakespeare's ability to imagine in terms of Christian certainty of Doomsday shows itself in Macbeth's words when he hears of his wife's death. He looks forward into time, seeing day followed by day right up to the moment on the Day of Judgment when there will be no more history to be written, 'to the last syllable of recorded time' (V, v. 17–21). Then 'time shall have a stop'. Prospero looks forward in time to this same moment when he tells Ferdinand not to be dismayed by the sudden disappearance of the insubstantial spirits which seemed so substantial. Even so, he reminds the prince, human life is insubstantial, we ourselves have no substance, and the day will come when the whole world disappears into nothing, just like the insubstantial pageant of spirits. This being so there is no need to find consternation in the disappearance of spirits; the seemingly solid world will prove to have no more substance than 'the baseless fabric of this vision'. Prospero emphasizes the insubstantiality of this life again when he says 'we are such stuff/ As dreams are made on'. By 'dreams' he means imagining, fictions without substance; and just as dreams emerge into our consciousness out of darkness, to merge back into darkness, so does human life:

> These our actors,
> As I foretold you, were all spirits, and
> Melted into air, into thin air;
> And, like the baseless fabric of this vision,
> The cloud-capp'd towers, the gorgeous palaces,
> The solemn temples, the great globe itself,
> Yea, all which it inherit, shall dissolve,
> And, like this insubstantial pageant faded,
> Leave not a rack behind. We are such stuff
> As dreams are made on; and our little life
> Is rounded with a sleep.
>
> (*The Tempest*, IV, i. 148–158.)

Macbeth's fear of 'judgment here' before his death makes sense only in relation to an awareness of judgment after death on Doomsday, as usual for those who have not committed his particular brand of regicide.

Elizabethan Christianity, it will be recalled from Chapter Six, taught that everything that has ever happened and everything that may ever happen is foreseen by the Providence of God. What is to human comprehension a long sequence of events stretching out through time takes place simultaneously in a split second in the consciousness of God. Before creating the world, before the Fall of the Angels, God's prescience was aware of the assaults to be made by Satan upon Adam and Eve and all their descendants till the very moment of Doomsday; no event is regarded by this doctrine as too small, too insignificant for His prescience to take into account. Since the Creation this world has been governed by God's Providence, by what was known as his General Providence in larger, general matters; and by Special Providence so far as concerns individual persons and events. In the never-ending conflict with Satan in the course of this world before the Day of Judgment, Providence achieves its ends ultimately by working through Fortune and the free will of individual human beings.

It will be recalled that in Chapter Six we examined the function of the stars in their exerting of influence on human beings. Providence works through such influence as through everything else. The stars do not determine; they merely incline, give a tendency or impulse towards a certain kind of behaviour or action; but human beings possess free will; the rational soul is not subject to Fortune, to the influence of the stars; by the exercise of reason we cannot fight the stars, we can, however, negate them by a sort of spiritual jiu-jitsu, exercising patience and taking advantage of opportunity where it presents itself.

This is what Cassius tells Brutus, trying to involve him in conspiracy against Caesar:

Men at some time are masters of their fates;
The fault, dear British, is not in our stars,
But in ourselves, that we are underlings.
(*Julius Caesar*, I, ii. 139–40.)

Later, the relationship between Brutus and Cassius is reversed, when, before Philippi, the former urges action:

> There is a tide in the affairs of men
> Which taken at the flood, leads on to fortune;
> Omitted, all the voyage of their life
> Is bound in shallows and in miseries.
>
> (IV, iii. 216–19.)

The difficulty is to recognize whether the opportunity has indeed come; whether in fact the stars are not auspicious and human effort will be frustrated. Brutus and Cassius do not succeed, partly because of faults in themselves and partly because of faults in their stars.

Helena, in *All's Well that Ends Well*, makes their mistake of thinking that human will can prevail, that the stars and Fortune can be fought and beaten:

> Our remedies oft in ourselves do lie,
> Which we ascribe to heaven. The fated sky
> Gives us free scope; only doth backward pull
> Our slow designs when we ourselves are dull.
>
> (I, ii. 202–05.)

As she will find, her speed, her determination to act, not wait, to force matters to a head, does not bring her married love quickly. 'The fated sky,' under the government of Providence, lets her win her husband, and lose him immediately. Her 'scope' is 'free' to make mistakes, her designs are pulled 'backward' when she herself is not 'dull'.

Shakespeare's plays show what Milton calls 'the ways of God' as mysterious and inscrutable. Milton justified them, not by apology, but by bearing triumphant witness to their justice in an epic poem of twelve books. So far as Shakespeare gives an indication of an attitude to God's 'ways', it agrees with Milton's. Men cannot see enough; their 'scope' can therefore lead them into error as well as truth. 'Patience' is essential; Fortune can be circumvented only by means of Christian fortitude, a combination of passivity and action.

Thus when, in *The Winter's Tale*, Hermione recognizes the useless-
ness of fighting against events, she reaches the classic decision:

> There's some ill planet reigns.
> I must be patient till the heavens look
> With an aspect more favourable.   (II, i. 105–7.)

She has to wait patiently for sixteen years, during which time
Providence works through Fortune and human beings to bring
back Perdita, Polixenes, Camillo and a new son, Florizel. This is an
extreme case in a romantic tale, but it confirms the accepted
doctrine.

Not inappropriately (if it was the last of Shakespeare's plays),
The Tempest is imagined coherently in terms of the doctrine of
Providence, from which comes the ability to face humanity as
fallen, but not beyond redemption, which gives the play so stable a
maturity. In the past Prospero fell into error, neglecting his duty as
ruler, exposing his subjects, a brother among them, to temptation.
The error brought disaster; but the disaster was not irreparable,
thanks to a number of facts and persons. The conspirators did not
dare destroy Prospero and Miranda outright, but set them adrift in
a rotten, unseaworthy boat. Thus was Gonzalo able to perform his
act of 'charity', providing them not only with obvious necessaries
for survival, but with the apparent luxury of Prospero's books.

Well does Prospero ascribe their survival to 'Providence divine'.
The presence of his infant daughter saved him from despair at sea;
her angelic fortitude inspired him with 'an undergoing stomach':

> O, a cherubin
> Thou wast that did preserve me! Thou didst smile,
> Infused with a fortitude from heaven,
> When I have deck'd the sea with drops full salt,
> Under my burden groan'd; which rais'd in me
> An undergoing stomach, to bear up
> Against what should ensue.   (II, ii. 152–8.)

Once Providence has brought them ashore, Prospero takes advantage of the books given him out of Gonzalo's love and loyalty.
Twelve long years are spent partly in self-examination, in a prepara-

tion to take advantage of a second opportunity should that ever present itself; for Fortune may as easily advance as she casts down. When the play opens the opportunity has come. Fortune has brought the Neapolitan fleet within striking distance; Prospero's study of the books has given him the necessary 'prescience', power and determination not to let this chance go by. He has not brought the King of Naples' ship to the island; Fortune has done that; but he can raise the storm, separate the fleet, bring the royal vessel to shore:

> By accident most strange, bountiful Fortune,
> Now my dear lady, hath mine enemies
> Brought to this shore; and by my prescience
> I find my zenith doth depend upon
> A most auspicious star, whose influence
> If now I court not, but omit, my fortunes
> Will ever after droop.   (I, ii. 178–184.)

It is soon clear that Prospero's self-preparation has not been to take vengeance on these enemies; punishment they will receive, but after it forgiveness and reconciliation. No man, loving his daughter as he loves Miranda, can make certain that she will fall in love with his enemy's son unless reconciliation is intended. Anything else will make her life a hell. And so the action develops until the richly satisfying moment when Prospero states explicitly what his actions have implied:

> Though with their high wrongs I am struck to th' quick,
> Yet with my nobler reason 'gainst my fury
> Do I take part; the rarer action is
> In vertue than in vengeance; they being penitent,
> The sole drift of my purpose doth extend
> Not a frown further.   (V, i. 25–30.)

Wilson's *Christian Dictionary* (1612) tells us that *Vertue* means 'Christian fortitude' and gives examples of its use in the New Testament. Providence working through Fortune and human beings with 'free scope' has brought events to a position in which it is affirmed in word and deed that to suffer and act as a Christian should is both more precious and less usual than to pursue vengeance.

Despite the happy ending of this play, Shakespeare does not give us a sentimental picture of a delightful world with all evil cast out. The world is brave and new to Miranda; in some respects it is better for most people present; but this is still the world that has suffered the Fall. Antonio and Sebastian are unchanged; they are made ineffective, that is all. But they, or others like them, will still inhabit Miranda's new world.

Three more plays are important as an expression of a view of Providence governing the world in accordance with what was commonly believed on that subject in Shakespeare's time—*Romeo and Juliet*, *Hamlet* and *King Lear*. Unlike *The Tempest* and *The Winter's Tale*, each of these is a tragedy; but in each the ends of Providence are attained as a result of an inter-action between Fortune and the 'free scope' of individual human beings, making mistakes or avoiding them. The Chorus before Act I of *Romeo and Juliet* might appear to contradict this assertion; it seems to say that the stars alone are responsible for the outcome of the play, that the deaths of Romeo and Juliet are predetermined, not the result of anything done by them in free will:

> From forth the fatal loins of these two foes
> A pair of star-cross'd lovers take their life'.
>
> (Prologue, 5–6.)

But *fatal* should be read in the sense of 'death-dealing' not in a false sense of 'fated' or 'imposing fate upon', 'determining'. There is a hidden pun here; *loins* are defined as 'life-giving parts', which means that we can gloss the statement as 'the death-dealing life-giving parts of these two enemies'. In giving these lovers life, the enemies unintentionally have given them death. And this is in part, but only in part, due to the stars. The lovers are indeed 'star-cross'd'; but this means no more than 'obstructed by the stars', not 'doomed by them to destruction'. As we shall see, human choice plays its part, as well as Fortune, in their tragedy.

We must first consider what is the end of Providence to be attained in Verona. That is easily stated as peace, the avoidance of civil war, a victory of love over hatred; order must not disintegrate into chaos in the city. The play begins with a powerful example of the possibility of this disintegration, one to which the Prince is very much alive. His rebellious subjects, 'enemies to peace' are told that they are 'beasts' in their 'canker'd hate' which has now led to three 'civil brawls' caused by nothing more than an 'airy word' (I, i. 79–100). He insists upon an end to the disturbances.

By the time that Romeo and Juliet are committed to one another in their love, there is quite a strong possibility that a marriage between them might at last reconcile their families. Old Capulet has assured Paris that it should not be too difficult to keep the peace; and in his reply Paris expresses the common-sense view of those exposed to threats from this feud, though not directly involved in it:

> *Cap.* But Montague is bound as well as I
> In penalty alike; and 'tis not hard, I think,
> For men as old as we to keep the peace.
> *Par.* Of honourable reckoning are you both,
> And pity 'tis you liv'd at odds so long.
>
> (I, ii. 1–5.)

Capulet's determination easily survives the test when Tybalt rages at the presence of Romeo at his 'enemy's feast':

> I would not for the wealth of all this town
> Here in my house do him disparagement.
> Therefore, be patient, take no note of him;
> It is my will; the which if thou respect,
> Show a fair presence and put off these frowns,
> An ill-beseeming semblance for a feast.
>
> (I, v. 67–72.)

Friar Lawrence sees the opportunity to reconcile the two families when Romeo tells him about Juliet. The Friar marries them primarily to that end:

> In one respect I'll thy assistant be;
> For this alliance may so happy prove
> To turn your households' rancour to pure love.
>
> (II, iii. 90–92.)

Until the moment of Tybalt's death there is a stronger and stronger possibility that this 'rancour' will turn to 'pure love' in the happiness, not misery and death, of Romeo and Juliet. When first insulted by Tybalt, Romeo shows a truly heroic fortitude, refusing to be provoked by the man who is now unwittingly his cousin. Ironically, Romeo's determination to keep the peace leads to his undoing. His apparent cowardice deceives Mercutio into fighting Tybalt for the honour of the Montagues; stepping between them to end the fight, Romeo inadvertently causes Mercutio's death. Now, with Mercutio dead and Juliet and Tybalt both absent, Romeo takes a new decision; this time it is not for peace and love but for hatred. He made a free choice not to fight when insulted, he made a second free choice to stop the fight; he makes a third. Even before the news of Mercutio's death he regrets Juliet's power to soften 'valour's steel' in his 'temper'. The news brings from him:

> This day's black fate on more days doth depend;
> This but begins the woe others must end.
>
> (III, i. 116–17.)

The reappearance of Tybalt lets Romeo put his new decision into action. In fact he has been no more forced to kill Tybalt now than he was earlier, when he would not be provoked. Circumstances have changed, and with them his intention. Here is human choice inter-acting with Fortune.

Once Tybalt is dead there is less and less chance of a happy ending for the lovers, married though they be. Capulet cannot be expected to realize that his daughter has married in secret, and consummated the marriage. He has always given her and others to understand that her consent will always be asked before she is married. And she has let her mother know that she will not even become involved in a relationship without her parent's approval (I, ii. 6–19; I, iii. 64–100). And so Capulet makes the decision, thinking his daughter's grief is for Tybalt, not for the killer of Tybalt, her husband (III, iv. 1–21). With the desperate resort to the drug, followed by the message to Romeo not reaching him, and with his reception of the false news of Juliet's death, the chances of a happy outcome diminish still more. Now Romeo defies the stars

(V, i. 24) and his doom is virtually sealed. Patience is the only defence, and he has all too little patience. The interaction between chance and human choice ends in his suicide followed by hers. But the Prince is able to impose forbearance and 'let mischance be slave to patience'. (V, iii. 219–20.) When all has been told by the Friar, peace at last reigns in Verona. The two families are reconciled in misfortune; the end of Providence is attained.

This end might have been attained happily so long as Romeo was prepared to use patience. Before going to the feast at which he sees Juliet for the first time, he has a premonition:

> my mind misgives
> Some consequence, yet hanging in the stars,
> Shall bitterly begin his fearful date
> With this night's revels and expire the term
> Of a despised life clos'd in my breast,
> By some vile forfeit of untimely death.
> But He that hath the steerage of my course
> Direct my sail! (I, iv. 106–113.)

So long as Romeo puts his future into the hand of God, all goes well. The decision to kill Tybalt wrecks everything, as Romeo admits: 'O, I am Fortune's fool!' (III, i. 133). This is not the way to circumvent the 'crosses' (obstacles) put in one's way by stellar influence. Because he is who he is, and because she is who she is, Romeo and Juliet, in circumstances influenced by the stars, 'with their death bury their parents' strife.' Fortune is involved to be sure; but Fortune determines nothing; the stars incline, provide crosses, do not determine. The outcome always involves human choice.

Elsewhere I have dealt at length with the inter-action between Fortune and human choice to attain the ends of Providence in *Hamlet*.[1] But the essential details need to be repeated here, to give a balanced account of Shakespeare's imagining in terms of the views of his contemporaries on the subject of Providence. In brief, Hamlet does not achieve his vengeance before leaving for England, either because he distrusts the Ghost or because he rationalizes his disinclination to kill Claudius into this distrust; he spares the seemingly praying Claudius once the play-scene has shown the Ghost's honesty either because he wants to send his uncle to Hell, or because he seizes another pretext to avoid what he does not want to do. Whichever of these possible motives we ascribe to Hamlet, it still remains true that he departs for England without having tried deliberately to kill the King; the thrust through the arras is more a reflex action in self-defence than a deliberate action to achieve revenge. Gazing down at the body of Polonius, Hamlet begins to understand just how little control he has over events. Who would have expected to find Polonius there?

But when Hamlet has returned to Denmark he has had time to reflect on the many things which have happened since his father's death, among them the secret death-warrant which he has altered, the fight with the pirates and its outcome, as well as his own failure to avenge his father. And now, not only is he certain that events are outside his control, but that they are under the control of Providence. I am not suggesting that this is the result of a revolution in his thinking, that he has moved from scepticism to faith; rather has his experience converged to emphasize a truth which he has taken for granted and neglected to apply to his own circumstances. Now he is convinced:

> let us know,
> Our indiscretion sometimes serves us well,
> When our deep plots do pall; and that should learn us
> There's a divinity that shapes our ends,
> Rough-hew them how we will.   (V, ii. 8–11.)

Horatio agrees: 'That is most certain.' This need not surprise us, for it was Horatio who, hearing Marcellus' comment on 'something rotten in the state of Denmark', replied confidently: 'Heaven will direct it.' (I, iv. 91.)

After the shock of Ophelia's funeral and the scuffle with Laertes, Hamlet waits upon events. In generous resolve to reconcile himself to Laertes whom he has unintentionally wronged he accepts the challenge to a duel of honour, seemingly an entirely harmless exercise in ceremony which will repair Laertes' honour.

When Hamlet mentions a slight misgiving Horatio is unable to persuade him to postpone the duel of honour. The Prince is convinced that Providence, Special Providence, for which nobody and nothing is too small for attention, is in control, and will use him living or dying, if he is to be used. And he is used. The treachery rebounds; Laertes, dying, confesses and betrays Claudius whose responsibility for Gertrude's unintended death is now plain. What Claudius is and what he has done can now be made clear in detail. Horatio has the authority to tell:

> th' yet unknowing world
> How these things came about. So shall you hear
> Of carnal, bloody and unnatural acts;
> Of accidental judgments, casual slaughters;
> Of deaths put on by cunning and forc'd cause;
> And, in this upshot, purposes mistook
> Fall'n on th' inventors' heads.   (V, ii. 371–77.)

Hamlet's awareness that something like this might happen is his reason for refusing to let Horatio postpone the duel; he rejects 'augury', an attempt to foretell the future. 'There's a Special Providence in the fall of a sparrow,' Providence is in control. If 'it' does not happen now, and it is the will of God for it to happen, it will happen in His time by means of His Providence. In the Good Quarto (1604) we may read the end of this speech as follows:

> since no man of ought he leaves, knowes what ist to leave betimes.

If we take 'of ought he leaves' in parenthesis, the sense is clear: 'since no man, of ought he leaves, knowes, etc..' Now we can gloss the whole statement as:

> since no man knows enough about anything he leaves to know what it is to leave it betimes.

He does not know if he leaves it at the right moment or in the right state of development. Hamlet then adds that 'the readiness is all'. When the moment is ripe for Providence, if he is always ready to die, if he is prepared to take an opportunity should the moment be ripe; that is what matters. And so, 'Let be': let it happen, do nothing more about it.

The moment is ripe. Claudius contrives that he shall himself be killed while about some activity which will send him to damnation; but the guilt for his damnation does not lie on Hamlet, as it would if the Prince had deliberately planned to trap his uncle in such a situation. Hamlet has given up planning; his death and his revenge occur as the result of the contriving of others. The play has been written like a triumphant assertion of the power and justice of Providence; Shakespeare may not have believed in this power, but he has imagined Hamlet as if he did.

In *King Lear* the person whose fortunes make us aware of the power of a guiding Providence is Edgar. And just as Hamlet in his play says 'the readiness is all' at a moment of pause before the development of the catastrophe, so Edgar in *King Lear* asserts 'Ripeness is all' when the critical battle has been fought, but before its worst consequences have taken place. There is one great difference between the two, however; Hamlet's words come after he has relinquished planning, although previously he has tried to control events; but Edgar makes his statement when for the first time he is about to put into action a preconceived plan. Hamlet is confident that if Providence will use him his moment will come; but Edgar after waiting long and patiently has had an opportunity presented to him, has acted and planned to make the most of it; Cordelia's defeat in the battle means that his moment for decisive action has come. Where Prospero's prescience tells him in *The Tempest* that everything is in his favour, Edgar knows from experience that his opportunity is waiting.

Edgar, like Prospero, has exercised patience, has not given in to despair. But his position has been much worse than Prospero's; Edgar at first thinks that father, not brother, has turned on him unnaturally; he has no companion to console him, no books, no memory of a former servant's 'charity'. All he has is a determination to survive without despair. As I have explained more fully elsewhere,[2] Edgar has spent most of the play in the conviction that he will have to wait until his reputation is cleared once more without his struggling to defeat events, just as he did nothing to bring about his outlawing by his father. Eventually Edmund's own machinations have not only brought his father and brother together; his departure from Regan's castle to try to kill Gloucester, his plotting with Goneril, have put into Edgar's hands the incriminating letter carried by Oswald. In a better disguise than that of a Bedlam, Edgar informs Albany; they agree on a plan in the event of a British victory.

Now the victory has come; after enduring mental and physical misery for so long he knows the moment for action has arrived; 'Ripeness is all'. By the time that Shakespeare wrote *King Lear* this statement in English had become associated with the Latin motto, *festina lente*, which expresses the notion of prudence combined with daring. Events are allowed to make themselves while a slow, quiet, unperceived strength grows to its own maturity. Now, suddenly, the concealed force is released devastatingly against the unprepared enemy. The moment has come for Edgar as for Hamlet; but Hamlet does not know, where Edgar sees clearly. So Prospero knows, but he does not need to destroy his enemies. Nevertheless, while Hamlet and Edgar are used by Providence as they kill, they each show charity. Hamlet shows it in his forgiveness of the treacherous Laertes; Edgar exchanges it freely with the half-brother who does not deserve it. And after all his vicissitudes it is Edgar who is to rule Britain as the play ends. What he has done, his suffering and action, suggests that if the end of Providence is to let the country recover from the harms brought on it unintentionally by Lear, Edgar is a well-chosen instrument.

As Shakespeare's mention of the stars has led to some confusion among modern readers it is necessary to dwell a little longer on this one play, *King Lear*. Kent is often misunderstood in his words marvelling at the difference between Cordelia on the one hand and Goneril and Regan on the other:

> It is the stars,
> The stars above us, govern our conditions;
> Else one self mate and make could not beget
> Such different issues. (IV, ii. 32–5.)

It is easy for the modern reader to misread this as an assertion that human beings have no free will, that our actions are determined by the stars. It is therefore very important to note that the word, 'conditions', does not have the sense of 'will' or 'decisions'; it is used of all that was seen as physical, as distinct from spiritual, in a living human being. As will be remembered, Elizabethan belief in the influence of the stars restricted its range; the stars influence only what is physical and mortal, having no power on the rational soul, which is not in any way physical. Differences like those between her two sisters and Cordelia we would ascribe to the laws of heredity. Shakespeare's contemporaries ascribed them to the influence of the stars on physical *conditions*. He imagined Kent subscribing to the normal view.

Providence, in the view of Shakespeare's contemporaries, has not only governed the course of the world by means of the inter-action of Fortune and human free will, using the stars as an element of Fortune. In addition unusual physical phenomena are used as portents to warn human beings of a divine summons to a repentance which will avert punishment. It was usual to interpret a comet, an eclipse of sun or moon, an earthquake, strange sights in the sky (real or imaginary) and such an occurrence as the Ghost of Hamlet's father, as portents; a portent is a warning of something which is about to happen; it is an advance symptom of what has not yet taken place. Shakespeare imagines characters in *Julius Caesar*, *Hamlet* and *King Lear* believing in portents.

The night before the murder of Caesar, Casca insists in the face of the scepticism of Cicero, that the strange things happening are portents:

> A common slave—you know him well by sight—
> Held up his left hand, which did flame and burn
> Like twenty torches join'd; and yet his hand,
> Not sensible of fire, remain'd unscorch'd.
> Besides—I ha' not since put up my sword—
> Against the Capitol I met a lion,
> Who glar'd upon me, and went surly by,
> Without annoying me; and there were drawn
> Upon a heap a hundred ghastly women,
> Transformed with their fear, who swore they saw
> Men all in fire walk up and down the streets.

And yesterday the bird of night did sit,
Even at noon-day, upon the market-place,
Hooting and shrieking. When these prodigies
Do so conjointly meet, let not men say
'These are their reasons—they are natural';
For I believe these are portentous things
Unto the climate that they point upon.   (I, iii. 15–32.)

The next day Calpurnia tries to dissuade Caesar from going to his assassination telling him of the portents seen by the watch:

A lioness hath whelped in the streets,
And graves have yawn'd and yielded up their dead;
Fierce fiery warriors fight upon the clouds,
In ranks and squadrons and right form of war,
Which drizzled blood upon the Capitol;
The noise of battle hurtled in the air;
Horses did neigh and dying men did grown,
And ghosts did shriek and squeal about the streets.
O, Caesar, these things are beyond all use,
And I do fear them.   (II, ii. 17–26.)

Caesar insists that if his death is 'purpos'd by the mighty gods', there is no point in trying to avoid it. He refuses to interpret the portents as applying to him in particular. His eventual decision to go as planned is responsible for his death; that is the way Providence works, through human choice as well as Fortune. But the portents are shown as having meaning.

The repeated appearance of the Ghost in *Hamlet* is interpreted by Horatio, once he himself has seen it, as a portent: 'This bodes some strange eruption to our state' (I, i. 69). Bernardo's reference to it as a 'portentous figure' brings from Horatio (whom many critics insist on regarding as a sceptic) an account of what happened during a period of great prosperity in Rome:

A little ere the mightiest Julius fell,
The graves stood tenantless, and the sheeted dead
Did squeak and gibber in the Roman streets;
          . . . and the moist star

Upon whose influence Neptune's empire stands
Was sick almost to doomsday with eclipse;
And even the like precurse of fear'd events,
As harbingers preceding still the fates
And prologue to the omen coming on,
Have heaven and earth together demonstrated
Unto our climatures and countrymen.

(114–125.)

Another well-known account of portents is given by Lennox, telling Macbeth what happened during the night of Duncan's murder (II, iii. 52–59). Modern critics are usually disposed to take this account as expressive of Shakespeare's own views, possibly because the portent relates to the death of Duncan, and the play of *Macbeth* suffers as a whole in interpretation if we discount the inter-action between natural and supernatural. Nevertheless critics who raise no objection to the presence of superstition in Lennox's speech, or in *Macbeth* as a whole, see a superstitious folly in Gloucester's reference to portents in *King Lear*:

These late eclipses in the sun and moon portend no good to us: though the wisdom of nature can reason it thus and thus, yet nature finds itself scourged by the sequent effects. Love cools, friendship falls off, brothers divide; in cities, mutinies; in countries, discord; in palaces, treason; and the bond cracked between son and father.   (I, ii. 99–107.)

This passage tends to be misread as if Gloucester were talking about the influence of the stars. But in fact he is not; he is talking about eclipses as portents. He does not say that the late eclipses cause harm, but that they 'portend no good to us'. That is, they are un-natural physical happenings (like the prodigies in *Caesar* and *Hamlet*) which are a sign of harm to come. As we have seen in Chapter Six, people who were equally religious could have two views of portents; one was that the prodigious events were the result of entirely natural causes; God's Providence has ordered things so that the prodigies will take place at the right time as a sign of divine anger. According to the second view, portents are the result of a deliberate divine interference with nature, again to give warning of God's anger to call erring human beings to repentance. As I have just remarked, each of these views is equally religious. Natural science, 'the wisdom of nature', was not necessarily irreligious; it merely ascribed a different method of procedure to Providence. In each case Providence leaves it to human beings to react to the portent in free will. We saw that Elizabeth and her counsellors took the earthquake of 1580 seriously and instituted special prayers and fast days, which were regarded by contemporaries as responsible for the avoidance of divine punishment. But Gloucester is remembering portents which were not acted upon, much as they seem to have been discussed. That the eclipses were portents of divine anger is now obvious in the actual events which have since taken place, 'the sequent effects'; he lists them. And events prove him correct in his lament, 'we have seen the best of our time'. It seems to me that Shakespeare, whether he believed in portents or not, imagines characters believing in them, as many of his contemporaries did in fact. And Edmund's remarks on the stars are in no way applicable to what his father has just said about the eclipses as portents. Gloucester has not asserted that the eclipses cause 'no good'; they merely 'portend no good'; he is not talking about stellar influence. But Edmund is certainly considering the contemporary doctrine on the influence of the stars; and he shows himself basically in agreement with orthodox opinion. The orthodox view, as we have seen in Chapter Six, is that stellar influence can incline us to evil, but that it does not determine our behaviour. By the exercise of will we can overcome inclinations resulting from the stars. Edmund agrees; but he is not concerned with resisting impulses for evil; he insists that his will allows him to overcome any inclinations for good which the stars may have evoked in him. Aquinas, to mention only one of the most important of Edmund's predecessors, had also insisted that we must not try to use the influence of the stars as evidence that we sin 'by a divine thrusting on'. Many a contemporary of Shakespeare's who believed in stellar influence (and that includes Bacon and Raleigh) would have agreed that Edmund would be what he is 'had the maidenliest star in the firmament twinkled on' his bastardizing; he can degrade himself by the exercise of his own corrupt will; nothing more is required. Just as the will can overcome inclinations towards evil, so it can overcome inclinations to good; this is sound, orthodox doctrine. In this Edmund does not represent any kind of new thinking on the relation of human will and sin to the stars; his view is normal to Shakespeare's contemporaries, except in his devotion to evil instead of good.

So far as we can tell, Shakespeare's plays assume the old view of the world beneath the moon as composed of four elements, with everything beneath the moon subject to mutability, and all above it perfect and incorruptible. He writes as if he believes the primal matter out of which the world was created to have consisted of the four elements in perpetual conflict. Othello's 'Chaos is come again' appears to be a complete collapse of all order in the speaker as well as in the world. We cannot be sure that the sarcastic reference in *Hamlet* to man as 'this quintessence of dust' betokens more than a familiarity with the belief of some Elizabethans that the immutable heavens were composed of a fifth element, comprehending the other four, but Lear is certainly imagined invoking the four to turn and destroy the world, and with it man, for being ungrateful to him. In his first scene in the storm he calls first on Air in the demand for the winds to blow until they burst their own cheeks; next Water is asked to drown the earth; then Fire, the lightning, is invoked and last of all, the element, Earth, is asked in the shape of 'all-shaking thunder', the thunder-stone, or thunder-bolt, to strike the globe into utter flatness with one tremendous blow (III, ii. 1–25). And the belief that of the four elements, Fire and Air are superior to Earth and Water, appears in Cleopatra's farewell:

> I am fire and air, my other elements
> I give to base life. (V, ii. 287–8.)

So, the Dauphin says of that Perseus, his horse, 'he is pure air and fire; and the dull elements of earth and water never appear in him' (*Henry V*, III, vii. 10–17). Without getting ourselves involved in the complications of *Hamlet* we may note that Shakespeare writes in terms of contemporary doctrine of humours, the physical secretions, the form in which the elements are present in human beings.

Antony's tribute to Brutus may be intended to have no more than metaphorical meaning, but it certainly assumes the existence of the elements. 'The noblest Roman of them all' had 'the Elements/So mix'd in him' that he was a perfect example of what a man should be (V, v. 73–5).

Again, while there is no detailed exposition of the organization of the heavens with the planets in their spheres, the 'Ptolemaic' account of these seems to be taken for granted. Similarly, there are frequent references to angels, but no detailed account of their hierarchies as of the hierarchies of things on earth. That an angel is a messenger he knows, as we see from Romeo's, 'winged messenger of heaven'; that the Cherubim are bright seems to be implied by the reference to Juliet as 'bright angel' in a passage whose imagery is very like that of the soliloquy in which Macbeth is terrified by his vision of 'Heaven's cherubim'. As Tillyard pointed out, it is possible that Shakespeare remembered that, in the Dionysian account of the angelic hierarchies, the cherubim have charge of the fixed stars;[3] which is why in *The Merchant of Venice* Lorenzo says to Jessica:

> There's not the smallest orb which thou behold'st
> But in his motion like an angel sings,
> Still quiring to the young-ey'd cherubims.
>
> (V, i. 60–2.)

Shakespeare gives most attention to hierarchy in the life of human beings, and in the effect of human beings in turn upon the order imposed and maintained by Providence on what would otherwise be corrupted by Satan into chaos. Man has been rendered vulnerable by the Fall. In 'natural life', that is, mortal life in the flesh in this world, man is an inseparable fusion of body-soul for Shakespeare in his imagining of Macbeth and Leontes. As has been mentioned in Chapter Six, the usual renaissance belief was that body and soul are inseparable in a living human being thanks to the existence of the substance 'spirit', at once the grossest form of soul and the subtlest form of body. The doctrine of the three aspects of the soul, it will be recalled, centres the vegetable soul in the liver, where its spirit, natural spirit, is concocted out of the blood; the sensible soul, centred in the heart, operates in vital spirit, refined in the heart out of natural spirit; and the rational soul, enthroned in the brain, functions through animal spirit, refined in that organ out of the baser form which rises to it with the blood. Fish, birds, beasts and insects, wanting a rational soul, have no corresponding 'animal spirit'. This is behind the conceit in which Polixenes lightly tells Hermione how he and her husband behaved in boyhood, 'as twinn'd lambs'. Lambs, devoid of a rational soul, have no animal spirit; they do not share original guilt. Had the two boys stayed young, remained as lambs, they would have remained innocent; had the blood never gained strength to rise to the brain, the conceit suggests, they would have had no rational soul, no animal spirits, keeping their innocence, instead of losing it as adults:

> Had we pursu'd that life,
> And our weaker spirits ne'er been higher rear'd
> With stronger blood, we should have answer'd heaven
> Boldly 'Not guilty', the imposition clear'd
> Hereditary ours.   (*The Winter's Tale*, I, ii. 71–5.)

The inseparable entity of body-soul is referred to by Macbeth as 'my single state of man'. Before Descartes set forth the notion of man as a dualism, he was envisaged as a single state. This state of body-soul operates in 'function'. 'Function' does not mean that body obeys soul, but that they work together as a single unit. Macbeth knows that he is only imagining a murder; but he does so with such strength that the operation of body and soul simultaneously in *function* is 'smother'd in surmise' (in imagining) so that nothing exists for him except what he knows rationally to be non-existent. His rational knowledge does not stop him responding to the imaginary as if it were real because the single state is so shaken that body and soul no longer operate inseparably as one unit. 'Function' is used in this sense in *The Spanish Tragedy* when the Ghost of Andrea says that while his body and soul were one in life 'each in their function' served the 'other's need' (I, i. 4). Macbeth' actual words are as follows:

> My thought, whose murder yet is, but phantastical,
> Shakes so my single state of man

> That function is smother'd in surmise,
> And nothing is but what is not. (I, iv. 138–141.)

He can distinguish between appearance and reality, but the single state is so shaken by imagining that the body continues to respond to the appearance despite the rational knowledge that it is not real. Macbeth is in the same state when he hears the knocking on the door and any kind of noise terrifies him. Then he asks himself what is the matter when rational knowledge that a noise is quite normal does not stop it appalling him because he imagines it as ominous. Hamlet uses the word, 'function', in the same sense when he remarks on the power of the Player's imagination, 'his whole function suiting/With forms to his conceit'. Powerful imagining makes body and soul in their function conform to his 'conceit'. (II, ii. 549–50.)

Many modern commentators interpret Macbeth's reference to 'my single state of man' as involving a correspondence between the individual and the body politic. They find Macbeth drawing attention to the fact that the disturbances within him, a microcosm, are related to equally profound disturbances which are affecting the larger world, the macrocosm. This is, indeed, probable, despite the fact that at the same time he is remarking upon the nature of the disturbance within him; it has rendered null the usual single functioning of body-soul. For us to understand clearly what Shakespeare could have communicated at this moment, we need to remind ourselves that those who studied human psychology, physiology, anatomy, like the philosophers, regarded the human body and mind as literally, not metaphorically, possessing details which are the equivalent of those existing in the larger world. It was because man was regarded as literally containing within himself in miniature everything existing in the world outside him that he was called a microcosm. The Gentleman is speaking more than metaphorically when he describes how Lear:

> Strives in his little world of man to out-scorn
> The to-and-fro conflicting rain and wind.
> (III, i. 10–11.)

Shakespeare's plays assume the key position of man, the little world, in the ordering of the world by Providence. That he should concentrate on human beings as the centre of his interests is no more than natural in a dramatist, for drama deals essentially with character in action. In general Shakespeare assumes the acceptance of a belief in hierarchy and deference, brotherhood and natural-ness, as essential to the preservation of order, not only in human society, but in the world as a whole. Human society is but one sec-tion of the Chain, but one whose importance lies in the fact that it is particularly vulnerable to human passion disorganized by human sin. In the history plays he deals specifically with recent English history which confirms the political theory; quite naturally much attention is given to the relationship of subject to monarch, the duties of each, the need to maintain order. These matters are obviously of much importance to his treatment of *Macbeth*, *Romeo and Juliet*, *King Lear*, *Julius Caesar*; but in the plays as a whole we may find at any moment a speech or incident which assumes the rightness of a hierarchical society dominated by an *élite*, with each rank showing correct deference to those above it. One mark of deference is kneeling, another the removal of hats by men and boys. Comparatively rarely do we get an explicit reference to such conventions, as when Richard II tells his companions:

> Cover your heads, and mock not flesh and blood
> With solemn reverence; throw away respect,
> Tradition, form, and ceremonious duty;
> For you have but mistook me all this while.
>
> (III, ii. 171–4.)

And Hamlet, irritated by Osric's obsequious antics, bids him:

> Put your bonnet to his right use; 'tis for the head.
>
> (V, ii. 93.)

Shakespeare thinks in terms of the ordering of creation in the Chain of Being, with each kind of created thing or being observing its own hierarchy beneath its superiors. It is natural to defer to those above, to rule those below and to co-operate in a spirit of brotherhood with those of equal rank. We find Shakespeare think-ing in terms of primacies in each kind when he likens, or imagines the characters likening, Richard II to fire, as the prime element, to the sun among the planets, the eagle among birds, the rose among flowers, the lion among beasts, for he is a king among men. The dolphin, the king among fish, is used by Cleopatra to describe Antony:

> His delights
> Were dolphin-like; they show'd his back above
> The elements they liv'd in. (V, ii. 88–90.)

And Aufidius likens Coriolanus in Rome to the osprey, an eagle; fish were believed to offer themselves willingly to this king among birds:

> I think he'll be to Rome
> As is the aspray to the fish, who takes it
> By sovereignty of nature. (IV, vii. 33–5.)

The often-quoted speech of Ulysses in *Troilus and Cressida* will bear quoting once again, as it contains so much that is essential in the view of a Providential ordering of the world which we considered in Chapter Six. It is pertinent to ask why Shakespeare puts these words into the character's mouth; it was obviously not an idiosyncratic view to which he wanted to call people's attention; nor do I think the speech is there deliberately to remind contemporaries of basic principles which they denied or ignored. It is more probable that the speech says what is normal to the situation in the play, things which the Jacobean did not dispute, but which he might not always feel so acutely as when he receives the message in this imagined experience. Ulysses gives an account of 'degree', a justification for it and a vivid picture of the chaos which is its opposite. This chaos is a state of opposition between everything which works harmoniously when organised hierarchically in accordance with degree; Ulysses' occasion for speaking is his recognition of the evil effects of ignoring degree:

> The speciality of rule hath been neglected;
> . . . Degree being vizarded,
> Th' unworthiest shows as fairly in the mask.
> The heavens themselves, the planets, and this centre

Observe degree, priority and place,
Insisture, course, proportion, season, form,
Office and custom, all in line of order;
And therefore is the glorious planet Sol
In noble eminence enthron'd and spher'd
Amidst the other, whose med'cinable eye
Corrects the ill aspects of planets evil,
And posts like the commandment of a king,
Sans check, to good and bad. But when the planets
In evil mixture to disorder wander;
What plagues and what portents, what mutiny,
What raging of the sea, shaking of earth,
Commotion in the winds! Frights, changes, horrors,
Divert and crack, rend and deracinate,
The unity and married calm of states
Quite from their fixture! O, when degree is shak'd,
Which is the ladder of all high designs,
The enterprise is sick! How could communities,
Degrees in schools, and brotherhoods in cities,
Peaceful commerce from dividable shores,
The primogeniture and due of birth,
Prerogative of age, crowns, sceptres, laurels,
But by degree stand in authentic place?
Take but degree away, untune that string,
And hark, what discord follows! Each thing melts
In mere oppugnancy: the bounded waters
Should lift their bosoms higher than the shores,
And make a sop of all this solid globe;
Strength should be lord of imbecility,
And the rude son should strike his father dead;
Force should be right; or, rather, right and wrong—
Between whose endless jar justice resides—
Should lose their names, and so should justice too.
Then everything includes itself in power,
Power into will, will into appetite;
And appetite, an universal wolf,
So doubly seconded with will and power,

> Must make perforce an universal prey,
> And last eat up himself. Great Agamemnon,
> This chaos, when degree is suffocate,
> Follows the choking. (I, iii. 83–126.)

It is relevant to notice how the early part of this speech is in agreement with the views of Gloucester on the eclipses in *King Lear*. Ulysses also believes in portents:

> What plagues and what portents, what mutiny,
> What raging of the sea, shaking of the earth,
> Commotion of the winds.

He and Gloucester both give a picture of a descent into Chaos which includes portents and a dividing in discord of those who should co-operate in harmony.

Ulysses does not treat monarchy in his account of order (apart from the reference to 'the commandment of a king'), but for Shakespeare the king has primacy in the state. Although *Macbeth* does not deal directly with the office of kingship in the way in which it is treated in the history plays, the basic assumptions are the same, and from time to time our attention is focused explicitly on some central point, as when Macbeth assures Duncan:

> The service and the loyalty I owe,
> In doing it, pays itself. Your Highness' part
> Is to receive our duties; and our duties
> Are to your throne and state, children and servants,
> Which do but what they should by doing everything
> Safe toward your love and honour. (I, iv. 21–7.)

When she receives the King, Lady Macbeth gives the same protestations of utter dependence upon him as both the fount of honour and the source of all material rewards:

> All our service
> In every point twice done, and then done double,
> Were poor and single business to contend

> Against those honours deep and broad wherewith
> Your Majesty loads our house.

And:

> Your servants ever
> Have theirs, themselves, and what is theirs, in compt,
> To make their audit at your Highness'
> Still to return your own.   (I, vi. 14–18; 25–28.)

This play is imagined not only in relation to contemporary belief on the Divine Right of Kings, and the inevitability of punishment for regicide, but it assumes a ceremonial of degree. Macbeth invites Banquo to 'a solemn supper', a very formal 'feast' to honour a 'chief guest'. This means exact observance of degree with everything to honour the recipient of the royal favour. But when the hour arrives Macbeth (expecting Banquo to be dead) reverses his commands. The Court is told that instead of a solemn supper there will be a much less formal occasion. The Queen 'keeps her state', remains in her chair of state and preserves a formal superiority and distance, but her husband plays 'the humble host'. So far as the courtiers are concerned at this point, he is treating them with genuine condescension; in seating themselves they must still pay their respects to the Queen, and they know how to acknowledge their 'own degrees', but they are given permission not to make formal acknowledgement of the King's rank; he will sit 'here . . . i' th' midst'. We know that Macbeth does this to have an opportunity to talk to the Murderer informally; but to create this opportunity in this society some such arrangement is necessary. At the same time, as a matter of art, not of history, we note that this ignoring of degree emphasizes the fact that Macbeth is fighting order throughout the play, a man ready in his own interests to let the world crash into chaos.

The very story of *Hamlet* with its killing of a king by his brother who usurps the throne can be expected to have suggested to an Elizabethan broader implications of kingship and obedience. The well-being, spiritual as well as material, of Denmark is bound up with the spiritual health of the occupant of its throne. The hypocritical guilt of Claudius corrupts the moral judgment of his sub-

Y

jects. And, paradoxically, his usurpation gives him rights over his subjects once they have mistakenly accepted him. As Rosencrantz assures the King:

> The cease of majesty
> Dies not alone, but like a gulf doth draw
> What's near with it. It is a massy wheel,
> Fix'd on the summit of the highest mount,
> To whose huge spokes ten thousand lesser things
> Are mortic'd and adjoin'd; which when it falls,
> Each small annexment, petty consequence,
> Attends the boist'rous ruin. Never alone
> Did the king sigh, but with a general groan.
> (III, iii. 15–23.)

The Gentleman who brings Claudius news of the revolt deplores that it is:

> as the world were now but to begin
> Antiquity forgot, custom not known,
> The ratifiers and prop of every word.   (IV, v. 100–103.)

In passing we may note Shakespeare's reflection of the contemporary insistence on 'every word' in matters of kingship being ratified and propped by antiquity and known custom. In this he can be likened to the opponents of royal prerogative who consistently discovered past precedent justifying their own words and actions. In *Hamlet* it is not surprising that the hypocrite, Claudius, can invoke divine protection of kingship, in virtue of which, if the truth were known, he would be the last to benefit:

> There's such divinity doth hedge a king
> That treason can but peep to what it would,
> Acts little of his will.   (IV, v. 120–2.)

The divinity which hedges a king is the central interest of the history plays. As a body they communicate in imagined experience a certainty that kingship is an essential element in the organization of the world by means of which Providence defeats Satan and prevents order becoming chaos. A monarch rules by Divine Right;

to rebel against him is to commit an irreligious act of disorder; the subject's duty is absolute obedience. Carlisle is immovable on that point when he denies Bolingbroke's claim to ascend the throne:

> I speak to subjects, and a subject speaks,
> Stirr'd up by God, thus boldly for his king.
>
> (*Richard II*, IV, 1. 131–2.)

On the other hand, while the subject must obey, the monarch is bound to rule justly in the interests of his people. Richard II is anything but a just ruler; it is his denial of an heir's right to inherit that makes York remind him that he is denying the very principle in accordance with which he rules as king. And when Bolingbroke returns, insisting he has come only to enter into his rightful inheritance, the justice of this claim disarms the Duke of York. York tries to be neutral, incapable of judging between two nephews, each of whom has right on his side. But the strict doctrine is that however wrong the King may be, he is to be obeyed. Unfortunately kings such as Richard do not carry out their function of protecting their subjects from such dilemmas as York's. Richard himself woefully misunderstands the Divine Right by which he rules. He thinks it means that he is divinely protected against rebels, who are bound to fail in any attempt to subvert order. And he has associated that protection with the existence of a loyal army sufficient to crush rebellion. When on his return from Ireland he finds that his large forces no longer exist, his confidence in divine protection deserts him.[4]

Once Richard has been dethroned and killed all England is involved in the sin and suffers from disorder. With the coronation of Henry IV it is impossible to avoid the sin of rebellion; to obey Henry is to be guilty by association; to defy him is an act of rebellion against an anointed king; this is literally disorder. Shakespeare, as has often been pointed out, surveys English history from Richard II to Henry VII, imagining events subsequent to the first act of disorder. Henry lives under the threat of punishment, never able to undertake his pilgrimage, plagued by rebellion, and punished by the seeming corruption of his heir. But the real punishment of England is held off until the third generation of the usurpers. Henry V, also plagued by insurrection, expects punishment for his father's sin the night before Agincourt (IV, i. 288–301). But divine punishment makes use of his success to embroil the English in France, so that when Henry dies suddenly his infant successor cannot lead the nation. The earlier victories in France lead to disaster in the reign of the infant king, whose nobles wrangle selfishly in opposing factions.

Now, in the third generation, comes dire punishment, not only for the ruling dynasty, but for the land as a whole. The scene in *Henry VI, Part III* in which a father finds he has killed his son and a son his father (II, v. 1–124), compresses all the agony of civil war, and shows the inability of this king, in himself a saint, to take control. And in the third act of this play the dialogue between the two Keepers and the King treats the dilemma of the common people, who can only take force as right if they are to survive. They insist that they have not broken their oaths to him in swearing allegiance to King Edward:

> For we were subjects but while you were king.

In this reign, disorder grows until finally the land is ready for the final punishment. This comes in *Richard III*, with Richard functioning as the scourge of God, tyrannising so appallingly over the land that when he is killed by Henry Richmond, the nation is only too happy to settle down once more with a rightful king.

Whether Shakespeare believed what has become known as the Tudor view of the Wars of the Roses cannot be proved; but he certainly imagined the histories as if he believed. Anyone who accepted the Tudor account completely would find nothing to cavil at in the treatment of English history in these plays. One more characteristic point is worth attention; Shakespeare seems to perceive in the period treated in these plays a conflict between love and hate like that which he perceives in the story of *Romeo and Juliet*. In that play civil strife and hatred are more obviously associated on the surface with the relationship of the lovers. But *Richard III* shows us Shakespeare conceiving of Richard himself as an embodiment of discord. Richard knows that to gain his ends he must undermine all attempts at reconciliation between the noble factions.

That is why in his first soliloquy he deplores the new peace and the new fashion of loving former enemies. He cannot thrive by love; he can become supreme only by manipulating the resentments of others. This opposition of love and hate is not explicitly an element of the Tudor account of history; but it is certainly implicit, and Shakespeare shows his quality as an artist in making that implication more apparent in his imagining of characters in action.

From the plays we get a background of a stable society in which, despite the possibility of disorder, the gentry and nobles function healthily beneath the monarch. The infection of faction at Court is known to Shakespeare, though he views it in the past in the reign of Henry VI rather than at the Courts of Elizabeth and James. Whether in Italy, Bohemia, Illyria or England the life of nobility and gentry seems to flow in an orderly course. Only in England, naturally, do we meet such personages as justices of the peace, bailiffs, village constables. Robert Shallow impresses Slender with his status as a superior justice of the peace of Gloucestershire. He was once, fifty-five years ago, a gay young spark at the Inns of Court. Now that he is a squire, his legal training has put him in the select number of justices who were known as of the 'Quorum', one of whom was always required for certain actions or the exercise of certain powers. And Slender adds that Shallow was also one of those very superior justices who could act as Clerk of the Peace and keep the records for the Lord Lieutenant, thus acting as 'custos rotulorum', or, in Slender's dog-Latin, 'and "Rato-lorum" too; and a gentleman born'. These lines reflect Elizabethan preoccupation with 'armigerous' ancestry. We see also we are in a country in which justice can often be received on appeal to the special court of Star Chamber (*Merry Wives of Windsor*, I, i. 1–9). Dr Rowse has pointed out the close similarity between what Shakespeare has written of Dogberry and Verges (*Much Ado About Nothing*, III, iii) and the details of a report of an actual incident which took place during the Babington conspiracy in August 1586.[5] It is not surprising that his picture of the gentry has a conventional counterpart in his scorn for and distrust of the 'rabble', whether in ancient Rome or Tudor or Stuart England. He obviously has contemporary England in mind when he imagines the plebeians cheering Caesar, scorning Coriolanus or succumbing to Richard III. His treatment of the Cade rebellion conforms to the conventional view of the poorer landless members of society as irresponsible and not to be relied on for political common sense. The kind of scorn for the lower orders which we found in Herbert in the shipwreck in an earlier chapter is imagined by Shakespeare as moving Tybalt at the beginning of *Romeo and Juliet* when he finds Benvolio with a drawn sword confronting common serving-men: 'What, art thou drawn among these heartless hinds?' No man of honour would sully his sword with such ignoble blood.

It remains to consider once more how far *King Lear* is to be interpreted as a communication of a prophetic insight into the mutability of much that Shakespeare would prefer to see enduring into a new age. We have seen that Edmund does not represent a new view of society and his father Gloucester is not drawn as a superstitious believer in views of the past outmoded by a new science. His reference to the wisdom of science does not imply conflict between religion and astronomy. It is true, nevertheless, that injustice is denounced, particularly when it emanates from those whose duty is to dispense justice. It is also true that in Edgar as the Bedlam we are introduced to the appalling lot of the itinerant beggars, whipped and maltreated from parish to parish. Lear and his companions learn what it is to be outside the law, what it is like in England if you have no land, no money, no status. Nevertheless, we must distinguish between a call to reform ourselves individually and a call for political and social reform. *King Lear* calls on us as individuals to feel for others, not as individuals to rebel against the existing order because it can be fallible. Gloucester associates the gods with injustice at one point; but he is of a different mind before he dies. Albany says that if the gods do not send down justice, humanity will prey on itself like monsters; but justice comes, Cornwall is struck down. And in the end Edgar is justified in the sight of all. Albany who would like to be a just ruler survives his adversaries. Even if the cost is great, those who are evil are overcome by the end of the play. Edmund finds that all his machination has done no more than bring him back where he started, stripped of honours and now on the point of death. This is a sombre play, but it shows the world as it was to be seen by a realist of Shakespeare's time, a place where, thanks to the Fall, human beings could inflict the most appalling torments on one another, a place where Fortune smiles and frowns alternately, but a place subject like everything else to the control of Providence.

When we say that Shakespeare writes like a man who accepts what is commonplace to his age in thought and society we do not necessarily diminish his stature as a mature and coherent artist. His stature comes not from originality of ideas about the world but from the originality of an artist who expresses himself in a fusion of thought and imagination. His stature comes in part from his insight into human beings; we in the twentieth century find it possible to be involved in what he has imagined in relationships of character to character some four centuries ago. Albany's reluctance to ascribe the worst to a wife whom he has loved and who has apparently loved him, is something we can understand; it is within our range of experience. So is the bitterness of his contempt for her once he has received news of her treatment of Gloucester and of the King. As we imagine Macduff (who has not yet heard of the slaying of his household) taunted by Malcolm for having left wife and family at the mercy of the tyrant, we remember similar exiles in the modern world, their families exposed to the malice of a dictator in their absence.[7] In the case of Kent we find ourselves entering into an experience which is essentially of Shakespeare's age. Those who attend the few remaining Courts of monarchs do not speak Kent's words and put them into practice as he does in the play. He is an ideal courtier imagined come to life. Threatened by his master with death, he replies that he regards his life as something lent to him by God to be used in the service of the King, and to be rendered back again to God when required once more.[8] Such loyalty has existed in many ages; but this was the way it was envisaged as ideal in Shakespeare's age, and this is how he presents it to us in his work. The idea is commonplace; Shakespeare's ideas are, more often than not, but his art transforms them, giving them an individual quality so that we receive from them a remarkable insight into fundamental truths; these we have often known about as commonplace, but he makes us experience their truth imaginatively as if for the first time in our own individual experience. What he himself believed or disbelieved is beyond absolute proof; but he wrote as if he shared the beliefs of his contemporaries in the society which he shared with them, untouched by fundamental doubts.

REFERENCES

¹ *Conscience and the King: A Study of Hamlet* (1953); see also 'The Theme', a re-written chapter of the above, in *Twentieth-Century Interpretations of Hamlet*, ed. D. Bevington (1968).
² *King Lear*, ed. Joseph (1966), pp. 32ff., 209.
³ Tillyard, *The Elizabethan World Picture* (1943), p. 42.
⁴ *Richard II*, II, i. 189-208; II, iii. 152-161; III, ii. 36-177.
⁵ Rowse, *The England of Elizabeth* (1962), pp. 356f.
⁶ *King Lear*, I, iv. 295-348; IV, ii. 3-15, 29-97.
⁷ *Macbeth*, IV, ii. 25-31.
⁸ *King Lear*, I, ii. 154-6.

Bibliography

Allen, J. W., *A History of Political Thought in the Sixteenth Century* (London and New York 1960).

Andrews, K. R., *Drake's Voyages* (London 1967).

Ascham, R., *The Schoolmaster* (1570).

Ashley, M. P., *England in the Seventeenth Century* (London 1952).

Aylmer, G. E., *The King's Servants* (London 1961).

Bacon, Sir Francis, *Essays*, ed. Reynolds (London 1890); *The Advancement of Learning* (tr. Wats, 1640); *Works*, ed. Spedding (London 1841).

Bacon, N., *The Official Papers of Sir Nathaniel Bacon*, ed. H. W. Saunders (Camden Society, London 1915).

Bald, R. C., *Donne and the Druries* (Cambridge 1959).

Baldwin, T. W., *William Shakespeare's Small Latine* and *Lesse Greeke* (Urbana 1943).

Bamborough, J. B., *The Little World of Man* (London 1952).

Beckingsale, B. W., *Burghley* (London 1967).

Black, J. B., *The Reign of Elizabeth* (2nd ed., Oxford 1959).

Boethius, *The Consolations of Philosophy*, tr. H. F. Stewart (London 1918).

Bowen, C. S. D., *The Lion and the Throne* (London 1957); *Francis Bacon* (London 1963).

Brinsley, J., *A Consolation for our Grammar Schools* (1622).

Browne, Sir Thomas, *Works*, ed. G. Keynes (London 1928-31).

Bulwer, J., *Chirologia* and *Chironomia* (1644).

Burton, R., *The Anatomy of Melancholy* (1621).

Butler, A. J., ed., *Public Record Office Calendar of State Papers, 1579-80* (London 1904).

Cantor, N. F., *The English* (London 1968).

Chambers, Sir Edmund, *William Shakespeare* (Oxford 1930).

Cheyney, E. P., *A History of England from the Defeat of the Armada to the Death of Elizabeth* (London 1914, 1926).

Cranmer, T., *Works*, ed. J. E. Cox (London 1844, 1846).

Cruikshank, C. G., *Elizabeth's Army* (Oxford 1966).

Davies, G., *The Early Stuarts 1603-1669* (Oxford 1937).

Dillenberger, J., *Protestant Thought and Natural Science* (New York 1960).

Dunlop, I., *Palaces and Progresses of Elizabeth I* (London 1962).

Elizabeth, Queen, *Letters*, ed. G. B. Harrison (London 1935).

Elton, G. R., *The Tudor Constitution* (Cambridge 1960).

Elyot, Sir Thomas, *The Governor* (1531).

Erasmus, D., *De Ratione Studii*, tr. W. H. Woodward as *D. Erasmus, Concerning the Aim and Method of Education* (Cambridge 1904).

Everett, A., 'Social Mobility in Early Modern England' in *Past and Present*, No. 33 (April, 1966).

Fraunce, A., *The Arcadian Rhetoric* (1588), ed. Seaton (Oxford 1950).

Gilbert, Sir Humfrey, *Queene Elizabethes Achademy* (1572), ed. Furnival (E.E.T.S., London 1869).

Griffiths, G., *Representative Government in Western Europe in the Sixteenth Century* (1968).

Hall, A. R., *The Scientific Revolution, 1500-1800* (London 1954).

Harrison, W., *The Description of England* (1587), ed. Edelen Ithaca 1968).

Harvey, W., *Works*, ed. R. Willis (London 1847).

Hexter, J. H., *Reappraisals in History* (London 1961).

Hill, C., *The Century of Revolution, 1603-1714* (London 1961).

Hobbes, T., *Answer to Davenant* (1650), ed. J. E. Spingam, *Critical Essays of the Seventeenth Century* (Oxford 1908).

Holles, G., *Memorials of the Holles Family, 1493-1656* (Camden Society, London 1937).

Johnson, F. R., *Astronomical Thought in Renaissance England* (Baltimore 1937).

Joseph, B. L., *Elizabethan Acting* (London 1951; 2nd, revised ed. 1964); *Conscience and the King, A Study of Hamlet* (London 1953); *Acting Shakespeare* (London 1960; 2nd ed. 1969); 'The Theme' in *Twentieth Century Interpretations of Hamlet*, ed. D. Bevington (Englewood Cliffs 1968).

Kempe, W., *The Education of Children* (1588).

Kenyon, J. P., *The Stuart Constitution, 1603-1688* (Cambridge 1966).

Lambarde, W., *The Perambulation of Kent* (1596).

Latimer, H., *Sermons*, ed. Corrie (Parker Society, London 1884).

Lee, Sir Sydney, *The Life and Letters of Sir Henry Wotton* (London 1907).

Mason, S. F., *A History of the Sciences* (London 1953).

Melsen, Van, A. G., *From Atmos to Atom* (New York 1960).

More, Sir Thomas, *Utopia* (1551).

Mulcaster, R., *Positions* (1581).

Neale, Sir John, *Essays in Elizabethan History* (London 1958); *Elizabeth I and her Parliaments* (London 2 vols. 1966); *The Elizabethan House of Commons etc.* (Harmondsworth 1963).

Notestein, W., *The English People on the Eve of Colonization* (New York and London 1954).

Peacham, H., *The Compleat Gentleman* (1622).
Prestwick, M., *Cranfield: Politics and Profits under the Early Stuarts* (1966).
Purchas, S., *Purchas His Pilgrimage* (1619).
Puttenham, G., *The Art of English Poesy* (1589).
Raleigh, Sir Walter, *The History of the World* (1614).
Ramsey, P., *Tudor Economic Problems* (London 1963).
Read, C., *The Government of England under Elizabeth* (Washington 1960).
Roberts, C., *The Growth of Responsible Government in Stuart England* (1966).
Rowse, A. L., *The England of Elizabeth: The Structure of Society* (London 1964).
Rye, W. B., *England as Seen by Foreigners in the Days of Elizabeth and James I* (London 1865).
Selden, J., *Titles of Honour* (1614).
Sidney, Sir Philip, *The Countess of Pembroke's Arcadia* (1593); *An Apology for Poesy* (1593), ed. C. G. Smith, Elizabethan Critical Essays (London 1931); *Poems*, ed. W. A. Ringler (1962).
Smith, Sir Thomas, *De Republica Anglorum* (1583), ed. Alston (Cambridge 1906).
Stone, L., *The Crisis of Aristocracy* (1965).
Stubbes, P., *The Anatomy of Abuses* (1583).
Tanner, J. R., *Constitutional Documents of the Reign of James I* (Cambridge 1930).
Tawney, R. H., *Religion and the Rise of Capitalism* (London 1926).
Tillyard, E. M. W., *The Elizabethan World Picture* (London 1943).
Trevor Roper, H. R., 'The English Aristocracy', *Economic History Review*, 2nd Series, III (1951); 'The Gentry, 1540-1640', *Ibid.*, Supplement (1953); *Historical Essays* (London 1957).
Wedgwood, C. V., *The Trial of Charles I* (London 1964).
Whitelocke, R. H., ed., *Memoirs Biographical and Historical of Bulstrode Whitelocke* (London 1860).
Wildebloode, J., and Wilson, P., *The Polite World* (Oxford 1965).
Williams, C., *Thomas Platter's Travels in England, 1599* (London 1937).
Winney, J., *The Frame of Order* (London 1957).
Woodward, G. W. O., *Reformation and Resurgence 1485-1603* (London 1963).
Wyn, Sir John, *The History of the Gwydir Family* (London 1770).

Index

Accommodation, doctrine of, 268f.
Acting, Elizabethan, 310ff.
administrators, 52, 120ff.
Admiral, Lord (office of), 123f.
Agrippa, Cornelius, 269
ambassador (office of), 127f.
Andrewes, Lancelot, 246
Angels, 158ff., 249f.
apprentices, 47f.
aristocracy, 277ff., 34ff. (expenditure), 74ff.
Aristotle, 18
Arminianism, 219f.
arms, coats of, 39f.
army, ranks of, 131
Artificers, Statute of, 70
Arundel, Earl of, 105
Ascham, Roger, 286, 298
astrology, 31f., 255f., 258ff., 261ff., 329ff., 340f.
astronomy, 18ff., 21ff., 31f., 247ff., 255ff., 263ff.
Augmentation, Court of, 132

Bacon, Sir Francis, 20, 25f., 31f., 111f., 206f., 211, 228, 269ff.—*Advancement of Learning*, 25f., 262, 265, 270f., 277, 280ff.
Bacon, Sir Nicholas, 195f.
Baker, Sir Richard, 306f., 309, 322
Baldwin, William, 246
banquets, 101f.
Bailey, Nathaniel, 21
baronet, 174
Barrow, Henry, 197
base, the (as distinct from gentle), 34ff.—burgesses, citizens, 42f., —masses, 46f.; yeomen, 43ff., 47
Bate, John, 187, 202
blazon, 84
blood, circulation of, 266ff.
Blundevill, Thomas, 248f.
Boethius, 257f.

Borough, the, 126
Breton, Nicholas, 250
Browne, Robert, 197
Browne, Sir Thomas, 245f.
Buckingham, Charles, Duke of, 188, 209, 225, 229f., 231ff.
Bulwer, John, 25, 107, 270, 314
Burbage, Richard, 312f.
Burghley, William Cecil, Lord, 80, 128
Burton, William, 165f.

Campion, Thomas, 306
Castelvetro, Lodovico, 304ff.
ceremony, 97ff.
Chain of Being, 158ff., 178ff., 251f., 255f.
Chamber, the (division of royal household), 119ff.
Chancellor, Lord (office of), 138ff.
Chaos, 154ff., 166f.
Charles I., 11, 103f., 188, 199, 210, 218ff., 225, 231ff.
Chaucer, Geoffrey, 275f., 291f.
Cheke, Sir John, 168f.
'classis', 196f.
clergy, 52f.
clothes, 76, 90f.
Coke, Sir Edward, 118, 200, 204f., 212, 216, 218
common sense, 21
Commons, House of, 147ff., 150, 229ff.
commonwealth (idea of), 34ff., 176
conflict, *élite* with Crown, 192ff.
constable (office of), 125f.
Constable of Castile, 101f.
Copernicus, 17ff., 21f., 263ff.
Coroner (office of), 124
Council, of the Marches, 126f.; of the North, 126f.
Court, royal, 119ff., 236ff.
Cowell, John, 187f.
Cranmer, Thomas, 161, 172, 176, 177f.

Creation of the world, 154f.
Crooke, Helkiah, 134ff.

Daniel, Samuel, 237, 293, 306
Davenant, Sir William, 306f.
Davies, Sir John, 21, 156
Dee, John, 22f., 261f., 268
degree, 34ff., 143ff., 346f., 349ff.
defence, (army and navy), 128f.
Deloney, Thomas, 300f.
D'Ewes, Sir Simonds, 79
Digges, Thomas, 18, 23, 265
disorder, 70ff., 154ff., 350ff.
Divine Right of Kings, 11, 12, 178ff., 350ff.
'Doleman' (Father Parsons), 180f.
Donne, John, 17, 24f., 160, 254, 275, 295ff.; *Extasy*, 254; *First Anniversary*, 24; *Ignatius, His Conclave*, 25
Drake, Sir Francis, 105
drama, 305ff.
Drayton, Michael, 261
Drury family, 92, 174, 271
Dryden, John, 290f., 306f.
duelling, 174

Earls, 38f.
education, 107ff.
elements, the four, 24f., 154ff., 247ff., 345f.
Eliot, Sir John, 189, 190, 210, 219
Elizabeth I, 13, 16, 37, 39, 87, 96, 105, 149ff., 173f., 183f., 188f., 201, 206ff., 211, 212ff., 216, 220, 221ff., 271f.
Ellesmere, Lord, 139
Elyot, Sir Thomas, 161, 170f., 172, 180
Epaminondas, 275
Erasmus, Desiderius, 110
Esquire, 39, 87
evil spirits, 249f.
Exchequer, the, 136f., 138
ex officio, oath of, 196f., 215f.
ex-servicemen, 64ff.

Ferne, John, 79
First-fruits, Court of, 132
'Five Knights, the', 202
Fleming, Chief Baron, Abraham, 187, 202f.
food, 75f.

foreign policy, 223ff.
Forest, William, 167
Fortescue, Sir John, 157
Fraunce, Abraham, 207f.

Galileo, 19, 23f.
Gardiner, Stephen, 175
generosity, 80f.
gentle (classes), 34f., 40f., 73ff., 85f.
Gilbert, Sir Humphrey, 112
Godwin, Francis, 23
Googe, Barnaby, 264
grammar schools, 110ff.
Grimald, Nicholas, 292f.
Grindall, Edmund, Archbishop, 196

Hakewill, William, 208
Harrison, William, 45, 77, 125
Harvey, Sir William, 19f., 267ff.
hats, 94f.
Hayward, Sir John, 181
heart, the, 267ff.
Hentzner, Paul, 97f.
Heralds, College of, 81, 85, 86ff., 91, 173f.
Herbert, of Cherbury, Lord, 93, 96
heroic poetry, 281ff.
Hexter, J. H., 240
Heywood, Thomas, 301f., 311, 319; *Woman Killed with Kindness*, 51
hierarchy, 143ff., 349ff.
High Commission (Court of), 143, 203ff., 215f.
Hill, Thomas, 247
Hobbes, Thomas, 26, 283f.
Holles, Gervase, 77
Holles, Sir William, 96, 289
Homily, 34f., 171f., 176, 177
honour, 77
Hooker, Richard, 157f., 160f., 166f.
Hooper, John, Bishop, 175f.
'Household, the' (Court), 119ff.
Howard, Sir John, 306
humanism, 276ff.
humours (of the body), 250ff., 345
hundred, 124f., 128

imagination, 26, 255ff.
impositions, 208f., 227f.
income (of the Crown), 130ff.

James I, 37, 102f., 174, 183f., 185, 198f., 205, 207f., 211, 212, 216, 221ff., 227ff.

justice, 121f., 137ff., 143ff.
justice of the peace (office of), 124f., 143ff., 199

Kemp, William, 108
knighthood, 82, 85

Lambarde, William, 97
land, 10f.
Latimer, Hugh, Bishop, 109, 176
Latin, 110f.
Laud, John, Archbishop, 218, 219
Law (Common), 118
law, courts of, 138, 141
law (enforcement), 144ff.
Law (Statute) 116f.
law suits, 51
lawyers, 50ff.
Leicester, Earl of, 105f.
loans, forced, 135f., 199f.
Lord Chancellor, 53
Lord Lieutenant, 122ff., 128ff.
love, 168f.
Lyly, John, 298, 320f.
Lynche, Richard, 293

Manwaring, Roger, 218f.
marriage (and succession), 220ff.
masques, 76
medicine, 18f.
Merbury, Charles, 180
merchant (title of), 91
microcosm, 256ff.
middle classes, the, 26f.
Milton, John, 20, 154f., 157, 159f., 163f., 285f., 294f., 330f.
mobility (social), 49f.
Mompesson, Sir Giles, 228
monarchy, 177ff.
monopolies, 135, 200ff., 206ff.
Montague, Anthony, Viscount, 104
More, Sir Thomas, 172f.
Morice, James, 216
Mulcaster, Richard, 35f., 111
musters, 128f.

Neo-Classicism, 304ff., 322ff.
nobles, 36ff., 77ff., 80ff., 91
nobility (idea of), 76f.
Norden, James, 51
Norris, Lady, 271f.
Notestein, Wallace, 54f.

oratory, 316ff.
order, 175, 348ff.

Pace, Richard, 78
Palingenius, 22
Paracelsus, 24
parish, 125f.
Parliament, 106f., 115ff., 119f., 146ff., 185f., 193ff., 229f.
patronage, 48f., 100
Peacham, Henry, 77f., 161f.
peers, 37f., 92f.
Petition of Right, 189, 209f.
physicians, 53f.
Platter, Thomas, 97
poetry, justification of, 276ff.
poor, the, 54ff., 60f.
Poor Laws, 56ff.
Pope, Alexander, 178f., 291
portents, 31f., 255ff., 262f., 341ff., 352
precedence, 91f., 174
prerogative, royal, 193ff., 206ff., 216, 219ff., 224, 226f.
Presbyterians, 197ff.
Primaudaye, Pierre de la, 167f.
Privy Council, 63ff., 67f., 69f., 71f., 116ff., 121f., 128f., 141ff., 144, 233
proclamations (by Charles I), 218f.—
   (by Elizabeth I), 90, 115ff., 201—
   (by James I), 185f., 207f.
Providence, doctrine of, 244ff., 257ff., 262f., 271f., 329ff.
Purchas, Samuel, 24
Puritans, the, 195ff., 213ff., 216ff.
purveyance, 106, 135, 211
Puttenham, George, 277f., 290

quintessence, 247

Raleigh, Sir Walter, 31f., 161, 259ff.
Recorde, Robert, 22
religion, 194ff., 212ff., 216ff.
rhetorical figures, 287ff., 320ff.
rhyme, 306
Rowse, A. L., 45

Sebonde, Raymond de, 159, 164
Selden, John, 39f.
servants (of the Crown), 106f., 193f., 226ff., 236ff.
Shakespeare, John, 86f.

Shakespeare, William, 28ff., 327ff; *All's Well*, 330; *Antony and Cleopatra*, 320, 345, 350; *As You Like It*, 82ff.; *Coriolanus*, 311, 350; *Hamlet*, 78f., 95f., 181, 251, 254, 292, 302, 318f., 336ff., 342,349,353ff; *Henry V*,169,186; *Henry VI Pt III*, 356; *Julius Caesar*, 329f., 341ff; *King Lear*, 28ff., 31f., 44, 59f., 76, 92, 93f. 99f., 104ff., 261, 262f., 266, 275, 327f., 339ff., 343ff., 348, 358f.; *Macbeth*, 84, 101, 181f., 249ff., 253f., 321, 327f., 328f., 347ff., 352f., 359; *Richard II*, 30f., 349, 355f.; *Richard III*, 169f., 183, 345, 356f.; *Romeo and Juliet*, 93, 314ff., 333ff.; *The Tempest*, 94, 328, 331ff.; *Twelfth Night*, 83ff.; *Troilus and Cressida*, 350f.; *Sonnets*, 294, *The Winter's Tale*, 253, 331, 347
Sheriff (office of), 123ff.
Sidney, Sir Philip, 174, 275f., 284, 287f., 298f., 306
Smith, Sir Thomas, 36f., 38f., 40ff., 46f., 77, 82, 97, 106f., 120f., 127, 130f., 133f., 137, 147f.
ship money, 135
soul (threefold), 251ff., 346ff.
Spenser, Edmund, 157, 168f., 236f., 285, 288f.
spirits (natural, vital, animal), 252ff.
Star Chamber, 141ff.
Starkey, Thomas, 168f., 173

stars, 258ff., 329ff., 340f.
Statute of Uses, 90f.
spheres, 247ff.
Stone, Lawrence, 240ff.
Strickland, Sir Walter, 214
Stubbes, Philip, 90

Tawney, Richard, Henry, 239ff.
taxation, 131f., 146ff., 187f.
telescope, 23f.
theatre, Elizabethan, 307ff.
towns, 126
tragedy, 305ff.
Trevor-Roper, Sir Hugh, 240ff.
Tunnage and Poundage, 209ff.
Tyndale, William, 179f.

universe, the, 246ff.

vagrants, 56f., 58ff.

wapentake (hundred), 124
wardship, 132ff., 211f.
Webster, John, 237f., 324
Wentworth, Paul, 214f., Peter, 215
Whitgift, John, Archbishop, 196f.
Wilson, Thomas, 332f.
Wither, A., 155
Whitehall (Banqueting House), 100ff.
witches, 265f.
Wright, Thomas, 316
Wyatt, Sir Thomas, 293
Wynn, Sir John, 79
Whitelocke, Sir Geoffrey, 88
Wotton, Sir Henry, 92f.